CONSOLIDATED STATEMENTS

R. G. Walker

ARNO PRESS
A New York Times Company
New York • 1978

Editorial Supervision: LUCILLE MAIORCA

———◆———

First publication 1978 by Arno Press Inc.

Copyright © 1978 by R. G. Walker

THE DEVELOPMENT OF CONTEMPORARY ACCOUNTING THOUGHT
ISBN for complete set: 0-405-10891-5
See last pages of this volume for titles.

Manufactured in the United States of America

———◆———

Library of Congress Cataloging in Publication Data

Walker, R   G
    Consolidated statements.

    (The Development of contemporary accounting thought)
    A modification of the author's thesis, University
of Sydney, 1976.
    Bibliography: p.
    Includes index.
    1. Financial statements, Consolidated. I. Title.
II. Series.
HF5686.C7W33 1978   657'.3   77-87307
ISBN 0-405-10946-6

CONSOLIDATED STATEMENTS

A HISTORY AND ANALYSIS

R. G. Walker

PREFACE

The following material has been taken from a PhD thesis submitted
to the University of Sydney in 1976. In an effort to reduce the
length of the manuscript for publication, the last chapter of the
thesis was omitted. What remains is mainly historical. The last
chapter ("An evaluation of the information conveyed by consolidated statements") appeared in <u>Abacus</u> Dec. 1976, pp. 77-115.

There have been some minor modifications to the thesis text. I
have added an index and approximately two pages of additional
explanatory material. I have also removed some blunders, errors
and infelicities.

                              R. G. Walker,
                              Sydney.
                              April 1977.

CONTENTS

Section V

SECTION I

Ch. 1 General introduction

Consolidated statements are widely used in the U.S.A., U.K., Australia, Canada and New Zealand, and are common in other commonwealth and European countries. They are an accepted form of financial reporting. Data derived from consolidated statements are widely disseminated within the financial community.

Despite the popularity and acceptance of consolidated reporting, there are serious inconsistencies in the disclosure rules of various jurisdictions concerning the circumstances and conditions which make the preparation of consolidated statements warranted or appropriate. For example, some regulatory agencies have framed rules requiring or permitting the filing or submission of consolidated statements only, unaccompanied by the financial statements of holding companies. Other sets of rules provide for the presentation of consolidated statements in conjunction with the reports of holding companies - and merely establish consolidated reporting as one of a series of alternative forms of providing supplementary information.

Moreover, there are inconsistencies in the rules or recommendations promulgated by regulatory agencies or professional associations of accountants concerning the techniques to be used in the preparation of consolidated statements. There are differences in the tests used to identify "subsidiary" companies. Some of the rules or recommendations encourage the consolidation of parent companies and all of their subsidiaries; other rules or recommendations have permitted the omission of certain subsidiaries, or even the omission of parent companies from aggregative statements. Some rules or recommendations support the total elimination of "profits" arising from inter-company transactions from consolidated-statement data while others permit or advocate the elimination of only the majority interest's share of those profits. There are differences of opinion about the calculation and disclosure of minority interests and "goodwill on consolidation".

One might suppose that questions about when to prepare consolidated statements, and their status (relative to parent-company reports) could be resolved by recourse to analyses of the relative merits of consolidated and conventional reporting. But contemporary text-books hardly bother to consider these questions. Some discussions of consolidation accounting are written within the framework of specific disclosure rules - and simply outline procedures which firms must follow in order to comply with those requirements. Other discussions rely on the authority of convention: consolidated statements are an accepted form of reporting - they must be worthwhile. And some claim that consolidated statements are "better" than conventional reports - but do not back up these claims with extended arguments or evidence.

One might also suppose that disagreements about the choice of techniques for preparing consolidated statements could be resolved after consideration of the aims or objectives of using this form of reporting. But text-book discussions of the aims of consolidated reporting are often little more than a series of slogans. For example, it is said that consolidated statements are concerned with depicting the affairs of a "group" of companies; they show the affairs of holding companies and subsidiaries "as if" the subsidiaries were only "branches" of the parent firms; they depict the affairs of an "economic entity"; they brush aside "legal technicalities". The diversity of rules and recommendations concerning the preparation of consolidated reports testifies to the ambiguity of these propositions. None are adequate statements of the _function_ of consolidated reports. None indicate the precise signals that consolidated statements are intended to convey. None explain _why_ legal "realities" are to be dismissed as "technicalities", or _why_ it is useful to report on an "economic entity" or "group".

This study traces the history of the use of consolidated statements and of shifts in views about the most appropriate ways of accounting for inter-corporate investments. An attempt is made to relate the use of consolidated reporting over time to prevailing ideas about asset valuation and financial disclosure. And considerable attention is given to the legal and regulatory framework within which corporations were preparing and publishing consolidated statements. The tracing of these subsidiary themes serves to emphasise how disclosure rules have influenced the use preparation of consolidated reports, and how the adoption and retention of consolidated reporting were in large measure responses to deficiencies of accounting reports prepared in accord with "generally accepted" procedures.

The examination of the history of the use of consolidated statements focusses on U.S. and British experiences. The circumstances which led to the initial use of consolidated statements in the U.S.A. were quite different from those which were prevailing when British accountants adopted consolidated reporting several decades later. Moreover, American and British accountants held quite different views about the aims of consolidated reporting. Sections II and III trace the separate development of consolidated reporting in the U.K. and the U.S. until the end of the 1930's. By this time, consolidated reporting had become firmly entrenched as part of accounting practice in both countries. This is also a convenient point to summarise the views held by accountants in both countries about the function and status of consolidated reporting, and to take stock of conflicting ideas about the appropriate way to prepare these documents. Section IV summarises

the main "issues" in dispute at this state in the history of consolidated reporting, and identifies key areas of disagreement about
the aims of consolidated reporting.

In the post-war years some accounting writers attempted to
enunciate the assumptions underlying consolidation accounting, and
both the British and American literature began to pay lip-service to
the proposition that consolidated statements were intended to represent
the affairs of "single entity". At the same time consolidated statements
were regarded as amplifications of holding company statements, and as
representations of liquidity. Consequently, accepted rules and
procedures have continued to reflect uncertainty about the aims of
consolidation accounting; sets of rules and procedures lack consistency,
so that statements prepared in accord with these rules may be incapable
of fully achieving any particular objective. Despite this uncertainty
about the precise aims of consolidated reporting, consolidated statements
have come to be regarded as the primary vehicle for corporate financial
reporting.

Section V traces major changes in the rules and recommendations
concerning the preparation of consolidated statements during this
period. Some attention is given to the 1970's acceptance of equity
accounting by professional accounting bodies, for the possibility of
adopting equity accounting procedures in parent company statements
eliminates the major claim made about the advantages of consolidation
procedures: that of overcoming the limitations of the conventional
method of valuing inter-corporate investments at cost.

Sections II - V thus provide an extensive review of the history
of consolidated reporting, and of the shifts in ideas about the objectives and advantages of these statements. This review highlights the
fact that there has been little analysis of the "case" for using consolidated statements. Accounting writers or professional associations

have avoided spelling out exactly what information consolidated statements are supposed to show, and that there has been little critical assessment of the underlying assumptions that consolidated data are useful.

SECTION II

U.K. BACKGROUND TO THE INTRODUCTION OF CONSOLIDATED REPORTING

Ch. 2 Asset valuation

When consolidated statements were first introduced into British
accounting practice, they were regarded as useful supplements to the
legally-required financial statements of holding companies. The
British profession's initial attitude to consolidated statements was
primarily that they were a convenient means of overcoming the
misleading impressions that might be conveyed by holding company
balance sheets and income statements. These were prepared using
cost-based asset valuation and dividend-based revenue recognition.
It was recognised that the information prepared on this basis was
uninformative or potentially misleading - but there was a general
reluctance to abandon these treatments and to use alternative
procedures which were seen as leading to the recognition of
"unrealised" profits.

This and the following chapter outline the emergence and adoption
of distinct asset valuation rules for corporate businesses, and the
application of these rules to inter-corporate shareholdings. Chapter
4 then describes the development of British accounting practices for
the treatment of investments in "subsidiaries". It is then possible
to examine and analyse the conditions under which the British
profession accepted and adopted consolidated statements, and to consider
the claims made about the merits of this form of reporting.

The starting point for this discussion is the latter half of the
nineteenth century. By 1856 it was possible to form corporations with
limited liability by a fairly simple process of registration. By the
1890's the corporate form had become widely used in the UK and hence

corporations had become increasingly significant in the mobilisation
and allocation of resources. These developments led to increased
job opportunities for accountants - and new sorts of problems for
those who found themselves compiling or auditing corporate reports.
As record keepers for sole traders ventures or partnerships,
accountants were reporting to persons who usually were fairly inti-
mately connected with the business in question. As liquidators of
bankrupt estates, accountants had little difficulty in valuing assets
or identifying liabilities. But as the individuals responsible for
compiling or auditing the reports of corporations, accountants were
forced to work out ways of communicating financial information to
individuals who might otherwise have no contact with the day to day
conduct of a business. It was difficult enough to report on the
performance of an on-going venture; it was harder when there was no
opportunity to explain to the readers of financial reports exactly
what the figures meant.

Professional associations of accountants were formed in England
late in the nineteenth century - The Institute of Chartered
Accountants in 1880 and the Society of Incorporated Accountants and
Auditors in 1885. (The Institute of Chartered Accountants had been
established in Scotland as early as 1853). These associations were
not to play an active role in the formulation of rules of practice
until the 1940's. However, their journals and meetings did provide
a forum for the discussion of accounting issues. Moreover, their
admission requirements encouraged the preparation of materials for
use by students attempting examinations - and thus contributed to
the crystalisation of ideas about "best practice".

Within this setting, accountants developed some ideas about
accounting - as opposed to bookkeeping.

One of the first matters to be discussed in the newly-launched accounting journals and in the meetings of these professional associations was the valuation of inventories. By the 1890's accountants had reached agreement about the desirability of using the "lower of cost or market" rule for these assets. But this discussion was concerned only with goods-inventories and was not related to any broad framework of asset valuation.

It seems that Dicksee's Auditing[1] contained the first major attempt to develop a general framework for asset valuation. Published in 1892, Auditing included proposals for the application of distinct computational techniques for assets in different categories. Dicksee introduced this approach by considering whether company financial reports should follow the Double Account form of reporting then required of many parliamentary companies.   Under the Double Account system, these companies presented two reports: a "general balance sheet" and a "capital expenditure account".

> ... the form of the Double Account system arose from the statutory requirement that all capital raised should be used for the carrying out of the works for the execution of which the company was created; ... the principle that, so long as the works were maintained in a state of efficiency their actual value need not be periodically reconsidered, arose from the circumstances that it was contemplated that the work would be permanently carried on (p.119).

Dicksee noted that auditors were not compelled to follow the procedures prescribed for governmental organisations, but suggested that one was compelled by "a sense of logic" to admit an analogy between the accounts of parliamentary companies and those of other undertakings (p.119). The perpetual succession of "registered" companies enabled one to consider them "theoretically permanent".

---

1. L. R. Dicksee, Auditing - a practical manual for auditors (London: Gee & Co., 1892).

However, the fact that these companies were not bound to retain possession of any of their assets, and the impracticability of stating what were and were not their "capital assets", led him to conclude that it was inappropriate to follow the "double account principle" of stating the value of capital assets at cost, indefinitely. Rather, he proposed that assets should be depicted at their "value to a going concern" - a proposal which nevertheless retained the double account system's approach of applying different valuation procedures to different classes of assets.

To calculate "value as a going concern", Dicksee stated that assets should be divided into two classes: permanent and floating. Permanent assets were said to be "those with which [a firm] carries on business"; floating assets were "those in which [a firm] carries on business" (p.121). There were different ways of calculating "value" for these two classes. Dicksee's discussion of the valuation of floating assets was illustrated by reference to goods-inventories only, and in this context he claimed that "the element of immediate realisation" was an important factor, so that trading profits should only be recorded when sales were completed. As for the valuation of permanent assets, Dicksee claimed that "value to the going concern" was affected both by physical "wasting" (which reduced "value") and "fluctuation" (changes in price which might either add to or reduce "value"). Wasting clearly was an expense and was to be handled by recording "depreciation". But fluctuation was "something altogether apart from profit and loss", and "on no account" were the results of fluctuations to affect the Profit and Loss Account.[2]

---

2. Ibid, p.121.
   However Dicksee did claim that price changes should not be totally disregarded; he argued that the auditor's duty was "to sufficiently acquaint the shareholders with the facts of the case to enable them to intelligently exercise their own discretion as to whether they will pass the accounts in the form in which they are presented to them", and that substantial overstatements or understatements of assets should be mentioned in the auditor's certificate (p.136).

In other words, different approaches were to be used when valuing fixed or floating assets.

Dicksee's proposals for the classification of assets into these two categories may have been influenced by attempts to apply economists' notions of fixed and floating capital in the context of accounting. But the linkage between asset classification and valuation seems to have been Dicksee's own contribution. It would seem that this approach to valuation was not immediately popular. But within a few years a series of judicial decisions dealing with the availability of profits for distribution as dividends produced an urgent need for the profession to develop a systematic approach to valuation questions.

The catalyst was the 1894 case of Verner v. General & Commercial Investment Trust, Ltd.[3] Securities held by the trust had "depreciated" by about £240,000, of which it was estimated that about £75,000 was irrecoverable within any reasonable period of time. During the financial year the company's revenue from investments had exceeded its current expenses by more than £23,000. The court had to consider whether this trading profit could be used to pay a dividend without taking into account the capital loss of £75,000. The court decided that the income could be used to pay a dividend, and that there was no need to make good the loss of capital. This decision was not exactly startling in the light of earlier precedents.[4]

---

3. 1894, 2 Ch. 239.

4. The 1889 case of Lee v. Neuchatel Asphalte Company Lim. marked the abandonment of the previously-held view that a company was only entitled to pay a dividend if its "capital" was intact. 1889 41 Ch. 1. This decision was reaffirmed and extended in Bolton v. Natal Land and Colonization Co. Lim. 1892 2 Ch. 124. See commentaries in H. B. Buckley and A. C. Clauson The law and practice under the companies acts... (London: Stevens and Haynes, 7th ed., 1897) p.557ff. See also L. C. B. Gower, Modern company law (London: Stevens and Sons, 3rd ed., 1969) pp. 115-9; B. S. Yamey, "The case law relating to company dividends", in W. T. Baxter and S. Davidson (eds.) Studies in accounting theory (London: Sweet and Maxwell Ltd. 2nd ed., 1962) pp. 428-30.

But the judgment of the appeal court included the following pithy

summary of the state of the law at that time:

> Fixed capital may be sunk and lost, and yet ... the
> excess of current receipts over current payments may be
> divided [as dividends], but ... floating or circulating
> capital must be kept up ....

Moreover, the Verner judgment appeared at a time when auditors were

becoming painfully aware of their legal liabilities in the event that

dividends were wrongfully distributed.[5] Almost immediately, accountants

looked more closely at asset classification. It was acknowledged at

the time that the Verner case had prompted practitioner-interest in

asset classification.[6] 1894 was the first year in which a question

concerning the distinction between "fixed" and "floating" assets appeared

in an Institute examination paper.[7] By 1899 asset classification had

"been discussed over and over by various meetings of Accountants' and

Students' Societies".[8] This concern with asset classification was in

no way associated with the aim of grouping balance sheet items in order

to represent liquidity. It simply represented the profession's attempt

to ensure that profit calculations stayed within the courts' guide-

lines. The courts had been concerned with categories of capital.

Accountants quickly applied these distinctions to assets. As Spicer

and Pegler's Practical auditing (1911) argued

> The terms "Fixed" and "Floating" or "Circulating" Capital
> ... are equivalent to that portion of the Capital
> represented by "Fixed" or "Floating" Assets.

---

5.   Two cases that were of particular relevance were The Leeds Estate
     Building and Investment Society Lim. v. Shepherd 1887 36 Ch. 787
     and The London and General Bank case (No.1) 1895 2 Ch. 166.

6.   R. Warner, "Fixed' and 'circulating' assets", The accountant, 4
     March 1899 p.251.

7.   The accountants' manual, loc.cit. Vol.IV (1894) pp.362-3.

8.   Warner, idem.

9.   E. E. Spicer and E. C. Pegler, Practical auditing (London: H.
     Foulks Lynch & Co., 1911) p.358.

And the profession rapidly accepted that different valuation rules
were to be applied to the different classes of assets.

What valuation rules were to be used for each category?

There was a near consensus about treatment of floating assets.
Spicer and Pegler summarised the legal position as requiring that
"depreciation on Floating Assets must be made good before the payment of
dividends" (p.360) - in other words, as supporting use of the lower of
cost and market rule. This interpretation was actually contrary to that
arrived at by legal experts. Buckley, author of the standard text on
company law, interpreted the prescription that "floating or circulating
capital must be kept up" as requiring that both <u>depreciation and apprecia-</u>
<u>tion</u> of floating assets be "the subject of entry in the profit and loss
account".[10] But it does not appear that accountants seriously entertained
the possibility that they might be obliged to record appreciation. The
lower of cost and market rule became accepted. It should be noted that
the application of this rule to <u>all</u> floating assets was a substantial departure from the prior association of the rule with goods-inventories only.

The treatment of fixed assets remained an unsettled question. Much
of the diversity of opinion can be attributed to confusion over the legal
significance of the dividend cases. Further differences arose from the
view taken of an accountant's responsibilities: some writers merely
indicated which procedures would enable practitioners to avoid liability
for improper dividend distributions, while others aimed at devising
methods which would provide useful information.

One interpretation of the court decisions was that fixed assets could
be left at cost, without reference to market prices. As one practitioner
put it, circulating assets were "liable to revision for the purposes of
the annual Balance Sheet", while fixed assets were not.[11] It appears

---

10. <u>Op. cit.</u>, p. 360.

11. Warner, <u>idem.</u>

that this interpretation was widely held; undoubtedly it was a misstatement of the legal position. The law at the time said nothing about whether depreciation should be calculated or whether fixed assets need not be periodically revalued. The courts had not been called upon to answer these questions. The case law only established that the courts would not interfere with the payment of dividends from profits calculated one way or another so long as certain conditions prevailed - chiefly that the company's articles permitted the dividend in those circumstances and that creditors would not suffer. If the judgments contained any guide about the valuation of fixed assets, they certainly did not put the seal of approval on cost-based valuation if cost figures were greater than current market prices. In the Verner case, Lindley L.J. made the obiter statement that "capital lost must not appear intact"; in the London and General Bank case, an auditor's comment that investment values were "subject to realisation" was held to be an inadequate warning of balance sheet overstatement.[12]

Dicksee, on the other hand, cautioned against attaching undue importance to the legal decisions. It might be legally permissable to declare dividends out of profits calculated without regard for changes in the market prices of permanent assets - but that did not mean that it was appropriate to ignore these matters entirely.[13]

An intermediate position emerged soon after the Verner, London and General Bank, and Kingston Cotton Mill cases. The view was taken that a certain amount of latitude was permissible in asset valuation, so that fixed assets, for example, could be safely recorded at cost or other cost-based figure except when the discrepancy between recorded values and market selling prices became extreme. One summary of these views was as follows:

> There must always be a certain amount of margin between a
> Balance Sheet which improperly overstates and a Balance

---

12. London and General Bank (No.2), 1895 2 Ch. 673.

13. 7th ed., p.288.

Sheet which improperly understates the position of affairs; and, within the limits of that margin, it is clearly the privilege, as well as the duty, of directors to exercise a reasonable and honest discretion. It is only when these limits are exceeded that the auditor is called upon to intervene.[14]

Despite disagreements about matters of detail it is clear that by the late 1890's the British profession had firmly adopted the practice of linking asset classification with asset valuation. This is not to say that there was agreement about a clear cut set of rules. In the following years there were substantial changes in the terminology used to describe assets - the terms "permanent" and "floating" were supplanted by the tidier terminology of "fixed" and "floating"[15] and later "floating" was replaced by American references to "current assets".[16] More significantly, there were substantial changes in the criteria used to categorise assets into these groups. Dicksee originally had based his classification scheme on ex post judgments about patterns of asset utilisation. He stated that a firm's permanent assets were "those with which it carries on business"; its floating assets were those in which it carries on business" (p. 121). This distinction evidently found favour at the time.[17] But by the time of the sixth edition of Auditing (1904), Dicksee switched the criteria for asset classification from ex post to ex ante judgments about asset use.

---

14. "F.C.A.", "Some contested points in auditing practice", The accountant, 1 April 1899, p.365. See also (anon.) "Hidden liabilities and hidden reserves", ibid, 15 April 1899, p.413.

15. These terms were used by Dicksee in the sixth edition of Auditing (1904).

16. The Institute of Chartered Accountants in England and Wales used the term "current assets" in its Recommendation 8 (1944).

17. Model answers to the June 1894 Institute examinations reproduced this distinction and referred students to Dicksee's Auditing for further information. The accountants' manual, Vol. IV (London: Gee & Co., 1894), pp. 362-3. G. Lisle's Accounting in theory and practice (Edinburgh: William Green & Sons, 1899) also distinguished asset categories in terms of use in the business (p.67).

> The proper distinction between fixed and floating assets
> must, it is thought, always rest with the intention of
> the parties owning such assets, and the manner in which
> they propose to utilise them ... (p.291).

While there had been a few earlier isolated references to "intention"
as the basis of asset classification[18] it appears that Dicksee's
adoption of this rule was influential, and encouraged other writers
to accept similar classification criteria.[19] Some attempts to
formulate rules incorporating elements of both ex post and ex ante
bases of classification led to the adoption of mixed rules which did
not necessarily encompass all of a firm's assets.[20] But it appears
that accountants were not overly concerned with the niceties of asset
classification, and simply adopted a liberal interpretation of one
definition or another.[21]

Asset classification finally became entrenched in British
accounting practice in 1907 with the passage of legislation obliging
company accountants to describe how "fixed" assets had been valued.

---

18. e.g. (anon.) "Notes on balance sheets", The incorporated
    accountants' journal, Feb. 1898, p.66; A. L. Hellyer,
    "Depreciating assets, sinking funds and kindred subjects", The
    accountant, 29 July, 1899, p.811; W. Strachan, "Some remarks
    on balance sheets and profit and loss accounts", The incorporated
    accountants' journal, May 1903, p.173. Model answers to a 1901
    Institute examination described asset classification in terms
    of "intention", but solutions to later papers reverted to
    references to asset-use. See The accountants' manual, Vol. VIII
    (1902), p.220; Vol. X (1906), p.517.

19. e.g. See editorial, "Balance sheet values", The accountant, 11
    Jan. 1908, p.42.

20. See, e.g., M.Webster Jenkinson, Book-keeping and accounting
    (London: Edward Arnold, 2 ed., 1912), p.11; Spicer and Pegler,
    op. cit., p.133; F. R. M. de Paula, "Some further notes on
    auditing", The accountant, 22nd March, 1913, p.445. For a fuller
    discussion on these matters see R. G. Walker, "Asset classifica-
    tion and asset valuation", Accounting and business research,
    Autumn 1974.

21. e.g. Webster Jenkinson described investments as "practically
    fixed assets". Op. cit., p.84.

Until 1907, U.K. companies legislation contained no general requirements for companies to publish or otherwise disseminate financial
information. And then, the 1907 Act did not explicitly require that
information be transmitted to shareholders - though it was later
claimed that the Act "assumed" an audited balance sheet would be
tabled at annual general meetings.[22] The major 1907 innovation was
the requirement that firms lodge documents with the Registrar,
including

> a statement, made up to such date as may be specified in
> the statement, in the form of a balance sheet, audited
> by the company's auditors, and containing a summary of its
> share capital, its liabilities, and its assets, giving
> such particulars as will disclose the general nature of
> such liabilities and assets, and how the values of the
> fixed assets have been arrived at ...[23]

These provisions substantially followed the recommendations contained
in the 1906 report of the "Loreburn" Company Law Amendment Committee.[24]
Significantly, an earlier Company Law Amendment Committee under the
chairmanship of Lord Davey had unsuccessfully recommended that
companies should be required to publish annual balance sheets which
stated how the valuation of all assets had been calculated.[25]
Evidently in the space of eleven years the practice of linking asset
classification and valuation had become so accepted that the Loreburn
Committee could assume that only fixed assets might be overstated -
circulating assets would be valued at the lower of cost and market.

---

22. Companies Act, 1907, s.19; see discussion of this section in
     "Company law reform in relation to the accounts of public companies",
     The accountant, 14 February 1925, p.257.

23. S.21. Emphasis added.

24. Report of the Company Law Amendment Committee, British Parlia-
     mentary Papers, 1906, Vol. 97, No. 3052, para. 33; this section
     of the report was reproduced in The accountant, 14 July 1906,
     pp.52-3 and discussed 25 August 1906, pp.204-5.

25. Report of the Company Law Committee, British Parliamentary Papers
     1895, Vol. 88, No.7779.

The 1929 Companies Act extended this recognition of asset classification by requiring disclosure of "the amounts respectively of the fixed assets and of the floating assets",[26] but this provision was loosely drafted so that firms were not required to arrange assets in those categories. It was not until the 1948 Companies Act that British disclosure rules formally required the balance sheet arrangements of assets. Thereafter, discussions of asset classification tended to emphasise the representation of liquidity and solvency. Even so, it was widely accepted that different valuation rules should be applied to assets depending upon whether they were "current" or "fixed". In the 1940's a Committee on Company Law Amendment even went so far as to recommend that all fixed assets should be reported at cost, less the aggregate amount provided or written off since acquisition. If this recommendation had been adopted, firms would have been prevented from writing-up fixed assets. But the Committee also saw the need to accomodate situations where past records did not enable cost to be calculated, or where it was not practicable to maintain detailed records, or where assets had been obtained on the acquisition of an existing business for a lump sum.[27] Accordingly when the "fixed assets at cost" recommendation was incorporated in the 1948 Act it was overridden by provisions allowing the use of "valuation" figures (or "valuations" less amounts written off).[28]

In the 1940's the Institute of Chartered Accountants provided further support for the proposition that asset valuation should be linked with asset classification by issuing recommendations which

---

26. S. 124.

27. Report of the Committee on Company Law Amendment, (London: H.M.S.O., 1945), pp. 55-6, para. 100.

28. Companies Act, 1948, 8th Sch., clause 5.

clearly associated the two operations.[29] Subsequent pronouncements

have maintained this support.

---

29.   e.g. Recommendation 8 (1944) and Recommendation 10 (1945).

Resume

    In the 1890's British accountants attempted to develop a
systematic set of ideas concerned with asset valuation. In 1892
Dicksee proposed that asset valuation be linked with asset classification. This proposal seems to have been suggested by the reporting
practices developed for governmental undertakings under the "double
account" system. Later in the 1890's the British profession adopted
a rule which prescribed that fixed assets and floating assets were
to be valued differently. The main stimulus for the adoption of this
rule was the profession's wish to avoid liability for improper dividend
distributions. It seemed that the courts would not seek to interfere
with corporate dividend distributions provided that the profits being
distributed had been calculated after due allowance for current losses
of "floating capital". Hence accountants sought to apply the lower of
cost and market rule to all "floating" (current) assets. There was
greater disagreement about the valuation of fixed assets, though
perhaps the dominant rule to emerge in the late 1890's was that fixed
assets could be left at cost (or cost derivatives - after allowance
for depreciation through "wasting" or wear), provided the discrepancy
between that figure and market selling prices did not become extreme.

    This emphasis on the use of cost or cost-derivatives for asset
valuation was to survive for many years. The U.K. Companies Acts
of 1929 and 1948 effectively acknowledged that different categories of
assets should be valued differently. And the Institute of Chartered
Accountants issued recommendations which supported the practice.

    This approach to asset valuation was applied, in due course, to
inter-corporate investments. And the use of cost-based valuation
for these "fixed" assets was to be a major factor in prompting the
use of consolidated reports.

Ch. 3   U.K. accounting for inter-corporate investments

The U.K. companies acts did not impose any prohibitions on inter-company shareholdings. It seems that by the 1890's (when several American states were just beginning to permit the establishment of holding companies) inter-corporate shareholdings were fairly common in the U.K. However the British practice of inter-corporate share-holdings typically arose from the efforts of banks or "trust" companies to find profitable avenues of investment. There were some companies which held stock in customer or client firms with an eye to cementing business connections. And there were a few cases of holding companies being established to amalgamate various businesses.[1] But unlike later American experience the use of the holding company form was not aimed at avoiding statutory prohibitions on combinations in restraint of trade. Indeed, until 1918 there was little official British interest in the regulation of monopolies. Hence those who sought to effect amalgamations were free to choose from a variety of organisational devices. By 1907 several British firms had been organised as holding companies, with notable examples including the Nobel Dynamite Trust Co. (formed in 1886) and the English Sewing Cotton Company (formed in 1897).[2] But other organisational devices in use included simple price fixing agreements and the formation of syndicates, associations and "con-ferences".

The 1907 U.K. Companies Act established definite incentives for

---

1. These included some notable company failures. In 1892 the collapse of the Liberator Permanent Benefit Building Society and others in the Balfour group was followed by revelations of substantial losses arising from speculative ventures carried out by two subsidiaries. The end of the 1890's mining boom led to the collapse in 1901 of the London and Globe Finance Corporation and other companies in the Whitaker Wright group; again shareholders belatedly learnt of subsidiaries' losses.

2. H. W. Macrosty, The trust movement in British industry (London: Longmans, Green & Co. 1907),pp.15, 129, 200.

the formation of holding companies. The act introduced general
requirements for companies to publish financial information. All
companies (with the exception of newly-defined 'private' companies)
were to lodge financial statements with the Registrar of Companies.[3]
The intention of the legislature in relieving private companies from
the obligation to publish financial reports was presumably to encourage
company formation and also to avoid placing small businesses at a
disadvantage relative to unincorporated competitors.[4] But since
many firms were reluctant to submit to financial accountability, the
legislation encouraged the formation of subsidiaries. Within a year
of the passage of the legislation, commentators were describing this
privilege of not having to file financial statements as the chief
advantage of the private company form.[5] As the accompanying table
indicates, there was a marked increase in company registrations shortly
after the new act came into force.

---

3. The term "private company" had been in common use before the 1907
   Act. The definition adopted in the act was that recommended by a
   Departmental Committee appointed by the Board of Trade in February
   1905, (the 'Loreburn Committee'): the number of shareholders was
   not to exceed 20, there were to be restrictions on the transfer of
   shares, and private companies were not to appeal to the public to
   subscribe for their shares. See the Committee's Report, para. 45.
   (The report was reproduced in The incorporated accountants'
   journal, Jan. 1907, pp.96-103).

4. The Loreburn Committee had recommended that private companies be
   afforded several concessions: that they need not file statements
   in lieu of prospectuses, and they should be afforded releif from
   stamp duty on property transfers. However a majority of the
   Committee was firmly opposed to exempting private companies from
   the filing of financial statements with the Registrar (para. 45ff).
   However a bill incorporating the Loreburn Committee's recommendations
   was amended in the committee stages to exclude private companies
   from the filing provisions. See The incorporated accountants'
   journal, Sept. 1907, p.283.

5. "Auditor's duties under the new companies act", The incorporated
   accountant's journal, Aug. 1908, p.241. See also "Professional
   notes", ibid., Oct. 1913, pp.1-2.

U. K. registration of companies
with share capital and limited liability[6]

1896	4,658	1906	4,776	1916	3,317
1897	5,148	1907	5,152	1917	3,895
1898	5,065	1908	4,932	1918	3,385
1899	4,879	1909	6,268	1919	10,592
1900	4,859	1910	7,091	1920	10,861
1901	3,358	1911	6,371	1921	6,692
1902	3,850	1912	7,268	1922	8,368
1903	3,992	1913	7,321	1923	8,400
1904	3,765	1914	6,097	1924	8,420
1905	4,253	1915	4,002	1925	8,437

By 1918 no less than 50,000 of the 66,000 companies then on the register
were private companies[7] - though it is not possible to assess how many
of these were subsidiaries of public companies. However it seems likely
that there were few holding companies in Britain; certainly the use of
holding companies had not been a great source of contention. In 1907
a leading article in The accountant had warned that holding company
structures were "capable of producing transactions upon the Whitaker
Wright principle"[8] - meaning transactions at inflated prices between
related companies leading to firms reporting illusory profits. Subsequent references to holding company accounting in the British literature
were mainly references to American or Canadian experience.[9] And as late
as 1918 the announcement of the merger of two firms via the formation of
a holding company was unusual enough to warrant a news-item in an

---

6. Source: A. E. Hussey, thesis submitted in partial fulfilment of
   requirements of degree of M.Ec., University of Sydney, 1971;
   information obtained from British Parliamentary Accounts and papers
   1896-1908 and 1919-1925, Reports from Commissioners, Inspectors and
   others 1909-1918.

7. Report of Committee on Companies Acts, 1918, para.63 (The report
   was reproduced in The accountant, Oct. 1918, pp.182-7, 199-200 and
   213-5).

8. "Points in company procedure, loc.cit., 6 July 1907, p.2.

9. See, e.g., "The accounts of 'parent' companies", The accountant,
   18 March 1911, pp.413-5; D. S. Kerr, "Consolidated balance sheets",
   ibid, 20 Nov. 1915, pp.637-30.

accounting journal:

> The idea of a working arrangement through the medium of
> a holding company is not one which is very popular in
> this country, and it will be interesting to observe
> whether this example is followed in other instances.[10]

If holding companies were still few in number immediately after

World War I, business conditions were such as to cause more

businessmen to look closely at this form of organisation. A. E. Cutforth

later wrote that a short-lived post-war boom, together with a loss of

export trade, the challenge of imports, pressure for improved working

conditions and the formidable costs of replacing obsolete equipment

all encouraged business combinations as a means of reducing competition

and minimising costs.[11]

Part of the jump in the number of company registrations from

around 4,000 per annum during wartime to more than 10,000 per annum in

the immediate post-war years may have been due to the popularity of

holding companies as a means of effecting amalgamations, or the use of

subsidiaries to conceal the existence of business combinations from

customers and suppliers. Holding company structures may also have been

popular as a means of avoiding public scrutiny of financial affairs at

a time when there was considerable concern about the economic conse-

quences of the amalgamation movement. Since the 1898-1901 merger boom

in the U.K., "hostile sentiments" had been expressed about "the

organisation of combinations".[12]

There emerged an extensive economic literature describing the

tendency towards amalgamations and combinations and evaluating the

---

10. "A new holding company", ibid, 26 Oct. 1918, p.222.

11. A. E. Cutforth, "Amalgamations", ibid, 1 April 1933, p.425.

12. Industrial commission reports, Vol.xviii, pp.15-32 as cited G. R.
     Carter, The tendency towards industrial combination (London:
     Constable & Company Ltd., 1913), p.267.

likely effect of mergers on the British economy. A wave of bank
amalgamations led to the appointment of a parliamentary committee to
investigate the possibility of interfering with these mergers.[13] Later
another parliamentary committee was appointed to consider more general
questions about the effect of the formation of trade organisations
and combinations. This committee reported in 1919 that trade
associations and combines were soon likely to exercise "a paramount
control over all important branches of British trade", and recommended
the establishment of machinery to monitor and regulate all forms of
industrial combinations.[14] These recommendations were not followed
in their entirety, perhaps because events quickly demonstrated that
the power of combines and associations had been overestimated.[15] But
there was no doubting that by the 1920's business combinations - and
holding companies - were widespread. Certainly by the early 1920's the
use of the holding company as an amalgamation device was discussed
frequently in the columns of The accountant. And a series of
commentators described how holding companies had come into prominence
after World War I.[16]

---

13. "Bank amalgamations and the public", The incorporated accountants'
    journal, March 1918, pp.105.6.

14. Report of departmental committee on trusts, 1919, p.11, as cited
    P. Fitzgerald, Industrial combination in England (London: Sir
    Issac Pitman & Sons Ltd., 2nd ec., 1927), p.212. A summary of
    these recommendations was also reproduced in The incorporated
    accountants' journal, June 1919, p.16.

15. Fitzgerald, op.cit., p.213. The Profiteering Act of 1919
    established a central committee and a series of standing committees
    to investigate the operations of trusts. See The incorporated
    accountants' journal, Dec. 1919, p.51.

16. See, e.g., "Holding companies and their published accounts",
    The accountant, 6 Jan., 1923, p.2; D. Hickey, "Company law
    defects - suggested amendments", ibid, 1 Nov..1924, p.634;
    E. W. Jones, "Company amalgamations", ibid, 21 Nov. 1925,
    p.819 and "In parliament", ibid, 17 March 1928, p.387.

The popularity of holding companies was followed by an expanding literature on the accounting issues involved in handling inter-corporate shareholdings. And in 1922 British accountants began experimenting with the use of consolidated statements.

This chapter examines part of the background to the introduction of consolidated statements into U.K. reporting practices.

Publicly-traded securities

The accounting literature concerned with inter-corporate investments did not draw clear distinctions between the treatments appropriate for publicly-traded and other securities, respectively. However it is convenient to adopt this distinction and to consider the methods developed for readily-marketable securities before turning to other inter-corporate investments.

The previous chapter outlined how the British profession came to apply distinct sets of valuation rules to assets, depending upon whether the assets were classed as "fixed" or "floating". This rule was to be of especial significance to inter-corporate investments. There were few other items which might appear as either "fixed" or "floating" assets, depending upon the circumstances of individual firms or the "intentions" of managers.

In the 1880's and 1890's - before this valuation framework had been adopted - it was common for shareholdings to be valued at current market prices or approximation of those prices. There was support for this practice in the literature. Model answers to an 1886 Institute examination stated that in valuing listed securities accountants should examine a "stock and share list of the day, and take the mean price".[17] And in the late 1890's several accounting writers argued that these assets either could, or should be valued at current market

---

17. The accountants' manual (London: Gee & Co., n.d.), p.E59.

prices.[18]

However, in terms of the Dicksee-sponsored view of asset valuation, the appropriate basis for valuing listed securities would vary according to whether they were "fixed" or "floating" assets. For fixed assets, any "fluctuations in value" would be ignored and cost data used for valuation purposes. For "floating" assets, the use of the lower of cost and market rule was indicated.[19]

The introduction of these rules appears to have produced some conflict of opinion within the profession. In 1899 it was reported that there was a "good deal of opinion ... as to what is the advisable course where the value of investments fluctuates".[20] Some continued to favour the systematic use of market prices,[21] though this practice was described in the correspondence columns of The accountant as giving rise to "vain hopes" and "needless fears".[22] Conversely, the steadfast

---

18. See, e.g., F. W. Densham, "Depreciation of assets and goodwill of limited companies", The accountant, 28 May 1898, p.570; R. Whitehall, "Some notes on matters of opinion in connection with accounts", ibid, 1 July 1899, p.704.

19. However, Dicksee's Auditing (London: Gee & Co., 1892) did not spell this out in any detail. Evidently Dicksee had not considered the possibility that inter-corporate investments would be anything but fixed assets. His brief discussion of the matter obviously assumed that they would be classified as fixed; he asserted that investments "need not be depreciated unless of a wasting nature - such as shares in Mines or Single-Ship Companies" (p.128). It was not until the 8th edition (1910) that Dicksee extended the discussion to cover "temporary investments" which were to be "valued at either their original cost or realisable market price, whichever for the time being may be the lower" (p.220).

20. R. Whitehall, loc.cit.

21. See, e.g., "The valuation of assets in balance sheets", The accountant, 6 July 1901.

22. C. W. Moore, "Holding companies and depreciation", correspondence, loc.cit., 10 Nov. 1906.

retention of cost-based valuation of shareholdings was interpreted
by some as a happy symbol of financial stability:

> At such a time as the present, when all first-class
> securities stand nearly 20 percent lower than they
> did a few years since, it is only those companies that
> have in the past built up ample secret reserves that
> are able to produce accounts that do not show a falling
> off of the value of the securities held ...[23]

Banking companies appear to have been unaffected by the changing
attitude to asset valuation since they had long been accustomed to
record marketable securities at well below their current market prices.[24]
Distinctive practices were also developed for life assurance companies.
Although it was claimed that "the necessity for valuing ... investments
below market price" was "less urgent" for insurance firms than for
banks,[25] it seems to have become accepted that insurance companies should
also promptly write down all their investments.[26]

Otherwise it seems that most firms adopted the valuation framework
of retaining fixed asset-investments at cost (unless fluctuations in
value appeared "permanent") while valuing shareholdings which were
deemed "floating" assets at the lower of cost and market price. Most
variations in treatment arose from different interpretations of the
judgment in the Verner case - the 1896 judgment which had prompted the

---

23. (Anon.), "The fluctuation of investments", The accountant, 2 Nov.
    1901, p.1183.

24. In a model answer to an Institute examination it was claimed that
    there was "very much to be said in favour of secret reserves for
    banks" - presumably because of beliefs that the collapse of banks
    would be bad for the community, so that anything which might add
    to the strength of banks was a "good thing"; it was assumed that
    conscious under-valuation added to the financial strength of banking
    enterprises. See The accountants' manual, Vol.VI (London: Gee &
    Co., 1898) pp.117-8. See also Vol.II (1894), p.192 and Vol.IX
    (1904), p.417; "Secret reserves", The incorporated accountants'
    journal, March 1902, pp.120-1; E. Snowden, "What are profits?",
    ibid, April 1904, p.161.

25. The accountants' manual, loc.cit., Vol.IX, 1904, p.418.

26. See "The re-valuation of investments", The accountant, 14 Sept.
    1901, pp.977-9.

profession to link asset classification and valuation. Some
accountants interpreted the case as sanctioning the retention of
cost-based valuation for <u>all</u> fixed assets.[27] Others saw the judgment
as establishing that investment-trusts need not write-down their
investments[28] though strictly the case had not been concerned with the
propriety of this or that method of profit calculation but with the
circumstances under which the court should interfere with the payment
of dividends. Even so, the interpretation that "trust companies need
not write-down investments" was so popularised that on occasions
trust companies were commended for having prepared their financial
statements on a "sounder basis" than the form sanctioned in the Verner
case.[29] And some writers adopted a rule-of-thumb to the effect that
"trust companies could leave investments at cost" while "finance
companies should remedy depreciation out of current revenue". (The term
"finance company" was at that time applied to firms which traded in or
handled the issue of securities). Rather than approach asset valuation
from the consideration of whether investments were "fixed" or "current"
assets, distinct rules were applied to firms conducting one or other
style of business.[30] This rule-of-thumb may initially have been a way

27. e.g. F. N. Keen, "The balance sheet of a limited company", <u>ibid</u>,
    16 April 1898, p.407; (anon.) "Balance sheet values", <u>ibid</u>, 11 Jan.
    1908, pp.42-3.

28. e.g. M. Webster Jenkinson, "Some debateable matters in accounting
    and auditing", <u>ibid</u>, 20 March 1909, p.411.

29. "Trust companies and depreciation", <u>ibid</u>, 22 Feb. 1902, p.203.

30. See, e.g., (anon.), "Depreciation in investments", <u>ibid</u>, Feb.
    1918, p.121; E.H., "Trust companies and depreciation", <u>ibid</u>,
    4 June 1932; M. Webster Jenkinson, "Some notes on the audit
    of different businesses", <u>ibid</u>, 19 April 1913, pp.590-1. By 1930
    the distinction between trust and finance companies was also
    relevant to the form of balance sheet disclosure of details
    concerning inter-corporate investments: trust companies were
    expected to provide supplementary schedules of their investments
    while finance companies were not expected to do so "as a matter of
    course". See <u>The accountant</u>, 1 Nov. 1930, pp.627-8.

of overcoming troublesome questions about asset classification criteria
- but it was soon evident that this approach merely substituted
troublesome questions about what constituted a "trust" or "finance"
company.[31] Further the adoption of this rule-of-thumb led to some
conflicting proposals about the valuation of investments. For example,
a "finance" company might hold shares acquired for long-term investment
- so that these assets would (by most definitions) be classed as fixed
assets, and hence (by most valuation rules) recorded at cost price.
But in terms of the "trust or finance company" rule, these shares would
be valued at the lower of cost and market.

The view that the accounting treatment of inter-corporate investments would be approached in special ways for firms engaged in particular
classes of business has endured in the British accounting literature.[32]
However, the idea that different valuation rules were to be applied to
"fixed" and "floating" inter-corporate investments gradually became
widely accepted. Until the 1920's, accounting writers steadfastly
affirmed that "fixed asset" investments should be retained at cost
unless there had been "permanent", or "definite and permanent" declines

---

31. See, e.g. The accountants' manual, loc.cit., Vol.IX 1904, p.417;
    "Depreciation on investments", op.cit., p.121; "Payment of divi-
    dends and depreciation of investments", The accountant, 1 Nov.
    1930, pp.627-8.

32. Subsequent legislation permitted banks and assurance companies to
    conceal the basis upon which assets had been valued and profits
    calculated. See U.K. Companies Act, 1948, 8th Sch., paras.12(5)
    and 15(4); also sections 149(4), 150(2) and 152(3). The rationale
    for these concessions was discussed in the Report of the Company
    Law Amendment Committee (1945), paras.101-2. Notwithstanding these
    statutory rules, the Institute of Chartered Accountants in England
    and Wales has suggested that in principle, the treatment of inter-
    corporate investments for "banks, assurance companies ... investment
    trust companies and companies which deal in shares and similar
    investments" involves different considerations to the treatment of
    the investments of trading companies. See the preamble to the
    Institute's Recommendation N 18 (1958), "The treatment of investments
    in the balance sheets of trading companies".

is the value of those investments.[33] To some observers, the scale of
any losses was of some significance - it was suggested that investments
should be written down when price-falls were considerable.[34] But by
1916 "most mercantile firms" did in fact value investments at cost,
provided those investments had "reasonably maintained their value since
the time they were bought".[35]

The usefulness of cost-based valuation for inter-corporate shareholdings was questioned before and after World War I. In 1913, The
accountant provided a gloomy report of falling share prices - but
insisted that these were only "temporary", and could be disregarded when
valuing long-term investments.[36] Around this time there were severe
falls in the price of trustee securities, so that The accountant
suggested that 'gilt-edged' securities would soon have to be renamed -
"the adjective seems rapidly to be becoming a misnomer".[37] For a
time The accountant firmly supported the retention of cost-based
investment valuation:

> Securities which are really held for investment purposes
> need, under no circumstances, whatever, be valued for
> Balance Sheet purposes at the market price on the date of
> such Balance Sheet - indeed the market price ... has

---

33. e.g. E. Snowden, "What are profits?" The incorporated account-
      ants' journal, April 1904, p.162; "Depreciation on investments",
      The accountant, 18 June 1904, pp.802-3; M. Webster Jenkinson,
      "Some debatable matters in accounting and auditing", ibid, 20
      March 1909, p.411; P. D. Leake, "Depreciation and wasting assets",
      ibid, 3 July 1915; (anon.), "Writing down securities", ibid,
      5 Feb. 1910, pp.193-4.

34. E. M. Carter, "What is an annual balance sheet?", The accountant
      22 Oct. 1910, pp.563-4.

35. "Some notes on the preparation and audit of a balance sheet",
      The accountant, Feb. 16 1916, p.231.

36. (Anon.), "Depreciation of investments", loc.cit., 1 Feb. 1913,
      pp.147-8.

37. "Depreciation in bank investments", loc.cit., 17 Jan. 1914, p.69.
      See also "Gilt edged securities", ibid, 27 July 1912, p.114.

nothing whatever to do with the proper basis of valuation
of fixed assets under any circumstances whatever, and ...
it is only remotely concerned with the proper valuation
of assets in Balance Sheets in so far as it may throw a light
upon the loss (if any) that may fairly be expected to be
incurred on the realization of such assets as there is [38]
reason to suppose will, in fact, be realised at a loss.

However share prices continued to fall. Commentators became pro-

gressively dissatisfied with the customary accounting treatment of

inter-corporate investments. Two major proposals were canvassed. First,

it was argued that the basis of valuation of investments should be

disclosed in unambiguous terms - be it 'at cost' or 'at market price'.[39]

Balance sheets which showed investments as being valued "at or under

cost" (without explicit disclosure of the actual position) provoked

hostility from commentators.[40]

Second, it was argued that the market prices of securities should

be stated in parenthetical or supplementary notes to the balance sheet.

As early as 1911 Spicer and Pegler had proposed that notes be inserted in

balance sheets stating the market prices of investments - but only when

market prices were less than cost and when no provision for loss had

been made in the published reports.[41] This proposal seemed more concerned

---

38. "Minimum prices and balance sheets", ibid, 25 December 1915, p.766.
The last lines of this passage allude to the practice of providing
for losses on realisation. It appears that these provisions were
often entered on the equities side of the balance sheet and were
created by appropriations rather than charges against profits. For
a discussion of these and other practices concerning the valuation
of inter-corporate shareholdings see "Investment Accounts - II",
The accountant, 20 March 1915, p.373.

39. e.g. R. H. E. Wilkinson, "Balance sheets", The accountant,
1 Aug. 1914, p.159; J. H. McCall, "The principles of auditing",
ibid, 8 Dec. 1923, p.840.

40. e.g. "Auditors and investments", The accountant, 19 Feb. 1921,
pp.198-9, citing The daily mail; "Investments in tin", The
accountant, 25 Aug. 1928, p.278 and "Origin of a dividend", idem,
20 July 1929, pp.102-3.

41. E. E. Spicer and E. C. Pegler, Practical auditing (London: H.
Foulks Lynch & Co., 1911), p.389.

with the legal liabilities of auditors than with the usefulness of
financial reports. Even so by 1915 the disclosure of the market
prices of investments "in small figures under the book values" had
become a routine practice.[42] And it was to remain an accepted practice
in later years.[43]

Both of these proposals were essentially refinements of the cost-
based valuation framework advanced by Dicksee in 1892. But in the
1920's there was a short-lived change of attitude, as volatile prices
encouraged many accountants and commentators to support the systematic
use of market selling prices for the valuation of inter-corporate
shareholdings - regardless of whether these assets were classed as
"fixed" or "floating".

The accountant, it will be recalled, had unequivocally supported the
use of cost-prices to value investments. But since 1915 there were
gradual shifts in The accountant's position, so that in 1921 an editorial
writer could fairly note that

> the practice of bringing investments into a Balance Sheet
> at the present time at cost price has been frequently
> criticised in our columns.[44]

By 1921 The accountant supported both the writing-down of investments
and the inclusion of this "depreciation" as a charge against income.
Similarly a contemporary financial paper, The financial news wrote:

> If [a balance sheet] ... is to possess real value it must
> unequivocally declare the state of affairs at the date
> to which the accounts are made up, and investments should
> in all cases be valued as at that date ... Shareholders
> have the right to be told precisely what their assets
> will realise at the end of the financial year.[45]

---

42. (Anon.), "Investment accounts - II", op.cit., p.374.

43. See, e.g., R. N. Carter (ed.), Advanced accounts (London: Sir
     Isaac Pitman and Sons, Ltd., 1922), p.894; W. H. Castle, "Points
     on company accounts", The accountant, 28 June 1924, p.1063; N.
     Wilkinson, "Valuation of assets", ibid, 22 Aug. 1925, p.286.

44. "Valuation of investments", loc.cit., 4 June 1921, p.712.

45. As quoted in "The question of depreciation", The accountant,
     18 June 1921, p.789.

By 1922 <u>The accountant</u> was condemning the retention of cost-based valuation in the strongest terms;[46] and by 1924 the journal was even supporting the <u>writing-up</u> of investments where they were recorded at less than current market prices.[47] While several writers took pains to reject the suggestion that income statements should regard the "unrealised" gains of appreciation as revenues,[48] it seems that accountants had come to reject the long-standing view that market prices should be disregarded when valuing assets.

However this seems to have been a short-term response to unusual stock market conditions. Further unusual stock market conditions in the late 1920's ensured that firms had few opportunities to write-up marketable securities - even if they wanted to. By the early 1930's it seems that British accountants had once again embraced cost-based valuation of long-term investments and the use of the lower of cost and market rule for "temporary" shareholdings. There was general agreement that market prices should not be used to value publicly-traded securities.

Large parcels of listed securities

The overriding impression to be obtained from an examination of the meagre literature on this subject available before 1930 was that accountants were more sure of what <u>not</u> to do than of what was the "best" practice. Accountants were extremely reluctant to use unit market selling prices as the basis for calculating the worth of large parcels of stock. This reluctance stemmed more from a distrust of the significance of unit market prices to the holder of a large parcel than from a concern about the propriety of using market prices <u>per se</u>.

---

46. "Valuation of investments", <u>loc.cit.</u>, 4 March 1922, p.

47. "Writing up investments", <u>loc.cit.</u>, 12 Jan. 1924, p.44.

48. e.g. L. R. Dicksee, "Published balance sheets and window dressing", <u>The accountant</u>, 17 April 1926; A. E. Barton, <u>Australasian advanced accountancy</u> (Sydney: The Law Book Co. of Australia Ltd., 7th ed., 1922), p.433.

In the 1890's the question of how to handle large parcels typically arose in connection with the accounts of promoter or vendor companies. Here, the matter which seemed to cause greatest concern was not so much the valuation of shares *per se* but whether a sale of property in exchange for shares in a newly-floated company produced a *realised* profit - and, if so, how that profit could be calculated. It was reported in 1899 that a variety of methods were in use to record such transactions. The method popular with "the largest and most important of the finance and development companies" actually placed no value on the shares so acquired. A profit was recognised when the shares were sold; meantime particulars of the number of shares held and the prevailing market price of those securities were reported in notes to balance sheets. A less conservative method recorded a profit to the extent of year-end share values - a procedure which was forcefully criticised in the financial press as "misleading and erroneous". Other methods involved the recording of shares acquired at their par value, or at the original cost of the property exchanged for those securities. The method most favoured by one group of Institute members was to record the shares at par values for balance sheet purposes, while preparing a profit and loss account in two columns - one showing revenues in terms of "cash" and the other showing revenues in the form of "shares".[49] The advocates of these methods generally shunned the use of current selling prices for newly promoted companies. However, one critic of the use of market prices added that he withdrew his objection when the shares became "dividend paying, and the market value of the shares was based upon its earning powers".[50]

Evidently it was not unknown for promotors or vendors to support

---

49. "Report of meeting of Chartered Accountants Students' Society of London", The accountant, 18 Feb. 1899, pp.201-6.

50. Ibid, p.203.

stock prices in the market until it was opportune for them to "unload".[51]
The profession's fear of profit manipulations through write-ups or the
use of market selling prices was seemingly reinforced by the failure
of the London and Globe Finance Corporation and related companies in
1901. This group, under the general direction of Whitaker Wright, had
been active in promoting mining companies and in dealing in the shares
of its own and other promotions. The collapse of the mining boom brought
disaster. However an illusion of prosperity was sustained for a time
by a series of write-ups and intra-group transactions involving large
parcels of securities.

These events contributed to a decided reluctance on the part of
the accounting profession to sanction the use of market prices in valuing
inter-corporate investments. While there were few discussions of the
treatment of large parcels of shares, it was apparent that the underlying concern was to avoid a repetition of the London and Globe affair.
Indeed in 1906 several accountants expressed the opinion that no profit
should be taken into account on the acquisition of stocks in promotional
situations until these stocks were sold. (They did not indicate how
the shares should be treated for balance sheet purposes).[52] In 1911
Spicer and Pegler warned that it was "not always possible to rely on
market quotations in the case of newly-promoted companies":

> such quotations are frequently merely nominal and do not
> represent actual value.[53]

And in 1913 M. Webster Jenkinson cautioned against using selling prices
where the listing of a large block of shares could "bring down" a
market; accordingly he proposed balance sheet values should be at

---

51. Idem, p.202.

52. W. Strachan, "The audit of financial and land companies' accounts",
     The incorporated accountants' journal, Dec. 1906, p.74.

53. Op.cit., p.500.

cost (net of any underwriting commission or promotion profit) and
that profit and loss statements should be presented in two columns.[54]

In summary, since the 1890's British accountants were extremely
reluctant to base the valuations of large parcels of listed securities
on market prices. Where securities were obtained through transactions
with third parties, accountants generally favoured the use of cost.

Unlisted securities

Little attention was given in the U.K. literature to the recording
and reporting of unlisted inter-corporate investments until the 1920's,
when accountants were frequently confronted with problems arising from
the popularisation of subsidiaries. Nevertheless a review of the early
literature provides some sense of the basis from which accountants
approached holding company accounting.

When the treatment of unlisted securities was discussed in the
early U.K. literature, the question at issue was usually that of how
to ascertain the current "value" of those securities. For example,
model answers to 1886 Institute examinations said that unlisted
securities should be valued in the same way as listed securities: at
their current market price.

> To assess the correctness of valuations, one should make
> ... application to the secretaries of the various
> companies who are usually able to give a fair idea of
> the value. If not, the dividends paid for a series of
> years, and the financial position of the companies, as
> shown by the published accounts, might enable an opinion
> to be formed.[55]

The author of a prize winning essay published in The incorporated
accountants' journal in 1885 said that the "general rule" for valuing
intercorporate investments was "to put them down at cost price rather

---

54. "Some notes on the audit of different businesses", The accountant,
    19 April, 1913, p.590.

55. The accountants' manual, Vol.I (London: Gee and Co., n.d.), p.E59.
    See also pp.D27-28.

than estimated figures" - though "if the latter price is decided upon, then the auditor should satisfy himself as to the basis of calculation.[56]

Similarly, in 1899 a practitioner asserted - not very helpfully - that where there was no market quotation there was "no satisfactory basis upon which to calculate the actual value of the asset"; "it seemed to him" that the valuation of unlisted shares was "a matter of individual opinion".[57]

In summary, the "general rule" for valuing unquoted securities at this time may have been cost - but evidently estimates were also used. However, the failure of the London and Globe group in 1901 demonstrated that "estimates" could be wildly optimistic and deceptive. The London and Globe had written-up investments in related (listed) companies to totally unrealistic levels: in one case, shares were recorded at double market prices, while in another, shares "bought" from a subsidiary for £125,000 were instantly carried in the balance sheet at £500,000.[58] But the profession's response to these revelations of fraudulent upward revaluations was (for a time) a general antipathy towards the valuation of all inter-corporate investments. In 1906 one practitioner proposed that all inter-corporate investments should be recorded at the lower of cost and market value regardless of whether they were fixed or floating assets.[59] In 1911 Cropper commented that "unquoted investments and investments for which there is no ready market" could, in unscrupulous hands, lend themselves to "manipulation for the purpose of creating

---

56. A. W. Rooke, "The duties and responsibilities of an auditor to a public company", loc.cit., Jan. 1885, p.89.

57. H. E. Barham, "Report of discussion of the Chartered Accountants' Students' Society of London" The accountant, 18 Feb. 1899, p.202.

58. A. Vallance, Very private enterprise (London: Thames & Hudson, 1955), p.61.

59. W. Strachan, loc.cit., pp.70-1.

fictitious 'paper' profits".   Hence

> their valuation must be upon as conservative a basis as
> possible, and should lean to undervaluation rather than
> otherwise.[60]

And in 1914 another practitioner claimed that unlisted shares in highly

speculative enterprises should never be valued in such a way as to record

"unrealised" profits.[61]

At the time, some securities not officially listed on stock

exchanges were nevertheless the subject of "off-market" transactions:

the literature contains occasional references to the availability of

price data in respect of non-listed securities in the "Stock Exchange

Year Book" or "financial papers".[62]   But for lesser-traded stocks the

memory of price-propping during the 1890's mining boom may have prompted

comments that where a market was not "free" then the consideration reported

might "not always represent the actual value". Inspection of the

balance sheets of such companies was recommended as a means of helping

auditors "form an opinion" though warnings were issued to the effect

that the financial statements of these corporations were often unaudited

and "consequently liable to be strongly tinged with the optimism of

the company's officers".[63]

There were very few discussions of the treatment of unlisted

securities - but a theme common to these contributions was that it was

hazardous to write-up these assets to "estimated values". The most

highly regarded treatment was the retention of these investments at

---

60. L. C. Cropper, Book-keeping and accounts (London: Macdonald and
     Evans, 1911), p.450.

61. F. M. Hawnt, "The plea for greater detail in balance sheets of
     limited companies", The incorporated accountants' journal, Dec.
     1914, p.66.

62. S. E. Giles, "The verification of assets and liabilities", ibid,
     Oct. 1913, pp.16-17;   E. C. Pegler, "The principles of auditing",
     The accountant, 14 Feb. 1914, p.231.

63. H. Benington, "Limitations", ibid, Sept. 1916, p.290.

cost. When British practitioners found themselves concerned with handling investments in subsidiaries, the use of cost-based valuation was commonly regarded as best practice.

The well-publicised failure of Farrow's Bank in 1920 provided further support for cost-based valuations by focusing on the way upward revaluations could be used to disguise company losses. An investigation of the bank's affairs initiated by an American investor who had just acquired a controlling interest uncovered evidence of accounting manipulations. The bank had incurred heavy trading losses which had not been disclosed in the 1920 financial reports.[64] Further investigations by a liquidator revealed that while the bank had regularly reported profits, it had actually accumulated "working losses" of over £1,100,000 between 1909 and 1920; in addition £1,700,000 had to be struck off the book value of investments. The total losses of £2,800,000 had been concealed by writing-up assets, chiefly "investments":

> In the 1915 balance sheet the bank's investment in the Dreadnought Cement Company, formed to operate on some bank-owned land was put down at £435,000, though the amount actually spent on the company's development was then only £11,000. (Dreadnought was eventually written up, by 1920, to £780,000). Likewise, in 1912, an actual investment of £230 in the Gazeland China Clay Company figured in the balance sheet as an asset valued at £150,000; and in 1919 a holding in the Laminated Coal Co., costing £35,000, was promptly written up to £160,000.[65]

These revaluations could not have been justified by reference to the circumstances of the firms in which investments had been made. They had been carried out with the complicity of the auditors.[66] However, to some observers it may have appeared that asset revaluations were to blame for the undoubted misrepresentations of the bank's

---

64. The incorporated accountants' journal, Feb. 1921, p.84.

65. Vallance, op.cit., pp.106-7.

66. "Professional notes", The incorporated accountants' journal, July 1921, p.193.

affairs. There was not, in 1921, an immediate rejection of the practice of asset revaluations; quite the opposite, insofar as marketable securities were concerned. However it seems likely that the Farrow's Bank revelations reinforced preferences for cost-based valuation of unlisted securities.

Resume

As outlined in Chapter 2, around the turn of the century British
accountants adopted a framework for asset valuation which involved
the application of distinct sets of valuation rules to "fixed" and
"floating" assets. The early history of accounting for inter-
corporate investments is largely concerned with the application of these
ideas. If holdings of publicly traded securities were regarded as
"floating" assets, then they were to be valued at the lower of cost
and market price. If they were deemed to be "fixed" assets, then
"cost" was appropriate. Publicly-traded securities were a special
case since market prices for these assets were readily available.
Accountants accepted that market price data were useful information, and
the practice of supplying these prices as supplementary disclosures
became customary. The treatment of large parcels of listed securities
was generally consistent with the treatments advocated for small
parcels - except that commentators seemed conscious that the valuation
of similar assets had been a source of manipulation in several cases.
Accounting writers were similarly cautious about the treatment of
unlisted securities (in large or small parcels). Again, the use of
cost-based valuation was regarded as standard practice.

One feature of the treatment of publicly traded securities was
that for a time in the 1920's accounting opinion seemed to favour the
systematic valuation of these assets at market selling prices. This
attitude was short-lived, and by the late 1920's accountants again
favoured cost-based valuations.

Ch. 4   U.K. accounting for investments in subsidiaries

The title of this chapter might be interpreted as suggesting that the accounting procedures appropriate for "investments in subsidiaries" are somehow different from the procedures appropriate for other "inter-corporate investments". No such distinction is intended - though it must be recognised that accounting rules have been developed as though the treatment for one form of investment should be different from the treatment appropriate for the other. These artificial distinctions have led, at times, to anomalous treatments and manipulative practices.

However, the distinction drawn here between subsidiary and non-subsidiary investments is simply one of convenience. It was con-venient to postpone an examination of the development of U.K. accounting techniques for subsidiaries until after first examining the techniques developed for handling inter-corporate investments in general. This is so because in the U.K. and Commonwealth countries, little attention was paid to the specific question of how to handle investments in "subsidiaries" until the 1920's, when the use of holding companies was popularised. And by the 1920's British accountants had developed firm ideas about the techniques appropriate for valuing other inter-corporate investments.

Some discussion of the treatment of subsidiaries appeared in the columns of The accountant around the turn of the century - before and after the collapse of the London and Globe Finance Company and other companies in the Whitaker Wright group. Before the group's collapse, Wright told an annual meeting of shareholders that it was "not the auditor's duty to value securities [such as those held by] this corpora-tion", since in order to do so the auditors "would have to go to British Columbia, New Zealand, Western Australia and elsewhere". The editor of The accountant enthusiastically endorsed these comments, claiming that without local knowledge it would be impracticable for an

auditor to attempt to form an opinion on the value of such securities
- and adding that even an informed opinion would not be of "any
particular value". And then The accountant claimed that auditors
could not be expected to form a definite opinion about any asset
valuations since "the duties of an auditor in one case must necessarily
be his duties in all cases".[1] The logic was dubious, but plainly the
view was taken that auditors should not be held responsible for
verifying representations made about subsidiaries. Three years later,
The accountant expressed totally conflicting views. In 1901, some
months after the appointment of liquidators to the wreckage of the
London and Globe group, The accountant was extremely critical of
suggestions that auditors should not be held responsible for the accuracy
of the accounts of subsidiaries.

> It occurs to us that in some cases the entire income of
> a parent company might be derived from subsidiary com-
> panies, and in these cases an audit of the parent company's
> accounts would be singularly ineffective if it did not
> also contain some guarantee that the accounts of the
> various subsidiary companies were also correct.[2]

In 1908 similar observations were made about auditors' responsibilities in connection with the investments of holding companies -
The accountant claimed that it was "competent" of the auditor to ask
for copies of subsidiaries' balance sheets and of the reports of the
subsidiaries' auditors. Editorial writers expressed concern that
inter-locking corporate relationships could produce results similar
to those experienced in the London and Globe crash and the earlier
failure of the Liberator Building Society, and other firms in the Balfour
group. Nevertheless they claimed that subsidiaries should be valued
at cost despite "fluctuations in value".[3]

---

1.   "Auditors and the valuation of assets", loc.cit., 1 Oct. 1898,
      p.925.

2.   "The audit of subsidiary companies" accounts", loc.cit., 8 June
      1901, p.665.

3.   "Auditors' duties and affiliated companies", loc.cit., 18 Jan.
      1913, p.78

The major discussions of holding company accounting appearing
in the British literature before the 1920's were reprints of articles
previously published or presented in North America. In 1905 The
accountant published a copy of a lecture delivered by A. L. Dickinson
at New York University in which Dickinson described a series of
matters dealing with corporation accounting, including the newly-
introduced practice of preparing consolidated statements.[4] In 1908 The
accountant published W. M. Lybrand's "The accounting of industrial
enterprises" which had previously appeared in The journal of accountancy
and which similarly alluded to consolidated reporting.[5] And in 1915
The accountant published a short note by a Canadian chartered accountant,
D. S. Kerr, which dealt specifically with the use of consolidated
balance sheets.[6]

One of the earliest non-American discussions of holding company
accounting in the British literature concerned the reporting practices
of an Australian company, the Commercial Bank of Australia Ltd. In
1913 The accountant reproduced the bank's balance sheet and profit and
loss account following a reader's request for an explanation of an
item, "estimated deficiency in connection with the Special Assets
Trust Company Ltd." which appeared as a deduction from paid-up capital.
The explanation given was that the latter company was a subsidiary of
the bank, and that the subsidiary's assets and liabilities had been
incorporated with those of the parent in its published financial statement. The accountant commented that the treatment was "absolutely
unconventional" and certainly preferable to the "more conventional form
under which the bank's interest in the Trust Company ... would appear

---

4.   "Some special points in corporation accounting", loc.cit., 7 Oct.
     1905.

5.   "The accounting of industrial enterprises", loc.cit., 19 Dec. 1908,
     pp.786-99.

6.   "Consolidated balance sheets", loc.cit., Nov. 1915, pp.627-30.

among the assets at its book value".[7] It seems significant that The
accountant readily supported the principle of consolidated statements
- though its interpretation of the bank's financial statements was
unfortunately astray. The Special Assets Trust Company Ltd. had been
formed in October 1898 as part of a reconstruction scheme following
the failure of the Commercial Bank of Australia in the aftermath of
the Victorian land boom earlier in the 1890's. Special Assets Trust
assumed responsibility for unpaid deposits, and agreed to repay these
over an eighteen year period out of assets of the old bank and contributions from the newly reconstructed bank. Four years before The
accountant commented on the matter, the new bank had agreed to deduct
the outstanding liability of the Special Assets Trust from its paid-up
capital.[8] In effect the reconstructed bank made a token gesture to show
that it accepted responsibility for pre-reconstruction liabilities. The
1913 bank balance sheet (while similar to a consolidated statement) was
merely an attempt to reflect the bank's assumption of these obligations.

It appears that accounting writers did not always regard investments in subsidiaries as significantly different from other investments
so that one must look to general discussions of the treatment of
"interests in associated companies" for illustrations of pre-1920
views on valuation questions. One such contribution came from a
member of the Society of Incorporated Accountants who proposed in 1914
that "trading profits and dividends from other companies should be set
out separately, so that one could tell what profit is being made by
the company and what is received from 'associated companies'".[9] That

---

7.   "Bank balance sheets", loc.cit., 18 Jan. 1913, pp.78-9.

8.   Australian Associated Stock Exchanges, Investment service,
      File C18.

9.   F. M. Hawnt, "The plea for greater detail in balance sheets of
      limited companies", The incorporated accountants' journal,
      Dec. 1914, p.66.

was hardly a startling proposal. Another brief contribution to the early literature on holding company accounting came from a practitioner who sought advice as to the propriety of treating the unpaid dividends of subsidiaries as income of a holding company.[10] This enquiry also clearly presupposed the use of cost-based asset valuation.

Despite the infrequency of discussions of inter-corporate investments during this period, it seems that accountants readily adopted cost-based asset valuation for those items that were considered to be fixed assets. Later in the 1920's, as holding companies became more common, the usefulness of cost-based valuation and of the conventional methods of disclosing information about inter-corporate investments was reconsidered and reassessed.

Nobel Industries' use of consolidated statements

At the 1922 annual meeting of Nobel Industries Ltd. the firm's chairman referred to comments that "the balance sheet of a company like ours does not tell the full story about the position of the business, and that shareholders are quite in the dark as to what is really behind such an item as 'Cost of Shares in Constituent Companies, £17,334,564'". Nobel Industries wanted shareholders to have "the fullest possible information about the real position, and know what actually constitutes their assets". Shareholders were given an "aggregate balance sheet" dealing with the "real state of the merger companies taken as a whole". It was dated December 1920 - a year out of date. The chairman claimed that the statement was "practically an innovation for large concerns so far as this country is concerned".[11] The incorporated accountants' journal devoted more attention to Nobel

---

10. Correspondence, "Accounts of holding company", The accountant, 10 July 1920.

11. "Balance sheets of holding companies", The incorporated accountants' journal, Oct. 1922, p.6.

Industries' attempt to "standardise" the basis of asset valuations within the group than to the aggregate balance sheet. Even then it simply observed that the innovation of aggregative statement was unlikely to lead to an improvement in reporting standards unless they were made compulsory[12] - an odd comment since British practitioners were scarcely aware of how to carry out the techniques of consolidation. But it may be noted that this commentary treated the use of consolidated statements as an attempt to show that the "real" state of the holding company's affairs was better than the holding company's own financial statements revealed. In other words, consolidated statements were initially regarded in British accountancy practice as supplementary statements which amplified the reports of holding companies.

Garnsey's contributions to discussions of holding company accounting

Two months after reports of Nobel Industries' novel method of reporting was described in the financial press, a lecture to Institute members by Sir Gilbert Garnsey publicised the use of "aggregate" balance sheets. The lecture, "Holding companies and their published accounts", was reprinted at length in The accountant[13] and formed the basis of the first U.K. text on the subject.[14] Thereafter there were frequent discussions of holding company accounting and consolidated statements, particularly since revision of the 1908 Companies Act was then under active consideration.

Undoubtedly Garnsey played a leading part in the introduction of consolidated statements to the British profession. As a partner of Price, Waterhouse and Co., he was no doubt in touch with his American

12. "Professional notes", loc.cit., Oct. 1922, p.21.
13. 6 Jan. 1923, pp.13-26; 13 Jan. 1923, pp.53-68.
14. Holding companies and their published accounts (London: Gee and Co. (Publishers) Ltd., 1923).

partner A. L. Dickinson, the leading publicist of consolidated
reporting in the U.S.A. But Garnsey's contribution has been the
subject of some extravagant claims which have exaggerated his role in
relation to the adoption of consolidated reporting in the U.K.[15]
Further, Garnsey's contribution has been misrepresented by commentaries
that his 1922 lecture was met with "indifference or opposition"[16] and
that he "failed initially to persuade the accountancy profession and
British businessmen to the point of action".[17] The fact is that
Garnsey was mainly concerned to debate the pros and cons of a variety
of treatments of investments in subsidiaries - of which the use of
consolidated statements was only one.

Apart from cost-based valuation of subsidiaries with the corresponding recognition of revenues when dividends were received, Garnsey
also considered equity accounting - or as he described it, the "unusual
practice" of "taking up" subsidiaries' profits or losses regardless of
dividends. A third method was to supplement the financial statements
of holding companies with the balance sheets and profit and loss accounts
of all subsidiaries. Fourth, the financial statements of holding
companies could be supplemented by a "summary of the assets and liabilities of all the subsidiary undertakings taken together". Fifth,
he discussed the publication of a consolidated statement - as a
supplement or an alternative to the publication of the holding company's
financial statements. Finally, instead of preparing a consolidated

---

15. e.g. "The Garnsey lecture of 1922 was central to the development
    of accounting for holding company groups" - it was "a technical
    tour de force which made British accounting history". J. Kitchen,
    "The accounts of British holding company groups: development and
    attitudes to disclosure in the early years", Accounting and busi-
    ness research, Spring, 1972 p.114.

16. T. B. Robson, Consolidated accounts (London: Gee and Co. (Publish-
    ers) Ltd., 1946), p.7.

17. e.g. J. Kitchen, op.cit., p.115.

statement with minority interests shown as liabilities, Garnsey noted
that "a variation" sometimes suggested was to show "only the proportion
of each asset and liability of the subsidiary companies attributable to
the capital held by the holding company" - a procedure which Garnsey
did not recommend since it gave rise "to some peculiar results".[18]
But the other four methods were all presented as valid and useful
techniques.

Garnsey devoted considerable space to working papers and the
preparation of consolidated statements. However these illustrations
were explanatory rather than evangelistic. In fact, he gave more space
to a consideration of the propriety of cost-based valuation of shares
in subsidiaries[19] than to his discussion of the merits of consolidated
statements.

After 1922 the literature contained regular allusions to the
limited usefulness of holding company balance sheets. To some extent
accountants expressed concern about the utility of cost-based valuation
of inter-corporate investments. Unlike American experience with mergers
and combinations, there was relatively little concern about the use of
exaggerated asset valuations and exaggerated representations of paid-up
capital of newly-formed holding companies. Indeed it was said that
British use of holding companies had avoided the "evil of over-valuation"

---

18. "Holding companies and their published accounts", The accountant,
    6 Jan. 1923, p.16.

19. Garnsey generally supported the use of cost data (adjusted for
    subsequent dividends from pre-acquisition profits") for valuing
    subsidiaries. He noted that in some circumstances a case could be
    made out for the use of market prices - where subsidiaries were
    publicly listed or circumstances were such that the shares would be
    readily sold (p.21). And while acknowledging that a case could be
    made out for the valuation of subsidiaries' shares to reflect the extent
    of post-acquisition undistributed earnings, he pointed to the need
    to consider any losses of other subsidiaries, and strongly opposed
    the payment of dividends by holding companies out of the undis-
    tributed earnings of subsidiaries.

which had plagued American firms.[20]

Garnsey's writings had outlined the limitations of cost-based valuation of inter-corporate investments. It was fairly well understood that the consequence of cost-based valuation of investments in subsidiaries was to limit revenue recognition to the amounts of dividends and to ensure that the amount of subsidiaries' losses was not necessarily recorded by a holding company as an expense of the period in which those losses occurred. But British experience with holding companies in times of a booming economy did not prompt the accounting profession to seriously examine these matters. However considerable attention was given to the form of balance sheet presentation adopted by many holding companies.

Balance sheet disclosure of inter-corporate investments

British companies were subject to minimal disclosure rules at this time. Since the 1850's, the British legislature had steadfastly accepted the proposition that corporate business was entitled to privacy. This view of the role of corporate regulation was periodically challenged, and gradually disclosure rules entered the statutes.

In 1862 banks and insurance companies were obliged to publish financial information, and in 1870 similar requirements were imposed on life assurance firms.[21] Attempts were made in 1862, 1877 and 1884 to introduce general requirements for financial disclosure by companies, but they either failed or were allowed to lapse.[22] In 1894 a Company Law Amendment Committee (the "Davey Committee") recommended that

---

20. A.L.Boddington, "Company amalgamations, absorption and reconstruction", The accountant, 26 April 1924, p.689. Similar comments were made earlier by H. W. Macrosty in The trust movement in British industry (London: Longmans, Green & Co., 1907), p.333.

21. Companies Act, 1862, s.44; Life Assurance Companies Act, 1870.

22. See H. C. Edey and P. Panitpakdi, "British company accounting and the law 1844-1900" in A. C. Littleton and B. S. Yamey (eds.) Studies in the history of accounting (London: Sweet & Maxwell Ltd. 1956), pp.368-9.

directors should be obliged to make balance sheets available to shareholders each year, either by direct presentation or on request at
companies' registered offices; significantly, the Davey Committee
opposed the suggestion that balance sheets be filed with the Registrar
of Companies on the ground that these documents should not be made
available "for public use".[23] However even these relatively conservative proposals for corporate accountability were rejected. The Davey
Committee's draft bill was drastically amended by a House of Lords
Select Committee, so that the Companies Act of 1900 contained no requirements for the publication of financial information.[24]

It was not until 1907 that the Companies Act first included requirements for financial information. However, the legislature acted against
the advice of a Company Law Amendment Committee (the "Loreburn
Committee") in extending the privilege of privacy to "private" companies.
Even so, the information to be filed with the Registrar of Companies was
merely a statement "in the form of a balance sheet". Proposals that
these documents be supplemented by a profit and loss statement were
later rejected by another Company Law Amendment Committee (the "Wrenbury
Committee") on the ground that

> to require from a corporation a public disclosure of
> profit and loss which is not required from a firm or
> an individual gives an unfair advantage to a com-
> petitor in trade.[25]

While many companies regularly communicated considerable financial
information to their shareholders, at least some firms regarded the
1907 filing rules as setting maximum standards for disclosure. The Act
required that the document "in the form of a balance sheet" which was

---

23. Report of the Company Law Amendment Committee, British parlia-
    mentary papers, 1895, Vol.LXXVIII, Paper 7999, paras.51-2.

24. 63 & 64 Vict. c.48.

25. Report of committee on companies acts, 1918, para.60 (reproduced
    in The incorporated accountants' journal, Sept. 1918, pp.217-8.)

to be placed on public record was to be "made up to such date as may
be specified in the statement", "audited by the company's auditor, and
containing a summary of its capital, its liabilities, and its assets,
giving such particulars as will disclose the general nature of such
liabilities and assets, and how the values of the fixed assets have
been arrived at" (s.21). This prescription was loosely drafted.
Perhaps the most ludicrous loophole was the absence of any specification that the statement to be filed should relate to the current year;
some companies adopted the expedient of filing the same statement year
after year. Another failing was that the rule requiring disclosure
of "how the values of the fixed assets have been arrived at" could
be met by a vague statement such as "at cost, less depreciation, where
appropriate". And the rule that companies should "disclose the general
nature of ... assets and liabilities" was drafted so loosely that
companies could apparently lump all the assets or all the liabilities
under a single heading, provided the accompanying narration described
the "general nature" of the items. Thus the relative significance of
one or other asset or liability item to a firm's financial position
was impossible to determine.

The latter practice came under judicial scrutiny in 1912 when
the Board of Trade initiated a prosecution against a company which had
filed a statement which included the following description of its
assets

> Goodwill, trade-marks, machinery, furniture and
> fixtures £100,007

The Board of Trade claimed that goodwill should have been shown
separately and that it was not sufficient to place "one cumulative
value" on all the fixed assets. A divisional court found against the
company and stated that the lumping together of different items which
had been valued in different ways was not in compliance with s.26(3)

of the Companies (Consolidation) Act of 1908.[26] The accountant commented that the decision was "sound common sense" and advised auditors to ensure that "separate figures are given for each class of property in regard to which a varying method of valuation [had] been adopted".[27]

This decision concerned documents being filed with the Registrar of Companies rather than the reports being submitted to shareholders. One might expect, however, that published annual reports would have contained at least as much detail as the annually-filed documents since (i) the additional cost of producing (say) a ten-item rather than a one-item balance sheet would have been trivial, (ii) any concern to maintain "business privacy" could hardly be relevant since annual returns were matters of public record. However a decade later it was apparent that many companies were not prepared to disclose detailed information about their assets in published balance sheets.

Several firms produced balance sheets which listed assets under only one or two headings. For example, in 1918 a shipping company presented a balance sheet "lumping together such items as the value of ships, cash in hand, investments and goodwill"

> Out of assets amounting to £10,000,000 in all, no less than £9,316,000 [were] ... 'bundled up in one item'.[28]

In 1920 Dicksee alluded to several similar cases, including the following extract from the balance sheet of "a well-known company":

> Explaining an outlay of upwards of 5 3/4 millions sterling, it does it in five lines of print, as follows: - 'By land, water rights, reservoirs, effluent works, buildings, plant, machinery, office furniture, goodwill, designs, engraving, and sampling, as per last account, £5,776,212 19s 8d. Further capital expenditure at cost (less sales) for the two years

---

26. Galloway v. Schill, Seebohn & Co., Lim. as reported The accountant, 4 May 1912, p.677.

27. (Anon.), "Companies and their balance sheets", ibid, pp.671-2.

28. "The grouping of assets", The accountant, 24 Aug. 1918, p.96. The company was Frank Leyland & Co. Ltd.

ended 26th June, 1920, £14,922 16s 11d making a total
of £5,791,135 16s 7d.[29]

In 1921 another shipping company provided a classic example of obscure
reporting - the assets side of its balance sheet contained only one
item:

> By Steamers, Tugs and Launches; Payments on Account of
> New Ships; Coal, Naval and Victualling Stores, Freehold
> and Other Property, Workshops and Machinery, Wharves,
> Moorings &c., Sundry Investments, Cash at Bankers and In
> Hand, and Debts Owing to the Company ... £23,236,597.14.10.[30]

The shipping industry became notorious for its overly-condensed
reports.[31] But - as the following examples indicate - the publication
of obscure balance sheets was not confined to any one industry.

> The 1926 balance sheet of Associated Portland Cement
> Manufacturers Ltd. "... lumped together ... the following
> assets, totalling £6,654,155 ...: Freehold and leasehold
> estates, chalk and clay lands, ground rents, house and
> cottage property, works, buildings, plant, machinery,
> wharves, railways, tramways, locomotives, rolling stock,
> barges, tugs, goodwill, stamp duties and conveyancing
> charges. In another item investments and loans [were]
> lumped together at £1,704,928".[32]

> The balance sheet of Peter Walker (Warrington) and
> Robert Cain & Sons Ltd. showed total assets of
> £7,108,972 of which £6,493,277 related to "freehold
> and leasehold licenses and other properties &c., loans
> and advances on mortgages and sundry investments,
> including the ordinary share capital of [a wholly owned
> subsidiary], less depreciation of reserves".[33]

Dissatisfaction with reports as uninformative as these led to
demands for balance sheets to contain more detailed information.

---

29. L. R. Dicksee, "Published balance sheets and accounts", The
    accountant, Nov. 1920, p.564.

30. As reported by H. Parkinson, "Disclosure in published accounts",
    The accountant, 19 June 1937, p.875. The company was the
    Peninsular and Oriental Steamship Co. Ltd.

31. See also "Brevity in accounts", ibid, 9 June 1928; "Cunard com-
    pany's accounts", ibid, 30 March 1929, p.419; "Lacking in informa-
    tion", ibid, 29 June 1929, p.835.

32. "Uninformative balance sheets", ibid, 2 April 1927, p.498.

33. "Combined assets", ibid, 24 Nov., 1928, p.698.

And yet it also became clear that even a <u>detailed</u> balance sheet could be singularly uninformative if the reporting firm was a holding company. A holding company's balance sheet could set out its asset holdings under the customary headings, with the items "shares in subsidiaries" or "loans to subsidiaries" constituting the major proportion of its assets. Without supplemental information concerning those investments, a reader would be just as much in the dark as if the holding company had provided a highly condensed statement.

The following observations on the financial statements of holding companies are taken from <u>The accountant</u> during the late 1920's. They illustrate how commentators encouraged the search for better forms of reporting:

> ... one item [in the balance sheet of Aerated Bread Company Ltd.] stands out as requiring further explanation. This is the investment of £407,422 in subsidiary companies. The investments ... represent the use of nearly 25 per cent of the share capital.[34]

> Shareholdings in subsidiary and allied companies are stated at the cost price of £808,840. Thus from the balance sheet [of Gilstrap, Earp & Co. Ltd.] shareholders are unaware as to what actual assets stand behind more than half the total assets figure.[35]

> Amalgamations often take the form of an absorption of one company by another by an exchange of shares. Thereafter the company taken over is submerged under the heading "investments in subsidiaries". In the case of S. Smith & Sons (Motor Accessories) Ltd., the £342,928 in shares in subsidiary and allied companies is nearly half the £692,000 invested in capital. In all such cases it should be the endeavour of the directors to afford the fullest possible information.[36]

> Out of [Lewis Berger's] total capital of £925,750, £691,124 is represented by shares, advances and debit balances of current accounts in associated companies. ... To the extent, therefore, of nearly £700,000 shareholders are in the dark as to what material assets are represented by that amount.[37]

34. "Passing the dividend", <u>ibid</u>, 22 Dec. 1928, p.825.

35. "Subsidiary company assets", <u>ibid</u>, 1 Dec. 1928, p.731.

36. "Amalgamation in industry", <u>ibid</u>, 22nd Dec. 1928, p.825.

37. "Paint and varnish profits", <u>ibid</u>, 10 Nov. 1928, p.631.

The most pressing need was seen to be the disclosure of information about what assets were actually "represented" by the investments heading. Did the subsidiaries own substantial assets, or only intangibles? Were subsidiaries' resources committed to assets which could appreciate, or to those which could not? Were the subsidiaries reasonably liquid or were they likely to place cash demands on the parent?

No doubt these were the sort of questions that commentators wanted answered. But could consolidated statement provide this information? There was very little analysis of the usefulness of consolidated statements or of alternative forms of disclosure at this time.

Demand for legislative reform

Obscure reporting practices (such as those described earlier) prompted serious criticisms of the existing companies legislation, and proposals for amendment and reform. For example, in 1924 D. Hickey referred to cases "where shareholders did not know the actual extent of their companies' trading spheres, and had neither the knowledge nor the means of ascertaining the financial state of the subsidiary or other companies in which their companies' funds were invested" - this situation, Hickey claimed, was in need of remedy.[38] The Manchester Chamber of Commerce publicly urged the need for reform of the sections dealing with private companies, so that the "commercial community could be fully protected against ... prevalent dishonest practices".[39]

38. D. Hickey, "Company law defects - suggested amendments", The accountant, 1 Nov. 1924, p.634. Hickey suggested that companies holding shares in other corporations should be required to supplement their balance sheets with lists of those investments, and on demand "to supply to its members copies of the balance sheets of the companies in which it has money invested". Further where a private company was "controlled" by another corporation, it should be obliged to register as "public" company, and henceforth file financial statements with the Registrar.

39. "Company law reform", The incorporated accountants' journal, Dec. 1924, p.77.

And a parliamentary debate on the form of accountability to accompany
the payment of government subsidies produced serious criticisms of
disclosure rules included in the 1908 Companies Act. One member of
parliament claimed that it was common knowledge that audited balance
sheets frequently provided "very little information" while another
claimed that lax reporting requirements had "given rise to very great
scandals".[40]

In response to mounting criticism of existing legislation the
Board of Trade announced in January 1925 the appointment of a committee
to enquire into what amendments in company law were "desirable".

---

40. Debate on the British Sugar (Subsidy) Bill, 1925; a report of
    this debate was included in The accountant, 28 March 1925, pp.526-7.

Ch. 5 <u>Company law reform in the 1920's and holding company accounting</u>

The appointment in 1925 of a Company Law Amendment Committee (the "Greene Committee") was of some significance to the development of holding company accounting in the U.K.

The prime consequence of the Committee's deliberations was, of course, the passage of amendments to the Companies Act. The appointment of the Committee also prompted the accounting profession to crystalise its ideas about a range of accounting matters. At this state in the development of the profession, neither the Institute nor the Society had issued recommendations on accounting practice. But when the Greene Committee invited submissions on a number of accounting questions, the two bodies felt compelled to develop "official" views on a range of technical matters. These were, in due course, published - and in the absence of other, more formal, pronouncements, constituted a guide to practitioners as to what were regarded as "acceptable" practices. The deliberations of the Greene Committee are also of particular interest in relation to the development of holding company accounting because they occurred as accountants were showing increased interest in consolidated reporting.

Nobel Industries' report of 1922 had been followed by other instances of the use of consolidated balance sheets, and these were usually well publicised. <u>The incorporated accountants' journal</u> saw fit to comment in 1923 that when a consolidated balance-sheet was issued it frequently indicated "a preponderance of American influence on the Board of the holding company"[1]- suggesting that the practice was spreading. In 1923 Agricultural & General Engineers Ltd. provided figures depicting the "combined trading" of the firm's associated companies - later claiming to have been the first U.K. company to publish consolidated income data. In 1925 the company produced both

---

1.   "The accounts of holding companies", <u>loc.cit.</u>, Feb. 1923, p.112.

a combined balance sheet and a formal consolidated profit and loss statement. The firm was "virtually the owner of [subsidiary] concerns, holding 97 per cent of their capital". The chairman said:

> [it] is not always appreciated by the investing public that it is on the results of the parent company and the associated companies, grouped as a whole, that the concern must be judged and valued.[2]

When the English Electric Company produced a consolidated statement in 1925, these documents were still rare enough for the event to be newsworthy.[3] Shortly afterwards the Ebbw Vale Steel, Iron and Coal Co. Ltd. produced an annual report which included a statement amalgamating the balance sheets of four "associated" companies (but not the parent). The accountant was suspicious of the figures, evidently because the share capital figure conveniently agreed with the net price paid to acquire the subsidiaries; accordingly it claimed that the statement was a "rather ... meaningless document".[4]

More companies produced consolidated statements during the course of the Greene Committee's deliberations. In a 1926 lecture, Sir Gilbert Garnsey listed several "large commercial concerns" which were among those publishing consolidated balance sheets as supplementary information: Agricultural & General Engineers Ltd., Nobel Industries Ltd., Crosse & Blackwell Ltd., Meadow Dairy Co. Ltd., The Swedish Match Co. Ltd. and Jute Industries Ltd. Moreover he pointed out that "most of the large insurance companies of this country prepare nothing but consolidated balance sheets"[5] a point which had certainly appeared to have escaped the attention of The accountant's weekly commentaries on

---

2. "Holding companies' accounts", The accountant, 31 Oct. 1925.

3. See The accountant, 16 May 1925, p.788 for references to reports in the general press.

4. "Balance sheets in bulk", loc.cit., 18 July 1925, pp.63, 92-3.

5. The accountant, 20 Feb. 1926, p.275.

published reports. But Garnsey was in a position to know: he had
recently participated in an official investigation of the form and
content of insurance company accounts - an exercise prompted by the
failure of the City Equitable group.[6]

It seems fair to say that when the Greene Committee began its
hearings, consolidated statements were far from common. However
Garnsey's contributions to the literature and the publicity given to
early uses of consolidated reporting ensured that many members of the
accounting profession and the financial community were familiar with
the supposed advantages or disadvantages of this form of reporting.

The Greene Committee paid considerable attention to the desirability
of amending the Companies Act's disclosure rules and accordingly invited
and considered evidence concerning ways of overcoming deficiencies in
the reporting practices of British firms. Holding company accounting
came under special scrutiny. The evidence offered before the Greene
Committee thus provides a view of the attitudes of the accounting
profession, stock exchanges and industry towards the desirability of
various treatments of inter-corporate investments and of the utility of
consolidated statements.

The recommendations offered by various organisations and witnesses
about holding company accounting can be conveniently categorised as
follows:

> (i) proposals dealing with the non-disclosure privileges
> of private companies

---

6. The report of this investigation was not published until 1927.
   See "Insurance law reform", The accountant, 28 March, 1927,
   pp.455-6. The investigating committee recommended a series of
   amendments to the Assurance Companies Act of 1909, including
   several matters dealing with "accounts and returns". These
   included: (i)"any combined balance sheet or combined revenue
   account [shall] be so framed as to minimise the chance of
   being misinterpreted", and (viii)"investments in and loans to
   controlled companies are to be dealt with specially".

(ii) proposals dealing with the treatment in holding
companies' reports of interests in and dealings with
subsidiaries

(iii) proposals concerning the publication of consolidated
statements.

Filing and publication of balance sheets: The 1907 Act had required

public companies but not private companies to place financial reports

on file for public inspection. The concession extended to private

companies enabled small businesses to retain the privilege of business

privacy. But it also enabled holding companies to conceal their

affairs by forming or acquiring subsidiaries.

Several witnesses claimed that all companies should be required

to make some information about their financial affairs open to public

inspection. As a Scottish lawyer argued, it was "not right [these

companies] should get the benefit of limited liability [without facing]

some of the obligations".[7] But others argued that the corporate form

had fostered the development of British industry, and that exposure to

widespread publicity would deter investment, encourage foreign

competition, and subject small businesses to unwarranted pressures.

In particular, both the Society of Incorporated Accountants and the

Institute of Chartered Accountants strongly supported the claims for

business privacy for small firms. The Society pleaded that private

companies should continue to enjoy "relief" in filing a balance sheet

(p.lxxiv); the Institute argued that compulsory filing obligations

would be "harmful" to private companies carrying on family or private

businesses (p.lxx).

The Greene Committee finally accepted the case for business

---

7. Minutes of evidence taken before the departmental committee
appointed by the Board of Trade ... (London:H.M.S.O., 1925) pp.
278, xci. (page references in arabic and roman numerals refer to
oral evidence and written submissions, respectively).

privacy,[8] and in subsequent legislation businesses operating through private companies retained the right to privacy over their financial affairs.

While only some witnesses before the Greene Committee wanted public disclosure by private companies in general, many more were prepared to argue for some form of accountability by those private companies which were subsidiaries of other companies. There were disagreements about the form that these disclosure requirements should take - whether, for example, the subsidiaries simply should be required to place balance sheets on file with the Registrar, or whether holding companies should incorporate subsidiaries' reports in their own annual reports, or else make those reports available to shareholders on request - but certainly there was agreement by a significant number of witnesses about the need for reform in this area.

The Registrar of Companies suggested that holding companies should themselves issue information about subsidiaries (p.viii) and the same suggestion was made by representatives of an association of Scottish solicitors (p.lxxvi). In fact, a feature of the evidence was the consensus among Scottish witnesses concerning the need for public dis-closure of the affairs of subsidiary companies. The Scottish Law Agents Society proposed that subsidiaries' balance sheets should be "available for inspection" (p.lxxviii); the Faculty of Procurators in Glasgow argued for disclosure by all private companies but emphasised that the case was "even stronger" for subsidiaries (p.279). The Joint Committee of the Councils of Chartered Accountants of Scotland, which had joined with its English counterpart in claiming that there was no need to change the law to require private companies in general to file balance sheets

---

8. Report of the Company Law Amendment Committee (Reports of Commissioners, Inspectors and Others, 1926, Vol. 9, paper 2657), The recommendations of the Committee were reproduced in The accountant, 12 June 1926, pp.830-8.

(p.lvii), made a special point of recommending that holding companies should be required to publish information about their subsidiaries (p.lvii, p.191).

The need for access to the balance sheets of subsidiary companies was also firmly supported by the Council of Associated Stock Exchanges (p.lii), whose representative was one of the key witnesses in the discussion of holding company reporting. (The London Stock Exchange curiously made no submissions on this issue). Stock exchanges were in a position to require financial disclosures by holding companies as a condition for admitting the securities of those firms to quotation. However the Associated Stock Exchanges argued that legal requirements were needed: the exchanges would be unable to police listing rules chiefly because they had no means of identifying a firm's subsidiaries (pp.155-6).

A submission from the Manchester Chamber of Commerce recommended that private companies controlled by public companies should be compelled to register as public companies (p.287, p.xcv) - in other words, that they be required to file their financial statements for public inspection. (This recommendation followed an earlier public statement by the Chamber urging that something be done about the status of private companies [9] - a statement which was issued under the name of Sir James Martin, president of the Chamber. Martin was later appointed to the Greene Committee and in this capacity was highly critical of proposals favouring extensions of corporate disclosure).

The only concrete objections raised to proposals for the separate publication (or filing) of subsidiaries' statements were (a) that disclosure would uncover devices used to conceal the beneficial ownership of trademarks etc. (and hence hamper British industry in its

---

9. "Company law reform", The incorporated accountants' journal Dec. 1924, p.77.

competition with foreign competitors ...), and (b) that holding company annual reports would become very bulky if they had to include subsidiaries' financial statements.

Now even supposing that objection (a) had some validity, this objection could have been met by granting the Registrar the right to relieve certain companies of their disclosure obligations; whatever the merits of objection (b) they were irrelevant to claims that subsidiaries' reports should only be filed with the Registrar.

Despite the consensus of opinion among witnesses in favour of reform, and despite the absence of any plausible objections to arguments that subsidiaries of public companies should be required to file their balance sheets with the Registrar, the Greene Committee resolved to retain the status quo. Perhaps the Committee was swayed by recommendations of the accounting profession, for representatives of both the Institute and the Society had recommended that private companies should continue to be exempted from obligations to place their balance sheets on public record. Both bodies had recommended that company balance sheets should separately identify "investments", and yet both were opposed to any further amplification of the significance of that asset-item. When the Institute considered the possiblity of introducing prescriptions for holding company reporting, it cautioned against laying down "hard and fast rules" (p.lxviii) while the Society flatly opposed the imposition of "rigid and inflexible obligations" (p.lxxxiv).

The Greene Committee attempted to justify its position by reporting that it had received so many different proposals that it seemed wiser to avoid making detailed recommendations.

(ii) Annual reports of holding companies: The most criticised accounting practice of the 1920's was the presentation of highly condensed balance sheets. As outlined in the previous chapter widespread hostility to this practice appears to have been a factor in prompting the

British government to undertake a review of the companies legislation.
And in due course submissions about the need for reform in this area
reached the Greene Committee.[10]

The proposals put forward for rules which might prevent the
aggregation of asset items under one or two headings were not so much
concerned with the need for an overview of the pattern of investment in
a given firm as with the reliability or validity of the asset figures.
For example, the London Chamber of Commerce pointed out that a detailed
examination of the actual circumstances of firms could reveal that
"imposing" balance sheet figures could represent "paper values only".

> [They could include] such a hypothetical asset as
> goodwill, and investments in other companies which
> are subsidiary to or associated with the Company
> in question (p.xxii).

The Greene Committee accepted that the inclusion of intangibles
with other assets could be misleading, and so agreed that balance sheets
should separately disclose the amounts of "goodwill" and "preliminary
expenses". But the Committee for some reason was reluctant to follow
up recommendations that inter-corporate investments and loans should
also be separately disclosed. The London Chamber of Commerce recommended that

> investments, holdings in subsidiary companies and
> holdings in associated companies respectively should
> be shown under separate heads, in order that the
> creditors can appraise the extent of the resources
> of the company in fixed and floating assets (p.xxii).

Similarly the Association of British Chambers of Commerce suggested
that detailed disclosure would help shareholders assess a firm's
resources (pp.235, 237). Other witnesses argued for explicit disclosure requirements but differed on the amount of detail that should be
required. The Society of Incorporated Accountants recommended that

---

10. e.g. evidence submitted on behalf of the Council of Associated
     Stock Exchanges (pp.153-6) and the Joint Committee of the Councils
     of Chartered Accountants of Scotland (p.170).

firms be obliged to disclose "Investments in Stock Exchange Investments" - with any remaining holdings of securities to be lumped
together under the heading, "Other Investments" (p.lxxiv). (Presumably inter-company loans were to be described as debts and recorded
elsewhere). On the other hand, the Institute's representative thought
that it would be a good idea to separately show "interests in
subsidiaries" - the aggregate of both inter-company shares and loans
(p.222).

Most witnesses who supported the separate disclosure of inter-
corporate investments also considered the adequacy of prevailing
practices in connection with revenue or loss recognition. For example,
the Association of British Chambers of Commerce alluded to instances of
firms reporting dividend-income from some subsidiaries while ignoring
the losses incurred by others (p.235). Whinney observed that there
could be a case for framing special restrictions on the distribution
of dividends "in the case of holding companies" (p.48). Representatives
of Scottish Chartered Accountants thought that holding companies should
be obliged to "bring in all the losses" of subsidiary companies (p.178).
Even F. D'Arcy Cooper (chairman of Lever Bros., then one of Britain's
largest holding companies), who staunchly opposed any legislative
interference with the supposed right of the "owners of a business"
to determine what information should be made public, thought that it
would be "sound and wise" to introduce legislation which ensured that
the losses of subsidiaries were charged against a holding company's
income (p.lx). The representative of the Council of Associated Stock
Exchanges reported that there were "quite a few cases where losses have
not been taken up", and suggested that it was "very desirable that
something be done to prevent that" (p.153). A witness appearing on
behalf of the National Association of Trade Protection Societies
claimed that directors of holding companies should have "some respon-

sibility ... to have regard to the condition of ... subsidiary
companies and [their] trading results" (p.166) while a submission
from the Society of Incorporated Accountants asserted that in the
valuation of all unquoted investments, "directors should take into
consideration all losses sustained by such companies and all relevant
circumstances" (p.lxxiii). Moreover two members of the Greene
Committee commented at various times on the need for reform in this
area: Sir William McLintock regarded the failure to report
subsidiaries' losses a definite "abuse" (p.47) while G. W. Wilton K.C.
described a case in which non-disclosure of the source of holding company profits was "misleading" (p.153).

There was little direct opposition to suggestions that the
legislature should intervene to prevent the concealment of subsidiaries'
losses and the manipulation of inter-corporate dividend payments. The
Federation of British Industries agreed that some form of rule was
needed to ensure that subsidiaries' losses were introduced into a
holding company's books, but opposed suggestions that a holding
company should provide for all a subsidiary's losses: the "position",
it claimed, was already adequately protected by the duty thrown
onto the auditor" (p.292). And the Institute of Chartered Accountants
claimed that directors should be allowed to choose the method they
wished to use to report on the performance of subsidiaries.

While there was little direct opposition to proposals for
legislative intervention so as to prevent abuses in holding company
accounting, both witnesses and committee members seemed uncertain
about what should be done. In particular, witnesses were unsure as
to how a holding company might record the losses or undistributed
profits of subsidiaries. The Institute's representative argued that
shares in subsidiaries should be valued at cost "unless value was
less" - but evaded questions about what constituted "value" by

suggesting that each case would have to be considered on its merits. Scottish chartered accountants professed ignorance of how a holding company could take care of subsidiaries' trading losses in its own books (p.172). And, as noted earlier, the Society of Incorporated Accountants that accountants should examine "all relevant circumstances".

Even so, the dominant concern of the witnesses who discussed holding company revenue recognition was that the practice of recording subsidiaries' dividends as revenues while ignoring subsidiaries' losses was potentially misleading. The ultimate recommendation of the Greene Committee did not fully face up to this problem. The Committee recommended that holding companies should disclose <u>how they had "dealt with" the profits or losses of subsidiaries</u>. This proposal appears to have emerged from a discussion between D'Arcy Cooper and William Cash, the Institute's representative on the Committee. (Cooper favoured the use of equity accounting methods, but opposed the separate disclosure of subsidiaries' reports and objected to consolidated statements). The exchange ran as follows:

> Cash: I am not making this as a definite suggestion of which I want you to think I am in favour, but do you think the position might be met as against an agitation for more information which is mainly directed to this particular point as to whether the final profits of the combine are total profits after allowing for all assets if it were made obligatory on the directors that on the balance sheet of the holding company they should make a statement as to the basis on which the balance sheet of the holding company had been compiled - that is to say, that they should say in that statement, which might be confirmed by the auditors, that all the losses, if any, of the subsidiary companies had been provided for, or otherwise?

> Cooper: Yes, I think they should. I see no objection to that whatsoever. (p.186).

Cooper saw "no objection" to the method - it would "satisfy the shareholders that the associated or subsidiary company was not making huge losses and that the position of the parent company was sound" (p.186) - but it was not what Cooper regarded as best practice. Cash's suggestion was later discussed with other witnesses, but they also were far from enthusiastic about the proposal (pp.202, 221).

Shortly after publication of the Greene Committee report, Greene himself discussed holding company accounting at a meeting of Institute members. He readily agreed that the practice of recognising subsidiaries' revenues while ignoring their losses was open to abuse, and revealed that the Committee had actually considered whether to ban the payment of dividends from the prior profits of loss-making subsidiaries.

> We said: 'If this sort of thing is done, it is only
> fair that the shareholders should know it; because
> at present a shareholder may not know that he is
> receiving dividends out of a combine when the combine
> as a whole is running at a heavy loss.' We thought
> that if he was told what the real position was, and how
> the losses had been dealt with by the parent company,
> he would be getting information which would enable him
> to decide what should be done. Beyond that we felt
> we could not go.[11]

However the Committee's analysis of how to inform shareholders about the "real position" had been brief and tentative. The Greene Committee's recommendation was at odds with the arguments submitted by various witnesses. Nevertheless the 1928 Companies Act finally incorporated a clause requiring holding companies to disclose how subsidiaries' profits or losses had been "dealt with". Events would soon demonstrate that this requirement was so loosely drafted as to be useless.

) The preparation of consolidated statements: When the Greene Committee invited submissions on accounting matters it attached great significance to the reporting problems of holding companies. Never-

---

11. W. A. Greene, "The report of the company law amendment committee", The accountant, 13 Nov. 1926, p.683.

theless only seven out of thirty-nine witnesses gave extensive
evidence on the subject. And the seven did not include the Society
of Incorporated Accountants. The Society delivered a written
memorandum which expressed opposition to the introduction of
requirements for the preparation of consolidated reports, though it
recognised that "pressure of opinion on the part of the investing
public has already been sufficient to induce some holding companies
to issue amalgamated balance sheets" (p.lxxxiv). But the Society's
representative did not volunteer any further comments on this
matter. Nor was he asked a single question about consolidated statements.

The Committee's somewhat cursory examination of the usefulness
of consolidated balance sheets took place at a time when these reports
were still comparatively rare documents. Several witnesses were asked
whether more firms were using this form of reporting. The Institute's
representative and F. D'Arcy Cooper both denied that the practice was
"growing" (pp.184, 219); on the other hand a representative of
Scottish chartered accountants asserted that the practice was indeed
"growing", and as if to prove it, produced an "amalgamated balance
sheet" of a big firm that had "come out yesterday" (p.171). As to
why consolidated statements were not more common, the Scottish representatives attributed this to the practical difficulties which arose
when an auditor was not responsible for all the subsidiaries while
another chartered accountant witness suggested that the infrequent
use of consolidated reports was due to the fact that they were difficult
to prepare (p.167).

It seems significant that discussion dwelt on consolidated balance
sheets, and that few references were made to the use of consolidated

income statements,[12] even though the Greene Committee's recommendations were to lead to the first requirements for the publication of
profit and loss statements to appear in British disclosure laws.

Moreover, consolidated balance sheets were considered only as
possible supplementary statements. Not one witness was prepared to
argue that consolidated statements should be a substitute for the
balance sheets of holding companies - the "legal" balance sheets, as
they came to be called. The discussion of consolidated statements
centred on whether they conveyed a better sense of a holding company's
assets. Time and time again witnesses or committee members expressed
concern that the customary treatment of investments in subsidiaries
neither gave any indication of the "real value of the shares" nor the
pattern of a holding company's investments (e.g. pp.178,220,237).

On reviewing the arguments put before the Committee it is evident
that while there were differences of opinion about what constituted
the most appropriate method or combination of methods to be used in
holding company accounting, there was at least a consensus about the
need for fairly substantial reforms in the rules governing corporate
disclosure.

The Council of Associated Stock Exchanges wanted consolidated
statements to be mandatory, along with the filing of subsidiaries'
balance sheets with the Registrar (p.lii).[13]

---

12. Scottish chartered accountants and the British Chambers of Com-
    merce proposed that consolidated profit and loss information
    should be published to avoid misleading impressions of profit-
    ability being conveyed by the customary practice of recognising
    subsidiaries' dividends as income while ignoring subsidiaries'
    losses. See pp.171,235. Mr. A. V. Alexander,a parliamentarian
    who was associated with the Co-operative movement, was alone
    among the witnesses in expressing concern about the desirability
    of revealing whether "combines" were earning excessive profits
    (p.249).

13. The Stock Exchanges' representative before the Committee elaborated
    on these proposals by arguing that an aggregate balance sheet
    would be of little use unless it isolated "goodwill" as a separate
    asset item. (p.153). However he claimed that access to individual
    balance sheets (only) would be more useful than access to aggre-
    gate balance sheets (only).

Scottish chartered accountants and the Council of Associated Stock Exchanges both recommended that the publication of consolidated statements be established as a means of fulfilling minimal disclosure requirements. The various groups of the Scottish profession submitted in their formal memorandum that holding companies should be obliged to either separately publish subsidiaries' statements or to publish a summary of them (p.lviii); their representatives explained that while a consolidated balance sheet gave "a great deal more information than the ordinary balance sheet which simply states interest in associated companies" (pp.170-1) it was not the perfect form of reporting, merely a "step in the right direction". They argued that a better method of reporting would be for consolidated statements to be accompanied by separate statements for subsidiaries (p.171) - or, where practical, for this information to be provided in a multi-column presentation which separately detailed the affairs of the subsidiaries, in conjunction with the aggregate figures (p.173).

Witnesses who argued against the use of consolidated statements based their claims on the fact that creditors of holding companies or subsidiaries could be misled by aggregate figures. D'Arcy Cooper of Lever Bros., and a Mr. F. Whinney (who was said to have had "very extended experience of matters relating to company law") were the chief proponents of this position (pp.185, 47). It seems that these arguments were intended to support the adoption of alternative presentations. Cooper supported the use of equity accounting (p.188), while Whinney urged that the publication of subsidiaries' balance sheets was to be preferred to consolidated reports. (However Whinney did concede that a combined balance sheet gave "a truer picture of the position as a whole than the type of holding company's balance sheet we are generally familiar with today" (pp.47-8).

Members of the Committee often appeared to be more dogmatic critics

of consolidated statements than the most conservative of witnesses
(see pp.154, 155, 167, 171 and 173). In particular they laboured
the point that consolidated statements could mislead creditors. One
witness responded that under the then-existing regulatory framework,
creditors of subsidiaries had no legal right of access to financial
statements, and even if they did manage to see a consolidated statement
it could hardly be more misleading than the so-called "legal" balance
sheet (p.176). Overall, Committee members appeared to be so antagonistic to the proposals for the compulsory publication of consolidated
statements that sections of the evidence almost suggest that the
Committee was trying to curtail the use of this dangerous form of reporting.

In the end, it appears that the submissions of the Institute of
Chartered Accountants carried the most weight - even if they were hardly
the most persuasive. The Institute carefully avoided committing itself
about the merits or demerits of consolidated statements. It simply
submitted that the most appropriate form of reporting should be left
to directors and shareholders (p.lxviii). During discussion of this
submission the Institute's representative affirmed that consolidated
statements might be useful supplementary statements in some situations,
although their use as substitutes for "legal" balance sheets would be
entirely wrong. But the Institute's view was that it would be entirely
inappropriate to make the presentation of consolidated statements
compulsory, since this would expose businesses to unwarranted public
scrutiny (p.lxxx).

It is significant perhaps that The Law Society's written
submissions paralleled those of the Institute's, almost to the word,
but took a markedly different stance on the question of holding company
accounting. The Law Society argued that combined balance sheets should
be presented "wherever practicable", although it declined to urge

that they be made obligatory (p.xlix).

Except for the Institute's submissions, the evidence placed
before the Greene Committee supported the case for drastic changes
in the disclosure rules dealing with holding companies. It was
claimed that these firms should be required (i) to account for both
subsidiaries' losses and profits, or (ii) to publish subsidiaries'
financial statements, or (iii) to publish consolidated statements -
or some combination of these proposals.

When the Committee reported in 1926 it asserted that the evidence
before it disclosed "a considerable divergence of views" concerning
the form of accounts appropriate for holding companies. The Committee
acknowledged that traditional accounting treatments of investments in
subsidiaries did not produce useful information:

> Complaints have undoubtedly been heard from shareholders
> in such companies that the information given them by
> the accounts of the holding companies is unintelligible
> without fuller details as to the position of the
> subsidiary and associated companies.

Yet it rejected suggestions that the solution to these difficulties
lay in the introduction of requirements for the publication of
consolidated balance sheets "for the whole group of companies".
Two grounds were given for this decision. First, it was asserted
that shareholders could make such requirements "as they may think
proper" for the publication of financial information (p.33) - an
assumption which could hardly be relevant to the circumstances of
many shareholders who had to deal with secretive managements which
controlled a significant bloc of votes. The second assertion was
that the presentation of accounts in the form chosen by management
could in fact be "in the best interests of shareholders". The two
grounds were totally inconsistent - the one suggested that the remedy
for obscure reporting lay in shareholders' hands, while the other
suggested that shareholders were not entitled to object to managerial

decisions. Even so, one can hardly blame the Committee for not regarding consolidated statements as a panacea. What is remarkable is that the Committee chose to ignore the arguments of expert witnesses concerning the source of anomalies in corporate reporting.

The Committee focussed on disagreements about the remedy rather than on the consensus about the disease. And so: the "divergence of opinion" allowed the Committee to "only ... make recommendations of a quite limited character". These amounted to the recommendations reviewed earlier. First, it was suggested that "investments in, and loans to or from subsidiary companies" should be separately disclosed in balance sheets. And second, it was proposed that holding company balance sheets should be accompanied by a statement showing "how the aggregate profits and losses of any subsidiary company or companies" had been "dealt with in the accounts of the holding company" (p.36).

Resume

The Greene Committee chose to believe that directors and the
accounting profession could weigh the conflicting claims of business
privacy and corporate accountability so as to arrive at optimal
solutions to financial reporting problems. The Committee made a point
of emphasising that it wished to avoid imposing "restrictions which
would seriously hamper the activities of honest men" and which would
"inevitably react upon the commerce and prosperity of the country".
This laissez faire position was qualified only in minor respects. The
Committee accepted that shareholders were entitled to receive copies
of balance sheets, directors' reports and auditors' certificates (p.63).
However it was extremely reluctant to introduce rules affecting the
content of financial statements. In refraining from prescribing the
form and content of corporate reports, the Committee acted in accord
with the submissions made by the Institute of Chartered Accountants in
England and Wales. But these submissions were contrary to many other
recommendations. In fact, most expert witnesses who appeared before
the Committee had urged the need for immediate and extensive revisions
of the disclosure rules, especially in order to improve the reporting
practices of holding companies.

The major sources of the anomalies complained of by these
witnesses were the failure of firms to provide supplementary information concerning the financial position and activities of subsidiaries,
and the use of cost-based valuation and dividend-based revenue
recognition in recording these investments.

The Greene Committee showed absolutely no inclination to eliminate
these practices. The proposals that it eventually formulated to meet
these difficulties were virtually useless. The Committee did not
recommend the publication of any form of statement concerning the
position and performance of subsidiaries. Nor did it provide an

effective barrier to the manipulation of holding company income.

The Greene Committee overruled those who advocated the introduction of requirements to compel the publication of consolidated
statements. Nevertheless, the Greene Committee's recommendations
set the scene for the widespread adoption of consolidated statements. Had the Committee proposals led to requirements for the use
of equity accounting methods and for the publication of private
companies' financial statements, then the financial community might
have held different views about the advantages of consolidated reporting.
The fact is that the Greene Committee did not make these recommendations
- and early in the 1930's consolidated statements became extremely
popular.

The arguments advanced in support of consolidated reporting during
the course of the Greene Committee's deliberations all assumed that
public companies would be obliged to publish their own separate
financial statements. Contrary to U.S. practice, consolidated statements were not regarded as primary reports. Nor were they thought
of as depicting the affairs of an "economic entity" or of a "group"
of companies. They were simply treated as one way of supplementing
the financial statements of holding companies. Support for consolidated statements came from those who regarded them as the optimum way
of overcoming the limitations of holding companies' balance sheets.
In the 1920's, consolidated statements were regarded as supplementary,
remedial reports.

Ch. 6   Widespread acceptance of consolidated reporting in the 1930's

The early 1920's were a period of experimentation in British
accounting practice. Nevertheless in the mid-twenties (when the
Greene Committee was considering proposals for the amendment of the
companies legislation) the use of consolidated statements was still a
novelty. However by the mid-1930's, consolidated reports were not
only familiar but also widely accepted.

This chapter examines the circumstances which led to the wider
use of consolidated statements and which prompted the British profession to prefer the use of consolidated statements to other
procedures for reporting on investments in subsidiaries.

Expansion of the literature on consolidated statements

Before the Greene Committee's review of companies legislation
there had been few discussions of holding company accounting in the
British literature. But by the early 1930's there was an extensive
literature on the subject.

Garnsey's 1922 lecture had been published in book form in 1923.[1]
Three years later Garnsey published a paper on holding company
accounting which he described as "an amplification and extension" of
his earlier work on the subject;[2] once again Garnsey avoided making
firm recommendations concerning the superiority of one or other methods
of reporting on the standing of investments in subsidiaries. Other
contributors to the technical literature during the late 1920's
were similarly equivocal about the desirability or otherwise of
using consolidated statements; it was said that "the subject of
holding companies accounts is so comparatively new that few accountants

---

1.   Holding companies and their published accounts (London: Gee and Co.
     (Publishers) Ltd., 1923).

2.   "Holding companies and their published accounts", The accountant
     20 Feb., 1926, pp.267-79.

in England at the moment have really settled notions thereon".[3] But

it seems that commentators were in agreement that the recording of

"investments at cost" was potentially misleading.[4]

The most forceful comments on the subject of consolidated state-

ments came from those who regarded them as misleading documents. In

1925 one company chairman took the opportunity to launch an attack on

the use of consolidated statements at his firm's annual meeting. Since

his company was only "partly" a holding company, he claimed that no

consolidated balance sheet could present "atrue picture" of its affairs,

and so instead of a consolidated statement the company published the

balance sheet of its major subsidiaries. In support of this procedure,

the chairman read a letter from a leading practitioner, Sir Arthur

Whinney.[5] Whinney congratulated the firm on its performance and offered

the following comments on its financial statements.

> Although the balance sheet is silent as to the invest-
> ments in subsidiaries, I hope your Board will not be
> led into the prevailing error of issuing a balance
> sheet in which all the figures of parent and subsidiary
> companies are consolidated, which is necessarily wrong
> from the point of view of creditors and may be wrong
> as regards the shareholders ... There seems to be a
> general tendency among shareholders and others to call
> for consolidated balance sheets, to which there is, in
> my opinion, grave objection.[6]

These comments elicited a response from Sir Gilbert Garnsey. The

company chairman had suggested that there was a serious dispute between

"eminent accountants" on the subject, and alluded to a recent

---

3.   A. J. Simons, Holding companies (London: Sir Isaac Pitman and
     Sons Ltd., 1927), preface.

4.   See, e.g., Sir Josiah Stamp, "Audit of holding companies", The
     accountant, 21 Feb. 1925, p.312; editorial, "The accounts of
     holding companies", ibid, Aug. 1925, pp.201-4; V. Walton, "Some
     thoughts on accounts and financial statements", ibid, June 1926,
     p.891; H. Morgan, "Published balance sheets and accounts, ibid,
     25 June 1927, p.981.

5.   Whinney was vice-president of The Institute 1925-6 and then
     president until his death in mic-1927.

6.   "Consolidated balance sheets - Mr. Roscoe Brunner's statement",
     The accountant, 6 June 1925, p.926.

"long book" on consolidated statements which was identifiably
Garnsey's. However, Garnsey seemed intent on avoiding the appearance
of being the sponsor of radical views: he claimed that there was no
real dispute between himself and Whinney, since he (Garnsey) did not
advocate the substitution of consolidated statements for legal
balance sheets.

> What I do point out is that in some cases it is doubtful
> whether by itself the 'legal' balance sheet of a holding
> company as prepared nowadays really gives the share-
> holders all the information to which they are entitled
> ... This objection may be overcome, not, indeed, by the
> abandonment of the 'legal' balance sheet, but by
> addition to it and by way of supplementary information...[7]

Again Garnsey listed possible alternative ways of overcoming the
difficulty: by the separate publication of subsidiaries' balance
sheets, by the publication of statements combining the subsidiaries'
balance sheets, or by the publication of consolidated balance sheets
embracing both the holding companies and their subsidiaries. He acknowledged that one method might be "best" for a given company - but
avoided specifying the criteria whereby one could select one method
rather than another in particular situations. A similar stance was
taken in later editions of his book - published in 1931, and again in
1934 (after Garnsey's death) under the editorship of T. B. Robson.

A major addition to the volume of the pre-1930 British literature on consolidated statements was A. J. Simons' Holding companies.[8]
Apart from some fairly individual observations about the treatment
of dividends out of pre-acquisition capital profits, and other technicalities, Simons did not break much new ground. Much of his book
was descriptive material concerning the uses (and abuses) of holding
companies. However Simons did propose that control over subsidiaries
was a necessary (though not sufficient) condition for consolidation.
Similar proposals had a long history in American literature, but they

7. Idem.
8. Loc. cit.

had not been advanced in the U.K. Simons did not provide any support
for his contention that "control" was a key factor; he simply offered
an assertion:

> Where control is not and has not for some time past been
> exercised, then the investments should be treated as
> ordinary shareholdings (p.89).

This proposal would be canvassed more thoroughly in later years.
Meantime, Simons' text served an educational role in explaining the
techniques of consolidation. It was, as the preface stated, "intended
primarily for the accountant student".

There was some discussion at the International Congress of Accounting held in New York in September 1929. William Cash (a practitioner
who had served on the Greene Committee) contributed a paper which
summarised British attitudes to consolidated reporting. The title,
"Consolidated balance sheets",[9] underlined that at this stage British
practitioners had little interest in consolidated income statements.
The objectives of consolidated balance sheets were firmly associated
with efforts to represent the position and affairs of a particular
company - not of a group of companies (p.639 & p.653). And consolidated
balance sheets were regarded as one of several alternative presentations
available to accountants when they sought to supplement "legal"
balance sheets with further information about inter-corporate
investments (pp.651-2). However Cash did suggest that the English
view of "best practice" was the simultaneous publication of a legal
balance sheet and a combined statement "amalgamating the assets and
liabilities of the whole group together with information as to how the
trading results of the group have been dealt with" (p.645).

Perhaps the greatest influence in British reporting practices was
The accountant. Certainly The accountant must be credited with having

---

9. Proceedings - international congress on accounting (New York:
   International Congress on Accounting, 1930) pp.639-52.

made British practitioners aware of the use of consolidated reports:
the "Finance and commerce" column of this weekly journal regularly
highlighted the use of consolidated balance sheets and drew attention
to cases of good and bad financial disclosure. For example, when
Vickers Ltd. included a "statement of the combined assets and
liabilities of the company and its subsidiaries" in its 1926 report,
The accountant urged students to search out the document and study it
carefully.[10] When in 1928 Radiation Ltd. published a "combined" balance
sheet encompassing the assets and liabilities of its subsidiaries, The
accountant welcomed the move as a progression to a state of "enlightenment
in the matter of accountancy standards".[11]

However the use of consolidated statements in the late 1920's
is perhaps best seen as evidence of continued experimentation with
methods of disclosure rather than as reflecting agreement that consolidated reports were the optimum way of presenting financial information.
Some firms published summaries of subsidiaries' balance sheets rather
than full consolidated statements.[12] Several large companies such as
Lever Bros. and I.C.I. shunned the use of consolidated statements and
instead used equity accounting methods.[13] Cortaulds Ltd. chose to
make periodic (though not systematic) revaluations of its investments
in subsidiaries.[14] And at least one firm used a form of equity
accounting in conjunction with the publication of consolidated statements.[15]

---

10. "Vickers Limited", loc.cit., 30 April 1927, p.646.

11. "Radiation Ltd.", ibid, 25 Feb. 1928, p.268. This company had
    been noted for its earlier, "singularly uninformative" financial
    statements which listed assets under only two headings.

12. See, e.g. "Radiation Ltd.", op.cit., p.268; "A commendable principle",
    The accountant, 25 Feb. 1928, p.294; "Selfridge Provincial
    Stores", ibid, 22 Sept. 1928, p.394.

13. See discussion in W. Cash, op.cit., p.642.

14. "Cortauld's assets", The accountant, 10 March 1928, p.374.

15. "Vickers Limited", loc.cit.; see also W. Cash, op.cit., p.643.

However it appears that the use of equity accounting, the publication of consolidated balance sheets and the publication of statements aggregating the balance sheets of the subsidiaries were commonly viewed as alternatives. Until the late 1920's, at least, there was no discernable body of opinion favouring one or other of these methods.

Disclosure rules - the 1929 Companies Act

Four years after the Greene Committee commenced its deliberations, a new Companies Act finally came into force. The disclosure rules included in this act were based on the recommendations of the Greene Committee. As outlined in Chapter 5 these recommendations did not come to grips with anomalies in corporate reporting practices that had been evident in the early 1920's. To some extent these deficiencies were acknowledged and a series of modifications and amendments to the Greene Committee's recommendations were made during the course of the bill's passage through parliament.

One of the dominant concerns of critics of the 1908 legislation was that it enabled the presentation of highly condensed balance sheets which aggregated disparate asset items together under one or two headings. However the Greene Committee took little notice of these complaints, save for proposing that certain items should be separately identified in corporate balance sheets. These items were: preliminary expenses, goodwill, and investments in and loans to subsidiaries.

In due course the Committee's report was translated into the Companies Bill of 1927. But shortly afterwards there was widespread criticism of the Bill for its failure to ensure that balance sheets did not contain "omnibus" asset items. Even The accountant (which in 1926 had warmly approved the Committee's report and laissez faire attitude)[16] condemned the Committee for failing to compel the preparation of "more

---

16. "The report of the Company Law Amendment Committee", loc.cit., 12 June 1926, pp.805-6.

informative balance sheets". The accountant expressed the hope that
the asset disclosure clause would be amended during parliamentary
examination of the bill.[17] Politicians duly criticised this aspect of
the draft legislation[18] and possible amendments were discussed by the
House of Commons in committee. One member proposed an amendment which
would have required that no fewer than 20 items should be set out in
balance sheets under separate headings. Another member proposed that
a list of 12 items would be sufficient.

Finally the Government agreed to reconsider the matter.[19] But
when the Companies Act was finally enacted in August 1928 it included only
trivial modifications of the Greene Committee's proposals for the separate
disclosure of asset items. The Committee's recommendations were extended
somewhat with clauses requiring the separate disclosure of amounts
capitalised in connection with patents or trademarks and share or
debenture issues.

The 1928 Companies Act also included a new requirement for balance
sheet disclosure. Firms were not to only disclose the "general"
nature of the liabilities and ... assets", and how fixed assets had been
valued, but also

> the amounts respectively of the fixed assets and of
> the floating assets (s.40(2)).

The 1928 Act did not come into effect immediately. The government
had earlier announced its intention to delay implementation of the
legislation until a consolidating act could be prepared. Eventually a
further bill was enacted in May 1929. Meantime, the last minute amendments providing for the separate disclosure of "the amounts of fixed

---

17. "Company law reform", loc.cit., 23 April 1927, p.603.
18. See "In parliament", The accountant, 3 March 1928, p.326.
19. "Balance sheet reform", ibid, 19 May 1928, p.702.

and floating assets" were not well received. It appears that the
amendments were aimed at requiring that fixed and floating assets would
be segregated in balance sheets, with their values listed and neatly
sub-totalled. However, the drafting of the clause did not achieve
this effect. Both the Institute of Chartered Accountants and the
Society of Incorporated Accountants sought legal advice on this point;
these opinions concurred that to comply with the 1928 Act it would be
sufficient to simply describe the method of valuation adopted for
different asset categories.[20] But the fundamental objection to the
provisions arose not from their drafting but from their failure to come
to grips with demands for an improvement in the quality of the information
made available to the market place. Disclosure of the basis of asset
valuation did not, by itself, indicate whether a firm was in a strong
or a shaky position. As an editorial in The accountant indicated, the
mere "intimation that a certain asset is taken in the accounts at cost
price may conceal the fact that the property in question is now worth
considerably less than the amount for which it was acquired". Paradoxically, "investments" were frequently regarded as neither fixed
nor current assets - and the Act's draftsmanship meant that managers
would not be required to disclose the basis of valuation of these items.
The accountant's comment on this omission was as follows:

> It is precisely in regard to such assets that many
> balance sheets have in recent years proved so unsatis-
> factory. The bulk of the balance sheet total may be
> represented by investments acquired at inflated prices
> during a 'boom' period and now worth only a fraction of
> their cost figure, at which it is legal to show them
> year after year. Even if the book figures are qualified
> by the intimation that they are taken at cost, the
> accounts will not in such circumstances indicate the
> real value of the assets, and may, in fact, be grossly

---

20. "In re The Companies Act, 1929", The accountant, 31 Aug.
     1928, p.280; "Changes in company law", supplement to The
     incorporated accountants' journal, Dec. 1929. One of the joint
     authors of the opinion prepared for the Institute was W. Greene,
     K.C., former chairman of the Company Law Amendment Committee.

misleading.[21]

The usefulness of the 1929 Act's requirements for the disclosure of valuation methods was summed up in an editorial in The accountant eight years later. After describing the requirements as a "first timid beginning towards scientific treatment", The accountant commented:

> It is a matter of common knowledge, however, that the practical result of this enactment has hardly been helpful towards informed criticism for, in ninety-nine cases out of a hundred, the wording adopted is 'at cost less depreciation'.[22]

The second major amendment to the disclosure rules recommended by the Greene Committee concerned the reporting of gains or losses from investments in subsidiaries. This recommendation was in due course translated into the 1928 and 1929 Companies Acts; companies with subsidiaries were required to append a note to their balance sheets "stating how the aggregate profits and losses of any subsidiary company or companies during the period covered by the accounts presented have been dealt with in the accounts of the holding company". This rule did not spell out whether so-called "capital" profits and losses were also to be mentioned. Moreover, the requirement for disclosure of how profits and losses "had been dealt with" was so vague as to permit such useless responses as:

> In the accounts of X Co. Ltd., the aggregate profits or losses of X Co. Ltd.'s subsidiaries have been ignored.

The rule certainly did not prevent the use of cost-based valuation methods for handling investments in subsidiaries - methods which had been widely criticised throughout the 1920's.

Before the financial community had any experience with corporate reporting in terms of the new legislation, critics were damning the

---

21. "The companies consolidation bill III", The accountant, April 6 1929, p.425.

22. "The valuation of investments in balance sheets", ibid, 3 July 1937, p.2 .

new disclosures rules as inadequate. One critic wrote in 1927 that
the proposed amendments did not "go nearly far enough for the protection of shareholders".[23] In 1928, The accountant complained that the
Greene Committee's report was a "compromise which practically left
the position where it was",[24] while another critic said that the 1928
bill "only touch[ed] the fringe of the problem".[25]

The inadequacy of the disclosure rules in the 1929 Companies Act
was soon highlighted in the now famous Royal Mail case of 1931. This
litigation concerned financial statements issued before the 1929 Act had
come into force - and in any event the firm was a chartered company and
as such not subject to general companies legislation. But it became
very obvious that the manipulations complained of would not have been
averted by the tentative reforms introduced in the 1929 legislation.

Before turning to these matters, it may be noted that the 1929
Act did shape reporting practices in connection with consolidated statements in a way that was not strictly intended.

Defining "subsidiaries"

Both of the 1929 Act's major changes in the disclosure rules
necessitated the specification of the meaning of the term "subsidiary".
The Greene Committee proposed that the term be defined in the following
fashion:

> When a company includes among its assets and holds either
> directly or through a nominee or nominees shares in
> another company and (i) by means of such holding either
> (a) has more than fifty per cent. of the voting power in
> such other company, or (b) holds more than fifty per cent.
> of the issued share capital of such other company or (ii)
> has power to appoint or nominate the majority of the

---

23. C. L. Norden, "Contemplated changes in company law", ibid,
    15 Oct. 1927, p.507.

24. "Companies bill limitations", loc.cit., 19 May 1928, p.730.

25. H. G. Howitt, "Present day demands on auditors and the effect of
    the companies bill thereon", The accountant, 28 Jan. 1928, p.129.

directors or persons occupying the position of directors,
by whatsoever name called, of such other company then
such other company shall be deemed to be a subsidiary
company for the purposes of this section.

This proposal was accepted and a similar definition was incorporated
in the 1929 Companies Act.

Note that this definition of "subsidiary" was not intended to
specify the scope of consolidated statements. It was framed for the
purpose of requiring the disaggregation of data relating to a firm's
asset holdings, and some explication of the valuation and revenue
recognition methods adopted in respect of those assets. In the light of
British experience with the manipulation of profits by unscrupulous
promoters involving transactions with "controlled" companies, the use of
tests of control may have seemed reasonable.

Nor was the definition of "subsidiary" arrived at after any
discussion of the use of tests of control in the literature on
consolidated reporting. Some American accountants at that time argued
that the function of consolidated statements was to report on an
"economic entity", and accordingly argued that the area of consolidation
should be determined by the ambit of managerial control. These arguments
were not even mentioned in the Greene Committee's report.

Nevertheless, the statutory definition of "subsidiary" was later to
be interpreted as setting the scope of consolidated reports, and
discussions of the rationale for consolidated reporting began to allude
to "economic entities" and "groups of companies".

Stock exchange listing rules and "subsidiaries"

The stock exchanges had not involved themselves in the regulation
of corporate financial reporting prior to the 1930's. But the market
collapse in the last months of 1929 led to a reappraisal of the stock
exchanges' attitude.

Investors' losses were enormous. In November 1929, one financial paper reported that it had examined the stock prices of about 250 of the 280 public offerings made in 1928. "While the cash value of these issues was £74 million, the present market value of the issues in which dealings are recorded [was] only £48 million".[26] A government-appointed committee investigating Britain's "banking, finance and credit" later provided more comprehensive statistics. The total amount subscribed in 1928 for shares or debenture issues by some 284 companies was £117 million. By May 1931 the total market value of these issues" as far as ascertainable" was only £66 million, indicating a loss of £51 million or about 47% of the amount invested. The Committee pointed out that the public's loss may have been even greater since many of the issues may have sold at a premium. Moreover, some 106 of the 284 companies (involving issues of around £20 million) had already been wound up or were near collapse.[27]

Investor losses of this magnitude no doubt discouraged new investment (and may so have precipitated the failure of other firms, with further consequential losses). Certainly the losses of investors led to considerable public dissatisfaction with existing modes of corporate and stock market regulation.

The London Stock Exchange was prompted to review its attitude towards the regulation of the securities market by the failure of the "Hatry" group in 1929.

The Hatry failure itself pointed to the inadequacy of the regulatory framework at the time, but has little significance to an examination of the contents of financial reports. The major concern at the time arose from the fact that Clarence Hatry and his associates had issued forged securities in an attempt to stave off a financial crisis.

---

26. The statist, 2 Nov. 1929, as reported The accountant, 9 Nov. 1929, p.570.

27. Report of the committee on finance and industry ("The Macmillan report"), (London: H.M.S.O., June 1931) p.166.

However it appeared that the key company in the group, the Austin Friars Trust, had delayed publication of its annual report at the time of the collapse. Consequently the grave financial position of the Hatry group had been concealed from the investing public.[28] This highlighted the ineffectiveness of the policies of the Registrar of Companies in following up overdue submissions of financial statements.[29] It also pointed to the total lack of any stock exchange rules setting deadlines for the publication of reports to shareholders.

On 27 January, 1930, the London Stock Exchange appointed a Special Sub-Committee to investigate whether the Exchange's rules governing new issues and official quotations "could be strengthened". An interim report of this committee dated May 1930 was concerned with ways "to combat ... future share frauds of the 'Hatry' variety", and dealt with procedures for the handling of securities particularly when transactions involved the use of temporary documentation. A final report[30] five months later was more extensive, and marked the start of involvement by the Stock Exchange in the regulation of financial reporting.

This report noted that the Stock Exchange had long had a rule whereby firms seeking listing were required to publish some information about their history and prospects before their stocks could be traded. But this rule had been "greatly abused by companies whose prospects did not admit of their obtaining capital from the public by means of a prospectus", and accordingly the Committee recommended more stringent rules governing non-prospectus companies. A distinction was drawn

---

28. See "The Hatry trial", The accountant, 1 Feb. 1930, pp.157-61. The background to the failure and to subsequent criminal proceedings is described in A. Vallance's Very private enterprise (London: Thames and Hudson, 1955).

29. See "In parliament", The accountant, 8 Feb. 1930, p.209.

30. The interim and final reports are reproduced in The accountant, 8 Nov. 1930, pp.641-9.

between the offerings of companies which had, or had not, previously
published financial reports. The rules governing firms without a
published record of operations were particularly stringent, and
required the preparation and publication of detailed reports concerning
the circumstances of the applicant firm and of any contractual arrangements entered into by it or its promoters. However the Committee did
not come to grips with questions about the scope or quality of the
financial information that was to be prepared in these circumstances; for
the moment at least the Stock Exchange was prepared to rely upon the
judgment of qualified auditors.

Accompanying these recommendations was a brief "memorandum of
policy" which illustrated the Stock Exchange's misgivings about the
hazards of investment in subsidiary undertakings. Notwithstanding that
a firm seeking listing may have complied with all other requirements
for the publication of financial information, the Stock Exchange
indicated that it would

> in general, be disinclined to grant permission to
> deal in the shares of a subsidiary company until
> after the publication of the first annual report of
> the parent company and the fact that the principal
> asset is a patent, new process or invention, or
> undeveloped commercial enterprise will weigh heavily
> with the committee in considering its decision on this
> point.[31]

Such extreme caution in approaching the listing applications of
subsidiary companies could perhaps be interpreted as indicating some
hesitancy in accepting published reports at face value. Certainly it
understood the fact that accounting reports might not always be reliable

---

31. Ibid, p.645. In other clauses of this memorandum, the Committee
     indicated (i) that it might defer consideration of the applica-
     tion for permission to deal until after publication of the first
     annual report and accounts of firms which indicated that preliminary
     expenses, underwriting fees etc. were to form an "undue percentage
     of the capital it is proposed to raise", and (ii) that it would
     give close attention to the "desirability or not of allowing
     bargains in new issues to be recorded in the supplementary list".

in their representations of the affairs of holding companies.

As far as the stock exchange's influence on corporate reporting
was concerned, this was a very small beginning. But by the end of the
decade, the London Stock Exchange was to become far more concerned with
setting standards for corporate reporting, and would in fact take the
initiative in requiring the publication of consolidated statements.

The Royal Mail case

The Hatry case shook up the securities industry and persuaded many
conservatives of the need to abandon their laissez faire stance with
regard to the regulation of companies and the trade in securities. The
accountant described these changes in attitude in the following terms:

> ... a year which has seen the new Companies Act
> enter into force has also witnessed an unprecedented
> number of events in the financial world demonstrating
> the necessity for strengthening and amending the law ...
>
> ... some of the features of the past twelve months ...
> have not only led to the welcoming of the new Act, but
> have also created an influential body of opinion in
> favour of further strengthening of the law.[32]

And yet it seems that accountants tended to view the need for reform
only with reference to "underwriting and other promotion scandals".[33]

The near-failure of the Royal Mail Steam Packet Company Ltd.
quickly dispelled this attitude.

The reporting practices of R.M.S.P. during the late 1920's had
led to a breakdown of accountability - on that there was widespread
agreement. And yet the evidence of the failure of contemporary
accounting practices to adequately depict the situation of R.M.S.P.
was no more compelling than that available from a series of corporate
crises during previous years. What made the Royal Mail affair
important to the profession was that it underscored the vulnerability

32. Editorial, "Abuses and remedies", The accountant, 21 Dec. 1929,
    pp.785-6.
33. Ibid, p.787.

of accountants to legal sanctions even though they may have been performing tasks in accord with "acceptable" standards.

The difficulties confronting the Royal Mail and related companies came to light in 1929 when R.M.S.P. sought an extension of government guarantees of borrowings made just after World War I for the purpose of rebuilding its shipping fleet. The government commissioned an independent accountant (Sir William McLintock) to investigate the R.M.S.P. group's affairs. McLintock's report cast doubt on the adequacy of the Royal Mail's financial statements and prospectuses, and later led to the prosecution of the firm's auditor (Morland) and its well-known chairman, Lord Kylsant.[34]

In the words of the prosecutor, R.M.S.P.'s 1926 and 1927 financial statements reported large trading profits "whereas in truth and in fact ... it had made ... very serious losses".[35] McLintock later reported that fixed assets which appeared at £23,526,151 were overstated by £9,560,278.[36] Moreover, while "properly adjusted trading results" for the period 1926-29 would show "substantial losses", the Royal Mail had paid out over £1,000,000 in dividends over these years.[37]

---

34. "Lord Kylsant was ... not only a great shipping magnate but [also] ... one of the most respected figures in the country. He had been made a peer in 1923 ... He was the Lord-Lieutenant of the County of Hereford West. He had been president of the Chamber of Shipping of the United Kingdom and of the London Chamber of Commerce". Sir Patrick Hastings, Cases in court (London: 1949), extract reproduced in W. T. Baxter and S. Davidson, Studies in accounting theory (Homewood, Ill.: Richard D. Irwin, Inc. 1962), p.452. Kylsant (then Mr. Owen Phillips) had also been a member of the "Wrenbury" Committee Law Amendment Committee of 1918, which had passed judgment on the adequacy of the disclosure rules contained in the 1908 Companies Act.

35. As quoted by Hastings, op.cit.

36. "Royal Mail Steam Packet Co., The accountant, 21 Feb., 1931, p.234. The economist noted that "the group ... [had] been burdened not only with normal depreciation, but with a catastrophic decline in the value of ships built near the top of the short-lived post-war boom". 7 Feb. 1931, p.300.

37. "Royal Mail exposures", The accountant, 21 Feb. 1931, p.257.

An appearance of profitability had been maintained through the judicious use of two major accounting devices. The first was the writing-back of "reserves". R.M.S.P. had previously recorded a liability for taxation but when in later years it was discovered that no such liability existed the "taxation reserve" was written back as income. Similar procedures had been used by several wholly-owned subsidiaries in order to manufacture profits in unprofitable trading periods. The second device was that of basing the recognition of income from subsidiaries on the receipt of dividends. R.M.S.P's subsidiaries had paid dividends to the parent company in periods in which their trading activities had led to losses: the dividends were paid out of the trading profits of earlier years, or else out of surpluses obtained from writing back "reserves".[38]

The Royal Mail case was undoubtedly a turning point for the British accounting profession. It swept aside long-standing assumptions about the right of managements to decide what information should be made available to shareholders. It initiated a debate about the desirability of the profession issuing "recommendations" on accounting.

And it prompted a series of changes in accounting practice. In particular it seems that the Royal Mail case was a major factor in encouraging the publication of consolidated statements.

Most commentaries on the Royal Mail affair have concentrated on the firm's supposed use of "secret reserves". F. R. M. de Paula, for example, suggested that the case taught the accounting profession that "if secret reserves were drawn upon to bolster current earnings, this fact would have to be disclosed in the accounts".[39] To some extent,

38. For a convenient summary of these manipulations see the report of the opening address of counsel in preliminary proceedings, reproduced in The accountant, 13 June 1931, pp.785-88.

39. F.R.M.de Paula, "Accounting principles", paper delivered 1946 and reprinted in de Paula's Developments in accounting (London: Sir Isaac Pitman & Sons Ltd., 1948); de Paula's interpretation is cited by S.A. Zeff in his Forging accounting principles in five countries (Champaign Ill.; Stipes Publishing Co., 1972), p.15.

this interpretation of the affair is borne out by the facts. It appears
that the manipulation of profit calculations by transfers to and from
reserves had been a fairly common practice in British accountancy.
Morland's counsel later recalled that he had based his client's defence
on whether the terms used to describe these transfers in the R.M.S.P.
report (i.e. that reported profits included "adjustments of taxation
reserves") were "well recognised in accountancy circles". It seems he
had little trouble in establishing that the practice of adjusting annual
profit by means of transfers from reserves was "well recognised".[40]
The practice had also been soundly criticised, and well before the Royal
Mail case there had been public requests for amendments of the Companies
legislation to ensure that firms which made these transfers were obliged
to disclose the fact that they had taken place.[41] But while these
attempts to institute change in accounting practices had been unsuccess-
ful, the publicity associated with the Royal Mail litigation was sufficient
to bring about a fairly rapid change in the profession's attitude.
Commentators concluded that it was dangerous to carry out transfers from
reserves to income summaries (or vice versa) without disclosing to
shareholders the fact that these transfers had taken place.[42] Soon many
firms were making a point of being quite explicit about these transfer
entries.[43]

---

40. Hastings, op.cit.

41. See, e.g. "Balance sheets of private companies", The accountant,
     18 June 1927, p.968; correspondence from A. Haslam, ibid, 14 Jan.
     1928, p.47 and 30 April 1927, p.649; "The P. & O. balance sheet",
     ibid, 14 Dec. 1929, pp.777-8.

42. See, e.g., "The auditing aspect of the Royal Mail case", ibid,
     8 Aug. 1931, p.195; "Auditors' responsibilities", ibid, 5 March
     1932, p.304; H.J.Lunt, "The liability of an accountant for negli-
     gence", ibid, 16 Jan. 1932, pp.73-8.

43. See, e.g., "Out of the hat", ibid, 20 June 1931, p.831; "Is it net
     profit?", ibid, 27 Feb. 1932, p.289. Some firms did not
     immediately modify their practices and were sharply criticised:
     see, e.g., "Profit - including reserve not required", ibid, 13
     Feb. 1932, p.225.

These disclosures eliminated the "secrecy" surrounding transfers from reserves. They did not meet the criticism directed at the presence of "secret reserves". This term has been variously applied to the presence of unrecorded assets, the understatement of specific assets, the overstatement of liabilities and the reporting of non-existent obligations. However while the term was used extensively during the Royal Mail court proceedings, it was clearly understood in that context that the matters at issue concerned the propriety of specific recording techniques: the retention of a supposed "liability" for taxation that was not an obligation of any sort, and the use of cost-based valuation for handling investments in subsidiaries.

Subsequent discussions of the Royal Mail affair in the accounting literature have obscured these facts. Indeed, it is fair to say that British accountants quickly developed a fixation about the need for disclosure of transfers to and from reserves but often overlooked the fact that the treatment of gains or losses associated with subsidiary-investments was a key factor in the Royal Mail's breakdown of accountability. During the early 1930's, The accountant frequently provided examples of financial reports which provided meticulous details of reserve accounts but only the barest of disclosures on the presence and profitability of investments in subsidiaries.[44]

However, there was some recognition of the fact that the Royal Mail's treatment of investments in subsidiaries had contributed to the misleading impression conveyed in its financial statements. In July 1931, when interest in the legal proceedings against Kylsant and Morland was at its height, The accountant reproduced an anonymously-

44. e.g. "Discouraging accounts", loc.cit., 23 Jan. 1932, pp.121-2;
      "Assisting profits", ibid, 19 March 1932, p.395; "£23,584,018
      mystery", ibid, 11 June 1932, p.816; "Reserves in one account",
      ibid, 23 May 1936, p.802.

contributed review of contemporary practices for handling the earnings of subsidiaries.[45] In all cases firms had complied with Companies Act requirements for disclosure of the manner in which subsidiaries' profits or losses had been dealt with. And yet the disclosures were (in The accountant's words) "so vague and uninformative ... as to be meaningless, or very nearly so". [46] It was generally agreed that the disclosure rules incorporated in the 1929 Companies Act were inadequate - for they would not have prevented manipulations of the kind uncovered in the R.M.S.P. accounts.

The Society of Incorporated Accountants appointed a committee to formulate recommendations for the reform of company law and accounting practices. The Committee's report included the following suggestion:

> ... where a holding company has investments in one or more subsidiary and/or sub-subsidiary companies, there should be stated on the face of the accounts of the holding company, the total amount of the ascertained profit or losses of such subsidiary and/or sub-subsidiary companies appertaining to the interest of the holding company in such subsidiary and/or sub-subsidiary companies, in so far as such profits or losses have not been brought into account in the profit and loss account of the holding company.[47]

The proposal for clear-cut disclosure of the monetary amount of subsidiaries' profits or losses was not new. Nor was the allusion to the earnings of sub-subsidiaries - for there had been earlier discussions of how these firms were not encompassed by the 1929 Act's requirements.[48] More significant perhaps was the fact that the Society's report did not canvass the suitability of using either equity accounting or consolidated

---

45. (Anon.), "The earnings of subsidiaries", The accountant, 11 July 1931, pp.40-1.

46. Editorial, "Earnings of subsidiaries", idem, p.37.

47. See The incorporated accountants' journal, April 1932. The report was reproduced in The accountant, 30 April 1932, p.601.

48. See, e.g. Sir Gilbert Garnsey's Holding companies and their published accounts (London: Gee & Co., 2nd ed. 1931); (anon.), "Balance sheet of the holding company" (correspondence) The accountant, 9 Jan. 1932, p.49.

statements as a means of reporting on investments in subsidiaries. The use of either technique would have prevented the manipulations of earnings from subsidiaries that had taken place in the R.M.S.P. group.

While post mortems on the Royal Mail affair did not lead directly to suggestions that holding companies should publish consolidated statements, it seems that the affair did in fact encourage the use of these reports. This encouragement stemmed from two factors. First, the Royal Mail case led to a reaction against the use of equity accounting. This virtually ensured that investments in subsidiaries would be valued at cost. Second, the Royal Mail case made accountants anxious to avoid situations in which users of financial statements might obtain a grossly misleading impression of a firm's financial position and performance; accordingly practitioners saw a need to supplement cost-based data on inter-corporate investments with additional disclosures about assets or income.

Antipathy to equity accounting

As noted earlier, several large British companies (notably Lever Bros. and I.C.I.) had used a form of equity accounting since the mid-1920's. It appears that cost-based valuation was the most common method used to record investments in subsidiaries: in 1931 a survey of balance sheet practices revealed that of 91 firms with subsidiaries,

> one-third valued shares of subsidiaries 'at cost' and another third stated the basis to be 'at cost, less written off', or 'at cost, less depreciation'. In 6 cases no basis of valuation was given, and the remaining 8 companies each had rather a special method of stating how the value had been arrived at ... Among the balance sheets of these companies we find the following:-

> Shares in Subsidiary Companies being the excess of the assets over the liabilities of such Companies as shown by their books ...

> Shares (taken at cost) and balance of Un-

distributed Profits.[49]

But even though cost-based valuation was the most common practice, equity methods were tried and tested.

However both the stock market collapse of 1929 and a series of corporate crises in the late 1920's and early 1930's seems to have engendered a fear of the overstatement of profits. This was evident in the treatment of marketable securities. As outlined in Chapter 3 in the late 1920's accountants suddenly rejected the writing-up of securities - even though this procedure had been strongly supported earlier in the decade. Similarly many accountants suddenly developed a strong distaste for equity accounting methods. The Royal Mail litigation appears to have contributed to a mood of conservatism in which the profession sought to adopt the "safest" solution to asset valuation problems that was available. And hence many accountants became antagonistic to the recognition of any form of "unrealised" income.

One early manifestation of this attitude was an attack on the reporting of "dividends receivable" by an anonymous contributor to The accountant in mid-1931.[50] Some weeks later, a member of parliament urged that companies legislation should prohibit the reporting of"dividends declared or receivable from a subsidiary company" until the dividend was actually received.[51] The accountant later discussed the propriety of reporting dividends receivable, and concluded that undistributed profits of subsidiaries could be "brought to credit, provided that before publication of the balance sheet, an event has occurred which definitely brings it into the class of receivables

---

49. J. Loudon, "Certain requirements of the Companies Act, 1929, as interpreted in published balance sheets and accounts", The accountant, 23 March 1931, p.681.

50. "The earnings of subsidiaries", ibid, 11 July 1931, p.41.

51. "In parliament", ibid, 25 July 1931, p.131.

for the period under review, i.e. if a dividend has been declared in that period".[52] This obviously precluded the recognition of subsidiaries' profits which were not to be paid out straight away.

The most prominent supporter of equity accounting was Mr. H. Morgan, president of the Society of Incorporated Accountants. During a discussion of the Royal Mail affair at a Society meeting Morgan took the opportunity to advocate equity methods.

> Personally, I consider that the most satisfactory method [of handling investments in subsidiaries] is to draw up the balance sheet and profit and loss account in such a form as to incorporate the results of subsidiary companies.[53]

Senior members of the Society acknowledged their respect for Morgan's arguments but withheld agreement with his proposals.[54] And The accountant claimed that equity methods would constitute a great departure from established accounting principles since they required "the bringing into the balance sheet of an appreciation of a fixed asset which has not been and may never be realised".[55] (It is not quite clear when the rule outlined by The accountant became "established". The valuation framework that had guided British practice since the turn of the century did not (as indicated in Chapter 2) specifically preclude the writing-up of assets. Moreover in the mid-1920's The accountant itself had vigorously supported the recognition of "unrealised" profits arising from increases in the prices of marketable securities).

---

52. "Practical points", ibid, 29 Aug. 1931, p.319. See also "Readers' queries and replies", ibid, 22 Aug. 1931, p.304 and 5 Sept. 1931, p.357.

53. See "Presidential address", The accountant, 4 June 1932, p.774. Morgan agreed that another "effective method" of handling such matters was the publication of consolidated statements.

54. Ibid, p.778.

55. Editorial, "The annual meeting of the Society", ibid, 4 June 1932, p.755.

While the Society's president favoured equity accounting the
Institute's president seemed to be against it (at least for income
recognition). Later in 1932 it was reported that the president, Mr.
C. Smith, told a meeting of Institute members that in his opinion

> undistributed profits of subsidiaries, if included
> in the accounts of the holding company, should be
> clearly described as such and not taken credit for
> in the same manner as a dividend.[56]

Subsequently a correspondent to The accountant took issue with the
tentativeness of these comments and claimed that "a holding company
has no right whatever to take credit ... for undistributed profits,
no matter whether or not it discloses and describes the item as such".[57]
And later, other writers expressed misgivings about the propriety
of recording a "profit" from the undistributed earnings of subsidiaries.[58]
The net result of this disparagement of equity accounting seems to
have been that accountants turned to other methods of reporting on
investments in subsidiaries. It was clear that cost-based valuation
was acceptable for "legal" balance sheets, but equally these reports
would not by themselves be very informative. It seems significant
that at a time when the use of equity methods was being discouraged,
one firm's footnote disclosures of "actual" income (i.e. that which
would have been reported using equity methods) was enthusiastically
commended.[59] But the method of supplemental disclosure most favoured
by commentators was the use of consolidated statements.

---

56. "Institute of Chartered Accountants", The accountant, 19 Nov.
1932, p.650.

57. "J.C.", "Holding companies' accounts", ibid, 10 Dec. 1932, p.753.

58. See, e.g., editorial, "The consolidation of accounts", The
accountant, 7 March 1936, p.346; F.R.M. de Paula, "The form of
presentation of the accounts of a holding company", ibid, 11 March
1939, p.325.

59. "A useful addition", The accountant, 28 Nov. 1931, p.727.

Throughout the 1930's The accountant played a leading part in fostering the use of consolidated reporting. In the late 1920's the "Finance and commerce" columns of this weekly periodical had made complimentary and encouraging noises about the occasional publication of consolidated balance sheets. But in the 1930's this attitude shifted to one of downright advocacy. Staff of The accountant had made up their minds that "there can be no shadow of doubt that the principle of the consolidated statement of accounts is the right one"[60] and accordingly promoted the use of consolidated reporting at every opportunity. If a holding company published its reports without any supplementary disclosures, The accountant would comment on the event under such headings as

Combined statement needed[61]

Consolidation accounts needed[62]

If a firm adopted consolidated statements, The accountant would compliment the firm's directors and report the event under such headings as

A great advance[63]

The way to do it[64]

and proceed to praise the use of consolidated reports as though these documents were the solution to all the problems of accounting. There had to this time been very little hard-headed thinking about the merits of consolidated statements vis a vis other disclosure methods, and there had been very little discussion of the appropriate basis for

---

60. Editorial, "Auditors and published accounts", ibid, 16 April 1932, p.510.

61. Ibid, 16 Jan. 1932, p.84.

62. Ibid, 6 Feb. 1932, p.186.

63. Ibid, 16 Jan. 1932, p.85.

64. Ibid, 11 June 1932, p.817.

preparing consolidated reports. (The area of consolidation, for example,

had been almost accidentally fixed by the 1929 Companies Act's definition

of "subsidiary" - which had been framed for a different purpose). Yet The

accountant was able to generate enthusiasm for the use of consolidated

statements with commentaries such as the following:

> Additional information is submitted by the directors
> of Ind Coope & Co., Ltd., with the 1931 balance sheet
> in the shape of a combined statement of the assets
> and liabilities of the whole undertaking ... The form
> in which this combined statement is drawn up follows
> the lines of a balance sheet reform advocated in
> 'Finance and Commerce' a short time ago. Its
> simplicity ... is its own recommendation. The fact
> that it has not been generally adopted shows how much
> custom more than convenience rules in accountancy.[65]

> Our congratulations are due to the directors and
> officers of Turner & Newall, Ltd., on the enormous
> improvement which has been made in the production of
> the 1931 report and accounts. In the first place,
> the legal balance sheet has been re-designed to
> distinguish more clearly between the fixed and the
> floating assets while the question of depreciation
> has been given more attention ... This, however,
> is but a minor part of the accounting reforms which
> have been introduced. By far the most important is
> the consolidated balance sheet of the whole undertaking,
> showing what real assets and liabilities lie behind
> the company's interests in subsidiaries ...[66]

In 1932 The accountant was able to report that "an increasing number

of parent companies has been persuaded to issue ... either a combined

statement of the assets and liabilities of their subsidiaries or a

consolidated balance sheet of the whole undertaking.[67] Of the two

methods, The accountant clearly favoured the all-encompassing state-

ment. Even so, until the mid-1930's few of the large prominent

British firms had published consolidated reports.

---

65. "Ind Coope's subsidiaries", ibid, 5 Dec. 1931, p.753.

66. "A great advance", op.cit., 16 Jan. 1932, p.85.

67. "The published accounts of companies", ibid, 13 Feb. 1932,
    p.194.

Dunlop Rubber Company's use of consolidated statements

In May 1934 Dunlop Rubber Co. Ltd. published its 1933 financial statements together with a consolidated balance sheet and a supplementary statement of profits. The accountant struggled to find superlatives to praise Dunlop's reports:

> It is almost impossible to find sufficient praise with which to acclaim the new standard in company accounting set by the 1933 accounts of the Dunlop Rubber Company Limited. Our best commendation is really their appearance in this week's issue of The accountant so that the accountancy profession itself may see the high level of informativeness that is possible in company accounts, particularly in the case of holding companies, if the determination of the management and officials is directed towards that end. These accounts answer all the present-day criticism regarding the obscurity that is possible in the earnings and assets of subsidiary companies when accounts are presented in the manner allowed by law.[68]

The economist was equally complimentary:

> The report of the Dunlop Rubber Company for 1933 places the company in the forefront of British concerns as regards the publication of clear, detailed and comprehensive accounts. The document embodies nearly all that The economist and other critics of obscurantism have advocated, in season and out of season, for years past, and gives the lie to the familiar assertion that a large holding company cannot afford to go beyond the meagre disclosure laid down by law, for fear of giving away valuable information to its competitors...[69]

Earlier reports by Dunlop had not been as well received. In 1922 the firm had suddenly reported a loss of more than £8 million which largely arose from earlier undisclosed futures contracts. In 1928 it was reported that that company had been "quite transformed" by new management - but even so its financial statements provided no details of the progress of a U.S. subsidiary.[70]

Late in 1929, F. R. M. de Paula was appointed chief accountant

---

68. Editorial, "Dunlop's new standard", ibid, 12 May, 1943, pp.676-9.

69. Editorial, "Dunlop's clear accounts", The economist, 12 May, 1934, p.1037.

70. "Dunlop Rubber Co.", The accountant, 21 April 1928, p.582.

to the group.[71] Dunlop's financial reports soon reflected a series of
innovations or reforms. In 1932 the directors' report was expanded
to "include a review of the balance sheet and an explanation of changes
during the year" while the balance sheet showed figures to the nearest
£, omitting shillings and pence columns. Dunlop was one of the first
British firms to provide comparative figures in its report and to
give effect to "the whole of the year's allocations and distributions
of profit" instead of showing shareholders' interest inclusive of
proposed dividends at the balance date.[72]

The 1933 report included a number of changes quite dissociated
from the use of consolidated statements (including: the treatment of
proposed dividends, the allocation of taxes in relation to preference
dividends and the disaggregation of income data between "normal"
earnings and non-recurring items).[73] The consolidated statements also
were of interest since they encompassed both subsidiaries and
sub-subsidiaries - a fairly rare practice at the time.[74] Commentators
also applauded the fact that Dunlop Rubber provided an explanation of
the scope of its consolidated statements. Of some significance to the
development of consolidated practices in the U.K. was the fact that

---

71. "Dunlop Rubber Co.", ibid, 21 Dec. 1929, p.811. F. R. M. de Paula
    was highly regarded within the profession. As chairman of an
    Institute committee he played a leading role in the drafting of
    the first British "recommendations on accounting principles";
    later he was the first non-practising member to be appointed to
    the Institute's Council. For biographical details see S. A. Zeff,
    "Profile - F. R. M. de Paula", The accounting historian, Oct.
    1974, p.6.

72. See "Dunlop sets a precedent", ibid, 14 May 1932, p.677; "A better
    style", ibid, 25 June 1932, p.883.

73. See editorial, "Dunlop's new standard", loc.cit.

74. An earlier instance was reported in "A correspondent writes ..."
    The accountant, 20 May 1933, p.697.

tests of "control" were used to specify what were or were not subsidiaries.[75]

The praise lavished on Dunlop's report may well have encouraged
other firms to attempt to follow Dunlop's example. Certainly The
economist predicted that the report would be a "source of inspiration
to other large companies" and The accountant claimed that it would be
a "model" to other firms. Meantime Dunlop's publication of consolidated statements indicated the growing acceptance of this form of
reporting by the British financial community.

Stock exchange requirements for consolidated data

The preparation of consolidated statements finally became part of
the established repertoire of the U.K. accounting profession when the
London Stock Exchange introduced its first significant disclosure
rules in 1939.

Australian stock exchanges had formally accepted the use of
consolidated statements some years earlier. The first initiatives for
introducing disclosure rules dealing with holding company accounting
were made in 1925 when the Melbourne Stock Exchange required companies
seeking listing to agree to supplement their own reports with the
financial statements of their subsidiaries. In 1927 this rule was
amended to allow the presentation of statements aggregating the
subsidiaries' data. The Sydney Stock Exchange then introduced a
requirement for the supplementary publication of either the separate
statements of subsidiaries or consolidated reports encompassing both
parent company and subsidiaries.[76]

---

75. The consolidated statements encompassed "all subsidiary and
    sub-subsidiary companies in which the Dunlop Rubber Co. Ltd. and
    any of its subsidiaries hold over 50 per cent. of the ordinary
    shares or stock of those companies or over 50 per cent. of the
    voting control".

76. R. W. Gibson, Disclosure by Australian companies (Melbourne:
    Melbourne University Press, 1971), pp.75-80.

Most Australian states later introduced companies legislation based on the 1929 U.K. Companies Act. New Zealand's 1933 Companies Act was similarly based on the U.K. legislation. But in 1938 the state of Victoria broke away from the British model by adopting a disclosure rule similar to that earlier instituted by the Sydney Stock Exchange: holding companies were to publish the separate statements of subsidiaries or an all-encompassing consolidated statement.[77]

The London Stock Exchange was slower off the mark, but finally in 1939 took action which ensured that the use of consolidated statements was expected of all listed British companies. The Hatry scandals in 1929 and the Macmillan Committee's criticisms of the content of prospectuses two years later prompted the stock exchange to look more critically at the protection afforded investors by existing rules and regulations. The first steps towards reform were taken late in 1930 with the adoption of a policy of caution towards the listing of subsidiary companies until after publication of the parent's first annual report. This policy towards newly-promoted companies was followed by rules aimed at publicising the names of unseasoned firms through the medium of italicised entries in the "unofficial list" until such time as the publication of financial statements satisfied the Stock Exchange committee that a firm could be safely listed and its securities traded.[78]

In the aftermath of the 1929 stock market collapse and the Royal Mail case there were repeated demands for review of the 1929 Companies Act. Commentators also began to express the belief that the stock

---

77. Idem; G. E. Fitzgerald and A. E. Speck, Holding companies in Australia and New Zealand (Sydney: Butterworth & Co. (Aust.) Ltd., 2nd ed., 1950), pp.6-9.

78. See "The stock exchange and investors", The accountant, 2 May 1931, p.56; "The stock exchange and investors", ibid., 16 May 1931, p.639.

market should also bear some responsibility for the regulation of financial disclosure.[79] But the next major initiative of the London Stock Exchange in connection with holding company reporting did not aim at improving financial disclosure. The stock exchange committee announced in 1936 that henceforth it would be reluctant to admit holding companies to the official list:

> The committee note a tendency for new companies to
> be formed as holding companies ... While the
> committee realise that holding companies in certain
> instances serve a useful purpose they will in future
> require to be satisfied that there are adequate reasons
> for this method of promotion.[80]

This action could be interpreted as a vote of no-confidence in contemporary methods of financial reporting. The accountant conceded that "the frequent obscurity of holding companies' accounts" was partly responsible for the committee' action.[81]

It was later reported that the stock exchange endeavoured to encourage holding companies to publish consolidated statements.[82] However in February 1939 the Committee for General Purpose of the London Stock Exchange took more positive action by formally requiring firms which applied for listing to agree to publish consolidated balance sheets and profit and loss accounts. The committee indicated that it would require "good reason to be shown before granting permission to deal in a stock or share of any company which does not

---

79. See, e.g., Editorial, "Company law and the Royal Mail case",
loc.cit., 15 Aug. 1931, p.250.

80. As reported by The accountant under the heading, "Holding
companies", 11 July 1936, p.43

81. Idem.

82. Letter addressed by the Committee of the London Stock Exchange
to brokers and issuing houses, 20 Feb. 1939, reproduced under
the heading "Consolidated accounts, the stock exchange ruling",
The accountant, 25 Feb. 1939, p.250.

publish consolidated accounts".[83]

This 1939 ruling has been described as a "landmark in the evolution of the movement for adequate disclosure.[84] It may have encouraged more firms to publish consolidated statements - and in particular, to adopt the practice of publishing consolidated income statements. Shortly after the Stock Exchange ruling, Imperial Chemical Industries Limited, the largest holding company in Britain, announced that it would publish a consolidated income statement that year. (It had only provided a consolidated balance sheet in 1938).[85] One commentator suggested that the combination of stock exchange ruling and I.C.I. example "should do much to stimulate the movements towards a more complete disclosure of results by holding companies and companies having many subsidiaries".[86]

There is little doubt that by 1939 consolidated reporting was "generally accepted".

Conflicting ideas about consolidated statements

The introduction of consolidated reporting into the mainstream of British accounting practice brought new problems to the profession. Practitioners were quick to find matters on which there were as yet not settled views. For example, if consolidated statements were so useful, what should an auditor do if a firm did not publish them?[87]

---

83. Idem.

84. H. Parkinson, "Disclosure in published accounts", The accountant, 15 April 1939, p.503.

85. I.C.I.'s consolidated statements were reproduced in the "Finance and commerce" section of The accountant, 13 May 1939, pp.657-60; the "full consolidation" was described as "one of the most important accounting achievements of recent years" (p.659).

86. (Anon.), "London notes - consolidated accounts", The accountants' journal (New Zealand), 20 May 1939, p.339.

87. See, e.g. H. Greenwood, "Balance sheet reform", The accountant 6 Feb.1937, p.198.

How should an auditor report on consolidated statements - or should he
offer any report at all?[88] What should an auditor do if the consolidated statements were not presented to him for his opinion?[89] How
should an auditor report on qualifications in certificates issued by
the auditors of subsidiaries?[90]

These particular matters could be "resolved" by considering the
state of the law regarding the responsibilities of auditors. But there
were other questions that could only be answered by the refinement of
ideas about the objectives of consolidated statements.

The background to the use of consolidated statements in the U.K.
indicates that the underlying aim of those who supported the use of
these documents was to provide a "better" representation of the position
and performance of holding companies than could be obtained from one-line
statements of "investments" and dividend-based income calculations.
Consolidated statements were intended to improve on the "legal"
financial statements. Yet the rationale for presenting consolidated
statements was phrased in an unfortunate manner. It was said that the
aim of consolidated statements was to "reflect the position and earnings
of a holding company group, viewed not as a series of separate entities
but as an economic unit".[91] The aim of amplifying holding companies'

---

88. See "Auditors and consolidated balance sheets", ibid, 26 Nov.
     1932, p.678. This issue was complicated by disagreements about
     the auditor's responsibilities in connection with profit and loss
     statements - consolidated or otherwise. See, e.g., "Holding
     companies' accounts", ibid, 6 June 1936, p.848; 20 June 1936,
     pp.921-2.

89. See, e.g., "Auditors' reports on consolidated balance sheets",
     ibid, 26 Nov. 1936, p.693.

90   See, e.g., "The audit of subsidiary companies", ibid, 21 March
     1936, p.443.

91. T. B. Robson, "The construction of consolidated accounts - some
     points to be taken into consideration", The accountant, 7 March
     1936, p.364.

reports was <u>not</u> the same as reporting on an "economic entity". The inconsistency between these two aims was most clearly reflected in attempts to specify the area or scope of consolidation. If the aim was that of "amplifying" holding company reports, then the criterion for determining which subsidiaries should be consolidated would be linked with the materiality of the investment in particular subsidiaries, or the extent to which statements of financial position might be distorted by the inclusion of the assets and liabilities of subsidiaries which were partly-owned. If the aim was that of depicting an "economic entity", then the appropriate criterion would be that of the existence of "controlling" relationships between firms.

There are other consequences of adopting one or other view of the aims of consolidated reporting. These matters will be explored more fully in Section IV of this study. The above outline may be sufficient to indicate that at the time British accountants adopted consolidated reporting, the theoretical basis of these practices had not been fully worked out. This may have been due in part to the fact that inconsistencies in the accepted rationale of consolidated reporting had not come under close scrutiny by the end of the 1930's.

There were portents of difficulties to come. The Dunlop Rubber Company's use of a test of "control" for determining the scope of consolidated statements did not attract much attention at the time it was first used. Nor did Dunlop's later well-publicised practice of excluding foreign subsidiaries from its consolidation[92] prompt discussion on the underlying rationale of consolidation. But these procedures were consistent with the "group entity" idea and as such in conflict with the general view that consolidated reports were amplifications of parent company reports.

---

92. See <u>The accountant</u>, 4 May 1935, pp.656-9.

Again, the underlying rationale for consolidated statements was to the effect that they were _supplementary_ reports. The financial statements required by the Companies Act were the "primary" documents; consolidated statements were one way of improving on this information. But in 1935 _The accountant_ attention to the fact that the English Electric Company emphasised the consolidated statements and relegated the "legal" balance sheet "to smaller type on the back page".[93] This, claimed _The accountant_, was "the right emphasis". The following year this journal again described consolidated statements as far more "important" than parent company statements.[94] The stock exchange's 1939 rules requiring consolidated statements may have added further support to the claim that consolidated statements were in fact (if not in law) the primary vehicle for corporate reporting. The obvious conflict between claims that consolidated statements were primary reports or supplementary schedules further highlights the fact that accountants were not clear about the objectives of this form of reporting.

The accountant had played a leading role in the popularisation of consolidated reporting. In 1939, after the stock exchange had taken the step of requiring firms to agree to prepare and publish consolidated statements, _The accountant_ surveyed the uncertainty surrounding several areas of consolidation practice, and stated that the accounting profession was faced with "a very serious responsibility" now that consolidated statements were formally required disclosures.

> it seems ... necessary that steps should be taken towards the formation of standardised professional opinion.[95]

---

93. "The right emphasis", _ibid_, 16 March 1935, pp.405-6.
94. "Emphasis on consolidation", _ibid_, 23 May 1936, pp.802-3.
95. "Consolidation: the stock exchange moves, _ibid_, 25 Feb. 1939, p.246.

Ch. 7 Section summary

The introduction, acceptance and widespread adoption of consolidated statements in the U.K. as a means of reporting on the affairs
of holding companies appear to have been responses to the inadequacy
of customary procedures for asset valuation and revenue recognition
to cope with inter-corporate shareholdings.

Until the 1920's few British companies had used the holding-
company form as a means of organising their affairs or carrying out
mergers, There had been some earlier uses of the holding company form -
and in fact several of the more notorious business failures in the U.K.
had involved holding companies which had previously managed to conceal
the actual state of their affairs by their use of conventional asset
valuation and disclosure procedures. Despite these scandals it was not
until the 1920's that the accounting profession examined holding
company accounting in any detail.

The procedures in general use during the 1920's to value inter-
corporate investments were those evolved in preceding decades to
determine a corporation's "distributable" profit. Assets were classed
as "fixed" or "floating" ("current") and distinct sets of valuation
rules were then applied to assets in those separate categories. Thus,
marketable securities were usually regarded as floating assets and
as such were valued at the lower cost and market selling price. (For
a time during the early 1920's accountants favoured the systematic
use of market prices to value these assets, but it appears that the
declining stock market prompted a retreat to the use of "cost" in
order to avoid the recognition of losses arising from "mere temporary
fluctuations"). Holdings of non-listed securities which were
regarded as "fixed" assets would typically have been valued at cost, or
a cost-derivative - without regard to estimated selling prices.

When the use of holding companies became fairly common, British accountants could rely on a long-standing framework for approaching asset valuation problems. Investments in subsidiaries were typically "fixed" assets, and as such declines in their value could be ignored for purposes of calculating a distributable profit. The customary valuation basis would be "at cost". Subsidiaries' losses could be ignored: there would be no need to write-down the investments. Subsidiaries' profits would only be recorded by the extent to which the holding company "realised" a gain through the receipt of dividends.

It was obvious to some observers that these traditional asset valuation procedures would not produce very informative calculations of a holding company's income. But of more immediate interest in the early 1920's was the fact that it was often extremely difficult to get any sense of a holding company's financial position. British reporting practices were largely governed by disclosure rules incorporated in companies legislation. The 1908 Companies Act had relieved "private" companies of the obligation to place financial statements on file for public inspection. And most subsidiary companies qualified as private companies. Hence holding companies were able to conceal particulars of their investments in subsidiaries. (In fact, the privileges extended to private companies appear to have been an incentive to the formation of subsidiaries). Under these conditions, many firms simply published a one-line report, stating the value of "investments in subsidiaries". This provided no indication of the subsidiaries' solvency, or of the assets underlying these investments. Nor did it provide any indication of the type of business activity conducted by the subsidiaries. Worse, while the monetary quantification of "investments in subsidiaries" might have provided some indication of the relative significance of these assets to a particular firm, the disclosure rules did not require the separate disclosure of this item.

Accordingly, holding companies' balance sheets often aggregated "investments in subsidiaries" with a multitude of other asset items.

It was against this background that a few firms sought to present financial information in a way that conformed with prevailing rules about the calculations of distributable income but overcame the obscurities of conventional reporting procedures. Some firms published consolidated balance sheets. Some published the balance sheets of the subsidiaries (but not including the holding company's data). A few firms used "equity" methods for valuing investments in subsidiaries, though commentators were often wary of this method in the belief that this could lead to the recording of an "unrealised" profit. In all cases, firms accepted that there was a definite need to publish parent-company balance sheets. Those which published consolidated statements were simply trying to supplement the "legal" report with additional, relevant data.

It must be stressed that these efforts to supplement the financial statements of the parent company were unusual in the early 1920's. It seems that most firms did not provide supplementary disclosures about the activities and standing of their subsidiaries. And most firms were content to present fairly condensed balance sheets and to obscure the profitability of their investments by the use of cost-based valuation.

The inadequacy of these methods of financial reporting was a key factor in prompting demands for reform of the companies legislation - leading to the appointment of the Greene Committee in 1925. The Greene Committee was confronted with evidence about the poor quality of holding company reporting. But the Committee's recommendations did little to prevent the continued publication of obscure and potentially misleading financial statements. In particular, the Greene Committee made no attempt to compel the amplification of holding companies' balance sheets, beyond proposing the separate identification of the aggregate amount of loans to and investments in subsidiaries. Nor did the Committee seek to prescribe methods of valuing these investments or methods of recording gains or losses arising from the commitment of resources to subsidiaries.

The process of considering reforms to company law appears to have contributed to an increased awareness within the accounting profession of shortcomings in customary procedures, and to have stimulated debate about the merits of different methods for the treatment of inter-corporate investments. But these discussions did not go far towards resolving disagreements, let alone key issues. Little attention was paid to the propriety of cost-based asset valuation, and there was virtually no attempt to sort out precisely the information that consolidated statements or other methods of disclosure were intended to convey.

After the stock market collapse of 1929 and following subsequent revelations of corporate frauds and failures, the financial community became disenchanted with _laissez faire_ attitudes towards company and stock market regulation. The London Stock Exchange responded to these conditions and made the first steps towards the establishment of fairly extensive disclosure rules affecting firms whose securities were publicly traded. The accounting profession was similarly moved to lessen its support for the rights of businessmen to dole out what financial data they thought appropriate. A major factor in prompting this ideological shift was undoubtedly the Royal Mail case. Accountants accepted a need for fuller financial reporting, and reacted strongly against practices involving the transfer of funds to or from "reserves". Paradoxically, despite the fact that the Royal Mail case had highlighted the manipulation and distortions possible through cost-based valuation of subsidiaries and dividend-based revenue

recognition, the accounting profession seems to have responded to
the affair by accepting these practices even more firmly. The overstatement of income by the Royal Mail group seems to have prompted a
more "conservative" attitude towards asset valuations. Accountants
emphasised the use of cost, and shunned upward revaluations in any form
- including equity methods for inter-corporate investments. This simply
exacerbated the inadequacy of holding company accounting. Had equity
accounting been more widely adopted, no doubt there would have been
demands for additional information about the assets "represented" by
inter-corporate investments. As it happened the emphasis on cost-based
valuation made the need for supplemental disclosures of one form or
another far more acute.

During the 1920's, the use of consolidated statements had been
viewed as one method of overcoming the limitations of conventional reporting
methods - along with other methods viz. publication of subsidiaries' statements, aggregative subsidiaries' statements or equity accounting. Few
contributors to the accounting literature of the 1920's or 1930's
expressed firm preferences for any one method. But during the 1930's,
consolidated statements came to be the preferred form of disclosure
through a combination of factors: the enthusiasm for this form of
reporting on the part of financial commentators, the well-publicised
example of some large firms, and finally the intervention of the stock
exchanges.

While the use of consolidated reporting by British firms did not
take place until well after these reports had become commonplace in
the U.S.A. it is clear that American influence on British practices
(before the late 1930's) was minimal.

There had been little discussion of American precedents in the
U.K. literature - as indeed little attention had been paid to early

European use of consolidated statements.[1] It is clear that some of
the leading British writers on consolidated statements had drawn on the
U.S. literature. And during the 1930's there were signs of American
influence on the techniques of consolidation. But the needs and
conditions which appear to have led to the U.K. use of consolidated
statements were substantially different from the circumstances giving
rise to the earlier American adoption of this form of reporting:
matters to be explored in Section III. However at this stage some key
features of the background to the British use of consolidated reporting,
relative to American usage, might be noted. British accountants had
been predominately interested in amplifying data under the heading,
"investments in subsidiaries". While the 1929 Companies Act permitted
the aggregation of the value of shares and loans under such a heading,
it seems that there was relatively little interest in unravelling the
effect of inter-corporate loans. In contrast, early American use of
consolidated statements placed far more emphasis on the use of these
documents to represent group liquidity - possibly because of greater
American reliance on debt-securities in corporate financing. Further,
there was relatively little U.K. interest in the use of consolidated
statements in order to eliminate the effect of profits on inter-company
transactions. Even though there had been a number of business failures
involving multi-company groups with consequential revelations of manipulative inter-company transactions[2] there was surprisingly little

---

1. Some exceptions were W.E.Seatree, "Consolidated balance sheets"
   (corresp.), The accountant, 4 Jan. 1930, pp.20-1; (anon.) "Emphasis
   on consolidation", ibid, 23 May 1936, pp.802-3. Seatree attributed
   the European use of consolidated statements to American influences
   on industrial enterprises or public utilities which had issued prospectuses in the New York market.

2. Following the failure of the Royal Mail group, there had been the
   long-delayed Scottish Amalgamated Silk trial (reported in The
   accountant, Feb. & April 1932), and overseas the collapse of the Kreuger
   empire (see ibid, especially March-May 1932). Other minor British
   failures included Combined Pulp & Paper (ibid, 30 April 1932, pp.
   594-8 & 7 May 1932, pp.637-8) and the Harman group (ibid, 21 May 1932,
   pp.685-6).

support for consolidated statements on the ground that they provided

a better indicator of the viability and performance of related

companies.

SECTION III

U.S. BACKGROUND TO THE INTRODUCTION OF CONSOLIDATED REPORTING

Ch. 8 The innovation of consolidated reports

Consolidated statements were first prepared in the U.S.A. at
least as early as 1894. They were widely discussed in early American
texts and the periodical literature, and widely used well before British
companies began experimenting with this form of reporting in the early
1920's.

These facts might suggest that the sequence adopted here - of
discussing American accounting after British - is singularly inappropriate.
The more so, perhaps, since it will be argued that the factors giving
rise to the use of consolidated statements in the American environment
were distinctly different from those prompting the adoption of this
form of reporting in later years by British (and commonwealth) practitioners.

However, the fact that U.S. accountants were the first to use
consolidated statements is not nearly so significant as the fact that
they continued to use them. In order to examine why consolidated
statements came to be popular, and why they were retained, and why
later they became required disclosures, it is necessary to look at the
use of consolidated statements against the broad background of U.S.
accounting practices since the turn of the century. And many of the
antecedents of U.S. accounting may be found in U.K. practices. Moreover,
many of the difficulties that arose in the American use of consolidated
statements and many of the doubts that were expressed about the usefulness or relative significance of consolidated data appear to have
stemmed from the American adoption of British approaches to asset
valuation.

However it appears that the circumstances which shaped the intro-

duction of consolidated reporting were significantly different from
the circumstances which led to the promotion of consolidated reporting
in subsequent years.

This chapter describes the setting in which consolidated statements were first used by American accountants. It considers the background to the use of consolidated statements by United States Steel
Corporation Ltd. (reputedly the first U.S. firm to publish these reports)
and finally reviews the arguments in support of the use of consolidated
statements that were advanced by Arthur Lowes Dickinson, the first
major advocate of this form of reporting.

Later chapters will relate the development of U.S. ideas about asset
valuation to the use of consolidated reports. They will also examine the
steps leading to the wider use of consolidated reporting, and the
adoption of disclosure rules requiring consolidated data.

Business combinations 1888-1903

"Combinations" were a familiar feature of American business history.
Even before the Civil War, "manufacturing corporations were growing
larger, groups of corporations were coming under unified control, and
the general field of industrial combination was being tentatively
explored" [1] - but evidently most of these early ventures met with little
success. In post-war years, the U.S. (and especially the northern states)
enjoyed a period of prosperity which was in part a consequence of
wartime industrialisation but which was sustained by the expansion of
international trade. Further the late 1860's and early 1870's were
years of rapid expansion of railroad construction. [2]

---

1.   V. S. Clark, History of manufactures in the United States (New
     York: McGraw Hill Book Co., Inc., 1929) Vol.II, p.39.

2.   See A. D. Chandler Jr., "The role of business in the United States:
     a historical survey" in E. Goldtern, H. C. Morton & G. N. Ryland
     (eds.) The American business corporation (Cambridge, Mass.: The
     MIT Press, 1969), p.43.

The railroad industry was at times fiercely competitive - with corporations striving to defeat competition and subsequently maintain a monopolistic situation. Attempts at exploitation in these situations were responded to by state regulatory action - and later in 1887 by the passage of the federal Interstate Commerce Act.[3]

Public hostility towards monopolistic practices was focussed on the activities of a variety of so-called "pools" and "trusts". Pools took such forms as agreements for the fixing of prices or the regulation of output, arrangements for the division of territories or outlets among firms, or arrangements for the exclusive purchase of manufacturing equipment.[4] The voting "trust" - as exemplified by the Standard Oil trust agreements of 1882 - was a scheme whereby a small group of "trustees" received the right to hold the stocks of a large number of corporations in exchange for a proportionate interest in the aggregate properties, thus empowering the trustees to appoint a central management to administer the various legally-distinct corporations.[5]

Antagonism towards pools and trusts was reflected in state laws or amendments to state constitutions aimed at banning combinations. In 1890 the federal legislature passed the Sherman Anti-Trust Act. In eight short sections the Sherman Act sought to "protect trade and

---

3. G. E. Roberts (ed.), Railroad regulation (New York: American Chamber of Economics, Inc., 1921), p.10; "Interstate Commerce Commission semi-centennial commemorative issue", The George Washington law review, March 1937; G. Kolko,Railroads and regulations 1877-1916 (Princeton University Press, 1965).

4. E. Jones, The trust problem in the United States (New York: The Macmillan Company, 1922), pp.6-18.

5. Ibid, pp.19-20. The Standard Oil trust agreement of 1882 "included about 40 companies, controlling from 90 to 95 per cent. of the refining capacity of the country". So successful was this trust that the form of organisation was rapidly imitated in other industries - with the American Cotton Oil trust (1884), the National Linseed Oil trust (1885), a "whiskey business" trust (1887), the National Lead trust (1887), the National Cordage Association (1887) and a trust among sugar refiners (1889). Ibid,pp.30-3.

commerce against unlawful restraints and monopolies". Section 1 of

the Act stated (in part):

> Every contract, combination in the form of trust or
> otherwise, or conspiracy, in restraint of trade or
> commerce among the several States, or with foreign
> nations, is hereby declared to be illegal.

This prevented the continued use of voting trusts to carry out

business combinations.

Lifting of statutory restrictions on inter-corporate shareholdings

Shortly before the passage of the Sherman Act, changes in state

legislation had enabled the formation of business combinations through

the medium of the "holding company".

The powers of corporations were limited by the scope of enabling

legislation. While companies formed by charter had been empowered to

purchase and hold shares in other companies[6] there was until 1889 no

general law permitting corporations to acquire the stocks of other

corporations.[7] In 1888 the state of New Jersey amended its constitution

so as to give corporations the right "to own, hold and dispose of

shares of stock in the same manner and with the same privileges as

individuals"[8] and this constitutional amendment was followed up in May

---

6. A. S. Dewing notes that some 5 or 6 corporations with "omnibus"
    charters were formed in Pennsylvania prior to 1873. The financial
    policy of corporations (New York: Ronald Press Co., rev.ed., 1926),
    pp.755-7. Haney suggests that the Pennsylvania Co. was the "first
    real holding company of large size in the United States". The
    Pennsylvania Co. was empowered by its charter to "make purchases and
    sales for investments in the bonds and securities of other companies";
    by 1879 it had a majority interest in the railway lines affiliated
    with the Pennsylvania Railroad west of Pittsburgh and Erie, and
    "over half its assets consisted of their securities". L. H. Haney,
    Business organization and combination (New York: The Macmillan Company,
    rev.ed., 1916), p.220.

7. Jones, op.cit., p.29.

8. H. E. Hoagland, Corporation finance (New York: McGraw-Hill Book
    Co. Ltd., 3rd ed., 1947), p.636.

1889 by specific amendments to the New Jersey corporation laws.
These amendments provided that the directors of any company organized
under the 1875 New Jersey act could purchase the stock of any other
company or companies "owning mining, manufacturing or producing
materials, or other property necessary for their business, and that
they could issue stock of their own company in payment thereof.[9] This
authority was amplified in 1893 to encompass general ownership rights,
and to explicitly include the right to own stock in corporations no matter
where they were incorporated.

Regardless of whether the New Jersey enactments were a calculated
stand against "the hysteria of the times"[10], a sophisticated attempt to
aid business interests or simply a crude effort to garner the revenues
obtainable from corporate registrations, the extension of corporate
powers in this direction offered hope of evading the anti-trust legislation. (As it happened, little attempt was made to enforce the
Sherman Act in the 1890's,[11] and it was not until 1904 that the
Northern Securities case settled the point that the Sherman Act trapped
not only consensual arrangements but also property transfers, as in the
acquisition of a controlling interest in competing firms).[12]

In a sense, combinations by means of one company holding stock in
other corporations were little different from the "trusts":

> The only apparent changes effected were: the
> substitution of the shares of the holding company

---

9. Jones, op.cit., p.30.

10. Hoagland, op.cit., p.636.

11. R. Sobel, The big board (New York: The Free Press, 1965), p.136.

12. Northern Securities Co. v. U.S., 193 U.S. 197 (1904). For a
discussion of this case, see T. W. Arnold, The bottlenecks of
business (New York: Reynal & Hitchcock, 1940), p.305; W. Z.
Ripley (ed.), Trusts, pools and corporations (Boston: Ginn and
Co., 1905), pp.x, 322ff.; J. C. Bonbright and G. C. Means, The
holding company (New York: McGraw-Hill Book Co., Inc., 1932),
pp.235-42.

> for the certificates of the old 'trust'; the
> substitution of the relation of owner for the
> relation of trustee; and the substitution of a
> board of directors for a board of trustees.[13]

One of the first holding companies was the United Gas Improvement

Company, which was formed in 1888 and (using an 1870 Pennsylvania charter)

acquired stock in several gas companies.[14] In 1889 the American Cotton

Trust took advantage of the New Jersey legislation to re-organise as the

American Cotton Oil Company - a holding company with 16 subsidiaries.

During this period, several states were actively competing for

corporate registration fees and taxes;[15] it is not surprising that

the New Jersey innovation was rapidly adopted in other jurisdictions.[16]

The availability of the holding company form attracted an increased

volume of "incorporation business" to New Jersey - as the data in the

accompany table indicate.

---

13. Jones, op.cit., p.28, citing Mead, Trust finance, p.36.

14. Dewing, op.cit., p.755-6.

15. "Such conspicuous phrases as 'Incorporate in South Dakota',
    'The corporation laws of the State of Nevada offer the greatest
    inducements' and ' We beat New Jersey' are not uncommon
    advertisements of our enterprising western states". D. E.
    Mowry, "The abuse of the corporation charter", from Central law
    review, Jan.1907 , reproduced in S. P. Orth (ed.), Readings on
    the relation of government to property and industry (Boston:
    Ginn and Co., 1915), p.180. See also W. Z. Ripley, Main Street
    and Wall Street (Boston: Little, Brown and Company, 1929),
    pp.16-37.

16. Haney reported in 1916 that since the 1890's "Delaware, Maine,
    West Virginia, New York and at least fourteen other States have
    followed suit." Op.cit., p.220.

Company incorporations[17]

(under general incorporation laws -
excluding incorporations under special charters or acts)

	1885	1886	1887	1888	1889	1890	1891	1892
Colorado	*	*	*	*	*	*	738	1,164
Connecticut	90	103	128	110	110	118	163	173
Maine	208	252	292	308	370	476	436	519
Maryland	92	114	147	142	144	206	216	193
Massachusetts	111	146	153	195	233	199	203	245
New Jersey	254	386	472	567	685	897	1,155	1,212
Ohio	515	626	832	661	725	768	834	854
Pennsylvania	*	*	*	477	717	667	572	760
Texas	221	157	284	264	331	416	337	304

	1893	1894	1895	1896	1897	1898	1899	1900
Colorado	822	829	1,164	1,841	990	781	912	1,008
Connecticut	137	141	139	131	137	165	179	198
Maine	456	405	457	432	490	452	697	631
Maryland	172	188	208	172	205	212	252	247
Massachusetts	227	228	251	235	259	232	256	239
New Jersey	970	890	964	859	1,118	1,104	2,186	1,915
Ohio	713	835	872	763	714	701	1,005	1,102
Pennsylvania	604	578	573	530	540	484	687	854
Texas	321	263	362	325	342	315	387	494

However use of the holding company form did not really take off until later in the 1890's. Perhaps this may have been due in part to uncertainty about the legality of holding-company structures as a device for maintaining or effecting combinations.[18] But the primary factor appears to have been the unsettled conditions of the stock market, which inhibited the large-scale merchandising of stocks.[19]

17. Compiled from data reported in H. E. Evans, Business incorporations in the United States 1800-1943 (New York: National Bureau of Economic Research, 1948), Appendix 3. Evidently data was not available for other states that were incorporating companies during this period.

18. Bonbright and Means, op.cit., p.68.

19. Sobel, op.cit., pp.132-9.

But confidence was restored in the stock market over 1896 and 1897 - marking the beginning of what was to be a ten-year bull market.

It has been claimed that "the periods of most marked merger activity have coincided with periods of speculative activity, characterised by rising security prices and broadened security markets".

> At such times a favourable opportunity is presented for refinancing and for the sale of new issues of securities, when the general business optimism is great and the expectations of investors run high.[20]

The 1890's were just such a period. Between 1887 and 1897 there were a total of 86 industrial "combinations" with a (reported) capital of $1,000,000 or more;[21] of these, it has been estimated that between 20-25 "secured a sufficient control of the industry to be called trusts".[22] Of these trusts, 11 were said to be particularly important - and, significantly, 7 of these 11 had been chartered in New Jersey.[23]

"The real trust movement, however, dates from 1898".[24] The number and scale of industrial combinations soon dwarfed the record of earlier years. The years 1898-1902 represented "the greatest merger movement in American history".[25] The following table provides some

---

20. *Mergers in industry* (New York: National Industrial Conference Board, Inc., 1929), p.26.

21. L. Conant, "Publications of the American Statistical Association", pp.207-226, March 1901, as cited Jones, op.cit., p.39. Note that these statistics include some multiple-counting: "The whiskey trust in its various forms is counted three times: while "the sugar trust" was listed twice. Jones, idem.

22. Jones, op.cit., p.40. Bonbright and Means, when reviewing this evidence, pointed out that "only one" of the 11 made use of the holding company "device" (op.cit., pp.68-9). However these authors were using the term to relate to so-called "pure" holding companies - firms whose activities were limited to the holding of stocks in other firms. Similarly Jones distinguished "holding company trusts" and "property owning trusts" - the latter being corporations which had acquired the assets formerly held by other firms, although they often functioned for a time as "holding companies" until the transfer of assets was effected.

23. Jones, op.cit., p.40.

24. Idem.

25. Chandler, op.cit., p.47.

indication of the scale of merger activities during this period:[26]

	Number of combinations	Total capitalization
	(a) capitalization in excess of $1 m.	(stocks and bonds)
1887-1897 (total)	86	$1,414,293,000
1898	20	708,600,000
1899	87	2,243,995,000
1900	42	831,415,000
	(b) contributed capital in excess of $1 m.	
1901	46	*
1902	63	*
1903	18	*

At first, the holding company device was used in relatively few of these cases. Before 1900, of the 41 "most important industrial combinations", only 6 were holding companies.[27] Of these, the most significant was the Standard Oil Company of New York, the one-time "voting trust". It has been suggested that Standard Oil's conversion to a holding company encouraged more firms to use this organizational device.[28] Of 29 major mergers between 1901-3, 29 were "important" and of these no less than 16 were formed as holding companies.[29]

The largest merger of all during this period - the "consolidation of consolidations" - was the formation in 1901 of the United States

---

26. Source: (a) Conant, loc.cit. (b) J. Moody, The truth about trusts, pp.453-67, as cited Jones, op.cit, p.43.. These figures may be understated. A. S. Dewing also examined the incidence of large mergers, though for one year only. For 1899 he listed no less than 259 combinations with a capitalization exceeding $1 m. (as opposed to 87 in the above table). See A. S. Dewing, The financial policy of corporations (New York: Ronald Press Company, 1920), Vol. IV, p.37. But by all accounts, the promotion of business combinations was at its height in 1899.

27. Bonbright and Means, op.cit., p.69.

28. Ibid, p.70.

29. Idem.

Steel Corporation. The first annual report of U.S. Steel took the
form of consolidated statements. U.S. Steel was not the <u>first</u> firm to
<u>prepare</u> consolidated reports. The 1893 report of General Electric is
said to have included both a consolidated balance sheet and a consolidated
income statement[30] - and evidently there were other early examples.[31]
But U.S. Steel may well have been the first firm to <u>publish</u> consolidated
statements. It was certainly one of the first large American corporations to undertake a programme of prompt and extensive public financial
reporting of any kind, so that its policies of disclosure may have been
more significant in the development of corporate accountability than the
actual content of its reports. (U.S. Steel's reporting practices will
be discussed in more detail below).

<u>Disclosure rules around the turn of the century</u>

The United States lagged behind the U.K. in developing a regulatory
framework for the protection of investors against stock frauds and
market manipulations. The date most commonly identified as marking the
introduction of any significant protective rules was 1911, when the
State of Kansas introduced the first "blue sky laws". But by that
time the corporate form of organization had become by far the most

30. M. B. Daniels, <u>Corporation financial statements</u> (Ann Arbor:
University of Michigan Bureau of Business Research, 1934). How-
ever Childs stated that General Electric first used consolidated
statement in its report for the year ended Dec. 1894. See W. H.
Childs, <u>Consolidated financial statements</u> (Cornell University
Press, 1949), p.44.

31 De Mond reported that Price, Waterhouse & Co. had issued consolidated accounts for other clients "a decade earlier" than U.S. Steel's
1902 report. C. W. De Mond, <u>Price, Waterhouse & Co. in America</u>
(New York: privately printed 1951), p.60. However it appears that
these earlier reports may not have been concerned with <u>corporations</u>.
"In a private letter George O. May states that the first consolidated statements were prepared for the American Cotton Oil Trust
in 1886". M. E. Peloubet, in M. Backer (ed.), <u>Handbook of modern
accounting theory</u> (New York: Prentice-Hall, Inc., 1955), p.31. Childs
stated that the National Lead Co.'s first annual report (1892) was
in consolidated form, <u>Op.cit.</u>, p.44. Brundage stated that in 1896
the Atchison, Topeka and Santa Fe Railroad issued a "system" balance
sheet. P.F.Brundage, "Consolidated statements", in T.W.Leland (ed.),
<u>Contemporary accounting</u> (New York: American Institute of Accountants,
1945), Ch.5, p.1.

dominant feature of the process of resource mobilization and allocation in the U.S. economy.

It may be that political forces forestalled efforts to introduce
reforms in some instances - but generally the relative slowness of
the U.S. to regulate corporate reporting and the conduct of securities
markets is understandable in the light of two factors. First, whereas
U.K. financial activities were centred on one major market and corporations were governed by a national statute, the American financial
activities and regulations were more fragmented and diverse. New York
was to become the key U.S. money market but there were a number of
rival financial centres around the turn of the century.[32] Moreover,
each state had its own corporation laws, many of which were designed to
attract registration revenues rather than to regulate corporate conduct.
Second, the major avenues of investment at this time did not suggest a
need for disclosure laws or protective provisions on the British model.
In the 1880's, the principal forms of investment were the bonds of railroad corporations. (It has been said that American railroads were
started "with practically no capital" - "for construction they relied
wholly upon bonds").[33] Events would soon demonstrate that railroads were
not exactly free of risk - but at the time, railroad bonds may have

---

32. In the 1850's there were large, competing stock exchanges in Boston and Philadelphia. See Sobel, op.cit., pp.52-3. Boston has
been described as "the early home of industrial securities". T.R.
Navin and M. V. Sears, "The rise of a market for industrial
securities, 1887-1902", Business history review, 1955, pp.105-38.

33. W. G. L. Taylor, "Promotion before the trusts", Journal of political economy, 1904, p.387. Kirshman claimed that by 1855 "over
41% of the capitalization of all the railways in the United States
was represented by mortgage bonds"; by 1899 "bonds and stocks
were about equal in amount; thereafter the low price of railway
stocks and legal prohibitions of the issue of stock for less than
par values, led to even greater bonds issues when the railroads
sought funds for new construction". J. E. Kirshman, Principles
of investment (Chicago: A.W.Shaw Company, 1924), pp.435-9.

seemed fairly safe investments. Holders of senior securities may
have been less concerned about financial disclosure than holders of
equity stock investments, and so may have been less insistent on
financial disclosure than holders of common stock. In any case, the
railroads and other public utilities were subject to governmental
regulation of their rate-setting activities, and the government
regulatory agencies were supposedly policing the reporting practices of
these corporations. Perhaps because of these existing forms of regulation the state corporation laws had little to do with the activities of
firms in the industries which attracted the bulk of public investment
in the late nineteenth century.

Some U.S. states did require corporations to periodically file
reports - but few required the public filing of information. The lack
of disclosure rules may have troubled some critics - but the literature
of the time appears to have been less concerned with encouraging
extensive disclosure than with guiding businessmen to those jurisdictions which were most amenable to corporate activity.[34] Among supposedly
"liberal" corporation laws passed prior to 1905 - "liberal" in the sense
that they encouraged the formation of corporations[35] - only a few required
the compilation and filing of any kind of report on financial condition.
The chief requirement was for disclosure of the names and addresses of
directors, particulars of shares on issue, and the location of the corporations principal office. (It is not clear that all states permitted public
access to these annual reports). Massachusetts went further in requiring
the inclusion in annual reports of a "statement of the assets and liabilities
of the corporation" - but there were no rules governing the content of these

34. See, e.g., W. C. Clephane, The organization and management of business
     corporations (St.Paul, Minn.:West Publishing Co., 1905), Ch. 1.

35. "The attention of the corporation counsel may well be confined to the
     following jurisdictions when selecting a domicile for a proposed com-
     pany, viz; Maine, Massachusetts, Connecticut, New York, New Jersey,
     Delaware, District of Columbia, Virginia, West Virginia, South
     Dakota, Nevada and Porto Rico (sic)". Ibid., Ch.1, para.17.

statements.[36]

New York's rules were complicated by a franchise tax which was based on a formula concerned with dividend rates and the proportion of a firm's assets that were held within the state. Hence New York's rules required disclosure of "the amount of real property owned", authorised and paid-in capital, the amount of intra-state investment, and "the amount of net worth.[37] Delaware's laws required annual reports to state how much of paid in capital was "invested in real estate and the annual tax thereon, and the amount invested in manufacturing or mining within the state, or both".[38] The District of Columbia's rules specified that annual reports "must be filed and published", and required that these documents state the "amount of capital and the pro-portion actually paid in, and the amount of existing debts", and that a schedule to be filed annually should state "tangible personal property".[39] West Virginia's rules simply required that corporations disclose the number of acres of land held in the state (if the number exceeds 10,000) and "such other facts as the auditor may require".[40] South Dakota's rules required publication of annual reports which disclosed authorised and paid-in capital, details of dividends, together with particulars of "indebtedness due to and by the corporation" and "net amount of profits".[41] (South Dakota was apparently the only state to explicitly require disclosure of profits. Several other states did not have detailed disclosure laws, but imposed penalties on directors

---

36. Massachusetts Business Corporation Laws, 1903, 45, as cited Clephane, op.cit.

37. N.Y. Tax Laws, 27, #189; N.Y.S.C.L. #30 - as cited Clephane.

38. Del. Franchise Tax Act, 1901, #2 - as cited Clephane.

39. D.C. Code, #617; 32 Stat.617 - as cited Clephane.

40. W. Va. Code, c.32, #88, as amended (Acts 1901, p.14, c.35, #36) - as cited Clephane.

41. S.D. Rev. Civ. Code, #430, #445 - as cited Clephane.

who issued false reports.[42] But the force of these strictures against "false" reports was negated by other statutory provisions establishing directors as sole arbiters of the value of assets acquired or services rendered in exchange for corporate stock. The effect of these provisions was to sanction the inclusion of fictional numbers in financial statements.

These early corporation laws were thus "enabling" rather than regulatory statutes. They provided for the formation, taxing and administration of the corporate form of organization, but contained few rules compelling corporate financial disclosure, and few guidelines for financial reporting.

It was noted earlier that the most popular form of investment around this time were the bonds of railroad companies. These securities dominated the trading of organised stock exchanges. But this is not to say that investment in non-railroad companies was negligible. "By the end of the 1880's the aggregate capital invested in industry may have equalled the capital tied up in the nation's system of rails". But while railroads were "large, well-established, widely-known enterprises with securities traded on organized stock exchanges" the industrials were "small, scattered, closely owned, and commonly regarded as unstable".[43] The development of the "trust" form of organization in the 1880's attracted a trade in "trust certificates". But general interest in "industrials" was not aroused until the early 1890's when the issue of "preferred" stock was widely practiced.[44]

---

42. New Jersey (N.J. Corp. Act, #29), Nevada (Nev. Gen. Inc. Laws, 1903, #110) and Virginia (Gen. Inc. Act, Va, c5, #26). New York and Massachusetts also made directors liable for issuing false reports.

43. Navin and Sears, op.cit., p.106.

44. Ibid, pp.116-7.

It has been reported that between 1890 and 1893, "at least 23 American industrial companies" (with a net worth of between $2 - $5 million) issued preferred stocks of "investment quality"; more than half of these were listed on the New York Stock Exchange and "frequently" a company's common stock was listed at the same time.[45] This was a dramatic innovation, and marked the start of more widespread ownership of non-railroad stock. A number of firms "went public" through a process of recapitalization, and others followed - seeking to produce vendors' profits through offerings on the "curb" exchange in New York.

> The number of issues traded on [the curb] is ... an indication of what was occurring. In 1890 less than 10 industrial companies, exclusive of mining ventures, had their prices quoted in the financial journals. By the crash of 1893 the number had grown to more than 30. In the next four years of depression another 170 names were added to the list.[46]

The curb exchange did not attempt to regulate corporate reporting. The New York Stock Exchange had made some tentative efforts to get firms to publish financial information[47] but it had no detailed formal disclosure rules, and moreover, since trading was concerned with railroad bonds and other senior securities there was little incentive to enforce the publication of detailed financial data. In general, the stock exchanges were concerned with maintaining their position against competition from second or third markets, and with weeding out wash sales and other manipulative devices. They took little active interest in regulating financial disclosure.

---

45. _Ibid_, pp.117, 119.

46. _Ibid_, p.127.

47. "By 1900, all corporations applying for listing had to agree to publish annual balance sheets and income statements, though this rule was not always enforced". M. Chatfield, _A history of accounting thought_ (Hinsdale, Ill.: The Dryden Press, 1974), p.232.

Accounting practices around the turn of the century

Relatively few corporations published detailed financial reports in
these years.[48] Furthermore, there were few discussions of financial
reporting in the press.[49] Certainly no journal documented accounting
and reporting matters as comprehensively and as pointedly as did The
accountant in the U.K. In any case, the geographic dispersion of
business activities across the U.S. meant that it was difficult for
contemporary commentators to have a general overview of American accounting at this time. While individual practitioners were accustomed to
travel widely in order to service their clients it appears that many
corporate activities were distinctly local ventures, so that the distribution of any financial reports would have been limited.

It appears that many British-trained accountants were practising
in the U.S. around the turn of the century.[50] As discussed in Section
II, there appears to have been little standardisation of British
reporting practices until the late 1890's. Hence immigrant British
accountants would not have been able to bring with them any well-developed
rules for measuring assets, calculating income or presenting financial

48. Hawkins provides some examples: Between 1897 and 1905 the West-
    inghouse Electric and Manufacturing Co. neither published reports
    nor held an annual meeting; in 1886 the treasurer of a railroad
    responded to a New York Stock Exchange enquiry by stating that
    it did not issue reports or statements and had done nothing of the
    sort for the past five years. Firms which were prepared to issue
    financial statements were reluctant to provide details: the American
    Tin Plate Company's 1900 balance sheet contained only four asset and
    five liability accounts. D.F.Hawkins, Corporate financial reporting
    (Homewood, Ill: Richard D. Irwin, Inc., 1971), pp.17-8.

49. See R. Sobel, op.cit., pp.175-9 for a discussion of the limited
    scope of corporate reporting and of the activities of financial
    journalists in this period.

50. Notable among these were Edwin Guthrie (active in the formation of
    the American Association of Public Accountants) James T. Anyon
    (first secretary of the Association), G.O.May, F.W.Thornton and A.L.
    Dickinson. See "A history of the American Institute of Accountants"
    in Fiftieth anniversary celebrations (Commemorative volume) (New York:
    American Institute of Accountants, 1937), pp.3-4; P.Grady (ed.)
    Memoirs and accounting thought of George O. May (New York: Ronald
    Press Company, 1962), espec. pp.30-1.

reports. They were, however, able to impress Americans with their
"professionalism".[51] And it appears that they were able to bring to
play a commonsense approach to auditing. As G. O. May later reported,
the many cases of defaults in railroad bonds around 1893 had "resulted
in demands for accounting examinations of the issuers and for the audit
of companies which emerged from the reorganization[s]".[52]

British-trained accountants were able to secure many of these
engagements, and under the circumstances paid considerable concern to
representations of a firm's solvency. It was later claimed that the
signature of a public accountant on the financial reports of a corporation put "the question of solvency and standing beyond doubt.[53]

However, it appears that while accountants were extremely cautious
about representations of liquidity, they nevertheless were prepared to
sanction financial reports which contained exaggerated asset valuations.

Blatant exaggeration of balance sheets was apparently commonplace
in the early days of the U.S. railroad industry. As noted earlier,
the railroads relied heavily on bond issues to finance expansion. While
these issues were not entirely free of fraud and deceit, some effort
was made to ensure that bond investments were associated with productive
investment. But stocks were another matter. Stock issues were regarded
as highly speculative, and the asset backing attributable to these
securities was often highly fanciful. It was openly said that "since
the American railroad was built on bonds, the stock issued amounted to
an overcapitalization to that extent".[54]

---

51. See, e.g., H. C. White, introduction to D. A. Keister's Corpora-
    tion accounting and auditing (Cleveland: The Burrows Bros. Co.,
    12th ed., 1907; introduction dated 1896), p.iii.

52. Memoirs, loc.cit., p.20.

53. White, op.cit., p.iii.

54. Taylor, op.cit., p.387.

In later years, the conscious exaggeration of asset magnitudes was associated with the early stages of the "trust movement". Unsophisticated stockholders in many smaller companies were (supposedly) attracted by the face-value of certificates offered for their shares. Hence in the 1880's "the total par value of the 'trust' certificates typically exceeded the combined pars of ... constituent companies".[55]

G. O. May has recounted that his U.S. experience in the years 1897-1901 was chiefly in connection with two types of business arrangements - the re-organization of railroad companies and the consolidation of industrial companies.

> One feature common to the two types was that the normal capitalization was usually far in excess of any reasonable valuation of the assets acquired. In both cases the practice was to set up the assets in the books in amounts equal to the capitalization.

The bankruptcy of hundreds of railroad companies was followed by a wave of re-organizations. May explained that "there was usually no attempt to reduce the nominal capitalization below that of the predecessor corporations".

> All that was done was to replace securities with preferential rights by securities carrying less in the way of priorities. But all the securities, good, bad, and indifferent, were recorded at their face value.

As for industrial consolidations, May indicated that

> It was customary to issue preferred stock, or occasionally bonds, up to the reasonable value of the assets acquired, including intangible value, and to issue common stock to represent hopes for the future.[56]

The state corporation laws enabled the overstatement of asset values, for they contained provisions to the effect that stock could be issued for cash or property (or, in some jurisdictions, for services).

---

55. Navin and Sears, op.cit., p.114.

56. Memoirs, loc.cit., p.22.

Newly established corporations were able to record the value of
properties at an amount equal to the par value of the stock issued to
acquire them. In situations where stock was "paid up" in consideration
for services provided by promoters or others, then there may have been
some incentive to record "preliminary expenses" (or the like) as asset
items. (Moreover, these "preliminary expenses" could be judiciously
grouped with other assets to convey an impression of financial strength).
Several state corporation laws in force around the turn of the century
went even further in expressly granting directors the final say as to
the value of any property (or services) acquired as consideration for
stock issues. Other states included provisos that directors' valuations
would only be acceptable in the absence of fraud. It appears that the
District of Columbia was alone in requiring that the issue of stock
be for cash or for property "at its actual value".[57] Hence the majority
of corporations in the U.S.A. at this time would have been formed in
terms of legislation which allowed promoters considerable lattitude in
the preparation of financial statements.

Many early textbooks were concerned only with bookkeeping
techniques and did not discuss asset valuation matters. One exception
was Keister's Corporation accounting and auditing which described the
procedures involved in recording the formation and subsequent life of
a corporate enterprise. Keister's illustrations of the entries on the
incorporation of an existing business showed the issue of stock to previous owners being recorded at face amounts, with an asset "franchise"
being recorded as a balancing item.[58] Further Keister asserted that it

---

57. See Clephane, op.cit., pp.13-27.

58. Loc.cit., pp.63, 70. Keister noted that "some accountants object
     to using fictitious accounts to get the real accounts upon the
     books" and observed that "it would be very gratifying indeed to
     know how to open the books ... without their use" (p.64).

was entirely legitimate to place "nominal values" on such properties
as "Mine, Plant, Franchise, Steamer, Machinery, Land, etc." when
opening the books of a corporation (p.79).

To summarise the state of accounting around the turn of the
century: apart from a concern with the accuracy of representations
of liquid assets, it would seem that accountants were prepared to
sanction financial statements which contained exaggerated (or "nominal")
representations of asset values. State corporation laws did not regulate
financial reporting in any detail but some afforded directors considerable
latitude in attributing values to assets. In this environment it seems
likely that the content of corporate financial reports would have been
largely moulded by the interests and wishes of promoters.

United States Steel Corporation's use of consolidated statements

U. S. Steel was the biggest business combination in U.S.A.'s
history. The first annual report of this corporation has been described
as a "landmark" in the history of American corporate reporting.[59] The
reporting contained consolidated statements and U.S. Steel's use of
this form of report has often been described as a major factor in the
adoption of consolidated reporting by other corporations.[60] But at the

---

59. G. O. May, "Improvement in financial accounts", Dickinson lectures
    in accounting (Cambridge, Mass.: Harvard University Press, 1943),
    p.12.

60. See, e.g., G. R. Webster, "Consolidated accounts", The journal of
    accountancy, Oct. 1919, pp.258-72; M. Moonitz, The entity theory
    of consolidated statements (American Accounting Association, 1944),
    p.7; G. Garnsey, Holding companies and their published accounts
    (London: Gee & Co. (Publishers) Ltd., 3rd ed. by T. B. Robson, 1936),
    p.117; G. Mulcahy, "History of holding companies and consolidated
    financial statements", Canadian chartered accountant, July 1956,
    p.61. W. H. Childs simply records U.S. Steel's report along with
    five other early examples of consolidated reporting. Op.cit., p.44.
    However Dickinson later asserted that in 1902 U.S. Steel issued
    "the first consolidated balance sheet"; this claim was later repeated
    by M. Murphy. See A. L. Dickinson, "The American Association of
    Public Accountants", The accountant, 28 Nov. 1925, p.846; M. Murphy,
    Selected readings in accounting and auditing (New York: Prentice-
    Hall, Inc., 1952), p.169.

time, the use of consolidated statements hardly attracted any attention.
Whad did seem important was the fact that a major firm had voluntarily
published reports on its profitability and position. It appears that
the extent of the detail in U.S. Steel's report was unparalleled in
early U. S. corporate history. In G. O. May's words, U. S. Steel's
1902 report amounts to a recognition of "an obligation to give to
stockholders a substantial amount of information in regard to their
investments".[61]

The use of consolidated reports is the primary concern here; an
examination of the circumstances surrounding U.S. Steel's use of these
reports sheds some light as to the objectives of accountants in selecting this form of presenting financial information.

The formation of the United States Steel Corporation was the
culmination of a period of merger activity that had gained momentum in
the late 1890's. The amalgamation of the major interests in the steel
business may have been promoted by a desire to stabilize an industry
which was then unsettled as a number of recently-amalgamated firms
jostled for sources of supply and for markets.[62] Or it may have
offered the means whereby the promoters of these earlier combinations
could avoid the risk of losses to the value of their portfolios that would
follow from a prolonged trade war.[63] The immediate stimulus for the
merger came early in 1900 with the announcement by the Carnegie
interests of plans to enter into active competition with some of the
newly-organized or re-organized firms.[64] This threatened the creation
of excess capacity in steel production and the termination of the

---

61. G. O. May, "Improvement in financial accounts", loc.cit., p.12.

62. H. L. Satterlee, J. Pierpont Morgan (New York: The Macmillan
     Company, 1940), p.346.

63. Jones, op.cit., p.202.

64. J. K. Winkler, Morgan the magnificent (New York: The Vanguard
     Press, 1930), pp.2,7,8.

monopolistic or semi-monopolistic status of several firms engaged in steel fabrication.[65] It has been suggested that the Carnegie announcement was merely strategic: that Carnegie wished to dispose of his holding and was merely cultivating the interest of potential buyers.[66] But, in the event, J. P. Morgan & Co. arranged the purchase of the Carnegie companies which were to be added to the Morgan-backed Federal Steel Corporation (organised in 1898) and combined with half a dozen other corporate groups.

Finally in February 1901 U.S. Steel was incorporated under the laws of New Jersey and proceeded to acquire the securities of the corporations involved in the prospective merger. With the exception of Carnegie (who received bonds) shareholders of the various firms were offered U.S. Steel stock, and eventually more than 98% accepted the offer. The "combination of combinations" brought together under unified control over sixty per cent of the steel producing capacity of the United States.[67]

Credit for some of the innovations in U.S. Steel's 1902 report has been attributed to Arthur Lowes Dickinson, a British-trained accountant then senior partner of the American branch of Price, Waterhouse. C. W. De Mond, author of Price, Waterhouse & Co. in America,[68] has described Dickinson's role as follows:

> Despite the views of the corporation's lawyers and
> bankers that the accounts presented to stockholders
> should be those of the parent company alone and that

65. Jones, op.cit., p.201.

66. Winkler, op.cit., p.206; A. Cotter, The authentic history of the United States Steel Corporation (New York: The Moody Magazine and Book Company, 1916), pp.13-14.

67. E. S. Mead, Corporation finance (New York: D. Appleton and Co., 1924), p.71.

68. New York: privately printed, 1951.

> the results of operations of the subsidiaries should be
> included only to the extent of the interest and dividends
> they had paid over to the parent company, Dickinson was
> firmly convinced that only consolidated accounts would
> provide shareholders with adequate information relative to
> the position of their company (p.60).

There are several grounds for doubting that Dickinson was responsible for
the use of consolidated statements. First, ever since U. S. Steel's
formation the firm had been engaged in what has been described as "a
thoughtful program of public relations"[69] - it had been issuing quarterly
financial reports, and these interim reports had been prepared on a
consolidated basis. The American branch of Price, Waterhouse _may_ have
been involved with the preparation of these reports, for it had acted
for J. P. Morgan prior to the formation of the American Steel and
Wire Co. (one of the constituents of the U. S. Steel amalgamation).[71]
But Dickinson himself did not step foot on American shores until 1901.[72]
And Price, Waterhouse & Co. were not appointed auditors of U.S. Steel
until the first meeting of stockholders in February 1902.[73]

Further, at this February 1902 meeting the first unaudited "annual
report" of U.S. Steel (covering a nine month period of operations) was

---

69. Idem. See also J. D. Edwards, History of public accounting in
    the United States (East Lansing: Bureau of Business and Economic
    Research, Michigan State University, 1960), p.77.

70. See, e.g., The commercial and financial chronicle, 5 Oct. 1901,
    p.694.

71. Edwards, op.cit., p.77.

72. M. Murphy, "Arthur Lowes Dickinson: pioneer in American profes-
    sional accountancy", Bulletin of the Business Historical
    Society (later Business history review), April 1947, p.28.

73. U.S. Steel became "the first important industrial company [in the
    U.S.A.] to adopt the British practice of having the auditors elec-
    ted by shareholders rather than selected by officers or directors".
    De Mond, op.cit., p.59. Price, Waterhouse & Co. was originally
    the name of an English firm which had been operating in the U.S.
    in conjunction with Jones, Caesar & Co. G. O. May later recalled
    that the appointment of the American partnership as the auditor
    of U. S. Steel under the name of Price, Waterhouse & Co. was a
    matter of "intense surprise". Memoirs, loc.cit., pp.26-7.

made available - and this report on 1901 operations was also in consolidated form. The much-praised 1902 report was U.S. Steel's first "full" annual report, and was not made available until some months later. Under these circumstances it seems likely that the initiative for producing consolidated statements may have come from U.S. Steel directors or staff.

The February 1902 report included a "condensed general balance sheet" dated November 30, 1901. The directors' report explained:

> It exhibits the assets and liabilities represented by the capital stock of the Corporation and by outstanding stocks of subsidiary companies except that, for simplicity, it omits indebtedness from company to another, as such sums though assets of one company are liabilities of some other company.[74]

A leading article in The commercial and financial chronicle eulogised the company's report, saying that its appearance was "in its way as important as the creation and organization of the company itself"

> In the clear and full manner in which information is imparted and the frankness with which policies are outlined the report sets a standard in corporation reporting as to which other industrial concerns, we are confident, will be obliged to conform if they would command the favor of either investors or the general public.[75]

But there was only brief mention of the use of consolidated statements. It was a "striking feature" to note that the balance sheet was consolidated: "striking" because there had been "for all practical purposes a complete consolidation" with 99 3/4% of the stocks of the constituent companies being exchanged for the securities of the new corporation. This was seen as "able testimony" to the universal

---

74. The report is reproduced in The commercial and financial chronicle, 1 Feb. 1902, pp.272-4. The directors noted that the balance sheet was dated November 30 and not December 31, 1902 because of the short time available to prepare the report before the time set down for the first shareholders' meeting.

75. "The United States Steel report", loc.cit., 1 Feb. 1902, p.233.

confidence accorded J. P. Morgan. The accounting significance of the
use of consolidated reports was ignored.

Why did U.S. Steel prepare and publish consolidated statements
rather than statements dealing with the holding company alone? There
seem to be two possible explanations.

One possibility is that consolidated statements just seemed to be
the natural way to depict the affairs of the corporation. Business
combinations in the U.S. were typically carried out through mergers of
existing businesses rather than through the incorporation of subsidiaries or through takeovers. And where the constituent firms had
previously prepared their own financial statements, it may have seemed
a fairly obvious procedure to aggregate the income statements of
those firms after the merger. Only thus could managers or others
assess the performance of the new combination compared with the
aggregate prior performance of the constituent firms.

In the case of U.S. Steel, the promoters' plans had been subjected
to enormous publicity. There was widespread interest in the prospects
of the combination. Some commentators had been prompted to aggregate
the profits of the constituent firms before the merger was consummated.[76]
The subsequent publication of consolidated data was the obvious way
to satisfy the public demand for reports on the combination's profitability.

The second possibility is that the use of consolidated statements
may have enabled the presentation of a more encouraging view of
U.S. Steel's position and performance than would have been available
from using conventional reporting techniques. There seem to have been
several reasons why those associated with the corporation would have
wanted to provide early reports of the firm's prosperity.

---

76. e.g. E. S. Mead, "The genesis of the United States Steel Corpora-
    Corporation", Quarterly journal of economics, 1901, p.528.

U.S. Steel was formed as a "pure" holding company, and funds for the acquisition were raised by a syndicate which was to sell U.S. Steel stock to the public.

> The syndicate which undertook to secure a majority of the stock of the eight companies originally acquired by the Corporation incurred cash expenses of $28,000,000 of which amount $25,000,000 went to the Corporation for working capital. In return for this outlay and its underwriting services the syndicate was given ... a total of 1,229,975 shares of stock (half preferred and half common) ...[77]

The syndicate aimed at unloading these securities onto the market. Listing of U.S. Steel stock was accompanied at first by well-organised support of share prices.[78] Later in July 1901 the syndicate's efforts to cash in its holdings were no doubt aided by the corporation's surprise announcement of a maiden dividend on both preference and common stock.[79] The syndicate recovered its $25 million investment after only eight months,[80] and received further distributions of profit during 1902.[81] But it is clear that when U.S. Steel published its first consolidated statements, the syndicate members had not finished cashing in their portfolios. If the syndicate had arranged to manipulate stock prices and had arranged for apparently premature dividend distributions[82] it seems highly likely that it could also arrange for

---

77. Jones, op.cit., p.288, citing the Report of the commissioner of corporations on the steel industry, part I, p.244.

78. Winkler, op.cit., p.215; Sobel, op.cit., pp.162-3.

79. The commercial and financial chronicle, 6 July 1901, p.2.

80. Ibid, 30 Nov. 1901, p.1167.

81. e.g. The commercial and financial chronicle reported distributions of $10m. profits - the fourth taking place in October 1902. Loc.cit., 4 Oct. 1902, p.736. The final profit was calculated to be $90,500,000. Jones, op.cit., p.288 again citing the Report ... on the steel industry, part I, p.244.

82. E. S. Mead, "Capitalization of the United States Steel Corporation", Quarterly journal of economics, 1902, pp.2,4,5.

financial statements to depict the firm's affairs in an attractive light. And it is possible that cost-based dividend recognition would not have provided as high a profit as was obtained from the consolidated income statement.

This possible explanation does not fully explain the choice of consolidated statements rather than equity methods; the permissiveness of American reporting practices at this time was such that no great objection could have been made to the use of equity methods.

It will be recalled that the early 1900's were a period of widespread political opposition to the combination movement. It was feared that the newly-created trusts would exploit the public by virtue of their monopolistic position. Against this it was claimed that business combinations were a natural expression of American capitalism and free enterprise and indeed were desirable as a means of enhancing business efficiency. With this background, it is understandable that managers of the biggest industrial combination on record would have liked to show that size could be linked with economies of scale. In any event, there had been moves to hold the "trusts" accountable for their profits. In 1900, the Industrial Commission made the following recommendation to Congress:

> The larger corporations - the so-called trusts - should be required to publish annually a properly audited report, showing in reasonable detail their assets and liabilities, with profit or loss; such report and audit under oath to be subject to Government inspection. The purpose of such publicity is to encourage competition when profits become excessive, thus protecting consumers against too high prices and to guard the interests of employees by a knowledge of the financial condition of the business in which they are employed ...[83]

The publication of extensive financial data by U.S. Steel was consistent with the ideals of disclosure described in the above recommendation. It

---

83. As cited Hawkins, op.cit., p.20.

seems unlikely that the publication of the holding company's balance

sheet alone (however "investments" were described or measured) would

have satisfied the demand for accountability by large combinations.

And the supplementary publication of the reports of every U. S. Steel

subsidiary would have been utterly confusing. The use of a consolidated

report solved these difficulties. Moreover, if these reports would

project U.S. Steel as being economically efficient, so much the better.

Finally, U.S. Steel soon found itself in need of additional working

capital.

> Obligations entered into by constituent companies before
> the merger, it was discovered, called for the expenditure
> of approximately $15,000,000, and fully $10,000,000 was
> needed to refund what was classed as 'purchase money
> obligations'. It was also thought desirable that expen-
> ditures should be made for improvements and additions
> which, it was estimated, would increase the big company's
> earning power at least $10,000,000 a year. Furthermore,
> it was deemed advisable to add from $10,000,000 to
> $15,000,000 to the corporation's fluid assets to provide
> for further expansion and to strengthen reserves ... [84]

A complex scheme to raise funds was put to shareholders on May 19,

1902 - not long after the publication of the first consolidated

balance sheet. There is no doubt that U.S. Steel's balance sheet

included many intangibles or over-valued assets. It was later revealed

that much of U.S. Steel's capitalization was "water".

> ... the securities issued directly by United States
> Steel Corporation exceeded the value of the securities
> acquired from the constituent firms by a substantial
> amount (omitting underlying bonds, purchase money
> obligations of constituent companies), $440,484,732. [85]

---

84. Cotter, op.cit., p.48

85. W. T. Hogan, Economic history of the iron and steel industry in
the United States (Lexington, Mass: D.C.Heath & Co. 1971) Vol.II,
p.476. In 1911 the Bureau of Corporations (then part of the
Department of Commerce and Labor) attempted to reconcile the
nominal capitalization of U.S. Steel with data concerning the
assets and earnings records of the merged corporations, using three
bases; in each case "the figure arrived at was substantially
lower than the ... authorized capitalization". Idem. See also
M. H. Robinson, "The distribution of securities in the formation
of the United States Steel Corporation", Political science quarterly, 1915, pp.277-300.

For the time, the extent of this "water" was hidden in the balance sheet figures. It seems reasonable to suppose that those involved with the choice of U.S. Steel's reporting methods would have been conscious of the need to convey an impression of substantial asset backing before the proposed issue of second-mortgage bonds. The publication of a consolidated balance sheet enumerating massive inventories, plant and real properties would have made the corporation seem more solid than the balance sheet of a "pure" holding company which only depicted holdings of unlisted securities.

It has been recorded that "combined" statements had been prepared in the 1890's for "voting trusts". Hence the use of "combined" statements for holding companies and their subsidiaries may not have been the consequence of a conscious decision to disregard legal relationships. Rather, the adoption of consolidated reporting may simply have followed from a minimal analysis of the legalities of the situation.

Dickinson's advocacy of consolidated statements

Regardless of whether Arthur Lowes Dickinson and his Price, Waterhouse colleagues were responsible for U.S. Steel's adoption of consolidated reporting, they were certainly involved with the publication of these documents. And Dickinson was soon to urge that all holding companies publish consolidated statements.

Dickinson published three papers between 1904 and 1906. A common theme was that accountants should ensure that financial statements were not misleading. The first paper, titled "The profits of a corporation", was presented at the International Congress of Accountants, held in St. Louis in September 1904.[86] It dealt with a wide range of issues, and touched on "consolidated earnings statements" and pre-acquisition profits. The second paper was a lecture at New York

---

86. Official record of the proceedings of the congress of accountants (New York: George Wilkinson, 1904), pp.171-91.

University and was later published in The accountant.[87]   Again this

paper was wide-ranging, though it concentrated a little more closely

on holding company accounting and consolidated statements. Then in

1906 Dickinson contributed an article to the initial volume of The

journal of accountancy which dealt squarely with the desirability of

the "form of balance sheet".[88]

The three papers were progressively more critical of contemporary

accounting practices and of attempts to manipulate reported profit or

asset figures. And so: Dickinson argued that assets acquired from

existing businesses should be revalued rather than kept at book value.

He supported a form of the lower of cost and market rule for inven-

tories, and argued against the allocation of non-factory overheads to

inventories. And, in particular, he expressed considerable distaste

for attempts to manipulate financial statements through the recognition

of pre-acquisition or pre-incorporation profits.

In 1904, Dickinson gave this example of the dangers of the

relationship between holding and subsidiary companies:

> ... it is within the power of the directors of the
> holding company to regulate its profits according not
> to facts, but to their own wishes, by distributing or
> withholding dividends of the subsidiary companies; or
> even to largely overstate the profits of the whole
> group by declaring large dividends in those sub-companies
> which have made profits, while entirely omitting to make
> provision for losses which have been made by other
> companies in the group (pp.189-90).

In 1905, Dickinson provided examples of other forms of inter-company

transactions which could give rise to manipulations, and he extended

the analysis by considering the possibility that accounting reports

might misrepresent liquidity.

---

87. "Some special points in corporation accounting", The accountant,
     7 Oct. 1905, pp.402-10.

88. "Notes on some problems relating to the accounts of holding
     companies", The journal of accountancy, 1906, pp.487-91.

> ... Corporation A may own the whole stock of Cor-
> poration B, both carrying on a similar business.
> Stockholders in A may know this fact, but have no means
> of ascertaining the real position of Corporation B. A,
> having control of B, may turn over to B all its un-
> remunerative work, with the result of showing large
> profits in its own accounts, while the accounts of B
> show correspondingly large losses. Corporation A, in
> its Balance Sheet, carries its investments at cost,
> probably merged under the general head of "Cost of
> Properties" with all its other capital assets. Corpora-
> tion B may obtain its loans from Corporation A, which
> largely exceed its assets, and may be expended in
> construction work, or even lost in operations, while
> Corporation A carries in its Balance Sheet these same
> loans as current assets recoverable on demand (p.409).

The papers became progressively stronger in their support of consolidated statements as the solution to the hazards of manipulated holding companies' reports. For example, in 1905 Dickinson was content to observe that balance sheets which weren't accompanied by details of the financial position of subsidiaries should be "looked upon with suspicion" - with the added observation that

> even then a collection of Balance Sheets cannot show
> the true financial position of the whole group until
> they are all combined into one and the inter-company
> interests eliminated (p.410).

But in 1906 Dickinson went so far as to claim that only consolidated balance sheets showed "the actual position of the whole group of companies in their relations to stockholders, and to the general public outside the consolidation".

> It is submitted that no statement which does not so
> disclose the true facts is permissible or should be
> allowed by any public accountant to be put forth over
> his signature (p.490).

Several features of Dickinson's arguments and proposals stand out in the light of inconsistencies which later emerged in the literature concerning the status, function and scope of consolidated reports. First, Dickinson saw consolidated statements as primary documents, not as supplements to other forms of reporting. To Dickinson, the balance sheets and earnings statements of holding companies would

only be correct if they showed the aggregate performance and position
of "the whole group of companies". Second, while Dickinson referred
to consolidated statements as dealing with "groups of companies", he
did not consider the complications which might arise from linking the
scope of consolidated statements with "groups". In 1904 Dickinson
simply described situations in which the holding company form of
organisation had come into favour. In 1905 he again described the
trend towards the use of holding companies and again emphasised that
ownership of "the whole or practically the whole" of a company's
capital stock carried with it absolute control of that company's
operations. In 1906 he alluded to situations in which one firm owned
either all of another's shares or "such a substantial proportion thereof
that it practically controls the operations". In all of these papers
Dickinson was simply trying to persuade his audience of the need to
adopt consolidated reporting. He did not propose that "similarity of
business" should be a criterion for determining whether or not a given
company should be encompassed by consolidated reports. And while he
drew a distinction between ownership of a large proportion of shares
and ownership of a controlling interest (arguing that consolidated
statements should be used where one firm controlled the operations of
another) he was not proposing it was necessary to delineate an economic
entity" as much as explaining that without consolidated reports it
would be hard to assess profitability and liquidity.

However it may be noted that Dickinson's support for consolidated
statements was partly based on the "misleading character" of representations of a holding company's affairs when investments in
subsidiaries were valued at cost. While the state of American accounting was such that firms could have readily used equity accounting had
they chosen to do so, Dickinson (perhaps because of his British background) seemed to assume that cost-based valuation was the norm. But

even had equity methods been widely used it seems likely that
Dickinson would still have supported consolidated reporting on the
ground that conventional balance sheets could still provide a misleading impression of corporate liquidity.

Resume

Around the turn of the century a few U.S. firms (notably the United States Steel Corporation) began using consolidated statements as a medium of financial reporting. At the time, the use of consolidated reports evoked little interest. State corporation laws contained few rules requiring financial disclosure, there was no federal regulation of corporations or corporate reporting, and the stock exchanges had yet to develop and enforce reporting standards. And it was rare for corporations to subject their financial reports to an independent audit. The fact that firms like U.S. Steel were prepared to publicise their financial performance was considered to be far more significant than the use of one or other device for the calculation of income or the representation of financial position.

U.S. Steel's choice of consolidated statements may have been a response to a variety of factors. Consolidated income statements may have enabled the corporation to report a greater profit than would have been possible using dividend-based revenue recognition at a time when the corporation's promoters were selling U.S. Steel stock in the market, and when business combinations were trying to impress the public with their efficiency. Consolidated balance sheets might have provided a more impressive picture of the security which would be offered prospective bond holders at a time when the corporation's management was becoming aware of a need to go to the market for additional working capital. Or, more generally, the use of consolidated statements may have seemed a natural extension of the reporting methods adopted earlier by "voting trusts".

While it is doubtful that A. L. Dickinson (as senior partner of U.S. Steel's auditors) was responsible for the initial use of consolidated reporting, he was to become the leading advocate of this style of presenting financial data. Dickinson's arguments appear to have assumed that conventional balance sheets would use cost-based valuation of inter-corporate investments. Hence, Dickinson argued that consolidated statements would avoid misrepresentations of holding company income. But he also emphasised the dangers of profit manipulations through inter-company transactions, and placed a considerable stress on the advantages of consolidated reports as a means of representing a firm's liquid position.

The contrast between the background to American and U.K. uses of consolidated reports is striking. American corporate reporting was largely unregulated; British reporting was subject to disclosure rules. American accountants were introduced to consolidated statements as examples of "correct" reporting; British accountants saw consolidated statements as a means of overcoming some of the inherent limitations of "legal" balance sheets. American accountants viewed consolidated state-ments as primary reports while British accountants simply saw them as one way of supplementing parent company reports. The first American firms to publish consolidated reports presented both income statements and balance sheets; the first British uses of consolidated reports were limited to balance sheets. Despite this British emphasis on balance sheets, it was the American literature on consolidated statements which placed the greater stress on the need to accurately represent liquidity.

Ch. 9   U.S. asset valuation practices before the 1930's

As outlined in the previous chapter, the initial use of
consolidated statements in the U.S. was not entirely a reaction or
response to the 'limitations' of established asset valuation practices.
It was certainly recognised that cost-based valuation of inter-corporate
investments could lead to obscure and misleading reporting. But other
methods of asset valuation were readily available to American practitioners
should they care to use them.

Around the turn of the century consolidated reports were fairly
radical presentations, prepared by only a handful of firms. By the
1930's consolidated statements were the customary method of reporting.
The preparation of consolidated data was sanctioned and supported by
the accounting profession, and corporations were required by government
agencies and stock exchanges to prepare or publish consolidated data.

This shift in the popularity and status of consolidated reporting
can be attributed in part to changes in ideas about the appropriate
methods for valuing inter-corporate shareholdings. This chapter examines
general developments in ideas about asset valuation; later chapters
relate these developments to the valuation of inter-corporate shareholdings and consider the evolution of ideas about consolidated reporting up to the 1930's.

Around the turn of the century, American accounting practice
seems to have been extremely permissive. By this time, some tentative
efforts had been made to organise the accounting profession.[1]
The 1890's and 1900's had seen efforts to formalise the teaching of
accounting,[2] and the launching of an indigenous journal

---

1.   See (anon.) "A history of the American Institute of Accountants"
     in Fiftieth anniversary celebrations (New York: American Institute
     of accountants, 1937), pp.3-4.

2.   See Webster, "Public accountancy in the United States", ibid,
     p.111. See also J. D. Edwards, History of public accounting in
     the United States (East Lansing: Bureau of Business and Economic
     Research, Michigan State University, 1960), p.80.

literature.[3] But these activities had yet to lead to any standardisation of practice or even to debate about what constituted "best"
practice.

The methods used to calculate profit and depict financial
position appear to have been influenced by the wishes of promoters,
the conflicting authority of early textbooks, the information requirements of credit institutions and the example of accounting procedures
developed in the railroad industry to support claims before regulatory
bodies. And while corporations such as U.S. Steel published detailed
financial reports, others maintained a policy of providing shareholders
and the investing public with bare scraps of data. There were frequent
cases in which firms issued highly condensed reports which showed asset
and liability items aggregated under a few headings, and reported
profit or loss figures without supporting descriptions or explanations.
In 1909 Montgomery described the publication of reports by industrial
corporations in the following terms:

> ... great divergence of form still obtains and some
> of [the reports] seem to be prepared with the thought
> that the less shown the better, otherwise the stock-
> holders may really learn something about the operations
> and financial condition of his company.[4]

The exaggeration of asset magnitudes upon the formation of new corporations remained a fairly common practice. Assets acquired in
exchange for the issue of stock were recorded at a figure calculated
by multiplying the par value of the stock by the number issued - leading
to "stock watering" and the overstatement of assets.[5] Thereafter, it

---

3. See Webster, _ibid_, p.114.

4. R. H. Montgomery (ed.), _Dicksee's auditing_ (New York: Ronald Press
    Company, rev. American ed., 1909), p.209.

5. In the United States there was a "prejudice ... for full paid
    stock" whereas in the U.K. it was customary for shares to be issued
    as "partly paid". The U.S. prejudice appears to have contributed
    to the incidence of stock watering. E. S. Mead, _Corporation
    finance_ (New York: D. Appleton and Co., 5th ed., 1924), p.69.

appears that some firms declined to charge any depreciation on durable assets lest they be correspondingly forced to reduce their calculated income.[6] Other firms reportedly adopted the practice of charging the cost of replacement plant or equipment to the operating expenses of the year in which the replacement was made.[7] And various methods were used to record investments and inventories.

Railroad regulation

Governmental regulation of railroads led to the introduction of "uniform" methods of presenting the financial statements of these firms - but seems to have encouraged the use of replacement prices for valuing assets, and thus contributed to the range of "acceptable" U.S. practices.

The state of Massachussetts established a form of railroad regulation in 1869 which was to serve as a model for a number of other states.[8] A Railroad Commission was established "with power to investigate railroad management and to report its findings". The Commission relied on publicity and the force of public opinion to secure obedience to its orders concerning levels of rates which protected consumers while affording the corporations a "fair" rate of return. Later, other states instituted more direct controls over the railroads by prescribing maximum rates. By 1890 there were 22 states with this form

---

6. See, e.g., commentary in L. Greendlinger, Accounting theory and practice, Vol.III of the Modern business series (New York: Alexander Hamilton Institute, 1901), p.357; P. Grady (ed.), Memoirs and accounting thought of G. O. May (New York: Ronald Press Company, 1962), p.23.

7. May, loc.cit.; F. J. Reynolds (ed.), The American business manual, Vol.III (New York: P. F. Collier & Son, 2nd ed. 1914), p.91.

8. C. E. Roberts, Railroad regulation (New York: American Chamber of Economics, 1921), p.10. See also J. E. Suelflow, Public utility accounting theory and applications (East Lansing: Michigan State University, 1973), pp.34-5 for a discussion of uniform accounting systems prescribed for railways (and later, gas and electric utilities).

of legislation.[9]

Federal legislation establishing the Interstate Commerce Commission was passed in 1887 though this statute was not sufficient to give the I.C.C. effective power to enforce its rulings.[10]

The 1898 case of Smythe v. Ames was "the first authoritative pronouncement upon the economic bases for the determination of rate reasonableness" - it "was a landmark in the development of public regulation.[11] The court held that the basis of such calculations "must be the fair value of the property being used by it for the convenience of the public".

> And in order to ascertain that value, the original cost of construction, the amount expended in permanent improvements, the amount and market value of its bonds and stock, the present as compared with the original cost of construction, the probable earning capacity of the property under particular rates prescribed by statute, and the sum required to meet operating expenses, are all matters for consideration, and are to be given such weight as may be just and right in each case.

On the face of it, the decision amounted to little more than a list of factors which might be taken into account in specific instances. But "as a practical matter ... reproduction costs, less observed depreciation, came near to being the controlling factor in the determination of the rate base".[12] There had been virtually no precedents in

9. W. Z. Ripley, Railroads rates and regulation (New York: Longmans Green & Co., 1916), p.630.

10. For a discussion of these developments see J. E. Kirshman, Principles of investment (Chicago: A. W. Shaw Company, 1924), p.449; Ripley, op.cit., pp.456-86. However, it was not until 1907 that the Interstate Commerce Commission was given authority to prescribe the forms and methods of keeping accounts of common carriers: thereafter there was a "rapid development in accounting regulations in the United States". See W. G. Bailey and D. E. Knowles, Accounting procedures for public utilities (Chicago: A. W. Shaw Company, 1926), p.35.

11. W. Z. Ripley, Railroads finance and organization (New York: Longmans Green & Co., 1915), p.318.

12. G. O. May, testimony before the Arkansas Public Utilities Commission, reproduced in Memoirs, loc.cit., p.156

either the U.S. or the U.K. for the use of replacement prices. But the Smythe v. Ames decision made the use of replacement prices (or strictly, "reproduction cost less observed depreciation") respectable not only for railroads and public utilities but for corporations in general.

Subsequently a number of U.S. texts alluded to the suitability or acceptability of replacement prices for valuing durable assets,[13] and the use of replacement prices was to remain acceptable until the late 1930's and early 1940's.

Influence of bankers and analysts on reporting practices

Considerable reliance was placed on borrowings in the financing of American corporate enterprises. U.S. businesses had always made extensive use of credit facilities.[14] With the popularity of the corporate form of organization, this use of borrowings had continued - notably in the financing of the railroads. Indeed, the securities markets of the late nineteenth century were predominately occupied with the trade in government, state, municipal and corporate debt securities. It was not until the turn of the century that a market developed for "industrials" - the stocks and shares of manufacturing firms. And even then, the trade in bonds and debentures was dominant for some years.

Individuals concerned with evaluating the risks attaching to bonds and notes were bound to consider the solvency and liquidity of the corporations which had issued those securities. Likewise bankers

---

3. e.g. W. A. Paton and R. A. Stevenson, Principles of accounting (New York: The Macmillan Company, 1920), p.451ff; C. H. Porter and W. P. Fiske, Accounting (New York: Henry Holt and Co., 1936), pp.364-5; M. B. Daniels, Corporation financial statements (Ann Arbor: University of Michigan Bureau of Business Research, 1934), p.32.

4. For an account of the development of credit institutions in the United States see R. A. Foulke, The sinews of American commerce (Dun & Bradstreet, Inc., 1941).

assessing the risk of discounting promissory notes would assess the credit standing of parties to the instrument. In such an environment, the demands of the "credit men" appear to have been of considerable influence on accounting. The appointment of auditors to pass judgment on financial reports stemmed largely from a desire to "put the question of solvency and standing beyond doubt".[15] If creditors or potential creditors were to be able to use balance sheets so as to assess the solvency and liquidity of corporations, it was necessary for balance sheet statements of asset values to bear some relation to the ability of firms to generate cash inflows. Perhaps the clearest indication of the concern of accountants to accommodate the needs of financial analysts is the fact that the profession's earliest rule-making activities were associated with interpretations of the liquidity or credit-worthiness of corporations.

At the 1894 annual meeting of the American Association of Public Accountants, members passed a resolution to the effect that balance sheets should show assets and liabilities "in the order of quickest realization".[16] This resolution probably constitutes the first attempt by a professional association of accountants to develop a standard for practitioners. The next major rule-making enterprise

---

15. H. C. White, introduction dated November 10, 1960 to D. A. Keister's Corporation accounting and auditing (Cleveland: The Burrows Brothers Co., - as reproduced in 12th ed., 1907), p.iii. Also note that in 1908 the American Bankers Association sought to establish as a condition of registration of commercial paper the requirement that the issuing firms "have their affairs audited at least once a year by certified public accountants, the audit to include an appraisal of all receivables, inventories, plants, and other investment, by competent experts ...". "Credit information", Journal of the American bankers association, July 1908, p.9.

16. Webster, op.cit.

was not initiated until 1917 when the American Institute collaborated
with the Federal Trade Commission and the Federal Reserve Board in
the production of a statement titled "Uniform accounting".[17] The
statement was intended to set out guidelines for the preparation
of statements to be submitted to bankers by potential borrowers.

"Uniform accounting" (which was reissued in 1918 under the title
"Approved methods for the preparation of balance sheet statements")
included recommendations on two major areas: standardisation of the
form and content of financial statements, and the procedures to be
followed in verification of these reports. The latter recommendations
were mainly concerned with "balance sheet audits", though they
included some forthright support for the valuation of inventories by
the use of the lower of cost and market rule. The discussion of the
valuation of non-current assets dwelt on the calculation of cost and
the calculation of depreciation, though it suggested that these values
were not always significant in connection with loan proposals.

> When the loan is greater than the quick assets seem
> to justify the auditor should suggest a reliable
> verification of the cost of property prior to the
> period under audit. Such action may become necessary
> even to the extent of calling for an appraisement
> by disinterested outside experts.

After the profession's involvement in the exercise of preparing
the document, the Institute began publicising the advantages of
balance sheet audits in connection with loan applications[18] - an
initiative which may have contributed to the more extensive engagement
of auditors to report on published corporate financial statements.
Credit analysts and bankers, for their part, took steps to ensure

---

17. Federal reserve bulletin, April 1917, pp.270-84, reprinted in
     The journal of accountancy, June 1918, pp.401-33.

18. D. F. Hawkins, Corporate financial reporting (Homewood: Richard
     D. Irwin, Inc., 1971), pp.26-7.

that accountants were aware of their views as to what constituted
adequate disclosure.

Tax legislation

Federal tax laws appear to have played a part in shaping the
early development of American financial reporting.

In 1909, the Federal government introduced an "excise" tax on
corporations. The U.S. Constitution did not at that stage enable
taxes to be imposed on incomes. The proposed tax base disregarded
accounting calculations of profit in favour of a formulation
encompassing "all items of income received" from a variety of sources.

Despite objections from the accounting profession,[19] the
legislation was passed. However, the proposed tax base "was so imprac-
tical that it was never put into effect".[20]

> ... the law as written was never enforced, for
> enforcement officials permitted determination of
> income on the accrual basis.[21]

Apparently corporations did not raise strong objections to the tax.

> The rate was only 1 per cent of net income, and the
> Treasury Department followed the liberal policies set
> forth in its regulations.[22]

It has been reported that "this ... encouraged income tax proponents

---

19. See, e.g., "Accounting errors in corporation tax bill", The
    journal of accountancy, July 1909, pp.212-3; "An open letter on
    the corporation tax bill" and editorial, "Amend the corporation
    tax law", ibid, Oct. 1909, pp.456-8 and pp.362-4; "Current
    comment on corporation tax bill", ibid, Nov. 1909, pp.51-2;
    editorial, "Official interpretation of the corporation tax",
    ibid, Jan. 1910, pp.132-5. Extracts from the legislation were
    reproduced in The journal of accountancy, Oct. 1909, pp.373-7.
    See also J. L. Carey, The rise of the accounting profession,
    Vol.I (New York: American Institute of Certified Public Account-
    ants, 1969), pp.64-7.

20. G. O. May, "Historical foreword" in D. T. Smith and J. K. Butters,
    Taxable and business income (New York: National Bureau of Economic
    Research, Inc., 1949), p.xvii.

21. Edwards, op.cit., p.96.

22. Ibid, p.97.

to sponsor an amendment to the United States Constitution which would
authorise Congress to levy a tax on income without resorting to the
subterfuge of continuing an excise tax measured by net income".[23]
The constitutional power of Congress was clarified in 1913 with the
passage of the sixteenth amendment to the American Constitution, and
a revised income tax law was enacted on October 3, 1913, effective as
from March 1, 1913.

The 1909 and the 1913 legislation opened up a new field of
practice for accountants, as well as fostering traditional activities
by necessitating the maintenance of records so as to facilitate the
preparation of income tax returns. The levying of taxes at higher
rates in 1917 made the maintenance of records which detailed revenues
and expenditures a matter of even greater significance to corporate
business. And then in 1918 rulings were introduced which aimed at
keeping tax calculations of income in line with the figures reported
to shareholders.

> The net income shall be computed upon the basis of the
> taxpayer's annual accounting period (fiscal year or
> calendar year as the case may be) in accordance with
> the method of accounting regularly employed in keeping
> the books of such taxpayer; but if no such method of
> accounting has been so employed, or if the method
> employed does not clearly reflect the income, the
> computation shall be made upon such basis and in such
> manner as in the opinion of the Commissioner does
> clearly reflect the income.[24]

The amendment was the first in a series of rulings which later imposed
serious constraints on U.S. accounting practice. Calculations of
asset values, revenues and expenses came to be influenced by the
acceptability or otherwise of those calculations for tax purposes.

1917 also saw the introduction of an "excess profits tax".

---

23. Idem.

24. Extract from s.212(b) of the Revenue Act of 1918, as cited May,
op.cit. "Historical forword", p.xviii. Emphasis added.

This tax was applied to the difference between taxable income and a "fair return" - the latter being assessed in relation to invested capital. Over the years 1917 - 1921 the rate of return on invested capital that was deemed to be "fair" was set at between 7% and 10%. The excess profit tax was as high as 80% in 1918.[25]

A key issue was the calculation of <u>invested capital</u>. The rule adopted was that invested capital included the value of stockholder's contributions at the time of the contribution, plus earned surplus. Specifically excluded were "additions because of values developed since incorporation but not realized through <u>bona-fide</u> transactions with outsiders".[26] The effect of this rule may have dampened enthusiasm for upward re-statements of the values of fixed assets. But the rule did not prevent the use of exaggerated asset valuations for initial entry at the time of a corporation's formation. However, it may have been recognised that a variety of inter-corporate transactions could be resorted to in order to manipulate transactions and so evade taxation. The legislation was applied to holding and subsidiary corporations as a "group" rather than in isolation. (Details of this regulation are discussed in Chapter 11).

Ideas about asset valuation

The picture which emerges is that American practitioners did not adopt a general framework for approaching asset valuation questions until 1910, or later; meantime, the choice of asset valuation practices was influenced by a variety of environmental and institutional factors.

One commentator has suggested that in its earlier stages, American accounting was "based on a concept of income as an accretion of new

---

25. E. L. Kohler and P. L. Morrison, <u>Principles of accounting</u> (Chicago: A. W. Shaw Company, 1928), p.317.

26. <u>Idem</u>. The authors noted that the power of Congress to limit net-worth values was upheld by the Supreme Court in <u>La Belle Iron Works</u> v. U.S., 256 U.S., 377.

worth" - and that "capital appreciation was treated as income even when unrealized".[27] Now there certainly is evidence that some firms used contemporary selling or replacement prices as the basis for valuing assets - and that some firms made artificial adjustments to recorded values. Some firms even treated revaluation increments as part of periodic income.[28] But in general, the use of upward revaluations seems to have been rare, probably because of the moderate movements in prices in these pre-war years.[29] Other commentators have placed a different interpretation on asset valuation practices in these early years. Chatfield, for example, asserted that

> in 1900 conservatism was the dominant accounting principle.[30]

And Storey claimed that

> essentially, asset valuation and income determination were based on an incomplete application of the going concern convention tempered by conservatism.[31]

---

27. G. O. May, Financial accounting (New York: The Macmillan Company, 1961), p.28.

28. See, e.g., W. H. Lough, Business finance (New York: Ronald Press Company, 1917), p.419.

29. The following series of "composite prices" is indicative:

1900	7.8839	1906	8.4176	1912	9.1867
1901	7.5746	1907	8.9045	1913	9.2076
1902	7.8759	1908	8.0094	1914	8.9034
1903	7.9364	1909	8.5153	1915	9.8530
1904	7.9187	1910	8.9881	1916	11.8251
1905	8.0987	1911	8.7132	1917	15.6565

Source: Bradstreet's, Dec. 15, 1917 - as reproduced in L. Middleditch's, "Should accounts reflect the changing value of the dollar?" The journal of accountancy, Feb. 1919, p.116. The series was "not computed to a base year" and was "not an index number in the strict meaning of the word but rather a composite price"; however it was said to "agree surprisingly ... with the elaborately computed index number of the United States bureau of labor statistics ..." Idem.

30. M. Chatfield, A history of accounting thought (Hinsdale, Ill.: The Dryden Press, 1974), p.232.

31. R. K. Storey, "Revenue realization, going concern, and measurement of income", The accounting review, April 1959, p.237.

The evidence of massive write-ups by promoters for prospectus
purposes seems to run counter to these claims about "conservatism".
In any event, there is little evidence to suggest that accountants
approached asset valuation from the standpoint of specific "principles"
or "conventions". In fact several early U.S. texts outlined the valuation of assets simply by describing one procedure for plant, another
for goodwill, another for receivables, and so on. At times, several
procedures were said to be equally suitable for valuing a given asset.
In short, a general basis for asset valuation was not described in the
early U.S. literature. And this lack of a framework was reflected
in a lack of uniformity in U.S. accounting.

After 1910, or thereabouts, the situation seems to have changed
with the importation and dissemination of British ideas.

In the U.K., the writing of Dicksee and the stimulus of hostile
litigation had prompted the profession to value assets by applying
different sets of valuation rules to assets classified as "fixed" or
"floating". In the U.S., accountants were using balance sheet
classification or arrangements to depict liquidity; asset classification
had not been linked with a choice of valuation procedures. However the
British ideas gradually found their way into the American literature.

The appointment of British-based firms as auditors of U.S.
corporations around the turn of the century, and the on-going immigra-
tion of British-trained accountants both contributed to the importation
of ideas. The English journal, The accountant, was widely read in
the U.S.[32] But the most important factor in the translation of British
thinking to the American context was the influence of British publications on early U.S. textbooks. MacNeal later selected four textbooks
as the "most representative works on accounting" in the U.S.A., and
he claimed that the authors of these books had "exerted a dominating

32. J. L. Carey, op.cit., p.49.

nfluence on the formation of current American accounting thought".[33]

he four were:

A. L. Dickinson's Accounting practice and procedure[34]
P. J. Esquerre's The applied theory of accounts[35]
H. R. Hatfield's Modern accounting[36]
R. H. Montgomery's Auditing theory and practice[37]

t seems to be no coincidence that three out of the four bore close links
ith the U.K. literature. Dickinson was an English chartered accountant
ho worked in the U.S.A. between 1901 and 1911. His writing reflected
is British background particularly with regard to a concern with
etermining what profits were available for distribution as dividends.
atfield's textbook drew heavily from overseas literature (and
articularly from Dicksee's Auditing) for ideas about asset valuation.
inally, Montgomery had produced American editions of Dicksee's
diting (1905 and 1909) before publishing another version of this text
der his own name in 1912; clearly, Montgomery's Auditing was
irectly based on Dicksee's earlier publications.

All of these four texts appeared around 1912-1914. Signs of
itish influences on the American literature can be found earlier,
articularly in the contributions of Dickinson and others to technical
urnals and the release of the American editions of Dicksee's text.
wever the most significant factor in the American adoption of British
proaches to asset valuation seems to have been the publication of
ntgomery's own edition of Auditing theory and practice.

Montgomery reproduced much of Dicksee's analysis. He distinguished

---

. K. MacNeal, Truth in accounting (Philadelphia: University of
   Pennysylvania Press, 1939), p.25.

. (New York: Ronald Press Company, 1914).

. (New York: Ronald Press Company, 1914).

. (New York: D. Appleton and Co., 1916).

. (New York: Ronald Press Company, 1912).

categories of assets in terms of how they were used in a business, and then proposed different valuation methods for current and for fixed assets. In light of the American practice of stock-watering Montgomery offered his own warnings of practical difficulties facing auditors:

> The chief difficulties in the way of preparing such a statement are, first, the over-valuation of assets to balance large capital stock issues, and the consequent temtation to hide the real facts by lumping all the fixed assets; and, secondly, the large number of cases of holding companies and consolidations where the fixed assets have passed through so many stages that their original identity is lost.[38]

Montgomery's proposals for the valuation of fixed assets at cost less depreciation were not agreed to by all other text writers and were certainly not followed in practice. But the idea of associating distinct valuation procedures with different categories of assets was rapidly accepted and became quite familiar in the U.S. literature. While some writers continued to adopt the traditional American approach to classification as a procedure for depicting a firm's liquidity or of giving shareholders some idea of the pattern of a firm's investment,[39] the adoption of a Dicksee-style approach to asset valuation was implicit in several early texts.[40] And soon the valuation-classification link was spelled out more and more clearly.

---

38. Dicksee's auditing (1909), loc.cit., pp.220-1.

39. H. C. Bentley, The science of accounts (New York: Ronald Press Company, 1911), pp.51-2; F. J. Reynolds (ed.), The american business manual, Vol.III, (New York: P. F. Collins & Son, 1914), pp.308-9; W. M. Cole, (with the collaboration of A. E. Geddes) The fundamentals of accounting (Boston: Houghton Mifflin Co., 1921), p.344; F. E. Reeve and F. C. Russell, Accounting principles (New York: Alexander Hamilton Institute, 1922 ed.), p.193; J. H. Bliss, Financial and operating ratios in management (New York: Ronald Press Company, 1923), p.211.

40. e.g., L. Greendlinger, Accounting theory and practice (New York: Alexander Hamilton Institute, 1910), p.359; J. R. Wildman, Principles of accounting (Brooklyn, N.Y.: The William G. Hewitt Press, 1913), pp.115-6.

Hatfield wrote in 1916 that "there is coming to be recognised a difference in the basis of valuation of two classes of assets".

> In general it is considered legitimate to continue
> fixed assets at their cost despite subsequent
> decline in their value. But in valuing circulating
> assets regard must be had to current values, although
> there is some question as to whether the market value,
> even of circulating assets can be accepted where that
> exceeds the original cost.[41]

Hodge and McKinsey (1920),[42] S. Racine (1923)[43] and W. A. Paton (1924)[44] all distinguished fixed and current assets and described corresponding valuation procedures. Stockwell (1925)[45] and Kohler and Morrison (1928)[46] similarly described a two-fold approach to asset valuation, but used different terminology.

Kester described a threefold classification:

1. For the current assets, the principle of valuation may be stated as valuation on the basis of cost or market whichever is the lower ...

2. The principle of valuation involved in deferred charges to operation is simply the principle of equitable prorating between periods on the basis of a going concern ...

3. For the fixed assets, the principle of valuation generally applicable may be stated as valuation on the basis of cost less depreciation ...[47]

This analysis was followed by a number of later texts.[48] Essentially

41. Op.cit., pp.81-2.

42. A. C. Hodge and J. O. McKinsey, Principles of accounting (Chicago: University of Chicago Press, 1920), pp.71-2.

43. S. F. Racine, Accounting principles (Seattle: The Western Institute of Accountancy, Commerce and Finance, 3rd ed., 1923), pp.94-5.

44. W. A. Paton, Accounting (New York: The Macmillan Company, 1924), pp.259-61.

45. H. G. Stockwell, How to read a financial statement (New York: Ronald Press Company, 1925), p.5.

46. Kohler and Morrison, op.cit., pp.284-5, 312-3.

47. R. B. Kester, Accounting theory and practice (New York: Ronald Press Company, 1922), pp.96-7.

48. e.g. E. A. Saliers (ed.), Accountants' handbook (New York: Ronald Press Company, 1923), p.449; W. J. Goggin and J. V. Toner, Accounting - principles and procedure (Cambridge, Mass.: Houghton Mifflin, 1930), pp.308-9.

it was little different from the framework outlined earlier; the only difference was that prepayments were segregated instead of appearing under the "current" asset category. And no matter how prepayments were classified, they were still valued by an apportionment of "cost".

By the late 1920's and early 1930's the idea of categorising assets and applying different valuation procedures had become well and truly part of the U.S. literature. Authors like Rorem,[49] Hatfield,[50] Porter and Fiske,[51] MacFarland and Ayers,[52] McKinsey and Noble[53] and Finney[54] all reproduced some form of this valuation framework. And, as had occurred in the U.K., there was some confusion about the appropriate basis for distinguishing asset categories. Montgomery had at first reproduced Dicksee's pre-1904 distinction based on the way assets had been used in business activities.[55] But it was not long before Montgomery (and others) adopted Dicksee's post-1904 distinction which was based on managerial intentions.[56] This led to further confusion about which set of managerial intentions were relevant - with some writers stressing current intentions,[57] some stressing intentions that were held at the time that assets were purchased,[58] and others attempting

---

49. C. R. Rorem, Accounting method (Chicago: University of Chicago Press, 2nd ed., 1930), p.292.

50. H. R. Hatfield, Accounting - its principles and problems (New York: D. Appleton and Co., 1927), p.75.

51. Op.cit., p.250.

52. G. A. MacFarland and R. D. Ayers, Accounting fundamentals (New York: McGraw-Hill Book Co., 1936), pp.13-15.

53. J. O. McKinsey and H. S. Noble, Accounting principles (Cincinnati: South-Western Publishing Co., 1935), pp.21-2, p.220ff.

54. H. A. Finney, Introduction to principles of accounting, (New York: Prentice-Hall Inc. 1932), pp.495ff.

55. Auditing theory and practice (1912), loc.cit., p.117. Other writers who adopted similar definitions included Hatfield (1916) op.cit., p.81; Stockwell, op.cit., p.5.

56. See e.g. Auditing theory and practice, 5th ed. (1934), p.247.

57. Idem; Hodge and McKinsey, op.cit., pp.71-2.

58. e.g. Racine, op.cit., pp.94-5.

to formulate classification schemes incorporating references to both contemporary and past intentions.[59]

Accounting writers were generally in agreement that current assets should be valued in terms of the lower of cost and market rule. But what was meant by "market"? Texts variously took this to mean market selling[60] or market replacement[61] prices. It appears that the relative popularity of replacement prices can be attributed to the influence of tax regulations. Bell (1926) reported that

> the United States Treasury Department takes the view ...
> that replacement or reproduction cost rather than sale
> value is the logical basis of valuation of merchandise
> when cost is not a proper measure of present values[62]

Upward revaluations of assets

There were similar disagreements about the treatment of "fixed assets", particularly in respect of the propriety of upward revaluations.

Dicksee's original proposals for asset measurement had not ruled out the use of revaluations of fixed assets. "Fluctuations" in the value of these assets could safely be ignored, said Dicksee, but "permanent" declines in value should be recognised. Conversely, there was no obligation to record upward movements in the value of fixed assets, but in the interests of representing the true facts about a corporation's financial position it was appropriate to make such adjustments when increases had become definite. So ran Dicksee's analysis. The rough-and-ready practitioner's interpretation of these proposals was that circulating assets were liable to revision, while permanent

---

59. e.g. Goggin and Toner, op.cit., p.309.

60. e.g. L. Greendlinger, Financial and business statements (New York: Alexander Hamilton Institute, 1922), p.156.

61. e.g. H. C. Cox, Advanced and analytical accounting (Vol.IV of a series titled Business accounting) (New York: Ronald Press Company, 1920), pp.223-6; Kohler and Morrison, op.cit., p.303; Rorem (1930), op.cit., p.298.

62. W. H. Bell, Auditing (New York: Prentice-Hall, Inc., 1926), p.165.

assets were not. Nevertheless, some U.K. firms did adopt the practice of periodically revaluing fixed assets. But after the 1929 stock market collapse, accountants were extremely reluctant to record "unrealised" gains and so chose to retain cost-based measures.

In the U.S., Montgomery (1912) was opposed to recording upward revaluations even when it could be "clearly established" that the value of certain assets had increased.[63] He emphasised that some state corporation laws permitted revaluation surpluses to be considered as distributable income, and railed against such foolishness:

> ... it remains for the professional auditor to educate
> the public to the principle that it is not only foolhardy
> but unscientific to write up the value of an asset which
> is not for sale and which therefore cannot be represented
> by cash or its equivalent (p.194).

On somewhat different grounds Esquerre (1914) was opposed to upward revaluations, and likewise urged the retention of cost-based data.[64] But other writers saw the use of replacement or resale prices as perfectly proper. Herr expressed approval of writing-up assets when "general or trade conditions" had brought about "a real or permanent increase in values"; he also argued that it was legitimate to adjust book values when "errors have been made in calculating depreciation".[65] May (1915) indicated that no objection could be taken to either revaluations or credits to surplus, provided the accounts disclosed the matter.[66] Page (1916) included "cost of reproduction" and "sale

63. Auditing theory and practice, loc.cit., p.120.

64. Op.cit., p.230.

65. J. P. Herr, "The appreciation of assets - when is it legitimate"? The journal of accountancy, Nov. 1906, pp.1-13.

66. G. O. May, "Qualifications in certificates", The journal of accountancy, 1915; reproduced in Twenty-five years of accounting responsibility (New York: Price, Waterhouse & Co., 1936; reprinted by Scholars Book Co., 1971), Vol.I, pp.33-4.

or realization price in a list of acceptable valuation methods.[67]

Similarly Bennett (1916)[68] and Cox (1920)[69] acknowledged the propriety

of recording asset appreciation. Paton (1924) claimed that the upward

revaluation of assets was contrary to "orthodox opinion", though he

conceded that these "orthodox opinions and doctrines were not very

solidly grounded".[70] Kohler and Morrison also noted that according to

orthodox opinion the appropriate basis for valuing capital assets was

at cost, less depreciation: however they acknowledged that this

attitude was not substantiated. "Future attitudes towards asset valuation",

they claimed, would be "based on public policies towards business in

general",[71] thus acknowledging the influence that tax legislation and

rate regulations were exerting on accounting practices at this time.

Meantime authors of books dealing with financial analysis raised

no great objections to the upward revaluation of assets but indicated

that when these adjustments had taken place, the financial statements

should clearly state that the basis of the valuation was an appraisal

carried out on a specified date.[72]

Around the mid-1920's it appears that a significant number of firms

had carried out upward revaluations of fixed assets. Unfortunately

67. E. C. Page, "Balance sheet valuations", The journal of accountancy,
     April 1916, p.243.

68. R. J. Bennett, Corporation accounting (New York: Ronald Press
     Company, 1916, 4th printing 1919), p.336.

69. Op.cit., p.231.

70. Op.cit., p.623.

71. Op.cit., pp.312-19.

72. e.g., J. H. Bliss, op.cit., p.212; se also W. E. Lagerquist,
     Investment analysis (New York: The Macmillan Company, 1921), and
     H. G. Guthman, The analysis of financial statements (New York:
     Prentice-Hall, Inc., 1925), pp.92-3. Neither writer opposed
     write-ups per se but they both objected to the inclusion of
     surpluses from write-ups in profit calculations.

available data do not distinguish between write-ups of properties
and write-ups of plant and equipment. Nor do they indicate the basis
of the valuation. But the figures are still indicative. Of a sample
of 153 large industrial firms which were in existence throughout the
years 1925-1934, some 32 reported write-ups of these assets.[73] It may
be that smaller firms made even greater use of the revaluation process.
The point made is that the practice of writing-up these fixed assets
was apparently acceptable in the 1920's. Even so, the upward revaluation of assets was an unusual procedure. For the most part, company
reports retained cost-based valuations. And the accounting and financial
literature expressed caution about the use of upward revaluations and
indicated opposition to the inclusion of revaluation surpluses in
reported income.

However there seems to have been some confusion as to why upward
asset revaluations were to be handled cautiously. This confusion arose
because accounting writers had not agreed on the aims and objectives
of asset valuation procedures. Indeed, the four writers singled out
by MacNeal as "representative" of American thought and opinion at
this time advanced quite different rationales for asset valuation and
other accounting procedures. Esquerre, and to a lesser extent,
Montgomery, seemed to see accounting as a report on stewardship, so
that asset valuation was the representation of what had been spent, less
what had been written off. Hatfield approached asset valuation as
a process of estimating "value in use" - a concept which he related to
the present worth of expected benefits to be derived from using an
asset-item. Dickinson, on the other hand, spoke of accounting as being

---

73. Data from S. Fabricant, Revaluations of fixed assets, 1925-1934
    (New York: National Bureau of Economic Research, Bulletin No.62
    1936), Table 3, p.4. The sample was drawn from a total of 208
    firms, the relative size of which may be gauged from the fact
    that in 1934 the reported value of their total assets comprised
    13.9% of the total asset holdings in 1933 of all listed industrial
    corporations in the United States. Ibid, p.2.

concerned with showing "actual financial condition ... at any time" and saw the choice of asset measures as a process of selecting data which would not provide an overly optimistic or imprudent view of a firm's standing and performance. Little wonder, then, that there was disagreement about whether asset values should be adjusted periodically.

Resume

By the 1920's the idea of linking asset classification and valuation
had been well and truly established in the American accounting
literature. Consequently it was said that the choice of valuation
procedures for assets such as inter-corporate investments turned
on the intention of managers at some present or past point of time
Another consequence was that when assets such as inter-corporate investments were deemed to be "fixed" assets, the orthodox opinion was that
they should be initially recorded at cost and thereafter left at cost
unless there was evidence of permanent and/or significant changes in
their value. The spread of ideas such as those just described will be
examined in some detail in the following chapter. It will be argued
that while consolidated statements entered U.S. practice for reasons
largely unrelated to the "limitations" of conventional methods of asset
valuation, post-1910 developments in this area led to the crystallisation
of arguments in support of the preparation of consolidated statements
in lieu of the uninformative reports of holding companies.

Ch. 10   U.S. accounting for inter-corporate investments

The amendments to the New Jersey corporation laws which extended the powers of corporations to include the holding of stock in other corporations were passed in 1889 and 1893. Other states soon copied New Jersey, so that in the 1890's American accountants suddenly faced the problem of how to handle inter-corporate investments.

It will be recalled that the "trust" form of organization was under attack at this time, and the amendments to the corporation laws enabled the wide use of the holding company form of organization. It appears that the first occasions on which accountants had to handle inter-corporate investments were situations in which one firm held 100% (or near to 100%) of another firm's stock. The relative significance of holding companies as investors may be gauged from the following data concerning stock issued by American corporations at June 30, 1905:

> ... total visible outstanding securities issued by
> by American corporations aggregated ... $34,514,351,383.
> Of this amount $21,023,393,955 represent[ed] the par
> value of stocks, and $13,490,958,427 the par value of
> bonds ... It is apparent, however, that a considerable
> proportion of securities is owned by holding companies,
> which are themselves represented by securities ...
> Such inter-corporate shareholdings of securities
> aggregated, in 1905, approximately $10,120,418,699 ... [1]

It seems likely that non-subsidiary investments were fairly rare around the turn of the century. This chapter reviews the accounting treatment of marketable securities and other non-subsidiary investments, and then examines the procedures adopted for holding companies.

Marketable securities

As has has been outlined above, the 1890's and 1900's were a time in which U.S. accountants had not yet developed a general frame-

---

1.   S. S. Heubner, "Scope and functions of the stock market" in The annals of the American academy of political and social science, May, 1910, pp.1-2. Huebner cited data compiled by C. A. Conant and reported in the Atlantic Monthly, Jan. 1908; the figures do not encompass "all small local corporations".

work for asset valuation, and when there were no disclosure laws
prescribing reports to be published by corporations. However, it
seems reasonable to suppose that the treatment of inter-corporate
investments was subject to experimentation in these years. No doubt
cost-based valuations were used, but it seems that other valuations
reflecting upward and downward fluctuations were equally acceptable.
There is some evidence to indicate that firms did revalue their
investments[2] and it appears that the upward or downward revaluation of
securities was not in itself frowned upon. But the evidence is sparse,
so it is difficult to generalise about the popularity of one or other
technique. However many accountants had had some experience with the
reporting and valuation practices of life insurance companies and other
institutional investors.[3] These organisations held extensive portfolios of bonds and other debt securities. It appears that the techniques
developed to account for these securities later influenced American
accounting treatments of other forms of investments.

Sprague's The accountancy of investment[4] was probably the first
authoritative text to deal with the accounting valuation of bonds. But
other general texts devoted considerable space to the bookkeeping entries
required to record the purchase, retention and maturity of bonds,

---

2.   e.g. Lough recounted that in 1903 one firm disclosed earnings of
      $1,417,000 of which it later appeared that $487,000 "consisted of
      'profits' from estimated increases in the value of investments
      still held". W. H. Lough, Business finance (New York: Ronald
      Press Company, 1917), p.419.

3.   For a review of the early history of life and speciality insurance
      companies in the U.S., see R. A. Foulke, The sinews of American
      commerce (Dun & Bradstreet, Inc., 1941), pp.165-73. In New York
      State alone, the "admitted assets" of life insurance companies
      totalled $403,142,000 in 1875, $1,723,000,000 in 1900 and
      $10,016,000,000 in 1925. As for specialty insurance companies,
      admitted assets totalled $2,312,000 in 1880, rising to
      $47,326,000 in 1900 and $529,088,000 in 1920. Ibid, pp.171-3.

4.   New York: Ronald Press Company, 1904; revised edition by C.E. Sprague
      and L.L. Perrine, 1919.

notes and similar securities. Indeed as late as 1918 Paton's and Stevenson's Principles of accounting included almost two chapters on these matters but virtually ignored investments in common stocks.[5]

Discussions of the "mathematics of investment" focussed on the calculation of yields attributable to the holding of bonds purchased above or below their par or maturity value. While little attention was given to balance sheet valuations, these discussions usually concluded that it was inappropriate to record securities at market prices. (In any event, for a considerable time bonds or notes which were publicly traded constituted only a very small percentage of corporate securities in the hands of the public,[6] so that usually market prices would not have been available).

Holdings of debt securities were treated as receivables: they entitled the holder to receive a specified sum in the future, and in this context variations in the market prices of any publicly-traded securities may have seemed irrelevant. This was particularly so for those banks which were required to hold government bonds as a condition of their charter.[7] Sale of the bonds was not possible if banks were to remain banks. Hence resale prices were not regarded as being relevant to on-going business decisions.

The method adopted by banks and many other firms was that of valuing bonds at cost while accruing interest on those bonds which had been purchased below par.

The collapse of the stock market in 1907 was followed by considerable support for the use of cost-based valuation. It appears

5. W. A. Paton and R. A. Stevenson, Principles of accounting (New York: The Macmillan Company, 1918), Chs.XVI-XVII.

6. Ibid, p.416.

7. H. R. Hatfield, Modern accounting (New York: D. Appleton & Co., 1916) pp.90-1. See also Hatfield's Accounting - its principles and problems (New York: D. Appleton & Co., 1927), p.87.

that the support for cost which emerged at this time was not a response
to the earlier use of inflated or exaggerated valuations but rather a
reaction to the use of the lower of cost and market rule. "Conservatism" in valuation was unwelcome. The major reason appears to be
that the laws of New York state required that "the solvency of insurance
companies be tested by the sufficiency of the assets (valuing stocks
and bonds at market prices) to meet the present value of policy contracts
in force and sundry other liabilities).[8] The fall in stock market prices
meant that "the statements of almost all the life insurance companies
at December 31, 1907 showed a startling decrease in surplus" - with
consequential dislocation of the industry. Hence it was claimed that
the recognition of "temporary fluctuations" in the valuation of securities
was inappropriate.

The experience of New York life companies around 1907-8 may have
influenced the attitudes of P. J. Esquerre, who was associated with
the insurance industry. His Applied theory of accounts (1914) firmly
argued for the use of cost as the basis of measuring marketable
securities. Esquerre acknowledged that it was usually proposed that
"securities carried for speculative purposes" should be valued so as
to "reflect the fluctuations of the market". But he refused to accept
this view.

> It cannot be forgotten ... that nothing which has not
> been sold can bring profits, and that the Profit and
> Loss account is not intended to reflect what the profits
> or the losses would be if certain transactions had taken
> place, but what they are as a result of the transactions

---

8.   R. H. Montgomery, Auditing theory and practice (New York: Ronald
      Press Company, 1912), p.137. P. J. Esquerre's The applied theory
      of accounts (New York: Ronald Press Company, 1914) reproduced the
      form of balance sheet for life insurance companies that was then
      prescribed by the Superintendent of Insurance, State of New
      York (pp.422-3). Hatfield noted that "under the New York Banking
      law ... bonds are listed at their market value, although a change
      to the adoption of the cost value, properly amortized has been strong-
      ly urged by the state superintendent of banks". Accounting (1927),
      p.89 - citing Annual report of the superintendent of banks of the
      state of New York, 1907.

which have taken place.[9]

Esquerre's espousal of cost-based asset valuation placed him in a somewhat isolated position,[10] since at this time most other writers were prepared to acknowledge the significance of market prices to the valuation of securities, especially when prices had fallen below cost. And it was reported that the marking-down of investments when market price was less than cost (combined with footnote acknowledgements of appreciation in market price) was the "general practice" of conservative American accountants.[11]

It is difficult to tell from this early literature whether authors who described the treatment of "investments" were concerned with holding of bonds, or common stocks, or both. Certainly ownership of industrial equity securities was not as extensive then as it was to become in the post-World War I years. And those writers who explicitly referred to equity securities still gave the subject scant attention. Montgomery's editions of Auditing are a useful indicator of the minimal

---

9. Loc.cit., p.263. Esquerre maintained this hard line on the use of cost-based valuation. In a text published in 1927, Esquerre wrote that accounting was "not interested in what would have happened 'if' but in what has actually happened". Accordingly he argued that "generally speaking, there is no reason why a going concern should even take cognizance ... of the market value of its investments". He rejected both upward revaluations and the use of the lower of cost and market rule. Accounting (New York: Ronald Press Company, 1927), pp.171, 252.

10. Another writer to suggest strict adherence to cost for market securities was W. M. Cole, who wrote that "no accounting is involved except entry for purchase and sale of stock and for dividends received". The fundamentals of accounting (Boston: Houghton Mifflin Co., 1921), p.171,252. J. R. Wildman also supported cost valuation but for different reasons. Wildman was one of the first U.S. writers to argue that investments were fixed assets ("they represent an excess of capital over and above that required by the business") and as such should be valued without regard to market fluctuations (though it was "desirable" to use footnote disclosures of market values). Principles of accounting (Brooklyn: The William Hewitt Press, 1913), pp.115-6.

11. H. R. Hatfield, op.cit., pp.92-3. This observation was repeated in Hatfield's Accounting (1927), p.89.

interest in these matters in the pre-war literature. His 1909
edition simply retained Dicksee's text without further comment.
Readers were told that these investments "need not be depreciated
unless of a wasting nature".[12] But the 1912 version extended the
analysis and clearly adopted the British approach of valuing different
categories of assets differently. Lont-term investments could be
valued at cost; temporary investments were to be valued at actual or
estimated market prices.[13]

Wider acceptance of equity securities as a medium of investment
was apparently fostered by the U.S. Government's sale of "Liberty
Loan" bonds in order to finance involvement in World War I. The
sale of the bonds was said to have made the U.S. "a nation of
investors".[14] As a war-time economic measure the government imposed
a general restriction on the sale of corporate securities.[15] But
the issue of these bonds was to stimualte wider public interest in
the securities market as an avenue of investment. In post-war
years the ownership of common stock became more widely distributed.

---

12. R. H. Montgomery, Dicksee's auditing (New York: Ronald Press
    Company, rev. American ed., 1909), p.204.

13. Op.cit., pp.364-5.

14. W. Law, Successful speculation in common stocks (New York:
    McGraw-Hill Book Company Inc., 2nd ed., 1934), p.xiii. There
    were four "Liberty Loans" and one "Victory Loan" between
    1917-1919. Securities issued totalled $1,989,455,550,
    $3,807,864,200, $4,716,516,850, $6,993,073,250 and
    $4,500,000,000 respectively; they were said (in 1924) to represent
    "about ninety five percent of the total debt of the United
    States". A. W. Taylor, Investments (New York: Alexander
    Hamilton Institute, 1924), p.97.

15. H. G. Moulton, The financial organization of society (Chicago:
    University of Chicago Press, 2nd ed., 1925), p.197.

Estimated number of stockholders in U.S. 1900-1923[16]

Year	Total capital stock of all corporations in U.S.	Average number of $100 par value shares per stockholder	Estimated number of stockholders in U.S.
1900	$61,831,955,370	140.1	4,400,000
1910	64,053,763,141	86.3	7,400,000
1913	65,038,309,611	87.0	7,500,000
1917	66,584,420,424	77.3	8,600,000
1920	69,205,967,666	57.3	12,000,000
1923	71,479,464,925	49,7	14,400,000

This extension of public interest in the stock market was accompanied by a higher frequency of inter-corporate investments. Texts published in the post-war years made more and more references to the valuation and accounting treatment of these assets.

One can discern two distinct developments in this literature: the gradual adoption and modification of U.K. ideas about classification and valuation, and a shift in attitude against the use of upward revaluations.

As described in Chapter 9 this was a period in which accounting writers were embracing the idea of valuing assets in different ways according to whether they were "current" or "fixed" assets. The most common classification base was "managerial intention". Hence, most of the earlier discussions of the valuation of marketable securities set forth distinct rules according to the purpose for which those assets were acquired.

For example, Paton and Stevenson (1918) explained that bond investments could be regarded as falling within three classes. First, there were bonds which would be held until maturity; market prices should be ignored in valuing these securities. Second, there were bonds which were to be resold at some time before maturity. Insurance

16. H. T. Warshow, "The distribution of corporate ownership in the United States", Quarterly journal of economics Vol.39, No.1, p.28, as reproduced in R. E. Badger, Investment principles and practices (New York: Prentice-Hall, Inc., 1935), p.29.

companies were held up as an example of firms which might invest with these intentions or expectations. The appropriate method to handle these bonds was to keep book values at "approximately the market price" - "small fluctuations" could be ignored. The third category of investments was speculative holdings for which the "market situation" was said to be "the sole guide to the revision of book valuations".[17]

As was described in the preceding chapter, the process of reconciling the British idea of linking asset classification and valuation with the American approach of trying to represent corporate liquidity led to inconsistencies and confusion in the literature about classification criteria and categories. The items most affected by these conflicts were inter-corporate investments; some writers supported the separate grouping of these assets for purposes of balance sheet presentation, while others argued that they should be subsumed under other headings - and there were corresponding inconsistencies in text-book proposals for the classification of holdings of securities. Perhaps the dominant view was that "temporary investments" should be listed under current assets, while other investments should be set out under a separate heading - which was frequently labelled "permanent investments". But the literature was equivocal, with writers indicating that this or that procedure was usually followed, or might be followed. For example, Saliers described the classification of "invested capital" into "fixed assets", "permanent investments" and "investment of reserves", and then

---

17. Op.cit., pp.416-20. A somewhat similar analysis was provided earlier by Hatfield (1916) who drew a distinction between (i) holdings of the minimum amount of securities required by banks as a pre-requisite to doing any business (ii) additional holdings by banks of securities "to serve as the basis for additional circulation" and (iii) holdings as "an available reserve against emergencies". Hatfield argued that the first two categories should be left at cost, since neither losses nor gains could be realised while the firm continued to exercise its function; as for the third category, Hatfield proposed use of the lower of cost and market rule. Op.cit., pp.90-2.

weakly commented that "if such a detailed subdivision in the balance
sheet is thought necessary [this] classification is a good one".[18]
Wade noted that temporary investments "may be shown" as current
assets.[19] Woodbridge noted that investments of surplus funds would
"commonly be listed in the current assets group".[20] Rorem referred to
some investments as current assets, and noted that long-term investments
were among those assets which "sometimes ... [find] their place in the
balance sheet under separate headings".[21] Himmelblau asserted "permanent
investments should appear as a separate item between current and fixed
assets" - but he merely noted that "temporary investments ... are usually
listed as current assets".[22]

When investments were deemed "current" assets, the accepted valuation
treatment was the use of the lower of cost and market rule. There was
near unanimity that falls in the price of these assets should be
recognised one way or another - either by establishing "reserves" or by
directly writing down the recorded value of the asset concerned.[23]

Authors who regarded investments as warranting a separate heading
in balance sheets typically argued that these items should be examined
to identify the purpose for which they were acquired (or held) in order

18. E. A. Saliers, Accounts in theory and practice (McGraw-Hill Book
    Company, Inc., 1920), pp.209-11.

19. H. H. Wade, Fundamentals of accounting (New York: John Wiley & Sons,
    Inc., 1934), p.272.

20. F. W. Woodbridge, Elements of accounting (New York: Ronald Press
    Company, 1924), p.24.

21. C. R. Rorem, Accounting method (Chicago: University of Chicago Press,
    2nd ed., 1930), p.151.

22. D. Himmelblau, Principles of accounting (New York: Ronald Press
    Company, rev.ed., 1934), p.181.

23. Greendlinger(1922) stated that it was "safe" to apply the "general
    rule that investments should be carried at cost" but acknowledged
    that "even in this case, due attention should be given to a reserve
    for any possible loss in value thru (sic) a decline in the market
    price of such securities". L. Greendlinger, Financial and business
    statements (New York: Alexander Hamilton Institute, 1922), p.143.

to select valuation procedures. This approach was similar to the British
approach of using different procedures to value current and fixed assets.
But, unlike British writers, American commentators often devoted
considerable space to considering whether fixed assets should be
systematically revalued. However few American writers concluded that
upward revaluations were desirable.[24]

It is clear enough that the idea of selecting valuation procedures
according to whether it was planned to hold or to dispose of assets was
a significant influence on accounting treatments for investments in
securities.[25] However the introduction of tax regulations also seems to
have affected corporate reporting practices in these areas. It appears
that the tax regulations led many firms to ignore market prices and to
look only to cost-based data (notwithstanding that particular holdings of
marketable securities might be classified as current). In general, the
tax regulations prohibited the inclusion of write-ups of securities as
part of taxable income. An exception was made for bankers, brokerage
houses and dealers in securities. These firms could treat write-downs
of securities as an expense for tax purposes; correspondingly texts continued to claim that the lower of cost and market rule was entirely
appropriate for these forms of business enterprise. But otherwise
commentators and practitioners supported the "convenient" procedure[26]

---

24. Paton seemed to approve of periodic upward revaluations of holding
     of securities "where such adjustments are unusual and for serious
     amounts" - provided the credit went to surplus not income. W. A.
     Paton Accounting (New York: The Macmillan Company, 1924), p.366.
     W. H. Lough (1917) argued that profits on holding securities should
     not be credited unless realized, but "the case may be different"
     in the case of firms "engaged in the business of buying and selling
     ... securities". Op.cit., p.419. However there were apparently some
     aberrant treatments of marketable securities - notably the recording
     of these assets at par value.

25. See, e.g., J. E. Kirshman, Principles of investment (Chicago:
     A. W. Shaw Company, 1924), p.247.

26. See, e.g., Paton, op.cit., p.366.

of keeping tax records and business records in line. Hence the use of the lower of cost and market rule for securities seems to have soon faded into disuse. By the 1920's there seems to have been agreement that the most usual method of recording marketable securities was at cost or cost-derivatives.[27] In 1934 Daniels reported that out of a sample of 155 cases in which balance sheets included "temporary invest- ments", market value was <u>used or indicated</u> in less than one third of the reports. The valuation methods adopted by these firms were:

No basis indicated	54
Cost	50
Market	28
'Cost or market'	10
Miscellaneous	13

Among the miscellaneous bases were "book value", "lower than cost", "subject to a reserve", "lower of par or market", "listed securities at market, unlisted at cost", "par", "below par", "bonds at par, stocks at market".[28]

This practice of not stating (or concealing) market prices of securities was poorly received by analysts. Wall and Duning (1930) claimed that firms submitting financial statements for credit purposes should provide "a schedule of securities owned, priced at the market value".[29] Even when market prices were disclosed, at least one analyst urged individuals trying to interpret published reports to recast balance sheets and recalculate income to reflect actual values.[30]

---

27. Idem; D. C. Eggleston, <u>Modern accounting theory and practice</u> (New York: John Wiley and Sons, Inc., 1930), Vol.I, pp.175-6.

28. M. B. Daniels, <u>Corporation financial statements</u> (Ann Arbor: University of Michigan Bureau of Business Research, 1934), p.51.

29. A. Wall and R. W. Duning, <u>Analysing financial statements</u> (New York: American Institute of Banking, 1930), p.116.

30. H. W. Sieg, <u>The A B C of Wall Street</u> (New York: Gold Star Publica- tions, 1939), pp.80-3.

Large parcels of listed securities

The treatment of large parcels of listed securities did not appear
to trouble American accountants as much as it did members of the British
profession. The scale of the securities markets in the U.S. may have
reduced somewhat the difficulties associated with ascribing market
prices to large parcels. Few writers worried about the validity of
calculations of market prices in these instances;[31] the adoption of
alternative treatments was rarely considered.

The foregoing comments should not be construed as indicating that
all accountants favoured the use of market prices as the basis of
valuing these assets. On the contrary, the discussions of large parcels was tied in with discussions of the categorisation of assets in
terms of one or other classification scheme. Thus it was argued that
non-current holdings need not necessarily be recorded at current market
prices if the intention was to hold them "permanently". Alternatively,
it was suggested that large parcels could be recorded at cost
provided the market prices of the securities were reported in footnotes.
After the late-1920's stock market collapse it was accepted that the
formal recognition of price variations in respect of these assets was
anomalous. Bell and Graham (1937) described this shift in viewpoint:

> Stocks which represent a non-controlling interest in
> another corporation, and which are non-liquid in nature

---

31. One exception was W. H. Bell, who wrote that "except in the case
of small holdings, market value may be called a theoretical concept,
for the reason that in perhaps most cases where large amounts are
involved if the securities were offered for sale in the market
they would bring a price different from the current quotation or
might not be readily saleable at all". However he added that "if
good judgment" was used, market quotations were acceptable as
fairly accurate approximations of "the actual value" of securities.
Auditing (New York: Prentice-Hall, Inc., 1926), p.187. H. W.
Sieg also noted that securities might not realise their market
price if the market was unable to absorb a large parcel; however
he appeared to raise this issue in the context of forced sale on
liquidation. Op.cit., p.78.

or which the management intends to hold for a long
period of time, are ordinarily valued at cost;
more recently, however, with the rapid and often
very substantial fluctuation in stock prices, it has
become necessary to reflect in the value of such
investments any large and seemingly permanent declines
in value.[32]

Some writers expressed concern about the balance sheet classification of large parcels. This reflected the confusion which arose from
the evolution of classification schemes loosely founded on alternative
and contradictory objectives. Comments by Graham and Meredith
typify this confusion:

> Some investments stand midway between ordinary marketable
> securities and the typical non-marketable permanent
> commitment in a related company. This intermediate type
> is illustrated by du Pont's enormous holdings of General
> Motors, or the large investment of Union Pacific in the
> securities of various other railroads. Such holdings
> will appear among the miscellaneous assets rather than
> the current assets, since the companies regard them as
> permanent investments; but for some purposes (e.g.
> calculating the quick assets per share of stock) it is
> permissable to regard them as the equivalent of readily
> marketable securities.[33]

The sparseness of the literature on this topic may simply have
reflected the unfamiliarity of text writers with the problems faced by
practitioners. However, it is reasonable to conclude that contributors
to the accounting literature were not troubled by the possibility
that holdings of marketable securities might be so extensive as to
create a subsidiary relationship. No attention was given to the basis
of discriminating between "large parcels" and "investments in
subsidiaries". The literature described distinct treatments for the
two categories.

Non-marketable securities

Again, the treatment of non-marketable securities appears to have

32. S. Bell and W. J. Graham, Theory and practice of accounting (Chicago:
American Technical Society, 1937), p.331.

33. B. Graham, and S. P. Meredith, The interpretation of financial
statements (New York: Harper and Brothers, Publishers, 1937), p.20.

been accorded less attention in the U.S. than in the U.K.   One can
speculate about the reasons for this.   While the U.K.'s arrangements for
the trade in securities were centred on London the United States had
a variety of markets, including an active over-the-counter market.
Consequently, prices were available for many stocks not listed on
the major stock exchanges.   Moreover, U.S. accountants did not commonly
face the problems created in the U.K. with the introduction of private
companies, the shares of which could not be publicly offered for sale and
could not be transferred without the prior consent of directors.

However undoubtedly many U.S. corporations did hold inter-corporate
investments which were non-marketable or marketable only in very thin
markets.   There was little discussion of valuation matters in this
connection.   Of the writers who did consider the matter, Paton and Stevenson concentrated on the treatment of non-listed bonds, and ignored
equity securities,[34] while Kohler and Morrison clearly accepted the
need to use cost-based valuations but were more concerned with balance
sheet classifications than with valuation questions.[35]   Several writers
simply asserted that inter-corporate investments should be handled
differently according to whether or not they established a holding
company - subsidiary company relationship.[36]   The basis of distinguishing
holdings in subsidiaries from holdings in non-subsidiaries or affiliated
companies will be discussed in detail in a later section;   in general

---

34. Op.cit., p.416.

35. "... conservative valuation principles demand [the investment's]
     classification as an item falling between current and capital
     assets.   Unless it is soon to be disposed of, it may be carried at
     cost, because the possibility of loss or gain from it is not yet
     determinable".   Op.cit., p.287.

36. e.g. R. B. Kester, Accounting theory and practice (New York: Ronald
     Press Company, 2nd ed., 1925), p.197;   S. F. Racine, Accounting
     principles (Seattle: The Western Institute of Accountancy, Commerce
     and Finance, 3rd ed., 1923), pp.104-5;   Himmelblau, op.cit., pp.181-2.

the criterion adopted was that of more than 50% of the voting stock. The usual recommendation was that non-controlling investments should be recorded at cost.

Investments in subsidiaries and affiliated companies

Dickinson's pioneering discussions of the treatment of inter-corporate investments placed particular emphasis on the need to counter managerial efforts to manipulate financial reports. Dickinson apparently responded to cases within his experience by warning of the hazards of including the pre-acquisition profits of newly-purchased firms in a corporation's income. Dickinson assumed that inter-corporate investments would be valued at net cost, with revenues being recognised on the receipt of dividends; correspondingly he assumed that it was possible for holding companies to ignore subsidiaries' losses.[37] In advocating the use of consolidated statements Dickinson was arguing that holding companies' reports should reflect changes in the value of investments in subsidiaries. He speculated that corporation laws might eventually introduce similar requirements (p.190). Meantime his arguments for consolidated statements assumed that holding companies' income calculations would incorporate the effect of dividend-based revenue recognition, and the discretionary recognition of losses.

It appears that many holding companies were providing financial statements prepared in this way. Montgomery's 1905 American edition of Dicksee's Auditing noted that:

> the proper method of stating the accounts of ... 'holding' companies has received considerable attention recently because it is believed that the omission on the part of some corporations to take up the losses of subsidiary companies, when they have included among their own earnings all the profits, has resulted in erroneous opinions as to the actual net earnings of the corporations in question.[38]

37. A. L. Dickinson, "The profits of a corporation", Official record of the proceedings of the congress of accountants (New York: George Wilkinson, 1904), pp.189-90.

38. New York: Ronald Press Company, p.225.

The next extended discussion of the valuation of investments in subsidiaries came from Lybrand (1908) who similarly assumed the use of cost-based valuation of investments in subsidiaries. Lybrand claimed that investments in subsidiaries would be left at cost except in cases where it was apparent that the value of these investments had suffered "a radical and permanent decline".[39] Like Dickinson, he did not address the question of whether or not some other basis of valuation would be more appropriate but rather turned to consolidated statements as the means of resolving the income recognition (and other) problems that flowed from cost-based valuation. It seems reasonable to conclude that enthusiasm for the new form of reporting led accounting writers to disregard the question of how to value inter-corporate investments in a holding company's books and how to record gains or losses arising from those investments. If one agreed with presenting consolidated statements alone (rather than presenting a combination of reports) then the valuation of a holding company's investments was largely irrelevant since inter-corporate investments and inter-corporate dividends were eliminated and disregarded in the process of preparing "group" reports.

Hatfield (1916) touched on the recording of inter-corporate investments in subsidiaries as an illustration of how the intentions of managers should influence asset valuation. He posed the case of stock acquired by a railroad to give it "control in the management of another road or of some allied enterprise".

> The market price of this stock may vary, but such
> changes in value cannot be realized by the purchasing
> company while it still continues to exercise the
> function for which it acquired the stock - that is to
> control the road.[40]

39. W. M. Lybrand, "The accounting of industrial enterprises", The journal of accountancy, Nov. 1908, pp.38-9.

40. Op.cit., p.91.

Wildman discussed the treatment of investments in subsidiaries more directly, but in the context of describing the preparation of consolidated statements. Wildman's analysis of asset valuation applied different procedures to fixed and to current assets; presumably investments in subsidiaries would constitute fixed assets - and as such would have been valued at cost. But Wildman did not spell out this line of reasoning directly and simply described current practices. He claimed that "the profits of subsidiaries are taken up by the holding company through dividends on the capital stock".[41]

Until 1914 The journal of accountancy did not include any examination of the utility of consolidated statements relative to the use of alternative bases of valuing or reporting on investments in subsidiaries. Accounting writers seem to have been prepared to accept that consolidated statements were the answer to the difficulties of valuation posed by inter-corporate holdings. Or perhaps the on-going political concern with the powers and pricing policies of large organizations[42] continued to prompt accountants to look to methods of reporting on "groups" of companies. Whatever the reason, little attention was paid to the possibility of using anything but cost-based valuation practices. The valuation of subsidiaries was a non-issue.

The first discussions of holding company accounting in the journal literature did little to alter this lack of interest in the valuation of subsidiaries. H. C. Freeman attempted to draw attention to what he saw as unsettled questions about holding company accounting:

> 1. Is it good practice to present the accounts of a holding company independently, without incorporating in them in any way the accounts of the subsidiary company or companies?

---

41. Op.cit., p.294.

42. See, e.g., Woodrow Wilson, Annual address, American Bar Association, Chattanooga, Tennessee, 1910, reproduced in W. Z. Ripley, Main street and Wall street (Boston: Little, Brown, and Co., 1929). pp.3-15.

2. Is it legally defensible, and if so is it good accountancy practice, to introduce into the accounts of a holding company any so-called equity in the earnings of subsidiary companies?

3. Is it necessary to present individual accounts of each subsidiary?

4. Is it good practice to consolidate the accounts of holding companies and subsidiaries?

5. If the accounts are consolidated what amount of detail is necessary or advisable ..?[43]

He claimed that cost-based valuation of investments in subsidiaries and dividend-based revenue recognition were "undoubtedly justified on legal and technical grounds" (p.159). While Freeman acknowledged that this technique lent itself to manipulation or obsfucation, he concluded that it was possible to avoid these difficulties by establishing provisions for subsidiaries' losses. As for the systematic recognition of subsidiaries' gains (other than those distributed as dividends) Freeman discussed two methods: adjusting the values of the subsidiary-investments, or simply showing undistributed profits of the subsidiary as a separate asset item in the holding company's balance sheet. The latter proposal could not be reconciled with the legal position that shareholders did not hold a direct equity in a company's assets. The former - the use of an equity accounting method - was said to pose difficulties in determining and describing the holding company's distributable surplus. Another objection posed by Freeman was that shares in subsidiary companies were often initially recorded at an inflated value (following mergers in which acquired assets were valued at the aggregate par value of the holding company's shares issued in exchange); accordingly directors might resist making upward revaluations of already exaggerated numbers. But the danger that directors might be held liable to repay dividends wrongly distributed was the main reason for Freeman's conclusion that:

---

43. "The statement of accounts of holding companies", The journal of accountancy, Sept. 1914, pp.157-80.

> it does not appear that there is any method which is
> advisable or expedient from the accounting standpoint,
> which is at the same time permissible from the legal
> standpoint, of introducing into the accounts of a
> holding company, as such, the undistributed earnings of
> the subsidiary company or any proportion thereof.[44]

So Freeman fell back on the use of cost-based valuation and dividend-

based revenue recognition - and hence claimed there was a need for

consolidated statements to overcome the limitations of the formal

valuation procedures.

A. W. Wright, on the other hand, concluded that a holding company's

"equitable interest in the undistributed surplus" of certain companies

should be treated as an asset.[45] Wright's paper was possibly the first

attempt to come to grips with the problem of deciding what proportion

of stock ownership in another company warranted the treatment of inter-

corporate investments in one way rather than another. Most early

holding companies held 100% (or near to 100%) of the stock of

"subsidiaries". The status of these companies as "subsidiaries" was

thus not in question. But Wright looked at situations in which stock

holdings could constitute 2%, 5%, 50% or 95% of another firm's issued

capital. He described the anomalies of dividend-based revenue

recognition, and considered the alternative of using consolidated reports.

He rejected the use of consolidated reports for 50%-owned companies on

the ground that they would convey a misleading impression of the holding

company's affairs.[46]

---

44. Ibid, p.167. See also correspondence discussing Freeman's argu-
    ments, "Accounts of holding companies", The journal of accountancy
    1914, pp.397-9.

45. A. W. Wright, "Consolidation of balance sheets in holding company
    accounting" loc.cit., Jan. 1914, pp.21-33.

46. Wright also considered a form of consolidated report in which the
    holding company's assets were added to a proportion of the sub-
    sidiaries' assets in accord with the proportion of stock-ownership
    held. He rejected this treatment on the ground that these reports
    were confusing, while the practice was not supportable in terms of
    the legal rights associated with shareholdings. Ibid, pp.24-6.

Wright saw consolidated reports as purporting to be those of the holding company (not a "group") and so argued that the inclusion of 50% owned companies would overstate assets and liabilities, relative to the holding company's equity. This led him to conclude that in situations where there was 50% stock ownership, the optimal solution was to record the "subsidiary's" undistributed surplus as an asset. But he made no claim that this method was "best in all cases" - as when ownership was "nearly uniform and nearly complete". And, given that he proposed that different treatments for subsidiary investments were appropriate at different percentages of ownership, he made no attempt to draw the dividing line more closely than by referring to a range of 50% to 100%.

Neither Freeman's nor Wright's contributions excited controversy. The systematic adjustment of investments in subsidiaries continued to be a little-discussed topic. Institutional developments hastened the widespread acceptance of the propriety of consolidated reporting: tax regulations in 1917 required "group" statements while from around 1919 the listing rules of the New York Stock Exchange recognized consolidated statements as a legitimate and acceptable form of reporting. Text-book discussions of holding company accounting continued to give cursory treatment to the valuation of subsidiaries. Repeatedly, writers asserted that a holding company's balance sheet would show these investments at cost, or that a holding company's balance sheet would simply reflect dividends received. Or teaching illustrations of the preparation of consolidated reports were built around cost-based valuation of subsidiaries.[47]

Paradoxically, it was not until consolidated statements had become widely accepted that there was much written about the methods of handling a holding company's own valuation problems. A number of writers

---

47. e.g. S. Walton, "Consolidated statements", The journal of account-ancy, April 1918, pp.309, 316, 319; May 1918, pp.385, 388.

expressed sympathy for the abandonment of cost-based valuation of investments in subsidiaries, though their discussions were clouded by differing views about the relative status of holding company and consolidated reports.

The 1920's saw publication of two major texts dealing solely with the preparation of consolidated statements: H. A. Finney's Consolidated statements for holding company and subsidiaries[48] and G. H. Newlove's Consolidated balance sheets.[49] Neither text questioned the desirability or utility of consolidated reports. But notwithstanding that both authors accepted a framework in which consolidated reports were the norm and were not alternative presentations or supplements to conventional reports, both took pains to canvass the desirability of abandoning cost-based valuation of subsidiaries in favour of "equity" methods of accounting involving the accrual of post-acquisition profits or losses.

Finney argued for the systematic adjustment of a holding company's investments in a subsidiary to reflect the holding company's share of the profits or losses of the latter company.

> This practice is justified because the two companies
> are so closely related that the profits of the subsidiary
> are virtually profits of the holding company which owns
> the subsidiary.

Hence a holding company following this "approved method" of accounting would have an investment account balance which was "equal to the book value of the stock held, plus any goodwill and minus any negative goodwill arising from the stock purchase".[50]

---

48. New York: Prentice-Hall Inc., 1922.

49. New York: Ronald Press Company, 1926.

50. Op.cit., p.47. Finney did not canvass the possibility of the subsidiary having non-trading profits or losses which were not recorded in the subsidiary's income statement; however he did make some limited attempt to come to grips with difficulties arising from over-valuation of subsidiaries' assets, by proposing (p.74) that so-called negative goodwill be offset against the assets in question.

Newlove was less emphatic about the relative merits of the "cost method" and what he termed the "actual value" method of valuing subsidiaries. So he prepared extensive illustrations of the preparation of consolidated data from reports prepared on either basis. As will be discussed in a following chapter, the use of consolidated statements received a fillip when in 1917 the U.S. tax regulations were amended to require consolidated returns. Because consolidated statements were required for tax purposes, Newlove regarded them as a fact of life. He did not question their utility beyond noting at one point that the use of "actual value method" in holding company statements was an alternative to consolidations for internal reports to management.

> The Actual Value Method would enable the holding company's comptroller to get a true picture of his concern's net worth without making a consolidated balance sheet.[51]

Other contributions during the 1920's considered the use of equity accounting methods - though only in the context of describing the merits of consolidated reports. Kester (1922) argued strongly that holding companies' reports should recognise the undistributed profits of subsidiaries. However he described consolidated statements as the best way of representing this relationship; consolidated balance sheets were a "device for showing the valuation of permanent invest-ments", and were the "best and only intelligible presentation of condition".[52] Cox (1920) objected to the use of equity methods on the ground that readers of financial statements would still lack "essential details" as to the source of such profits.[53] Similarly, Stockwell (1925) illustrated the accrual of subsidiaries' undistributed earnings

---

51. Op.cit., p.321

52. R. B. Kester, Accounting theory and practice, Vol.II (New York: Ronald Press Company, 1922), pp.261, 510.

53. H. C. Cox, Advanced and analytical accounting (New York: Ronald Press Company, Vol.IV of Business accounting series, 1920), p.346.

but claimed that the resultant financial report was "very incomplete
as a proper expression of the facts, such as would be shown in
a consolidated balance sheet". [54]   Racine (1923) unequivocally
supported the use of equity accounting methods in cases where investments were acquired "to secure the control of a company which it is
intended to operate". Indeed, Racine argued that investments in
such companies should initially be recorded not at purchase price but
at the book value of the subsidiaries. Why? Merely "to facilitate
the consolidation of the balance sheets of the respective
companies". [55]

By 1930, the bulk of the U.S. literature on holding company
accounting had come to dismiss holding company balance sheets as unimpor-
tant. Consolidated statements were regarded as primary documents, and
correspondingly the valuation of a holding company's investments in
its subsidiaries was irrelevant for reporting purposes. Moreover, the
use of the "cost method" to record investments in subsidiaries was
said to be required by the tax authorities. [56]

Text books published during the 1930's continued to describe the
process of systematically adjusting the book value of investments in
subsidiaries to reflect losses or undistributed profits. But, like
texts published in earlier years, it seems that the primary objective
of these commentaries was to highlight the advantages of consolidated
statements. Sunley and Pinkerton illustrated the preparation of
consolidated statements where investments were valued at "cost" or by

---

54.   H. G. Stockwell, How to read a financial statement (New York:
      Ronald Press Company, 1925), pp.394-5.

55.   Op.cit., p.105.

56.   Newlove, op.cit., pp.31-2. This "requirement" was only an
      administrative directive aimed at simplifying analysis of post-
      acquisition gains or losses.

the equity method;[57] McKinsey and Noble,[58] and Finney,[59] provided
illustrations in which holding companies used equity methods
exclusively. Be-1 and Graham did not provide numerical illustrations
of the equity method but simply described the procedures involved while
commenting that holding companies' balance sheets still did not show
"the nature of the subsidiaries' assets" or "details of the subsidiaries'
profits or losses".[60] Himmelblau seemed to favour the equity method;[61]
Kester suggested that it was "not considered to be the best practice"
and that it was "objectionable from the legal standpoint".[62] And yet
Kester (and later Stempf) seemed to favour the equity method for
valuing investments in unconsolidated subsidiaries[63] - assuming, of
course, that published reports would be in consolidated form.

---

57. W. T. Sunley and P. W. Pinkerton, Corporation accounting (New York: Ronald Press Company, for the American Academy of Accountancy, 1931), p.454.

58. J. O. McKinsey and H. S. Noble, Accounting principles (Cincinnati: South-Western Publishing Company, 1935), p.633. See also 2nd ed. (1939), p.667.

59. H. A. Finney, Introduction to principles of accounting (New York: Prentice-Hall, Inc., 1932), pp.579-80, 585.

60. Op.cit., p.430.

61. Op.cit., pp.182-3.

62. R. B. Kester, Advanced accounting (New York: Ronald Press Company, 3rd ed., 1933), p.652.

63. Ibid, p.261; V. H. Stempf, "Consolidated financial statements", The journal of accountancy, Nov. 1936, pp.358-76. By 1936 it was widely recognised that the omission of individual subsidiaries from consolidated statements allowed scope for manipulation of the consolidated figures. Accordingly both the Securities and Exchange Commission and the New York Stock Exchange required the disclosure of details concerning the profits or losses of unconsolidated subsidiaries. Ibid, pp.358-76.

Resume

American accountants were slow to adopt a framework for approaching
asset valuation questions. Different procedures were developed for
different types of assets or for assets held by firms engaged in
different types of business. Under these circumstances, a range of
treatments were used to handle inter-corporate investments, though
there were signs that the American profession was leaning towards the
British idea of linking asset classification (or managerial intentions)
with asset valuation procedures. However the American accounting
literature contained very little discussion of the valuation of
investments in subsidiaries.

Meantime, accountants were attracted by the techniques of preparing consolidated statements. Indeed, consolidated reporting was
widely advocated and became "accepted" before the profession had settled
down to argue about the relative merits of one or other means of
handling inter-corporate investments.

Subsequently, the federal government reinforced the arguments
of supporters of consolidated reporting with requirements for the
taxing of corporations on a "group" basis. And the New York Stock
Exchange encouraged the use of consolidated reporting by listed firms.
As consolidated reporting was more widely adopted so the profession's
interest in consolidated reporting overwhelmed the debate about
the valuation of inter-corporate investments. To this extent, the
history of consolidated reporting in the U.S. is largely unrelated to
difficulties associated with asset valuation.

Ch. 11 Consolidated reporting - before regulation

After very little discussion or analysis within the accounting literature, the use of consolidated statements quickly became part of U.S.
accounting practice. It seems probable that U.S. Steel's adoption of this
form of report in the 1900's would have made some accountants aware of the
possibilities of using consolidated statements. Thereafter, text
books and the journal literature disseminated information about how to
prepare these documents. By 1912, the profession's entrance examinations
were including questions on the preparation of consolidated reports[1]
thus reinforcing the educative activities of writers like Dickinson,
Montgomery and Lybrand who had all urged the use of this method of
reporting. In 1915 G. O. May claimed that the practice of publishing
consolidated balance sheets was "generally adopted"; however, it
seems doubtful that this assertion could be supported by a survey of
financial statements published at that time. Perhaps May was talking
of listed corporations - or, more particularly, New York Stock Exchange
- listed corporations that were his firm's clients.[2]

---

1. Childs reported that his review of C.P.A. exam papers revealed
   that the first occasion consolidated statements were mentioned
   was a problem in the Illinois 'Practical Accounting' examination of May 1912"; "a more difficult problem was set in the
   same Illinois examination two years later. W. H. Childs, Consolidated financial statements (Cornell University Press, 1949),
   p.46. Childs made no reference to New York C.P.A. exam papers;
   however Esquerre reproduced a problem taken from the New York
   C.P.A. examination of January 1913 (but without any mention of
   how long such material had been in the curriculum). P. J. Esquerre,
   The applied theory of accounts (New York: Ronald Press Company,
   1914), p.449.

2. These observations were included in May's advice to auditors
   concerning how to deal with recalcitrant clients who were unwilling
   to publish consolidated statements; May suggested an appeal to
   the authority of "general" practice. G. O. May, "Qualifications
   in certificates", The journal of accountancy, Oct. 1915, reproduced in May's Twenty-five years of accounting responsibility (New
   York: Price, Waterhouse & Co., 1936, ed. by B. C. Hunt; reprinted
   by Scholars Book Co., 1971), p.37.

Some years later Paton and Stevenson referred to consolidated statements as being commonly "published in the various corporation manuals"
- though their comments suggest that consolidated reports were not
exactly "generally adopted".[3]

It appears that several institutional factors encouraged the more
extensive use of consolidated reporting after 1915. These included
the passage of tax regulations requiring a form of consolidated report,
the recommendation of an association of investment bankers that members
look to consolidated data when considering prospectuses, and the New York
Stock Exchange's acceptance of consolidated statements as the primary
forms of financial disclosure. The consequence of these influences
and activities seems to have been that by 1920 consolidated reporting was
uniformly accepted - if not uniformly practised. On the face of it,
the case for consolidated statements seemed unassailable; as astute a
commentator as W. Z. Ripley observed that without consolidated statements, a holding company's reports were not worth the paper they were
written on.[4] Yet at least some accounting writers were aware that there
were alternative justifications for using consolidated statements - and
that these alternatives suggested alternative technical procedures.

Moreover in the early 1920's bankers became aware of the hazards of
relying on consolidated data alone. But the accounting profession seems to
have ignored or disregarded suggestions that consolidated data was of
limited usefulness to those concerned with evaluating liquidity or assessing
credit-worthiness. Certainly the accounting literature of the 1920's contains
no extended analysis or assessment of these suggestions. The introduction

3.   W. A. Paton and R. A. Stevenson, Principles of accounting (New
     York: The Macmillan Company, 1920), p.597. These authors repro-
     duced a consolidated statement as it was published in the 1914
     edition of Moody's Manual of corporation securities - an invest-
     ment service.

4.   W. Z. Ripley, Main street and Wall street (Boston: Little, Brown,
     and Company, 1929), p.203.

in the 1930's of federal regulations for corporate reporting saw
consolidated statements finally established as the dominant and primary
means of financial disclosure.

This chapter reviews some of these steps in the adoption of
consolidated reporting in U.S. practice.

Supposed objectives of consolidated statements

The pre-1930 literature on consolidated reporting was repetitive
and entirely uncritical. The supposed advantages of consolidated statements were often asserted as articles of faith, without any assessment of
the usefulness of these reports relative to parent company statements
prepared using equity accounting procedures, or relative to other forms of
presenting financial data. Despite this lack of analysis, there were
several distinct shifts in the matters emphasised in text-book descriptions
of the aims and accomplishments of consolidated statements.

Dickinson's pioneering discussions of the use of consolidated
statements (examined in Ch. 8) placed particular attention on the need
to forestall the manipulations that could arise from inter-company
transactions or arrangements. Dickinson pointed out that traditional
forms of reporting could lead to a distorted impression being conveyed
of profitability and liquidity. And in 1914 he claimed that consolidated statements had been introduced to overcome "the misleading
character of the ordinary balance sheet".[5] Dickinson seems to have
assumed that holding companies would use cost-based valuation procedures
to handle investments in subsidiaries because of the hazards associated
with recording undistributed profits as revenues. Dickinson saw the
publication of consolidated statements as a bold gesture in that they
"brushed aside legal technicalities" by disregarding separate entities
and treating subsidiaries as if they were merely branches of a head-
office holding company. But when it came to calculating distributable

5.   A. L. Dickinson, Accounting practice and procedure (New York:
Ronald Press Company, 1914).

income, it appears that Dickinson and others were not so ready to be bold, imaginative and creative by ignoring "legal technicalities". There was fear that the upward revaluation of investments in subsidiaries might be deemed an overstatement of (distributable) income. Of course, it does not follow that adjustments of the recorded values of assets (such as investments in subsidiaries) would necessarily be recorded as revenue, and even if these revaluation increments were included in income it would be possible to then transfer them to some non-distributable reserve.

One of the changes in discussions of consolidated reports was from emphasising the dangers of misrepresentation of liquidity and profitability to the more simple argument that cost-based valuation of subsidiaries was potentially uninformative. The bulk of the literature on holding company accounting proceeded as if cost-based valuation was the norm. In this context, the case for alternative representations of a holding company's affairs had considerable appeal, though it does not follow that consolidated statements were necessarily the ideal or optimal form of reporting.

A second shift in emphasis was that consolidated statements came to be described as attempts to reflect the performance of a group of companies rather than attempts to amplify the reports of holding companies. However, those writers who advanced those proposals only seem to have been trying to outline the procedures involved in the preparation of consolidated reports. They made no attempt to describe the significance of the identification of a "group" or "economic entity" in terms of some criterion of "control". For example, Wildman described the use of consolidated statements as follows:

> They are usually prepared ... where it is desirable
> to consolidate the showing of the subsidiaries with
> those of the parent company.[6]

---

6. J. R. Wildman, Principles of accounting (Brooklyn: The William G. Hewitt Press, 1913), pp.294-297.

But when was it "desirable" to produce these reports? Wildman offered
no comments. Paton and Stevenson (1920) claimed that consolidated
statements revealed facts "which the average investor in the holding
company desires to have presented" - "the condition of the property
as a whole which is under the control of the holding company" - but
they did not discuss the ramifications of this argument.[7] Likewise,
Bennett (1919) referred to the "necessity" or "desirability" of
preparing consolidated reports - without indicating the basis for
determining necessity or desirability.

> ... it is frequently necessary or desirable to present
> all the financial details in one balance sheet, in order
> to reflect the financial position of the whole group of
> affiliated companies as one undertaking.[8]

None of these writers made unambiguous statements about the occasion for
preparing consolidated statements, or the utility of this form of report.

Excess profits tax 1917

U.S. Steel's publication of consolidated statements has been described as the first major landmark in the history of this form of
reporting; the second major event was said to be the official recognition of consolidated reporting for purposes of taxation.[9]

The U.S. Congress introduced an "excess profits tax" in 1917.
The tax legislation did not make any explicit reference to consolidated statements, but regulations later empowered the Commissioner of
Internal Revenue to require corporations classed as affiliates to
"furnish a consolidated return of net income and invested capital".[1]

7. Op.cit., pp.592-7.

8. R. J. Bennett, Corporation accounting (New York: Ronald Press Company,
   1919), p.456.

9. P. F. Brundage, "Consolidated statements", in T. W. Leland (ed.),
   Contemporary accounting (New York: American Institute of Accountants, 1945), Ch.5.

10. Regulation 41, articles Nos.77 and 78. These articles are re-
    produced in E. A. Kracke, "Consolidated financial statements" The
    journal of accountancy Dec.1938, pp.373-4. For a review of the
    early history of the use of consolidated return see J. W. Jones,
    "The consolidated return", ibid, April 1933, pp.255-271.

In the following year, this requirement for consolidated tax returns gained full statutory recognition. 1918 legislation provided that "corporations which are affiliated ... shall ... make a consolidated return of net income and invested capital".[11] However, 1921 legislation made consolidated returns no longer mandatory and permitted firms to "make separate returns, or, under regulations prescribed by the Commissioner with the approval of the Secretary, make a consolidated return" upon the condition that whichever basis was selected would be adhered to thereafter unless a change was approved by the Commissioner. Subsequent legislation (1924, 1926, 1928 and 1932) maintained the right of taxpaying corporations to elect to make either consolidated or separate returns.[12] However in 1934 the use of consolidated tax returns was dropped (except for railroad corporations).[13]

There seems little doubt that these tax rules encouraged practitioners to learn how to prepare consolidated statements. Correspondingly the literature on the subject expanded rapidly. It seems likely that as more accountants became familiar with the techniques of preparing consolidated statements, more firms used consolidated statements for their reports to stockholders.

But it should be noted that tax legislation requiring consolidated returns was not aimed at "groups" of companies. In fact, consolidated returns were required where firms had common stockholders. The 1917 definition of an "affiliate" relationship included the following test:

> ... two or more corporations will be deemed to be
> affiliated ... when one such corporation owns directly
> or controls through closely affiliated interests or
> by a nominee or nominees, all or substantially all of

---

11. Kracke, op.cit., p.374.

12. The 1932 act imposed a higher rate of taxation if a consolidated return was used.

13. Kracke, op.cit., pp.374-5.

the stock of the other or others, or <u>when substantially</u>
<u>all of the stock of two or more corporations is owned</u>
<u>by the same individual or partnership,</u> and both or all
of such corporations are engaged in the same or a closely
related business.[14]

It was thus possible for consolidated returns to cover a "group"

of firms which were not related by <u>any</u> inter-corporate sharehold-

ings.

It has been claimed that the levying of tax by the use of

consolidated returns was a tribute to the accounting profession's

creativity and common sense.[15] It is true that the American

Institute of Accountants made submissions in support of the use of

consolidated returns,[16] and that the committee which provided advice

on the administration of tax laws included J. E. Sterrett,[17] a

Price, Waterhouse partner who was no doubt thoroughly familiar

with the views of his former colleague, A. L. Dickinson. But the ambit

of the requirements for consolidated returns suggests that the

provisions were aimed at identifying firms to bear the burden of

additional taxation, rather than with acknowledging the superiority

of a form of accounting report. Indeed, the 1918 legislation was

accompanied by a statement from Congress that the use of consoli-

dated returns afforded an equitable method of taxing affiliated

---

14. As cited Kracke, <u>loc.cit.</u> (emphasis added). A Treasury decision
    later interpreted the reference to ownership of "substantially
    all of the stock" as meaning ownership of 95 per cent. or more
    of issued capital.

15. Kracke claimed that the recognition of consolidated accounts by
    government authorities was "evidence of the educational work
    done by the accountant". <u>Ibid</u>, p.373.   G. O. May observed that
    by 1917 consolidated accounts had become "so well established
    that the Treasury without specific legislative authority, re-
    quired consolidated tax returns". <u>Financial accounting</u> (New
    York: The Macmillan Company, 1961), p.33.

16. These submissions were reproduced in <u>The journal of accountancy</u>,
    Jan. 1919.

17. Brundage, <u>op.cit.</u>, p.2.

corporations, and would prevent tax evasion.[18]   In short the claims
of commentators that the Excess Profits taxes of 1917 marked official
government recognition of consolidated reporting were inaccurate.
The U.S. government chose to levy taxes on (inter alia) related
corporations as if they were a single entity. But the government did
not in any way approve of or pass judgment on the use of aggregative
statements as a means of financial reporting.

New York Stock Exchange listing requirements

Some support from the practice of preparing consolidated reports
was given by the New York Stock Exchange (NYSE) through its requirements
for the listing of new issues.

The NYSE's attempts to regulate the flow of information to the
stock market date back to the 1850's when the New York Stock and
Exchange Board resolved that every application for listing had to be
approved by a majority of members present and had to include a "statement
of capital, resources, number of shares, etc".[19] In 1861 the Exchange
formed a Committee on Securities, "which attempted to obtain information
concerning securities on the list", though without much success.[20] In
1869 (after a consolidation of exchanges) a new constitution for the
newly-named New York Stock Exchange was adopted. This constitution
provided for the establishment of several committees including a

18. The pre-occupation with tax evasion was certainly evident from
    the 1917 regulation, which declared that corporations would be
    deemed "affiliates" when one such corporation (a) buys from or
    sells to another products or services at prices above or below
    the current market, thus effecting an artificial distribution of
    profits, or (b) in any way so arranges its financial relation-
    ships with another corporation as to assign it to a disproportion-
    ate share of net income or invested capital".

19. B. E. Schultz, The securities market (New York: Harper and
    Brothers, Publishers, 2nd ed., 1946), p.9.

20. Ibid, pp.8-9.

Committee on Stock List which was to assume responsibility for vetting applicants for admission to listing.[21] Around the turn of the century this Committee began to require companies to sign listing agreements which included promises to publish annual reports.[22]

The significance of attaining "listing" was reinforced with the abolition in 1910 of the so-called "unlisted department"; this limited NYSE-trading to stocks officially accepted for "listing".[23] By the early 1920's the Committee on Stock List consisted of five members and employed "a high salaried clerk, in reality an important expert with a staff of assistants, to study [corporate] reports and go over them in minute detail".[24]

Evidently from 1919 onwards the requirements governing annual reporting were modified so as to permit the presentation of either the statements of all "constituent" companies or consolidated statements.[25] The 1922 version of the listing requirements stated that an applicant had to agree to publish "at least once in each year"

> a statement of its physical and financial condition, an income account covering the previous fiscal year and a balance sheet showing assets and liabilities at the end of the year; also annually an income account and balance sheet of all constituent, subsidiary, owned or controlled companies; or a consolidated income account and a consolidated balance sheet.[26]

Whatever the contribution of these rules to the frequency of consolidated reporting, they certainly added to confusion over the

21. Ibid, p.12.

22. Ibid, p.14.

23. This followed the New York State "Hughes Commission" investigation of speculative activities in the commodities and securities markets. Ibid, p.15; W. J. Eiteman, C. A. Dice and D. K. Eiteman, The stock market (New York: McGraw-Hill Book Co., 4th ed., 1966), p.211.

24. A. W. Atwood, The stock and produce exchanges (New York: Alexander Hamilton Institute, Modern business series, 1921), p.73.

25. W. H. Childs, op.cit., p.76.

26. As cited, J. E. Meeker, The work of the stock exchange (New York: Ronald Press Company, 1922), p.585.

scope of consolidated reports. The NYSE's allusions to "constituent, subsidiary, owned or controlled companies" implied a far wider area of consolidation than had been customarily adopted or recommended in earlier years. J. M. B. Hoxsey, the NYSE staff member who played a key role in formulating these requirements, indicated that the intention was to include all corporations in which there were direct holdings of a majority of the voting stock[27] - a view which was radical at the time but which was consistent with proposals that these statements depicted "economic entities". Eventually opposition and non-compliance forced the NYSE to take a less rigid view and accept consolidated reports prepared as corporations saw fit - provided they were accompanied by separate statements dealing with any unconsolidated subsidiaries. At the same time consolidated statements could be published as primary documents. Thus the June 1930 requirements called for applicant-corporations to publish either separate balance sheets and income statements for themselves and their subsidiaries, or a set of "fully consolidated" statements, or "a similar set of statements consolidated as to the applicant company and specifically named and described subsidiaries, with separate statements for each unconsolidated corporation ...".[28] By 1932 further amendments required additional disclosures to indicate inter alia the parent company's proportion of the profits or losses of unconsolidated subsidiaries.

> (a) The caption of the statements must indicate the degree of consolidation
>
> (b) the income account must reflect, either in a footnote or otherwise, the parent company's proportion of the sum of or difference between current earnings or losses and the dividends of such unconsolidated subsidiaries for the period of report; and

---

27. As cited W. A. Staub, "Some difficulties arising in consolidated financial statements", The journal of accountancy, Jan. 1932, pp.15-16.

28. Idem.

(c) the balance-sheet must reflect, in a footnote or
    otherwise, the extent to which the equity of the
    parent company in such subsidiaries has been
    increased or diminished since the date of acquisi-
    tion, as a result of profits, losses and distri-
    butions.[29]

These amendments also included a change in the criterion for

identifying subsidiaries. The key test had been whether or not a

given firm owned a majority of another firm's <u>voting</u> stock; this

became ownership of a majority of <u>equity</u> stock. This change can be

seen as reflecting disagreement about whether consolidated reports were

intended to give an expanded view of a parent company's affairs or

rather an impression of the situation of "economic entities".

While the NYSE was formulating more and more elaborate rules

concerned with the reporting practices of holding companies, the

accounting profession had yet to canvass these issues at any length -

and had yet to sort out the rationale underlying the preparation of

consolidated statements.

Bankers and consolidated reporting

The hazard of relying on a holding company's statement as an

indicator of liquidity was frequently described in the U.S. literature

from the time that Dickinson first discussed the subject in 1904. As

Dickinson pointed out, advances to subsidiaries might be reported as

"current" assets and yet be invested in long-term projects so that

there was no chance of the holding company calling up these loans

in the short-run to meet its own debts.

As early as 1917, the need to highlight the extent of inter-

corporate advances involving "controlled or allied concerns" was

acknowledged by credit analysts. The American Bankers Association

---

29. <u>Idem</u>. The requirements for footnote disclosures were said to have
     been introduced to prevent "the omission of unfavourable data".
     Childs, <u>op.cit</u>., p.77.

prepared sets of model accounting statements which would enable
analysts to "elicit all the information necessary to obtain an
intelligent insight into the financial and other conditions of [a] ...
business"; these forms gave prominence to inter-corporate borrowings.[30]
Notwithstanding these efforts, it appears that some bankers sustained
serious losses through loans to holding companies or their affiliates.
G. R. Webster, who saw consolidated statements as the appropriate
means to avoid misrepresentations about liquidity matters, wrote in 1919
that "if bankers had insisted on the preparation of such accounts they
would have avoided several unpleasant experiences".[31]

Evidently the Federal Reserve Board held similar views, for Webster
records that it had "taken occasion to point out to banks which are
members of the system that they do not get an adequate view of the
financial condition of a company which has subsidiaries unless they
secure consolidated accounts".[32]

In 1923 an auditing text by Montgomery and Staub reproduced a
letter written by the deputy governor of a New York bank stating that
it had long been the bank's practice to require the submission of a
consolidated statement "in order that we might have full information
in passing upon the eligibility as well as the desirability of the paper
for rediscount ...". Evidently the bank also required separate parent
and subsidiary statements since "it sometimes happens that the borrowing
is done not by the parent or principal concern but by the subsidiary".[33]
The letter indicated that consolidated statements were viewed as

---

30. "Report of committee on credit forms", Journal of the American Bankers Association, Nov. 1918, pp.351, 355.

31. G. R. Webster, "Consolidated accounts", The journal of accountancy, Oct. 1919, p.258.

32. Ibid, p.259.

33. R. H. Montgomery and W. A. Staub, Auditing principles (New York: Ronald Press Company, 1923) pp.418-9.

significant documents for the purpose of assessing commercial paper.

It appears that bankers turned to consolidated statements as the primary means of representing liquidity - but found these reports less than satisfactory on their own. The journal of The Robert Morris Associates (a bankers' organisation) later acknowledged that

> consolidated balance sheets with their intercompany accounts and opportunities for window dressing have long been a source of trouble.

The occasion for these comments was the announcement by the Federal Reserve Board of a reconsideration of its earlier advice concerning consolidated reports. In 1924 the Board issued new regulations dealing with promissory notes:

> Whenever the borrower has closely affiliated or subsidiary corporations or firms, the borrower's financial statements shall be accompanied by separate financial statements of such affiliated or subsidiary corporations or firms ...[34]

There were provisions affording some relief from this ruling, but the substance of the regulation was clear: consolidated statements were not to be presented alone since they could be misleading.

De facto acceptance of consolidated statements as primary reports

The Federal Reserve Board's 1924 rulings are an indication of the extent to which consolidated statements had become accepted as the main vehicle for corporate reporting. This view of the status of consolidated statements had first been advanced by Dickinson around the turn of the century, and had been repeated by other writers in later years - though it was not until after the passage of the 1917 tax regulations that much was written on the preparation of these reports. And, with the appearance of a more extensive literature on consolidation matters, attitudes in favour of consolidated reports as the primary form of financial disclosure gradually hardened.

---

34. Federal Reserve Board Regulations, Series of 1924, August 1924, Article A, Section IV - as cited in "Consolidated statements", The Robert Morris Associates bulletin, September 1924, p.130.

The first extended treatment of the intricacies of preparing consolidated statements was H. A. Finney's <u>Consolidated statements for
holding company and subsidiaries</u> published in 1922.[35] While
essentially a technical manual, Finney's book contained the first
lucid identification of the conflict of views about the objects of
these statements. Finney described alternative propositions about the
function of consolidated statements. The first was that they were
intended to represent the "financial condition of ... several related
companies". In effect, then,

> ... the consolidated balance sheet is virtually a
> balance sheet of the holding company, in which the invest-
> ment account is dropped out and replaced by the subsidiary
> assets and liabilities which it represents (pp.17-8).

The second proposition was that consolidated statements were intended
to represent the affairs of a single organization:

> ... if we look past the legal fiction of separate
> corporate entities and view the related companies as
> a single organization, we find that no single balance
> sheet shows the total assets and liabilities of the
> organization, and the total stock of the organization
> in the hands of the public (p.11).

Having identified these viewpoints, Finney then avoided discussing
the conflict between the two. "Thus", he wrote, "the consolidated
balance sheet ... has its advantages whether we view the affiliated
companies as separate entities or as a single organization" (p.12).

Finney did not discuss the relative status of consolidated
statements <u>vis a vis</u> holding company statements, beyond asserting
(somewhat ambiguously) that the former "avoided disadvantages" of
separate statements.[36] Nor did he discuss whether consolidated statements should be presented as solitary or supplementary reports.

---

35. New York: Prentice-Hall, Inc.

36. Note that Finney recommended the systematic adjustment of invest-
    ment accounts to reflect undistributed profits or losses of
    subsidiaries; the "advantages" he saw in this context were thus
    concerned with the adequacy of the "presentation of the holding
    company's financial condition" (p.12).

In 1926 a second book on the preparation of consolidated statements was published in the U.S.A.: G. R. Newlove's Consolidated balance sheets.[37] Like Finney's text, this was a manual of procedures rather than an extended discussion of theoretical issues. Newlove had worked as an auditor and reviewer in the Income Tax Unit of the U.S. Treasury Department and as such had been involved with the use of consolidated tax returns. Much of his book was concerned with the requirements of the tax regulations.[38] A feature of the book was the inclusion of two sets of exercises - illustrating consolidation procedures for cases where holding companies recorded subsidiaries at cost or used what Newlove termed the "actual value method".

Newlove, like Finney, did not comment on whether consolidated reports should be accompanied by holding company statements. However, he strongly advocated the use of consolidated reports, stating that they were necessary whenever "a correct financial statement of the majority interest in a group of companies is desired" (p.7).

Text books published during the 1920's and 1930's steadily added to the volume of material concerned with the preparation of consolidated reports. But usually these texts avoided any explicit discussion of whether consolidated statements should be presented alone or in company with parent company reports.[39] Texts on financial analysis were

---

37. New York: Ronald Press Company.

38. In particular, Newlove described the preparation of consolidated statements for "affiliations" - relationships deemed to arise between corporations by virtue of stock ownership without any necessary inter-corporate stock holdings as typically understood by references to "holding companies" and "subsidiaries".

39. See, e.g., Bell and Graham, op.cit., pp.417-48; R. H. Montgomery and W. A. Staub, op.cit., pp.417-31; W. A. Paton, Accounting (New York: The Macmillan Company, 1924), pp.470-3, 504-8; C. F. Rittenhouse and A. L. Percy, Accounting problems: advanced (New York: McGraw-Hill Book Co., 1924), pp.21-2; J. V. Tinen, Advanced accounting (New York: Ronald Press Company, 1927), Ch.5, para.41; H. R. Hatfield, Accounting (New York: D. Appleton & Co., 1927), pp.439-55; C. R. Rorem, Accounting method (Chicago: University of Chicago Press, 2nd ed., 1930), pp.437-440; J. O. McKinsey and H. S. Noble, Accounting principles, (Cincinnatti: South West Publishing Co., 1935), pp.629-32.

similarly vague.[40] Authors who <u>did</u> take up the question of when

consolidated statements should be used often took the position that

holding company statements and consolidated statements were alternative

representations - so that accountants could use either one, or the other

statement, not both.[41] One writer suggested that analysts should

attempt to examine both consolidated statements and the separate reports

of subsidiaries - though he claimed that the latter could be dispensed

with if the consolidated statements were "of sufficient detail"; in

other words, holding company statements were regarded as inadequate

and irrelevant when consolidated data were available.[42]

The failure of texts to take up the point of whether consolidated

statements should be accompanied by parent company reports seems to

indicate how little significance was attached to parent company

statements at this time. Consolidated statements were customarily

presented alone.

Some contributors to the accounting literature had suggested that

consolidated statements should be accompanied by parent company reports,

or that the submission of consolidated statements alone could, on

occasions, be "undesirable".[43] But these comments seem to have been

disregarded. In 1925, Stockwell wrote that the financial reports of

holding companies "usually" were consolidated balance sheets.[44]

---

40. e.g. H. G. Stockwell, How to read a financial statement (New York: Ronald Press Company, 1925), pp.382-99; J. H. Bliss, Financial and operating ratios in management (New York: Ronald Press Company, 1923), pp.214-5.

41. See, e.g., R. B. Kester, Accounting theory and practice (New York: Ronald Press Company, 1922), Vol.II, pp.602-3; D. W. C. Eggleston, Auditing procedure (New York: John Wiley & Sons, 1926), pp.368-8.

42. W. E. Lagerquist, Investment analysis (New York: The Macmillan Company, 1921), p.59.

43. e.g. P. F. Brundage, "Some shortcomings in consolidated statements", The journal of accountancy, Oct. 1930, pp.285-92.

44. Op.cit., p.375.

In 1929, another source included the comment that consolidated balance
sheets were "almost universally employed by every large holding company".[45]
And in 1934, Daniels wrote that the importance of the legal financial
statements of holding companies had been "lost sight of" in the U.S.A.".[46]

Consolidated statements were accepted. But even though they were accepted accountants had still not thoroughly analysed what they were meant to
show. In the accounting literature in the late 1920's and 1930's,
descriptions of the need for consolidated statements or of the
advantages of this form of reporting became increasingly repetitive.
Texts continued to reflect uncertainty as to whether these reports were
amplifications of holding company statements or representations of the
affairs of "economic entities". For example, some said that consolidated
balance sheets were prepared "to avoid the meagre and perhaps misleading
information which may be given by the balance sheet of the holding
company only".[47] Others claimed that consolidated statements were
intended to provide an impression of "the business as a whole"[48] or to
show "the condition of ... affiliated concerns as an economic operating
unit".[49] But the authors of these texts did not bother to provide a case
for using consolidated statements rather than some alternative
representation, or for reporting on "economic entities". Meantime, other
writers continued the pre-1920 practice of simply describing consolidated
statements as aggregative documents, without any attempt to specify the

45. Commercial Research Bureau, Accountancy reports and reference
     manuals (Chicago: 1929), Vol.IV, p.375.

46. M. B. Daniels, Corporation financial statements (Ann Arbor:
     University of Michigan Bureau of Business Research, 1934), p.3.

47. Rittenhouse & Percy, op.cit., p.21. See also, e.g. McKinsey and
     Noble, op.cit., p.629.

48. Bliss, op.cit., p.214.

49. Paton, op.cit., p.506-7.

aims of the exercise or assess the utility of the product.[50]

---

50. e.g. "The consolidated statement is a representation of the
     business aggregate of all the separate parts, as if the actual
     assets were brought together and consolidated under one roof
     covering several departments ...". Stockwell, op.cit., p.382.
     See also A. L. Prickett and R. M. Mikesell, Principles of
     accounting (New York: The Macmillan Company, 1937), p.460.

Resume

Consolidated statements became accepted as primary reports after little analysis by the accounting profession of the supposed benefits of this form of reporting vis a vis conventional financial statements or other methods of representation. Tax legislation in particular seems to have been a significant factor in widening the profession's awareness of consolidated statements. But discussions of the aims of consolidated reporting were little more than crude appeals to the commonsense of practitioners. There was said to be a need to avoid misrepresentations of liquidity, or to ensure that readers were aware of the resources to which funds had been directed, or to reflect the position of an "economic entity". None of these claims was subjected to extended analysis. However, support for the "solution" of consolidated reports came from several institutions: the Federal Reserve Board and the New York Stock Exchange. By the early 1930's consolidated balance sheets were part and parcel of corporate reporting practice. But the precise objectives of consolidated reports had still not been examined by academics, practitioners or regulatory agencies.

Ch.12   Regulation of corporate reporting in U.S.A.

The first consolidated statements were prepared and published in the U.S.A. at a time when there were virtually no disclosure laws regulating the flow of financial information to shareholders, creditors and the investing public. By the 1930's, consolidated statements had become widely accepted and were used by a majority of corporations.

This chapter examines the forms of regulation in operation during this period in order to enable an assessment to be made of the role of regulation in encouraging or reinforcing the use of consolidated statements as a vehicle for corporate reporting.

Public service commissions

As noted in earlier chapters, a number of states had established agencies regulating railroads and other public utilities out of concern about monopolistic trading and pricing practices. In order to supervise rate fixing, some of these agencies required the submission of financial reports supposedly prepared on a uniform basis. Further, several state agencies extended their operations to encompass the regulation of the issue of stocks, bonds and other forms of indebtedness.[1] However, the disclosure requirements of these public service commissions do not appear to have shaped financial reporting. The commissions' activities are notable because they represented the first incursion of government rule-making into the conduct of corporate business and because they established a process of "merit regulation" aimed at preventing the issue of "unworthy" securities. This form of regulation was to be used for a time as the main method of government supervision of the securities market.

Blue sky laws

State regulation of corporate activities was initially limited

---

1.   A. U. Ayres, "Governmental regulation of securities issues", Political science quarterly, 1913, p.587.

to the specification of rules governing the incorporation of enterprises within state boundaries. The statutes were little more than
enabling legislation; they permitted incorporation under certain
conditions but did not effectively regulate the quantity or quality
of information flowing to the marketplace. Some states (such as New
York) introduced requirements for the filing of financial reports -
but these were aimed at establishing a basis for taxing corporate
franchises rather than at ensuring that investors were informed about
the position and prospects of corporations. The content and scope of
financial reporting wereleft to the conscience of directors. And, far
from condemning the absence of regulation, some commentators regarded
disclosure rules as an unwarranted interference in the affairs of
businessmen. For example, one writer saw the filing rules of some
states as "a decided disadvantage of the corporate form" - claiming that
"the inconvenience and expense of compiling the report is not nearly so
serious as the concomitant disadvantage of disclosing the business
affairs of the enterprise".[2]

A stock market collapse in 1907 which nearly led to the paralysis
of the U.S. banking system seems to have contributed to changed
attitudes towards the propriety of government regulation. But the
first major steps in the introduction of controls over securities
issues did not take place until 1911, when the state of Kansas enacted
legislation aimed at curbing the activities of fraudulent promoters.
Apparently a local politician described Kansas securities salesmen as
being willing to sell building lots in the blue sky. The phrase stuck,
and the regulations became known as "blue sky laws". The approach
adopted by some of the public service commissions with respect to
utilities issues was applied in Kansas on a broader scale. The state's

---

2. G. W. Gerstenberg, "Special phases of corporation law", The journal
    of accountancy, Oct. 1909, p.446.

Bank Commissioner was empowered to review all proposals for the sale of securities and to issue permits to those proposed issues which (in his view) should be allowed to proceed. The first Commissioner to perform these functions was J. N. Dolley, a retired grocer, who claimed in his first annual report that the new laws had saved residents of Kansas at least six million dollars.[3] Evidently the accuracy of these figures was questionable; however the "paternalistic concept" of the new laws took hold.

> ... government officials in practically all of the
> states requested copies of the Kansas law. In 1912
> the legislatures of two other states enacted similar
> statutes. In the following year, twenty additional
> states, primarily Southern or Western, enacted laws
> which, for the most part, were either identical to or
> based on the Kansas statute.[4]

The constitutionality of various blue sky laws was challenged, and these attacks were generally successful on the ground that the laws imposed a burden on interstate commerce and as such were contrary to the 14th amendment to the U.S. constitution. However three cases were the subject of appeal to the U.S. supreme court; all were argued in 1916 and decided in January 1917.

> To the general surprise the Supreme Court confirmed
> the constitutionality of the Blue Sky legislation in
> all of the cases.[5]

By 1919, there were thirty-nine states with blue sky legislation, though it was later said that these first attempts at regulation "were

---

3. J. S. Mofsky, Blue sky restrictions on new business promotions (New York: Matthew Bender, 1971), pp.6-7.

4. Ibid, p.7.

5. E. S. Mead, Corporation finance (New York: D. Appleton and Co., 5th ed., 1924), p.144. The cases involved the Ohio, South Dakota and Michigan statutes; 242 US., 539, 559 and 568. "It was decided that the issuance of securities, the business of dealing in securities and the general flotation or sale of a particular issue or block of securities may be made subjects of executive license and control". R. R. Reed, "Blue sky laws" in Encyclopaedia of the social sciences (New York: The Macmillan Company, 1930), Vol.II, p.603.

hopelessly crude and unworkable".[6] As for the influence of these rules on corporate reporting, it should be noted that they were predominately aimed at correcting abuses arising in promotional situations, and did not necessarily encompass corporate reporting on an ongoing basis. The "enabling" legislation of various states could however require the filing of documents including financial reports. One writer observed in 1914 that "most states require all corporations to submit periodical and detailed reports to boards or officials".

> This causes considerable trouble and expense, but, as necessitating system in keeping corporate books and records, it is sometimes worth all the labor it entails.[7]

The 1919 Illinois blue sky legislation was seen by commentators as constituting a considerable refinement in the pattern of regulation insofar as it was aimed at issuers rather than at dealers in securities.[8] The necessity for obtaining permits or licences in various states before proceeding with the marketing of securities had been seen as an expensive impediment to the mobilization of capital; the Illinois legislation introduced exemptions with respect to a variety of securities, notably those dealt in on the New York, Boston, Baltimore, Philadelphia, Pittsburgh or Detroit stock exchanges.[9] The Illinois laws were soon copied in other states,[10] with the effect that responsibility for regulating the dissemination of financial information was left to the stock exchanges.

With its emphasis on the licensing of issuers rather than dealers

6. Reed, op.cit., p.603.

7. W. H. Lough, Business finance (New York: Ronald Press Company, 1917), pp.57-8.

8. J. W. Angell, "The Illinois blue sky law", Journal of political economy, 1920, p.30; H. G. Moulton, The financial organization of society (Chicago: University of Chicago Press, 2nd ed. 1925), p.191.

9. Angell, op.cit., p.308.

10. Mofsky, op.cit., p.12.

in securities, the 1919 Illinois legislation included requirements for
the submission of information to the Secretary of State. The requirements
differed according to the status of the issuer. The issue of securities
"based on an established income" necessitated the filing of

> a balance sheet of assets and liabilities, and income
> or profit-and-loss statement, and an analysis of the
> surplus account.

Issues of unseasoned stocks necessitated the submission of more detailed
reports, including "an inventory showing the assets of the issuer", and
"an appraisement" of these assets.[11]

The 1919 legislation may have been innovatory in focussing on the
status of issuers and in its approach to the licensing of proposed
issues. But it is apparent that blue sky legislation of this form
had little significance to corporate disclosure. Ashby reported in
1926 that there were then 3 states whose blue sky legislation consisted
only of "fraud laws", while a total of 42 states had enacted regulations which established a method of supervision of "dealers, agents
and of issues of securities prior to any selling or issuing". Ashby
described the basic elements of the regulatory statutes in force in
the mid-1920's as follows:

> ... a clause which may be thus expressed: 'No sale
> of a security shall be effected in this state without
> permission of the securities commission' ...
>
> Second, ... a list of securities and transactions to
> which the act shall not apply, such as government bonds
> and issues of regulated public utilities, or sales by
> or to banks ...
>
> Third, regulatory laws usually provide that dealers in
> securities must secure an annual licence ...
> An issuer, selling its own issue only, does not
> obtain an annual licence, but rather a specific permit
> to market the single issue.
>
> The fourth characteristic ... is the requirement that
> non-exempt issues must be individually accepted by
> the state before sales may take place. To obtain such
> approval the person qualifying the security must

11. Angell, op.cit., pp.309-10.

> furnish comprehensive information concerning the
> issuing company, its character, type of business,
> powers, properties, and financial structure ...
>
> Appraisal, investigations and audits may be made
> (at the expense of the applicant) if the commission
> so desires.[12]

The Illinois precedent had been followed and developed so that

by 1926 the state regulators could require the submission of quite

detailed financial information as a pre-condition of licensing.

But only three states (Illinois, Wisconsin and Michigan) maintained

supervision of new companies past the period of promotion, with require-

ments for the submission of periodic "financial and operating statements"

- but this (Ashby suggests) was aimed at compelling "the observance

of conservative business principles by inexperienced promoters"

rather than at preventing fraud or ensuring corporate accountability.[13]

Federal regulation

The stock market collapse of 1929 created a political climate in

which there were demands for governmental control of business and

the securities markets. The outcome of initiatives in these areas

was the passage of the Securities Acts of 1933 and 1934 legislation

which established federal government controls over corporate reporting.

These moves in the early 1930's were by no means the first occasion

on which federal regulation in these areas had been mooted. In the

aftermath of the 1907 stock market and banking "panic" there was some

discussion of the possibilities of federal action, though it appears

to have been generally assumed that the likely form of regulation

would take the form of federal enabling legislation or a federal

---

12. F. B. Ashby, The economic effect of blue sky laws, (Philadelphia:
     University of Pennsylvania, 1926), pp.9-11.

13. Ibid, p.17. The Michigan blue sky laws even empowered the state
     commission to require "investors' companies" to allow it to
     "countersign their checks in order to prevent dissipation of the
     companies' money in unbusinesslike projects". Idem.

form of "merit" regulation - as opposed to "disclosure" laws of the
style which were to develop in later years. Around 1910 there was
further talk of statutes requiring federal incorporation.[14] J. E.
Sterrett (then president of the American Association of Public
Accountants) acknowledged that state laws were "chaotic" but nevertheless was scathingly critical of proposals for the establishment of
an "army" of federal government examiners.[15] However, it seems
that American accountants were not strongly opposed to government
regulation of financial disclosure. Indeed, whereas British accountants
at this time were actively supporting claims for business privacy, many
leading American accountants argued for increased corporate publicity.[16]
This was not to say that U.S. accounting was regarded as being of high
quality. In 1912 one author described a series of "abuses" evident in
accounting data published in connection with stock issues; the
principal remedies suggested were that the accounting profession should
develop uniform procedures, agree on a standard audit certificate,
and endeavour to police promoters' references to audit reports.[17]
Moreover, it was said that there was a need for federal regulation
to prevent abuses in the sale of securities through the mails.[18]

---

14. A bill to this effect was introduced into Congress (H.R. 20, 142);
    see "Washington notes", Journal of political economy, 1910, p.221-2.

15. J. E. Sterrett, "Legislation for the control of corporations", The
    journal of accountancy, Feb. 1910.

16. See, e.g., E. W. Sells, "Publicity of financial affairs of corpora-
    tions", (an address dated August 1911) reproduced in the author's
    The natural business year and thirteen other themes (Chicago:
    A. W. Shaw Company, 1924), pp.129-42; R. H. Montgomery, "Federal
    control of corporations", The journal of accountancy, Oct. 1912,
    pp.272-4.

17. A. Smith, "The abuse of the audit in selling securities" The journal
    of accountancy, Oct. 1912, pp.245-8.

18. Power already existed for such regulation by virtue of section 215,
    Ch.VIII of the Criminal Code of the United States, 1909. For a dis-
    cussion of pre-SEC federal regulation of mail frauds in the sale of
    corporate securities see Mead, op.cit., pp.144-6, Ashby, op.cit.,
    pp.50-3 and C. B. Frasca, Stock swindlers and their methods (New
    York: privately printed, 1931), pp.64-5.

In 1911 a Commission was appointed to investigate and report on
the subject of federal regulation of the issue of securities by interstate railway companies, and there was some speculation that this
commission might make its investigations more general as a precursor to
the introduction of federal legislation. In 1912 the possibility of
the extension of federal controls over corporations became a political
issue following a revival of concern about business combinations and
monopolistic practices. As it happened, proposals for federal
incorporation "turned out to be politically impracticable on the one
hand and economically inexpedient on the other".[19] However the federal
government did introduce or extend its controls over banks and railroads,
and the Clayton Antitrust Act of 1914 led to the creation of the Federal
Trade Commission (FTC). The FTC's powers were sufficiently wide to
enable it to compel firms to make far more financial disclosures than
were required under state corporation laws or by the stock exchanges.
But the FTC was inactive in this area.[20]

Bills brought before Congress in 1919 and 1922 sought to impose
federal controls over the activities of corporations and promoters.
The 1919 bill aimed at extending corporate disclosure and making
corporate officers liable for losses suffered by virtue of material
misrepresentation in the securities offered; the bill was referred to
committee and there it died.[21] The 1922 bill aimed at regulating the
sale of securities by proposing the imposition of penalties on those
who used the mails or interstate agencies to circumvent the state blue
sky laws. This bill passed the House but was finally rejected by a

19. W. H. Lawton,, "Government regulation of securities", The journal
     of accountancy, Sept. 1911, p.357.

20. See W. Z. Ripley, Main street and Wall street (Boston: Little,
     Brown, and Company, 1929), pp.222-3 for a discussion of the FTC's
     record.

21. H. R. 188. See R. F. de Bedts, The New Deal's SEC (New York:
     Columbia University Press, 1964) p.5. A second bill was intro-
     duced in 1919; this too was not proceeded with. Ibid, pp.5-6.

Senate committee.[22] However in 1920 Congress passed the Transporta-
tion Act, which empowered the Interstate Commerce Commission to regulate
stock issues by railroads - a move which appears to have been aimed
at regulating monopolistic arrangements rather than at protecting
investors (though the legislation seems to have been modelled on
earlier state "merit regulations").

By the 1920's neither the state nor federal governments had become
involved in the regulation of corporate financial reporting. There
were some exceptions arising from the establishment of state and
federal commissions and the conduct of various forms of merit regulation.
But there were no rules requiring corporations to publish reports nor
were there statutory rules or guidelines spelling out the form and
content of any financial reports that might be issued. Nor were there
any rules prescribing that financial reports be audited - rules which
would have formally transferred authority for the regulation of financial
reporting to the accounting profession. Even so, it seems doubtful
whether such a rule would have been effective. By 1926 over ninety per
cent of all the industrial companies listed on the NYSE were audited[23]
- and this does not appear to have produced a high standard of financial
reporting. G. O. May has claimed that the information being given
by the great majority of listed companies during the early 1920's was
"reasonably satisfactory" - "certainly it was so if judged on the basis
of a comparison with the highest standards observed in other parts

---

22. Idem.

23. G. O. May, "Corporate publicity and the auditor" reprinted in
    Twenty-five years of accounting responsibility (New York:
    Price, Waterhouse & Co., 1936, reprinted by Scholars Book Co.,
    1971), Vol.I, p.54. In 1932 the NYSE required listed firms to
    be audited; meantime, of course, only a small proportion
    of U.S. corporations were listed on the NYSE.

of the world".[24] On the other hand, W. Z. Ripley's essays in the
Atlantic monthly and Main street and Wall street suggest that
financial reporting was characterised by misrepresentation and that
business affairs were conducted for the benefit of manipulators at the
expense of the small investor. Neither May nor Ripley were unbiased
observers. But certainly available evidence indicates that there
were some serious cases of misrepresentations during the 1920's,
notably in promotional situations and among corporations engaged in
electricity generation and transmission.

In short, financial reporting was virtually unregulated in the 1920's.
This situation may be contrasted with the position in the U.K., where
since 1907 the companies acts had required firms to file statements
"in the form of a balance sheet" with the Registrar of Companies,
and had required firms to have their financial statements audited.
With all their imperfections and loopholes, the British companies acts
established a system of regulation of financial disclosure.

It seems reasonable to suppose that this lack of regulation in the
U.S.A. encouraged experimentation in reporting. Whereas U.K. firms were
obliged to prepare a "legal" balance sheet, and seldom considered
expanding or supplementing these reports, U.S. corporations were free
to adopt whatever style of reporting was chosen by management. Consolidated statements were first prepared as the result of managers'
preferences. The introduction and popularisation of consolidated
reporting took place in the absence of disclosure rules.

However, the absence of any form of controls over American securities
markets was highlighted in the aftermath of the stock market collapse
of October 1929. The scale of this collapse was unprecedented. It
has been estimated that in the ten years before 1933, total investor

---

24. G. O. May, Financial accounting (New York: The Macmillan Company,
     1961), p.55ff.

losses through worthless securities were approximately $25 billion, "half of those issued".[25] But the immediate public reaction to the stock market collapse was not one of recrimination against fraudulent stock issues or even against stock market manipulations; de Bedts records that "public reaction in the light of the morning after tended to lump together indiscriminately bankers, promoters, and the professional market operator under the disrepute of the label 'speculator'".

Under the threat of federal government intervention the New York Stock Exchange took steps to monitor short selling while in September 1932 the Committee on Stock List pursued discussions with representatives of the American Institute of Accountants concerning the possibility of introducing standards for corporate reporting. But these activities did not forestall government intervention, and in March 1932 a senate sub-committee was set up to investigate the "buying and selling, and borrowing and lending of listed securities", and the effect of stock exchange practices on the value of securities. This committee soon uncovered evidence of market manipulations; moreover the committee's hearings coincided with further news of the collapse of the Insull utility corporations and the bankruptcy of the Kreuger and Toll group.

Proposals for the reform of securities markets became a campaign issue in the 1933 Hoover-Roosevelt presidential election. At first, no questions were raised concerning the quality of financial reporting. The Democratic party's 1932 platform included a clause advocating "protection of the investing public" by the disclosure of "true informa-tion as to bonuses, commissions, principal invested, and the interests of the sellers". The policy statement also alluded to the need for "regulation to the full extent of federal power" of holding companies,

---

25. de Bedts, op.cit. p.11.

26. Ibid, p.12.

the rates of utility companies, and exchanges in securities and commodities.[27] Nothing was said about balance sheets or income statements. Nor were any abuses or proposed remedies specified. It appears that it was only during the heat of the campaign that the idea of federal regulation of financial reporting was aired. R. de Bedts has reported that in August 1922 Roosevelt outlined the following concrete proposals:

> first, 'truth telling' concerning the stock to be issued,
> and pertinent facts concerning the issuing corporation
> itself; second, Federal regulation of holding companies
> that sell securities in interstate commerce; and third,
> the use of Federal authority in the regulation of stock
> and commodities exchanges.[28]

On March 29, 1933 President Roosevelt sent a message to Congress recommending legislation "for Federal supervision of traffic in investment securities in interstate commerce".

> There is ... an obligation upon us to insist that every
> issue of new securities to be sold in interstate commerce
> shall be accompanied by full publicity and information,
> and that no essentially important element attending the
> issue shall be concealed from the buying public.[29]

The response to this request was the Securities Act of 1933, which had a rapid and fairly uncontroversial legislative passage, and was finally signed into law on May 27, 1933. This act provided for a scheme of registration of security issues, administered by the Federal Trade Commission. The Securities Act was only concerned with new issues. Securities could only be issued if they were duly registered; one of the conditions of registration was the filing with the FTC of a "registration statement" and the contents of this were to be made available to the public. To be included in the registration statement

27. Ibid, p.25.

28. Ibid, pp.26-7.

29. As cited in B. Schwartz (ed.), The economic regulation of business
     and industry - a legislative history of U.S. regulatory agencies
     (New York: Chelsea House Publishers, 1973), Vol.IV.

were balance sheets and income statements "in such detail and such
form as the Commission shall prescribe".[30]

Another objective of the Roosevelt administration was to regulate
trading in previously-issued securities - particularly the activities
of "speculators". Roosevelt wrote to Congress in February 1934 that "it
should be our national policy to restrict, as far as possible, the use
of [securities and commodities] exchanges for purely speculative operations".[31] After a period of intense lobbying there emerged the Securities
and Exchange Act of June 1934. This act provided for the establishment
of the Securities and Exchange Commission to assume responsibility for the
administration of both the 1933 and the 1934 legislation.[32] The main
features of the 1934 Act were requirements for the registration of stock
exchanges and of the securities listed on each such exchange. Restrictions were placed on the trading in shares by directors, officers and
principal security holders, and controls were introduced with the aim
of preventing the unfair use of inside information. The registration
of brokers and dealers was required, and provisions were designed to
prevent fraudulent, deceptive and manipulative acts during the course
of trading on stock exchanges or in the over-the-counter market. The
Federal Reserve Board was empowered to establish margin requirements
so as to regulate the use of credit in securities transactions. Regulations were also imposed on the solicitation of proxies.

For the accounting profession, the most significant features of
the 1934 Act were those provisions subjecting listed corporations to
requirements dealing with the form and content of their financial reports.

---

30. Securities Act of 1933, Schedule A, paras. 25-6.

31. As cited Schwartz, op.cit., pp.2712-3.

32. Later the SEC was to administer other statutes - notably the Public
    Utility Holding Company Act of 1935, and the Investment Company Act
    and the Investment Advisers Act of 1940.

Section 12 of the act provided that, as a condition of registration of securities, issuers had to file such information as might
be required in terms of (later promulgated) rules and regulations;
issuers of registered securities were also obliged to subsequently
lodge (inter alia) interim and annual reports. The act thus extended
the ambit of SEC regulation beyond firms which were making new issues
to all firms whose stocks were traded on stock exchanges.

Both of the securities acts established the authority of the
regulatory agency to prescribe the form and content of financial reports
- including the methods to be followed in preparing those reports.
Section 19 (a) of the 1933 act stated:

> ... the Commission shall have authority ... to prescribe
> the form or forms in which required information shall be
> set forth, the items or details to be shown in the
> earning statement, and the method to be followed in the
> preparation of accounts, in the appraisal or valuation of
> assets and liabilities, in the determination of deprecia-
> tion or depletion, in the differentiation of recurring
> and nonrecurring income, in the differentiation of invest-
> ment and operating income, and in the preparation, where
> the Commission deems it necessary or desirable, of con-
> solidated balance sheets or income accounts ...

Similar provisions were contained in Section 13A of the Securities and
Exchange Act and section 14 of the Public Utility Holding Act of 1935.

The SEC's authority over the accounting profession was further
affirmed with the promulgation of regulations concerning rules of
practice before the Commission. Rule II effective July 1, 1938 stated
that

> The Commission may disqualify and deny, temporarily or
> permanently, the privilege of appearing or practicing
> before it in any way ...

As A. A. Berle Jr. later remarked, "the Securities Act of 1933 had
"subtended very nearly the whole arc of accounting" by legal rules. At
the same time the accountant had suddenly become "part of the mechanism
of government control".[33] The Securities Acts of 1933 and 1934

---

33. A. A. Berle, Jnr."Accounting and the law", The accounting review,
     March 1938, p.9.

established machinery which was to exert a dominant role in shaping accounting practice. The following chapter describes how the SEC used these powers and in particular how SEC practices and rulings have moulded the use of consolidated statements.

Ch. 13   Early SEC influences on the use of consolidated statements

The securities acts made explicit reference to the use of consolidated reports. Section 19 of the 1933 Act empowered the SEC to prescribe
the forms in which information was to be set forth and the accounting
methods to be used, including the methods to be followed in "the
preparation, where the Commission deems it necessary, of consolidated
balance sheets or income accounts". As if to remove any ambiguity,
Section 13 (a) of the 1934 Act varied the form of words to specify that
the SEC could prescribe the form and content of "separate and/or
consolidated balance sheets or income accounts of any person directly or
indirectly controlling or controlled by the issuer".[1]

As outlined in Ch. 11, by the mid 1930's neither the accounting
profession, nor the regulatory agencies had developed a clear-cut
rationale for the use of consolidated statements. And text-book
discussions of consolidated reporting contained inconsistent assertions
about what consolidated statements were intended to represent. However,
during the early years of the SEC's operations accounting writers
began assessing the theory underlying these reports.

The accounting profession's representations to the SEC

The newly-established SEC faced formidable tasks. One was the
designing of forms for registration under the Securities and Exchange
Act of 1934. The FTC's administration of the 1933 Act had been strongly
criticised,[2] mainly because of the complexity of its registration

---

1.   Note that the act defined "person" to encompass "an individual,
     a corporation, a partnership, an association, a joint-stock company,
     a business trust, or an unincorporated organization".

2.   Form A-1, promulgated by the Federal Trade Commission on July 6,
     1933 "was criticised by the profession as being inelastic and
     obviously designed primarily for public-utility companies, and,
     therefore, not suitable for industrial concerns". A. Stewart,
     "Accountancy and regulatory bodies in the United States", Fiftieth
     anniversary celebrations (New York: American Institute of Account-
     ants, 1937), p.137.

requirements. Indeed, large corporations in need of equity capital
consciously avoided the FTC's filing requirements by making private
placements.[3]

Accordingly, the SEC endeavoured to introduce less onerous
disclosure rules. The Commission consulted corporation executives,
and representatives of the legal and accounting professions and the
stock exchanges,[4] and retained the services of three consultants - a
security analyst from a leading banking house, a contributor to "one of
the leading investment services", and a "member of the faculty of the
Harvard Business School".[5] The SEC also asked the two national
accounting bodies (The American Institute of Accountants and the American
Society of Public Accountants) to form a joint committee to liase with
the Commission.

Officially-sponsored histories have placed considerable emphasis
on the contribution made by the American Institute of Accountants in
assisting the SEC to formulate appropriate rules for disclosure and to
design forms and registration procedures.[6] However the Commission's
files provide a somewhat different perspective. It appears that the
committee's report recommended that the SEC abandon the FTC approach

3. M. V. Freeman, "A private practitioner's view of the development of
    the Securities and Exchange Commission", The George Washington law
    review, Oct. 1959, p.18.

4. Stewart, op.cit., pp.136-7; G. G. Mathews, "Address before the
    Illinois Society of Certified Public Accountants, Jan 18, 1935"
    (Washington D.C.: Securities and Exchange Commission,mimeo), p.2;
    R. E. Healy, "Address before the Controllers Institute of America,
    Jan.31 1934" The controller, Feb. 1935, pp.28-9.

5. Mathews, op.cit., p.2. The three were Jerry Dunn, Donald McCruden
    of Moodys, and Prof. T. H. Sanders. See R. E. Healy, "The next
    step in accounting", The accounting review, March 1938, p.2.

6. Stewart, op.cit., p.137; J. L. Carey, The rise of the accounting
    profession (New York: American Institute of Certified Public
    Accountants, Vol.I, 1969), pp.194-5.

of requiring the use of standard forms for disclosure, and leaving management and independent accountants to decide what form of statement and what amount of detail would fairly represent the financial condition and operating results of a corporation.[7]

This submission was flatly rejected: the SEC continued the FTC's policy of prescribing the form of financial statements to be lodged with the Commission. However the SEC did relax the FTC's rules to a significant extent. The FTC's highly detailed Form A-1 was retained (with some modifications) for use by unseasoned corporations making issues to initiate new ventures. But the SEC promulgated a new Form A-2 for use by "seasoned corporations with a record of operations",[8] and a newly-devised Form 10 to be used by firms registering under the 1934 act. Both these forms allowed some latitude in the submission of financial statements. The instructions accompanying Form A-2 and Form 10 provided that "the statements and schedules are to be made in such form, in such order and using such generally accepted terminology as will best indicate their significance and character in the light of the instructions".

While the accounting profession's joint committee was opposed to the standardisation of the format of financial reporting, it did urge that the SEC should require balance sheets to disclose or provide:

1. The bases on which the principal assets ... are stated.

2. a reasonable classification and adequate description of the substantial items on the balance sheet, so as to display significant

---

7. A copy of this report dated Aug. 3, 1934 is filed in the public reference library, Securities and Exchange Commission, Washington D.C. Members of the committee were: S. J. Broad, J. F. Hughes, J. J. Klein, P. K. Knight, P. N. Miller, R. F. Starkey, A. Stewart, H. N. Sweet and C. O. Wellington (chairman).

8. Securities and Exchange Commission, First annual report (Washington D.C. 1935), p.26.

facts.[9]

These proposals seem to have been heeded - though not to the extent

of requiring firms to provide complete statements of the accounting

methods used to prepare their financial statements. Commissioners

Mathews and Healy, and SEC consultant T. H. Sanders all made public

addresses in which they took pains to emphasise the flexibility afforded

registrants in the filing of material with the Commission. At the

same time, it was emphasised that the SEC would not condone "any kind

of accounting" even though there might be full disclosure of the

methods employed. Sanders summarised the position as follows:

> The general preferences of the Commission are unmistakable
> and the alternatives allowed are not designed to furnish
> excuses for any subterfuge in accounting practice that
> registering companies might see fit to present.[10]

The joint committee's submission also outlined matters which might

be made required disclosures. The committee recommended that the

following statements should be filed with the Commission:

> (a) a balance sheet in comparative form;
> (b) an income statement in comparative form;
> (c) a surplus statement;
> (d) a statement of changes in reserves;
> (e) a concise statement ... as to the major accounting
>   principles and practices followed during the period
>   under review and changes in such principles and
>   practices since the preceding year;
> (f) similar statements for subsidiaries or consolidated
>   statements, whichever will more clearly set forth
>   essential facts.

This appears to have been the first attempt by the accounting profession

---

9. Idem, These recommendations echoed the propositions enunciated the
    preceding year by the American Institute's Special Committee on
    Co-operation with Stock Exchanges in correspondence with the New
    York Stock Exchange. This committee (under the chairmanship of
    G. O. May) had recommended that listed corporations should "cause
    a statement of the methods of accounting and reporting employed
    by it" to be prepared and made available to stockholders. The
    submission to the SEC urging disclosure of the bases of account-
    ing adopted by firms seems to have flowed from this proposal.

10. T. H. Sanders, "The influence of the Securities and Exchange Com-
    mission upon accounting principles", The accounting review, March
    1936, p.69. See also T. H. Sanders "Accounting aspects of the
    Securities Act", Law and contemporary problems, 1937, pp.196-7.

to come up with rules about the use of consolidated reports.[11] And
it will be noted that (contrary to established practice) the committee
regarded consolidated statements as being designed to supplement
holding company statements. Whereas consolidated statements were
presented (in practice) as the primary reports of holding companies,
the committee regarded them merely as an alternative to the supplementary
presentation of the subsidiaries' reports.

SEC rulings on consolidated statements

In line with the 1934 guidelines that prospective registrants could
complete their submissions by presenting statements and schedules "in
such form, in such order and using generally accepted terminology as
will best indicate their significance and character" it would seem that
in its early years the SEC avoided making hard and fast rulings about
the use and content of consolidated reports. Holding companies were
allowed considerable latitude in determining the scope of any consolidated statements that they might prepare, provided that the statements
of unconsolidated subsidiaries were also filed.   And it appears that
some firms were permitted to lodge the separate statements of their
subsidiaries, omitting a consolidated statement altogether.[12]

However while the SEC did not make formal rulings on these matters
it must be recognised that the SEC staff wielded considerable power in
relation to their review of documents filed with the Commission.

The authority of the SEC was primarily that of a licensing power.
Registration of securities under both the 1933 and the 1934 acts would

---

11. However two years earlier the American Institute's Special
     Committee on Co-operation with Stock Exchanges had suggested that
     one of the "broad principles of accounting" was that pre-acquisition
     profits of subsidiaries were not to be regarded as part of
     "consolidated earned surplus" nor part of the distributable profit
     of parent companies.   .

12. See references to pre-1934 SEC filings in S. Fabricant, "Revalua-
     tions of fixed assets, 1925-1934", National Bureau of Economics
     Research Bulletin No.62 (New York, Dec. 1936), pp.1-2.

come into effect automatically twenty days after an application had been formally filed; however if it appeared to the Commission that the registration statements included "any untrue statement of a material fact" or omitted to state any material fact required to be stated "in order to make the statements therein not misleading", the Commission could proceed by issuing a "stop order", thus preventing registration from taking effect.

In practice, applications for registration were reviewed by SEC staff who identified "deficiencies" and issued letters specifying the matters which (in their opinion) required rectification before the registration statements constituted full and adequate disclosure.[13] If an applicant received a deficiency letter, he could choose to comply, or else abandon his application, or (failing informal appeals to SEC staff) submit to the unfavourable publicity attendant upon stop-order proceedings. In practice, few applicants chose the latter course. As A. A. Berle put it, "only ... a merely irresponsible swindler" would or could afford to "try out an issue of accounting in the form of a hearing to determine whether or not he is about to commit a fraud".[14] So the determination of what was, or what was not the appropriate way to report on the position or performance of a firm was conducted as an administrative process by SEC examiners.[15]

It seems possible that in those early years of the SEC's existence the Commission's staff passed judgment on whether firms should present consolidated statements or the separate statements of subsidiaries. The

---

13. For a more detailed statement of these procedures, see C. A. Smith, "Accounting practice under the Securities and Exchange Commission", The accounting review 1935, p.326.

14. A. A. Berle, Jr., "Accounting and the law", The accounting review, March 1938, p.12.

15. "The result, naturally, is that most questions of accounting are settled by the star-chamber process, and chiefly by sub-examiners". Idem.

staff may have formulated fairly clear-cut policies on the matter.
Judging from the lack of reports about firms not presenting consolidated
statements, it seems likely that the SEC staff would have required the
presentation of consolidated statements in certain situations.[16]

The significance of SEC decision-making at an administrative level
was recognised by the editor of The accounting review, Eric Kohler, who
arranged for the SEC to provide reports on some case studies arising
from registration applications. Altogether 21 cases were reported (with
Kohler's commentaries) in The accounting review before the SEC introduced
"Accounting releases" in January 1937. Neither these cases, nor the
early releases, indicated that any applicant took issue with the need to
present consolidated reports.

One is left with the fact that consolidated statements (in some
form or other) were indeed prepared and filed by registrants, and one
can suppose that the SEC was instrumental in extending the use of
consolidated reports. The majority of corporations listed on the New
York Stock Exchange were apparently publishing consolidated statements
prior to the passage of the securities acts. However the reporting
requirements of the 1934 Securities Exchange Act were aimed at all listed
companies, and this in itself would have extended the ambit of regulation considerably wider than NYSE-listed firms. Moreover in 1936 the
Acts reporting requirements were applied to the larger unlisted

---

16. Staub reported that at first the Federal Trade Commission had rules
    that all subsidiary companies owned to the extent of 51 per cent,
    or more should be included, but it had been recognised in subsequent
    discussion that that was not a desirable compulsory requirement,
    and at the last discussion the matter stood that subsidiary
    companies owned to the extent of 75 per cent, should be normally
    included. Those between 50 per cent, and 75 per cent, should be
    included or omitted according as to to whether disclosure would
    be informative or the reverse. W. A. Staub (comments on Sir
    Albert Wyon's paper at the 4th International Congress of Accountants
    1933) The accountant, 5 Aug. 1933, p.233.

companies.[17] In any case the 1933 act gave the SEC the authority to require consolidated reports of all those corporations under its jurisdiction which sought to make new issues.

Not only did the SEC encourage or require the use of consolidated statements, but its rules and regulations appear to have reinforced or directed (or even acted as substitutes for) the profession's thinking on the role and status of these reports.

The accounting releases were to inform registrants about Commission decisions. In practice, the releases established rules which were rigorously followed.

The first release concerned with consolidated reports was No.3 published in September 1937. Outwardly it was fairly innocuous. It concerned the techniques of preparing consolidated statements. A registrant had not followed the customary procedure of eliminating the "cost" of its investment in its subsidiaries, and had only eliminated the par or stated value of those stocks. The release simply "pointed out the fallacy of retaining any of a subsidiary's surplus at date of acquisition in the consolidated surplus" rather than eliminating the total equity attributable to the parent at that date.[18] But in the process of requiring the total elimination of pre-acquisition profits, the SEC described the purpose of consolidated statements as being

---

17. By an amendment to the 1933 act so that each registration statement under that statute was to contain an undertaking by the issuer to file the same supplementary and periodic reports as would be required if the offered securities were listed; this undertaking was only to come into effect when the "aggregate offering price" of securities issued by the registrant exceeded $2 million. By 1946 "only about 470 companies" were required to report in terms of this provision; by 1958 the number reached 1151, "about one-third of the active domestic issuers of over-the-counter stocks (excluding registered investment companies) having more than 300 shareholders". P. A. Loomis, Jr., "The Securities Exchange Act of 1934 ..." in The George Washington law review, Oct. 1959, pp.226-7.

18. W. H. Childs, Consolidated financial statements (Cornell University Press, 1949), p.256.

> to reflect the financial condition of a parent company
> and its subsidiaries as if they were a single
> organization.

Now the procedures consistent with showing the affairs of a "single
organization" differ in some respects from the procedures which are
consistent with other propositions about the aims of consolidated statements. (This point is discussed in more detail in Section IV below).
Before this SEC pronouncement, the suggestion that consolidated statements were concerned with showing a "single organization" was usually
advanced to explain the procedures followed in preparing these documents.
But Accounting Release No.3 gave authoritative support to this proposition
as a statement of the aims of consolidated reporting. Thereafter, less
stress was placed on viewing consolidated statements as amplifications of
the reports of holding companies. Ironically, the point at issue in
Release No.3 had nothing to do with one or other of these viewpoints.
Moreover, the SEC ruling might even be seen to conflict with the supposed
objective of showing the affairs of a "single organization" insofar as
the release did not lead to the balance-sheet segregation of the total
distributable surplus of the constituent firms.[19]

Later SEC decisions or relaeses seemed to conflict with the firm
statement of objectives contained in Release No.3.

The substance of one early SEC "informal" decision was described
by T. H. Sanders (formerly a consultant to the SEC). A registrant's
consolidated reports had not been accepted for filing on the ground that
the inclusion of a 60%-owned subsidiary led to the portrayal of "a net
quick asset position better than that of the issuing corporation".[20]

---

19. It seems that underlying the SEC ruling was a belief that the non-
elimination of a subsidiary's surplus was a devious way of artifi-
cially inflating asset values. A preamble to the release stated
that it was concerned to "prevent write-ups arising in the consolidation of accounts by a parent company with those of its subsidiaries
through the elimination of only a portion of the investment account".

20. "Influences of the Securities and Exchange Commission upon accounting
principles", loc.cit., p.71.

Now the inclusion of 60%-owned subsidiaries in consolidated statements
was entirely consistent with attempts to report on a "single organization"
or "group". But evidently on this occasion the SEC regarded the practice
as misleading on the assumption that consolidated reports were intended
to represent the solvency of a corporation or corporations.

Another (unreported) 1937 SEC decision concerned the preparation
of consolidated statements which excluded several of a firm's subsidiaries.
The excluded subsidiaries conducted part of the firm's retailing operations. The parent company claimed that these retail outlets were
"insignificant" and that it was its practice to develop sales outlets
and then sell them to dealers. The SEC evidently considered that exclusion
of these subsidiaries from the consolidation was acceptable provided
that the procedure was adequately described. This decision could only
be regarded as being consistent with claims that consolidated reports
were concerned with the affairs of "a single organization" or "group"
if these terms were understood to relate to on-going enterprises.

And then Accounting Release No.7 (May 1938) indicated that the SEC
had changed its views about the supposed objects of consolidated reports.
Release No. 7 took the form of a list of "commonly cited deficiencies
in financial statements" and was published with the aim of avoiding
"inconvenience and expense to registrants" and reducing the work of the
Commission in reviewing filings. One clause reported that a common
deficiency was the presentation of consolidated profit and loss statements
on a different basis than the consolidated balance sheet. Evidently some
registrants had been lodging consolidated income statements which
encompassed the earnings of subsidiaries which had been excluded from
the registrants' consolidated balance sheets. The SEC called for
consistency of treatment between statements but did not attempt to show
how these practices were inconsistent with the supposed aims of consolidated reports. Nor did the Commission specify appropriate bases for

determining the scope of consolidated reports. The SEC thus condemned a practice without explaining why the practice was wrong.[21] But the condemned practices seem to have been entirely in line with previous SEC rulings on consolidations. Inclusion of all subsidiaries in the income report was consistent with showing the performance of a group of companies; exclusion of certain subsidiaries from a consolidated balance sheet was consistent with attempts to avoid distortions in representations of solvency.

SEC and public utility holding companies

The rating policies of public utilities were a preoccupation of F. D. Roosevelt before and after his election as U.S. president. The methods used by public service commissions and the I.C.C. to assess the validity of rate claims had encouraged massive "over-capitalization" of the utilities, particularly through the pyramiding operations of holding company structures. Correspondingly the rating practices of the utilities were widely viewed as leading to the exploitation of consumers. The public scandals associated with the failure of the Insull group of companies added further support to political initiatives which culminated in the passage of the Public Utility Holding Company Act in 1935. The most contested feature of this legislation concerned proposals to eliminate "unnecessary holding companies" so as to curb the concentration of economic power produced by pyramiding and other devices. In its final form this proposal was phrased as a requirement for the SEC to examine holding-company systems and to devise and if necessary implement a plan for the "simplification" of these corporate structures. Other elements of the legislation empowered the SEC to regulate securities issues, and to ensure that the financial reports of utilities

---

21. However Release No.7 did state that one of the commonly encountered deficiencies was the "failure to state, as required, the principle adopted in determining the inclusion and exclusion of subsidiaries in each consolidated balance sheet".

enabled investors to appraise the financial position or earning power
of the issuing corporations.

While the public utilities legislation was aimed at coping with
abuses within a specific industry it seems that the matters encountered
in this area influenced the SEC's approach to financial reporting and
the use of consolidated statements.

First, the activities of public utilities and railways had prompted
critical examinations of the use of the holding company device in the
American economy. In 1932 J. C. Bonbright and G. C. Means published
The holding company: its public significance and its regulation[22] in
which they documented the case for the introduction of "social controls"
over holding company systems. And later the Federal Trade Commission
completed a 6 year investigation of public utilities with the compilation of a massive, 90-volume report. In the political climate of the
time, there was considerable concern with the concentration of economic
power that arose from intercorporate shareholdings or contractual
arrangements. Economists and others were preoccupied with "controlling
relationships" at the same time that accounting writers were describing
consolidated statements as representing the affairs of holding companies
and subsidiaries "as if" they were a single organization. The 1930's
political concern with the conduct of "groups" of companies seems to
have added weight to the view of consolidated reports were intended to
depict the affairs of economic entities.   In turn this encouraged
writers and practitioners to specify the area of consolidation in terms
of the ambit of "controlling" relationships".[23]

---

22. New York: McGraw-Hill Book Co., Inc.

23. The Public Utilities Holding Company Act of 1935 defined "holding
     company" in terms of "controlling interests" (or alternatively
     ownership, control or voting power over 10% or more of the issued
     securities of another corporation); however the corresponding
     regulations only required the preparation of a form of consolidated
     statement in respect of majority-owned subsidiaries.

Second, the public utilities became notorious for manipulating
accounting reports through write-ups and inter-company transactions
at inflated prices. Robert E. Healy, one of the first commissioners
of the SEC, had been the FTC's chief counsel during the course of that
agency's investigations of public utilities. Healy later reported
to the Senate Committee on Banking and Currency that the investigation
had revealed over $1,150,000,000 in write-ups. Healy claimed that in
"many instances" these revaluations had been entirely arbitrary. Moreover, in some cases the figures had been "passed upon and approved by
a State commission" - indicating that existing regulations did not
prevent the manipulation of accounting reports. Healy attributed the
high incidence of write-ups to a U.S. Supreme Court decision which had
accepted the use of "reproduction costs" as one of the elements in
determining "present fair value" in rate cases.

One way of assessing the effect of inter-company transactions on
the reported income of members of a "group" would be to prepare
consolidated statements incorporating appropriate eliminations. It
might be supposed that the evidence of profit manipulations among public
utilities may have directed FTC or SEC attention to this apparent advantage
of consolidated reports. However, this does not seem to have been so,
probably because the cases examined by the FTC often had involved the
use of "dummy intermediaries".[24] So long as the intermediary was not a
subsidiary or affiliate, the transactions might have the appearance of
being at "arms length"; hence there was a possibility that inter-
company profits would not be eliminated. Perhaps in the light of this
experience, Healy's approach was not aimed at detecting and disclosing

---

24. In hearings before the Committee on Banking and Currency, United
    States Senate, 73rd Congress, Healy described one instance in which
    properties with a book value of $72,621,000 were sold to an inter-
    mediary and then to a newly-formed affiliate for a price which was
    inflated by $66,000,000. (April 1934, p.7594).

manipulations, but rather at preventing them entirely. He proposed a method of government supervision of public utility transactions and he argued for uniformity of the utilities' accounting methods. Eventually the Public Utility Holding Company legislation also provided for the "simplification" of holding company systems. But while Healy and others were very concerned to avoid the manipulation of profits through inter-company transactions, little attention was paid to the possibility of using consolidated statements to achieve this objective.

After the passage of the 1935 Act the SEC duly required the public utilities to publish consolidated statements - but in a special form. The utilities were to prepare consolidating statements. These were multi-column presentations showing the financial statements of individual subsidiaries and detailing the elimination of inter-company accounts. While it could be argued that the use of this form of presentation enabled creditors and others to form a clearer view of the affairs of a firm that would be obtainable from either a "group" statement on its own or a single-firm statement on its own, it seems that the SEC's requirements were simply aimed at highlighting the effect of inter-company transactions and to ensure that the utilities provided comprehensive, readily interpretable data.[25]

These requirements for consolidating statements were introduced in conjunction with a ban on the use of equity accounting by public utilities. During his appearances before the Senate Committee on Banking and Currency, Healy had complained about "the practice [of parent companies] taking onto their books the earnings of their subsidiaries, which the subsidiaries do not distribute in any form, as dividend or credit to the parent company or anything else".

> It may be proper to reflect earnings of subsidiaries
> in the consolidated statements, but I do not believe

---

25. Childs, op.cit., p.257.

> that it is proper to take those earnings without
> receiving them into a surplus account and then pay out
> cash dividends against them.[26]

These objections to "equity accounting" were based on Healy's view of

the impropriety of particular dividend policies rather than on claims

that equity accounting was deficient as a means of measuring assets.

Even so, Healy's proposals were adopted and the ban on equity accounting

was to remain in force until May 1975.[27]

Public utilities were also required to report plant at "cost ...

to the person first devoting it to public service". To these "original

costs" could be added "plant acquisition adjustments" (bringing the

figures to the level of cost to the present owner) and "plant adjustments"

(to reflect subsequent additions or betterments).[28] Consistent with

these rules for the identification of "original costs", consolidating

statements for public utilities were also required to disclose the

difference between the net cost of a parent's investments in subsidiaries

and the underlying book equity of those subsidiaries at the acquisition

date.[29]

In the long run, perhaps the most significant outcome of these

attempts to regulate the reporting practices of public utilities was

that Healy (who was later one of the first SEC commissioners) became

convinced that the writing-up of assets was an evil which should be

eradicated. The public utilities had been condemned for "arbitrary"

write-ups; later the SEC (under Healy's influence) was to ban all write-ups.

Attempts to develop a rationale for consolidated statements

During the 1930's the accounting profession attempted to re-appraise

---

26. Ibid, pp.7605-6. See also p.7612.

27. See SEC Accounting Series Release No.171.

28. Gilman noted that this public utility concept was "sometimes referred
    to as that of aboriginal cost", S. Gilman, Accounting concepts of
    profit (New York: Ronald Press Company, 1939), p.483.

29. "While such excess is to be accounted for in the notes to the state-
    ments of other types of statements, it may be merged in the assets or
    surplus on the face of the statement". Childs, op.cit., p.258.

its practices. The non-existence of federal or state regulations
dealing with corporate reporting and the failure of the profession to
develop self-regulation contributed to permissiveness in accounting
practice and enabled the publication of financial reports that were
later seen to have been grossly misleading. The American Institute of
Accountants had been active in the early 1930's in attempting to develop
rules of practice. It had set up committees to co-operate with stock
exchanges and investment bankers, to consider problems associated with
the valuation of inventories, and to develop "accounting principles".[30]
But by the time of the establishment of the SEC, the output of these
committees had been of little significance either in stating the underlying theory of accounting or in setting guidelines to practitioners.

In the belief that it had a role to play in the development of
accounting principles and in fostering accounting research, the American
Association of University Instructors in Accounting had changed its
name to the "American Accounting Association",[31] and in 1936 endeavoured
to make some contribution by publishing a five-page committee report
titled "Tentative statement of accounting principles affecting
corporate reports".[32]

A proposed follow-up to the 1936 AAA statement was a statement of
the rationale for consolidated reports. Chief responsibility for
writing this statement was left to E. L. Kohler, who presented a paper
at the AAA annual meeting in December 1937 titled "Some tentative

---

30. For an account of these initiatives and a description of their
    product see S. A. Zeff, Forging accounting principles in five
    countries (Champaign, Ill.: Stipes Publishing Co., 1972), pp.
    119-30.

31. Ibid, p.131.

32. The accounting review, June 1936, pp.187-91. It appears that this
    initiative was encouraged by the SEC's Commissioner, G. C. Mathews.
    See Zeff, op.cit., p.131. Moreover, C. G. Blough, the SEC's chief
    accountant, was a member of the advisory committee for this project.

propositions underlying consolidated reports". When published under
Kohler's name some months later,[33] it was said that the paper "represents
in the main the opinion of the [A.A.A. executive] committee and will
shortly be reissued, perhaps in altered form, as an official pronouncement of the Association". The paper was not reissued, perhaps because
of disagreements about some of the points raised in the draft. Nevertheless, the Kohler paper appears to have been of considerable significance
to the evolution of rules for the preparation of consolidated statements,
since it was the first extended attempt to come to grips with these
questions and also because of the SEC's obvious interest in the AAA's
"authoritative" statements on the theory of financial reporting.

Kohler listed ten propositions "each followed by interpretations and
applications" which were "designed as an approach to consolidated
statements". They can be seen as an extension of Finney's 1926 observations that consolidated statements were useful whether one viewed them
as amplifying a holding company's report or alternatively as reporting on
an "economic entity". But Kohler's approach was more complicated, for
he recognised that there were alternative ways of providing extra
information about a holding company's investments in subsidiaries
(such as by providing "group" statements dealing with some or all of the
subsidiaries, but excluding the holding company). At the same time
he endeavoured to accommodate and elaborate the idea that consolidated
statements dealt with a "consolidated group" of companies. The latter
view of the function of consolidated statements led Kohler to state
that these reports should deal with "controlled" companies, regardless
of the percentage of stock ownership, provided that their operations were
in some way related to those of the holding company and other companies
in the "group".

---

33. The accounting review, March 1938, pp.63-77.

It is difficult to escape the conclusion that Kohler's concern with "controlled" corporations was a product of the 1930's political criticisms of the economic significance of holding company systems. And yet Kohler insisted that consolidated statements (or other alternative representations of the affairs of subsidiaries) were "secondary rather than primary in character", and were intended to provide an "enlargement of the financial statements of a common controlling interest". Kohler did not explain how a report concerned with a "group" of companies defined in the manner indicated would constitute an "enlargement" of the financial statements of a holding company. At no stage did Kohler's report identify the specific factors which were represented by consolidated statements (or other forms of supplemental presentation). They were said to "reveal information", and "to assist in explaining ... relationships", but whether this information and these relationships concerned liquidity, or profitability, or some other factors was left unexplained. One cannot obtain enlightenment from Kohler's ten "propositions underlying consolidated reports". To illustrate, Kohler asserted that "the strongest case for consolidated statements" was the situation where "a parent company and its wholly owned subsidiaries together constitute an integrated line of endeavour under a common management".[34] Why was this a particularly "strong case"? Kohler did not explain - the matter was (supposedly) self evident.

Kohler's exercise did examine a series of questions about consolidated statements which had not been resolved in the accounting literature. But Kohler's approach was to provide unsupported assertions. And while some commentators later took issue with Kohler's propositions they did not come to grips with key issues but only disputed Kohler's claims about the desirability of one rather than another technique.[35]

---

34. *Ibid*, p.64.

35. See e.g., comments by H. T. Scovill in The accounting review, March 1938, pp.73-77; comments by H. W. Bordner, *ibid*, 1938, pp.289-91.

Before 1940 there were several other attempts to delineate the
"theory" of consolidated statements. These discussions were much
briefer than Kohler's; perhaps this is why they were less equivocal.
E. A. Kracke disposed of the "theory of consolidation" in about half
a page. Kracke saw the need for reports about an "economic entity".

> The 'concern' - to make use of the conveniently
> brief term which German practice has adopted for
> the 'affiliated organization' - is the property
> of the stockholders of the parent company; that,
> broadly stated, may be regarded as the underlying[36]
> premise of consolidated statements.

A report on the "concern" owned by majority shareholders would be
something different from an amplification of a holding company's statement. Beyond stating that consolidated statements gave "a comprehensive
overall view", Kracke did not indicate why such reports were necessary and
what exactly they revealed that was not or could not be shown in other
reports or in other ways.

A somewhat similar standpoint was taken by Sanders, Hatfield and
Moore in their 1938 report on "accounting principles". These authors
claimed that there was a need for reports on "systems of interrelated
companies". Why? At this stage they became very vague.

> Since ... the interests of most of the parties
> concerned are identified mainly with the financial
> welfare of the entire system, statements that will
> disclose the position and earnings of the system[37]
> as a whole are indispensable.

Why information about the position or earnings of "the system" was
"indispensable" was in no way explained.

Regulation S-X

In February 1940 the SEC adopted Regulation S-X, a uniform set

---

36. E. A. Kracke, "Consolidated financial statements", The journal
of accountancy, Dec. 1938, p.377.

37. T. H. Sanders, H. R. Hatfield and U. Moore, A statement of accounting principles (New York: American Institute of accountants, 1938;
reprinted by American Accounting Association, 1959), p.101.

of accounting requirements to replace several sets of accounting instructions which had been developed for registrants filing financial statements in accord with the securities acts. With few exceptions, the rules included in this regulation had been developed earlier. However the SEC's attitudes to the use and preparation of consolidated statements can be conveniently reviewed by examining the rules set down in this omnibus ruling.

The SEC maintained the view that consolidated statements should be accompanied by the financial statements of holding companies, and by the separate statements of unconsolidated subsidiaries. This is not to say that consolidated statements were regarded as supplementary documents: one could equally suppose that the separate statements of holding companies supplemented the consolidated statements - and in fact post-1940 SEC rules were consistent with claims that consolidated statements were primary documents. By 1940, however, it is clear that the use of consolidated statements was a significant element of SEC disclosure rules. And in the light of NYSE listing requirements and other practices it can be safely concluded that consolidated reports were an established method of financial disclosure - even though it was not clear from the accounting literature what these reports were intended to disclose.

In view of the familiar claim that consolidated statements amplified the information available in a holding company's reports, it is worth noting that in the late 1930's there were changes in SEC policies regarding the valuation of investments in subsidiaries - changes which would have affected holding company accounting. The initial SEC rules simply required registrants to disclose the methods used to value subsidiaries and to report profits (or losses) arising from those investments. This did not amount to the approval of one valuation method or another, though the usual procedure seems to have been that of

recording dividends received as income, while ignoring other gains
or losses. It appears that the SEC monitored the methods used by
registrants, and on occasions dissuaded firms from using techniques
deemed unsatisfactory. In particular, the SEC's antipathy towards
asset write-ups was extended towards the adjustment of "investment"
balances to record unrealized appreciation resulting from appraisals
of subsidiaries' assets. However SEC staff were also concerned about
the practice of making systematic adjustments to record a subsidiary's
losses or undistributed profits.[38] As described earlier, "equity
accounting" was banned for public utilities. Moreover it appears that
the NYSE had adopted a policy of dissuading companies from reporting
undistributed profits as part of holding company income (except for
wholly-owned subsidiaries in certain circumstances).

These rulings may be supposed to have encouraged the retention
of cost-based valuation for investments in subsidiaries. There were
cases in which firms under the SEC's jurisdiction made substantial
write-downs of their investments in subsidiaries[39] but it is difficult
to find evidence of the use of equity accounting. However, while
the use of cost-based valuation may be supposed to have created the
need for a fuller view of a subsidiary's affairs, it must be recognised
that the use of consolidated statements was already widespread well
before these policies were introduced.

Regulation S-X contained a series of rules governing consolidation
accounting and related practices. One key provision was that only
majority-owned subsidiaries could be consolidated. This rule was in
head-on conflict with Kohler's claims that consolidated statements should

38. See W. W. Werntz, "Some problems as to parent companies", The journal
of accountancy, June 1939, p.339.

39. See, e.g., Securities and Exchange Commission, Data on profits and
and operations 1936-1942 (Washington, D.C.: 1944), Vol.III, pp.41,
71, 79, Vol.IV, p.186.

encompass controlled firms. But other rulings prevented the consolidation of subsidiaries engaged in specific businesses. It was stated that subsidiaries engaged in the insurance business could not be consolidated (but should submit separate financial statements or a group statement).[40] And bank holding companies could only be consolidated with subsidiaries which were also bank holding companies. The exclusion of insurance subsidiaries and the segregation of banking activities appear to have been aimed at preventing a misleading impression of a firm's solvency being provided by the inclusion of large amounts of readily saleable securities or other liquid assets with the debts and claims of other firms. However these exclusions could also be interpreted as being consistent with the aim of reporting on an "economic entity" composed of firms engaged in homogenous or related activities.

The disclosure rules in Regulation S-X were fairly permissive. They did not require that consolidated statements encompass all majority owned subsidiaries. In effect, the SEC avoided taking a position on what subsidiaries should or should not be consolidated. This seems, in retrospect, to have been an absurd situation. Consolidated statements were a prescribed form of report and yet the SEC avoided prescribing what these documents should show - presumably because of uncertainty as to the objectives of these reports. This uncertainty was underlined by the fact that registrants often chose to adopt a different criterion for determining the scope of consolidation from that indicated by the SEC. It was reported - in the late 1930's - that most firms limited consolidation to subsidiaries in which the percentage of ownership was

---

40. In November 1940 Accounting Series Release No.18 announced that this rule had been modified to permit the consolidation of financial statements of a totally held insurance company subsidiary provided it was "primarily engaged in the insuring of risks arising in the course of business of the parent and its other subsidiaries".

for more than a bare majority.[41]

Other SEC rules in this area were similarly flexible. There was to be stated as a note to the consolidated balance sheet the amount and accounting treatment of differences between the parent's "investment" balance and the corresponding equity in the net assets of subsidiaries. (The same information with respect to unconsolidated subsidiaries was to be reported in notes). A reconciliation was to be provided of dividends received from subsidiaries and the current earnings or losses of subsidiaries that were allocable to the holding company. When intercompany items and transactions had not been eliminated from the consolidated statements, this fact had to be disclosed along with the reasons for the non-elimination and a description of the treatment followed. In all cases, the SEC did not formally require the use of a particular treatment. This policy no doubt avoided exposing the agency to criticism. Rather than try to publicly justify its stance on fairly contentious accounting issues, the SEC quietly handled these matters very firmly at an administrative level. But it appears that the SEC was just as confused as the accounting profession about the aims of consolidated reporting, and that this confusion was reflected in inconsistent or indecisive rules and policies.

41. W. Werntz, op.cit., p.338; Sanders, Hatfield, and Moore, op.cit., p.102. See also Benjamin and Meredith, who described consolidated statements as dealing with wholly owned subsidiaries while "partly-owned subsidiaries and affiliated enterprises may appear under the heading of 'non-current investments'". B. Benjamin and S. P. Meredith, The interpretation of financial statements (New York: Harper and Brothers, 1937), pp.19-20.

Resume

The securities acts made special reference to consolidated statements. The SEC was empowered to require the preparation of this form
of report. The SEC did not, in fact, promulgate specific rules
formally requiring consolidated reports. But it did establish
guidelines for the scope and content of any consolidated reports that
might be submitted. However this "official recognition" hardly seems
to have contributed towards the popularisation of consolidated
reporting since the use of these reports was widespread even before the
SEC was established.

The passage of the securities acts and the establishment of the
SEC were part of a political programme which focussed attention on
inequities resulting from the unregulated activities of large corporate
enterprises. The political scrutiny of "holding company systems"
assumed that "controlling" relationships merged corporations into one
"entity". And later it made good sense to attempt to regulate public
utility holding companies and their subsidiaries as single entities, for
otherwise the actions of the regulators could be avoided and evaded.
But it did not necessarily make good sense to regard these "economic
entities" as the focus of attention of accounting reports which were
prepared for the shareholders or creditors of specific corporations.
Nevertheless, it is a matter of record that in the years after the SEC
was established accounting writers began actively promoting the idea
that consolidated statements should be concerned with showing the
position and/or performance of "economic entities". SEC rules and
instructions may have appeared to support this position since they made
more than passing mention of the criterion of "control" as determining
the need for certain disclosures.

While the SEC's disclosure rules were introduced after consolidated
statements had become popular, they did have the effect of ensuring that

consolidated income statements became as commonplace as consolidated
balance sheets.

Even so, the _need_ for consolidated statements had not been analysed
before the end of the 1930's. The aims of consolidated statements
had not been spelled out, and there had been no assessments of whether
or not consolidated statements were the most convenient or the most
useful way of presenting particular types of information. The use of
consolidated statements held appeal to a variety of parties at interest
- and the SEC seems to have been disinclined to question the use of an
accepted, uncontroversial accounting practice.

It is possible with hindsight to identify underlying disagreements
about the aims of consolidated reports in the statements or rulings
of the SEC and in the discussions of consolidated reporting by accounting
writers at this time. But it appears that the SEC was fairly liberal
in its approach to practices in this area and accepted a variety of
techniques for preparing consolidated statements. When the SEC did
take a stand on technical matters it typically did so at an administrative level in a way that did not attract controversy or publicity.
Consequently major disagreements about the rationale of consolidated
reporting did not come out into the open. But meantime the SEC's rules
and Accounting Releases tended to support the view that consolidated
reports were concerned with "group" entities.

Ch. 14 Section summary

Consolidated statements were first used in the U.S. around the
turn of the century - several decades before this form of reporting
was used in the U.K. Nevertheless in summarising the background to the
general adoption of consolidated reporting in the U.S., it may be
useful to highlight some of the significant differences between U.S.
and U.K. experiences.

U.K. companies were able to hold shares in other companies from
a very early stage in the history of the corporate form. On the other
hand U.S. corporations faced statutory prohibitions or common law
difficulties in relation to inter-corporate shareholdings.

Around the turn of the century there were waves of industrial
combinations in both countries. The scale of mergers was far less
in the U.K. than in the U.S.; it appears that many U.K. mergers were
effected by new incorporations rather than by the use of holding
companies. However, the holding of shares in other companies was common
enough as a means of establishing "business connections" or simply as
an avenue of investment. British accountants soon developed techniques
for valuing these securities and for recording them in balance sheets.
Hence when holding companies became a popular mode of organization in
the 1920's British practitioners were able to handle their inter-corporate
investments by using well-established procedures.

American experience was quite different. Corporations were not
able to hold shares in other corporations without explicit statutory
approval. During the 1890's entrepreneurs had devised a number of
complicated schemes to carry out amalgamations. Government reaction to
these industrial combinations led to anti-trust legislation. The
liberalisation of state corporation laws so as to permit firms to hold
the stock of other firms took place at a time when "pools" and "trusts"
were under attack. The holding company form offered safety from the

Sherman anti-trust legislation and after some initial hesitancy U.S.
businesses readily adopted this style of organization.

Hence, American accountants suddenly found themselves confronted
with the task of reporting on the affairs of large holding companies.
They had had no previous experience in handling inter-corporate investments. Moreover, U.S. financial reporting was virtually unregulated.
Even though U.K. disclosure rules were only in an embryonic state, they
established a framework for corporate disclosure. Further, the 1900
U.K. Companies Act had required that balance sheets tabled at annual
meetings were to be audited,thus rather obliquely requiring the appointment of auditors as well as obliging firms to prepare balance sheets.
But, in contrast, the U.S. corporation laws contained virtually no
disclosure rules and provided no guidelines for company reports. In one
sense, the absence of rules in the U.S. may have been conducive to
experimentation. This lack of regulatory constraints was reflected in
the American response to the use of consolidated reports. In the 1920's
the adoption of consolidated reports by British accountants prompted a
spate of comments that these statements did not satisfy statutory
requirements and that firms still had to prepare "legal" balance sheets.
But in the U.S.A. consolidated statements were accepted on their own
without controversy.

The initial adoption of consolidated reports by newly-organised
holding companies seems understandable enough in the light of claims
by promoters about the scale of operations and profits that would follow
from corporate mergers. It does not follow that this method of reporting
was necessarily the optimum way to handle these kinds of situations -
but accountants made little effort to assess the utility of this or
that reporting device. It appears that U.S. accounting was extremely
permissive around the turn of the century - so that many methods of
holding company reporting would have been acceptable. Some practitioners

chose to use consolidated statements and were very taken with this
reporting format. It seemed to provide an overview of the complex and
tangled affairs of a number of related companies - and in particular
it gave some indication of the credit-worthiness of members of a group.
Notable among the practitioners who pioneered the use of consolidated
statements were Dickinson, Lybrand and Montgomery. All were fairly
prolific contributors to the accounting literature, and all readily
espoused the merits of consolidated reporting - without, it should be
added, actually setting down a well-argued case for this form of statement.   The second decade of the century saw American accountants
adopting British ideas about asset valuation. Fixed and current assets
were valued differently and fixed assets were often valued at cost.
Inter-corporate investments were generally regarded as "fixed" assets,
and hence were valued at cost even though the use of cost and of
dividend-based revenue recognition was patently a poor way to report on
a holding company's position or performance. Hence consolidated
statements were seen as amplifications of holding companies' balance
sheets which "overcame" the deficiencies of cost-based valuation.
The use of consolidated reports was not necessarily the best way of
overcoming these "deficiencies" - but in the 1920's,arguments in support
of consolidated statements were usually emotive rather than analytical.
The pros and cons of consolidated reporting and of alternative procedures
were not debated. Indeed, much of the accounting literature simply
outlined the techniques of preparing consolidated reports and stopped
short of stating what these reports were intended to show.

A variety of institutional factors reinforced the view that consolidated statements were desirable reports. The professional associations' examinations required some knowledge of consolidation practices.
Investment bankers (and others) regarded consolidated reporting as a
desirable means of unravelling the complexities of holding company

organizations. And the federal government levied its 1917 "excess profits tax" on groups of "affiliated" companies thus requiring the use of a form of consolidated report. These tax rules seem to have been of considerable importance to the popularization of consolidated reporting since they prompted an outpouring of material on the techniques of consolidation, and led to an expansion of educational activities. Then, in 1919, the New York Stock Exchange introduced a series of initiatives which collectively ensured that consolidated statements were entrenched in U.S. accounting practices and enabled these reports to become the primary source of financial data for corporate reporting. On the other hand state corporation laws and the activities of public service commissions were of negligible influence on the use of consolidated statements. And the accounting profession had yet to start formulating rules or guides as to what were regarded as the best accounting practices.

Consolidated statements had become part of U.S. practice without being imposed by public or private agencies. Later, the passage of the securities acts in 1933 and 1934 empowered the SEC to prescribe the form and content of financial reports. The accounting rules which emerged in due course included requirements for the use of consolidated statements and some specifications of what these reports could not encompass.

By the 1930's consolidated statements were in effect required disclosures and they had become the major vehicle for financial reporting.

And yet it was only in the late 1930's that any extended attempt was made to analyse the aims of consolidated reports and to assess the validity of their assumptions and the utility of their product.

At this stage, most British accountants regarded consolidated reporting as an attempt to overcome the limitations of historical cost data and perhaps to unravel the effect of inter-company loans and transactions so as to avoid misrepresentations of the affairs of holding companies. But American ideas about the objects of these reports were more complicated. Initially, consolidated reports were prepared as some kind of parallel document to that prepared by the "voting trusts" - the form of organization which holding companies had replaced. In these early years accountants may not have fully realised the ramifications of the holding company form on the interests of creditors and shareholders. Later the idea of amplifying holding companies' statements gained some support. The aim of providing the means of assessing the credit-worthiness of holding companies or subsidiaries also came to be significant, with banks seeking consolidated reports to assist them when they had to pass judgment on commercial paper. Finally, the New Deal political objectives of public utilities regulation had some influence on accounting ideas, particularly in encouraging the idea that the reports concerned the performance of an "economic entity".

The significance placed on consolidated balance sheets <u>vis a vis</u> consolidated income statements, and on consolidated reports <u>vis a vis</u> holding company reports would depend on whether the objective of these statements was seen as being that

      (i) of amplifying holding companies' statements, or
     (ii) of reporting on credit-worthiness, or
    (iii) of assessing the overall earnings of a group
           of "controlled" companies.

Moreover acceptance of one rather than another objective would indicate the use of a specific set of techniques for preparing the statement(s). This inherent conflict between the supposed aims of consolidated reports was not recognised in the 1930's. There are indications that different preparers or users of these reports held differing ideas about the aims and usefulness of consolidated data. It is understandable, then, that early attempts to regulate consolidated reporting or to discuss the theory of consolidated reporting were uneasy compromises, attempting to accommodate differing ideas and to justify the differing techniques which had been developed to prepare these documents.

Ch. 15 Consolidated reports: the issues

By the end of the 1930's, consolidated statements were regarded
as an acceptable vehicle for reporting and were in fact widely used
in both the U.K. and the U.S.A. Even so, the accounting literature
continued to contain conflicting arguments about the aims of these
statements and about the techniques to be used in their preparation.
However, these conflicts were not explored in any depth and until
the late 1930's there had been few attempts to settle disagreements
about matters of technique let alone resolve underlying disagreements
about the function and status of consolidated reports.

Accounting writers had not focussed on the aims of consolidated
reporting or endeavoured to spell out precisely what these documents
showed that could not be shown in other ways. Nor, in pressing the
case for consolidated statements, had they provided any explanation
of their position. The case for consolidated statements had been
sufficiently persuasive to be accepted. But the case lacked analysis
or supporting evidence.

While it is important to recognise that by the end of the 1930's
there were conflicting ideas about consolidated reporting, it is
equally important to recognise that over the years different views
about the need for these statements had been held by groups of
users of financial statements. For example, in the U.S. around 1900-1910
consolidated statements were seen as a means of circumventing dividend-
based revenue recognition in holding company reporting. During the
next decade American bankers saw merit in consolidated statements as
a means of better representing the ability of parent or subsidiary
companies to meet committments arising from the issue of negotiable
bills.

Different rules for consolidation were consistent with differing perceived objectives of the resultant statements. Hence it is understandable that there was considerable diversity in accounting practice, at least until some of the points of disagreement were "resolved" through the promulgation of rules by legislatures or by regulatory agencies. But many of these rules were left fairly wide - supposedly to permit the "exercise of judgment" in the selection of the "best" form of reporting.

This section summarises the differing views which accountants and others held about the function and status of consolidated statements in the years before 1940. These ideas about the function and status of consolidated statements are then related to conflicting ideas about what rules and techniques were appropriate for the preparation of the statements. It will be shown that attempts to accommodate differing viewpoints on consolidation led to compromises in the selection of rules of practice, with the consequence that statements prepared in accord with these rules may have been incapable of fully satisfying any particular objective.

The function of consolidated statements

As is evident from the earlier examination of the U.K and U.S. historical background to the use of consolidated statements, it was rare for accounting writers to spell out their ideas about the aims or function of this method of reporting with any clarity.

Some writers described consolidated statements as depicting a holding company and subsidiaries as if they were a single organization, or as if subsidiaries were mere departments of the holding company. These propositions might have been useful as rough and ready descriptions of consolidated reports. They are to some extent indicative of one point of view about consolidated statements - that they represent the affairs of an "economic" entity - and in some instances accounting writers have deliberately adopted this form of words with that intention. Even so, the description of consolidated statements as depicting "a single organization" does not constitute an adequate statement of the _function_ of consolidated reports. The description makes no reference to the factors or relationships these documents are intended to depict, and it does not indicate the information needs of particular users of financial statements that consolidated statements might be supposed to satisfy.

In other cases, writers indicated their ideas about the aims of consolidated statements by illustrating the uninformativeness of other accounting techniques. For example, many texts pointed to the likely treatment of subsidiary investments in a holding company's balance sheet, and claimed that "obviously" disclosure in that form was inadequate. In some instances texts contained further assertions to the effect that consolidated statements were developed or adopted to "overcome" these limitations. Commentaries of this sort did not spell out the function of consolidated statements, but merely left others to draw their own inferences.

In short, the literature on consolidated statements was messy. And yet, despite the fact that arguments and practices were often vague or inconsistent, it is possible to detect some main themes in those arguments and to observe some major uses or applications of consolidated data.

Prior to the 1940's the main ideas about the objectives of consolidated statements seem to be encompassed by the following assertions:

1. Consolidated statements depict the financial position and performance of holding companies.

2. Consolidated statements amplify the financial statements of holding companies.

3. Consolidated statements supplement the balance sheets of holding companies or subsidiaries to facilitate assessments of the ability of those firms to meet their debts.

4.   Consolidated statements supplement the financial
     statements of holding companies by depicting the
     position and performance of "economic entities".

This list is not comprehensive. (For example, it does not include

claims that consolidated statements were a useful means of assessing

the consequences of prospective mergers). Nor does the list include

all possible combinations of the factors listed. (There were several

writers who claimed that consolidated statements fulfilled several

apparently conflicting functions).[1] However it is claimed that the four

propositions listed above represent the main ideas about the aims of

consolidated reports that were advanced in the years before 1940.

In support of this claim, there follows a brief review of instances

in which these aims of consolidated reporting were discussed or implicitly

adopted.

Proposition 1:   Consolidated statements depict the financial position
                 and performance of holding companies.

This view of the "aims" of consolidated statements was implicit in

stock exchange requirements and in the practices of stock exchanges

and the financial press of emphasising consolidated rather than parent

company data. The New York Stock Exchange introduced a requirement

for consolidated reports into its listing requirements around 1919;

Australian stock exchanges permitted consolidated statements in 1927

while the London Stock Exchange required consolidated data in 1939. The

asset backing and earnings data supplied by stock exchanges to the

press for publication in conjunction with stock prices have long been

---

1.   For example, Sunley and Pinkerton asserted that consolidated
     statements (i) reported on the affairs of a single "economic
     entity", (ii) enabled fuller disclosure than was contained in
     holding company statements, (iii) avoided window dressing of
     the liquid position of a holding company, and (iv) avoided
     manipulation of inter-corporate profits. W. T. Sunley and P. W.
     Pinkerton, Corporation accounting (New York: Ronald Press Company
     for the American Academy of Accountancy, 1931), pp.447-9. Simi-
     larly-mixed descriptions can be found in H. G. Guthman, The
     analysis of financial statements (New York: Prentice Hall, Inc.,
     1925), p.398 ff.

extracted from consolidated statements rather than from the holding
company's own reports. In this sense, consolidated statements have
been treated as the primary source of financial information about
holding companies. However this view of the function of consolidated
statements was adopted much earlier. Dickinson's pioneering discussions
of consolidated statements emphasised that this form of report was
appropriate for holding companies.[2] Stempf later reported that most
of the early consolidated statements were published without accompanying
parent-company reports.[3] And Cox emphasised that a holding company's
statements were not for "public presentation"[4] but were only necessary
steps in the preparation of consolidated statements.

It will be recalled that most of the early holding companies were
the owners of 100% (or near to 100%) of the issued stock of subsidiary
corporations. The contention that consolidated statements reflected
the "real" position of a holding company may have appeared more plausible
in this context than (say) in situations in which holding companies
typically were at the apex of a five or six-tiered pyramid structure,
to which outside shareholders had contributed a high percentage of the
aggregate equity capital. Indeed, when U.S. accountants later began to
encounter situations in which holding companies did not own close to
100% of the stock of subsidiaries, they immediately expressed doubts
about the usefulness of consolidated statements. It was argued, for
example, that consolidation "purports to show the ... assets and
liabilities of the holding company" so that inclusion of a 50%-owned

---

2. A. L. Dickinson, Accounting practice and procedure (New York:
    Ronald Press Company, 1914), p.179.

3. V. H. Stempf, "Consolidated financial statements", The journal of
    accountancy, Nov. 1936, p.359.

4. H. C. Cox, Advanced and analytical accounting (New York: Ronald
    Press Company, Vol.IV of Business accounting series, 1920),
    pp.340-1, 346, 350-1.

subsidiary would overstate or inflate the stated amounts of the holding company's assets and liabilities.[5] Others spoke of "difficulties" in handling large minority interests[6] and it appears that one American response to these difficulties was the practice of only consolidating substantially-owned subsidiaries (leaving other majority-owned subsidiaries unconsolidated). Similarly in the U.K. there were writers who saw the use of consolidated statements as appropriate for 100%-owned subsidiaries but who expressed misgivings about the suitability of the device for partly-owned subsidiaries.[7]

Further support for the contention that consolidated statements were seen as attempts to depict the position of the holding company can be found in the short-lived practice of "proportional consolidation". Individual assets and liabilities of a parent company were combined with the assets and liabilities of subsidiaries, valued at (say) 70% of book value for a 70%-owned subsidiary, 60% of book value for a 60%-owned subsidiary, and so on. This method seems to have been used occasionally in the U.S. before the 1930's. In the U.K. "proportional consolidation" would not have complied with companies act requirements for the filing of a balance sheet by individual companies. However in both countries

---

5.   A. W. Wright, "Consolidation of balance sheets in holding company accounting", The journal of accountancy, Jan. 1914, pp.23ff.

6.   See, e.g. comments by M. E. Peloubet on a paper submitted by Sir Albert Wyon to the Fourth International congress in 1933. Proceedings of the fourth international congress on accounting (London: International Congresss on Accounting, 1933), p.149.

7.   e.g. B. H. Binder, "Holding companies' profit and loss accounts", The accountant, 13 May 1933, p.635.

the method was thoroughly condemned or dismissed as unworkable[8]
(though one firm evidently tried to use the method in an SEC filing in
the mid 1930's).[9] The advantages claimed for this method were that
it avoided the distortions incorporated in conventional balance sheets
when holding companies valued their investments at cost. Correspondingly
it may have been claimed that by excluding minority interests the
statement was concerned only with the holding company. The fact that
the method was used at all does, of course, suggest a concern with
showing the affairs of the holding company in a fuller or less distorted
form than would be available from conventional financial statements.

Proposition 2: Consolidated statements amplify the financial statements
of holding companies.

By the end of the 1930's, British, Australian and American disclosure
rules included provisions for the preparation by holding companies of
both conventional financial statements and consolidated reports.

The U.K. companies legislation did not make mention of consolidated
statements until 1947; the 1929 legislation simply required holding
companies to publish their own financial reports. In 1939 the London
Stock Exchange took the step of requiring firms seeking listing to
agree to furnish both holding company and consolidated data. Similarly
in Australia, the companies legislation (which was modelled fairly
closely on earlier U.K. statutes) did not require consolidated reports,

---

8. See, e.g. Wright, op.cit., p.27; Cox, op.cit., p.346; R. B.
   Kester, Accounting theory and practice (New York: Ronald Press
   Company, 1922), Vol.II, p.611; G. R. Webster, "Consolidated
   accounts", The journal of accountancy, Oct. 1919, p.264; D. S. Kerr,
   "Consolidated balance sheets", The accountant, Nov.20, 1915,
   p.629; Sir Gilbert Garnsey, "Holding companies and their published
   accounts", ibid, 6 Jan. 1923, p.16 and Holding companies and their
   published accounts, (London: Gee and Co. (Publishers) Ltd., 1923),
   p.14; A. J. Simons, Holding companies (London: Sir Isaac Pitman
   & Sons Ltd., 1927), p.105.

9. See W. W. Werntz, "Some problems as to parent companies", The
   journal of accountancy, June 1939.

and the stock exchanges played a key role in introducing this form
of reporting. The Melbourne Stock Exchange introduced listing requirements in 1925 which provided for the supplementary publication of the
financial statements of subsidiaries; in December 1927 an amendment to
the Melbourne Stock Exchange's rules allowed the presentation of an
aggregate balance sheet and profit and loss account covering subsidiaries.
In the same year the Sydney Stock Exchange (which had earlier copied the
1925 rules of the Melbourne Exchange) adopted a different amendment
which allowed the presentation of full consolidated statements (encompassing holding companies as well as their subsidiaries). In 1938
companies legislation in the state of Victoria broke away from the
British model by requiring holding companies to supplement their financial
statements with either the separate statements of subsidiaries or
consolidated statements covering holding company and subsidiaries.[10]
(More than twenty years later a similar rule was adopted in uniform
legislation passed by all Australian states).

It will be noted that these British or Australian rules referred
to consolidated statements as a means of supplementing holding company
statements. This was entirely consistent with Sir Gilbert Garnsey's
well-publicised attitude to consolidated reporting. Garnsey emphasised
that consolidated statements were simply one way of supplementing a
holding company's financial statements, and were always to "be in
addition to the 'legal' balance sheet and by way of supplementary
information only".[11]

In the U.S., the SEC required both consolidated and holding
company reports - while at the same time allowing considerable "flexibility" in the interpretation of the rules. The fact that a holding

---

10. For a fuller account of these developments, see R. W. Gibson Dis-
    closure by Australian companies (Melbourne University Press, 1971),
    pp.74-85.

11. Sir Gilbert Garnsey, "Holding companies and their published
    accounts", The accountant, 20 Feb. 1926, p.268.

company's statements had to be prepared while consolidated statements could be presented at the discretion of managers also suggests that consolidated statements were regarded as an optional form of supplementary reporting. But the SEC rule must be considered in conjunction with (a) the SEC's powers to refuse registration to corporations whose financial statements were not considered sufficiently informative, and (b) the SEC's administrative practice of negotiating with registrants regarding the acceptability of financial reports which had been lodged for filing. It seems quite likely that consolidated statements were informally "required". But the very fact that no SEC decision or Accounting Release dealt with the necessity for producing consolidated statements certainly seems to indicate that the SEC regarded them as supplementary reports.[12]

Early text books provide further support for the claim that consolidated statements were regarded as amplifications of the reports of holding companies.

As noted in earlier chapters many accounting writers described consolidated reporting as a process whereby shareholders and others were provided with more information than would be conveyed in holding companies' balance sheets, and better information than would be provided by cost-based valuation of investments and dividend-based income recognition. In the context of firms supplying conventional financial statements to shareholders as a matter of course, recommendations for the presentation of consolidated statements can be seen as consistent with this view of aggregative statements as supplementary reports amplifying or remedying the representations contained in the holding companies' "legal" reports. And one can readily find examples of textual material

---

12. It is recognised that SEC attitudes towards consolidated reporting were equivocal. As will be noted later, there were inconsistencies in SEC rules or pronouncements, relative to one or other of the supposed aims of consolidated reporting.

explaining that consolidated statements attempted to overcome the inadequacies of conventional reports. Dickinson wrote that the consolidated balance sheet had been evolved "by reason of the misleading character of the ordinary balance sheet".[13] Esquerre claimed that consolidated statements were intended to show the "exact status of the assets controlled by the parent company".[14] G. O. May, who in 1915 had indicated that he viewed consolidated statements as the more important document and implied that publication of consolidated statements (alone) was sufficient disclosure,[15] later wrote of the growing realisation among practitioners of the limitations of consolidated reports and of the fact that there had been an "undue extension of the practice" and that there was a need for both holding company and consolidated statements for "a reasonable interpretation of the financial picture".[16]

Proposition 3: Consolidated statements supplement the balance sheets of holding companies or subsidiaries to facilitate assessments of the ability of those firms to meet their debts.

One clear illustration of this view of consolidated reports is the 1924 ruling of the U.S. Federal Reserve Board directing banks to require the submission of both consolidated reports and the reports of the relevant holding company or subsidiary when the banks were assessing the credit-worthiness of commercial paper. At one stage only consolidated reports were required in these situations, but it was

---

13. Op.cit., p.176

14. P. J. Esquerre, The applied theory of accounts (New York: Ronald Press Company, 1914), p.448.

15. G. O. May, "Qualifications in certificates", The journal of accountancy, 1915, p.257.

16. G. O. May, Financial accounting (New York: The Macmillan Company, 1943), pp.33-4.

subsequently realised that it was necessary to use both kinds of reports to forestall "window dressing".

Much of the early U.S. literature placed special emphasis on the uses of consolidated reports to enable informed assessments to be made of the liquid position of a holding company. Dickinson gave harrowing examples of how holding companies could appear to be well able to meet their commitments when in fact their "short-term loans to subsidiaries" might be illiquid; he suggested that consolidated statements, by giving an overall view of the current assets and liabilities of a number of related companies, could provide a better indicator of the ability of the holding companies to meet their obligations.[17] (The use of different criteria for classifying assets might have improved holding companies' balance sheets and so eliminated the need to consider alternative forms of reporting - but Dickinson did not consider this alternative). Kerr provided similar examples of advances to subsidiaries which might seem to be "current assets", and claimed that consolidated statements avoided misinterpretations. Moreover, he suggested that without consolidated statements the fact that subsidiaries had issued senior securities would not be apparent so that creditors of a holding company might otherwise have a misleading impression of the resources effectively available to meet their claims.[18] Similarly Masters emphasised the usefulness of consolidated statements in depicting credit standing, and described these reports as showing "the true position of holding corporations".[19] In 1929 a commercial publication dealing with credit analysis likewise claimed that where there were inter-company shareholding relationships, "a consolidated balance sheet is most essential to properly establish the status of the risk".[20]

17. Op.cit., pp.175-6.

18. Loc.cit.

19. J. E. Masters, "Financial statements as a basis of credit", The journal of accountancy, 1915, p.337.

20. Commercial Research Bureau Inc., Accountancy reports (Chicago, 1929) Vol.V ("Preparation of statements for financing and credits"),pp.474-5.

But while consolidated statements were often claimed to provide useful data for present and potential creditors, this claim was rarely presented as a "prime" or "main" purpose of consolidated statements. As indicated in the summary proposition, consolidated reporting was seen as complementing the separate financial statements of other companies. The aim of assisting creditors was seen as ancillary to other aims of consolidated statements.

To illustrate, Sunley and Pinkerton described consolidated statements as a means of improving or expanding on the information contained in holding companies' financial statements, and then added that consolidated reports could also overcome any manipulation of inter-company balances intended to convey a misleading impression of liquidity or solvency.[21] The showing of solvency was not regarded as the prime aim, but it was regarded as important.

It should also be noted that many writers made a point of stating that consolidated statements could mislead creditors of subsidiaries - so that creditors would need to examine the individual financial statements of the subsidiaries to which they had lent (or were lending) funds. However it is clear that considerable credence was given to claims that consolidated data provided useful information to creditors.

Acceptance of these claims was of considerable significance to the development of rules concerning the scope of consolidated reports.

Proposition 4: Consolidated statements supplement the financial statements of holding companies by depicting the position and performance of "economic entities".

Early texts often described consolidated statements as depicting the affairs of a holding company and its subsidiaries as if they were a single organization or as if the subsidiaries were merely branches of the parent.

---

21. Op.cit., p.447.

SEC Accounting Release No.3 (1937) similarly asserted that consolidated statements showed "a parent company and its subsidiaries as if they were a single organization". No doubt these forms of words were convenient to communicate a general sense of what consolidated statements contained. But the suggestion that consolidated statements were aimed at depicting the affairs of a "single organization" or "entity" was decidedly ambiguous.

One interpretation of this claim is that consolidated statements were intended to reflect the "real" position and performance of a holding company (which would otherwise be distorted by accounting technicalities. Another interpretation is that consolidated statements were aimed at reflecting the economic performance of a multi-corporation monopoly or "economic unit". It seems that initially American writers were concerned more with reporting on holding companies. But later, American writers began regarding the presentation of information about a "group" of companies as an end in itself. Perhaps the first publication to spell out the aim of providing information about a "group" of companies was Finney's 1922 text, Consolidated statements. Finney did not take a strong position on what should be regarded as the aim of consolidated statements, and merely suggested the "group" idea as a plausible alternative.[22] But other writers were to express this idea more strongly. Writers who plainly adopted this aim of the function of consolidated statements included Porter and Fiske (1935),[23] Kohler (1938)[24]

22. H. A. Finney, Consolidated statements for holding company and subsidiaries (New York: Prentice-Hall Inc., 1922), p.11

23. C. H. Porter and W. P. Fiske, Accounting. (New York: Henry Holt and Co., 1936), p.297.

24. E. L. Köhler, "Some tentative propositions underlying consolidated reports", The accounting review, March 1938, p.63.

Kracke (1938)[25] and Sanders, Hatfield and Moore (1940).[26] The last-named writers gave one of the most explicit statements of the reasons for adopting this aim. They asserted that information about "systems" of related companies was indispensable since the interests of "most of the parties" involved in a given corporation were "identified" with the financial welfare of the whole system.

Other texts that might be interpreted as supporting this aim of consolidated reporting include those by W. H. Bell (1921),[27] Bell and Graham (1937),[28] Bennett (1919),[29] Paton and Stevenson (1918),[30] Paton (1924 and 1938)[31] and Rorem (1930).[32]

*   *   *   *

While the ambiguity of the literature makes it difficult to categorise the position taken by many writers, it appears that the four propositions outlined above are a reasonable summary of the main ideas about the aims of consolidated reporting. The effect of adopting one or other aim is apparent in relation to the choice of specific rules or procedures.

---

25. E. A. Kracke, "Consolidated financial statements", The journal of accountancy, Dec. 1938, p.372 ff.

26. T. H. Sanders, H. R. Hatfield and U. Moore, A statement of accounting principles (New York: American Institute of Accountants, 1938), (reprinted by American Accounting Association, 1959), p.101.

27. W. H. Bell, Accountants' reports (New York: Ronald Press Company, 1921, p.143.

28. S. Bell and W. J. Graham, Theory and practice of accounting (Chicago: American Technical Society, rev. ed., 1937), pp.430-1.

29. R. J. Bennett, Corporation accounting (New York: Ronald Press Company, 1916; 7th printing 1919), p.456.

30. W. A. Paton and R. A. Stevenson, Principles of accounting (New York: The Macmillan Company, 1920), pp.567, 592.

31. W. A. Paton, Accounting (New York: The Macmillan Company, 1924), p.471; Essentials of accounting (New York: The Macmillan Company, 1938), p.761.

32. C. R. Rorem, Accounting method (Chicago: University of Chicago Press, 2nd ed., 1930), p.337.

The area of consolidation

One of the most contested technical issues concerning the preparation of consolidated statements is the specification of the "area of
consolidation" - the corporations which are to be encompassed by the
consolidated report.

The first consolidated statements were prepared at a time when
the subsidiaries of holding companies were usually wholly-owned or nearly
wholly-owned. Around 1910 there was little dispute about the area of
consolidation. Within two decades the holding company form was used
more widely, and holdings of less than 100% of subsidiaries' stock
were far more common. Even so, in 1914 Dickinson still argued that
consolidation was only warranted when there was almost 100% ownership:

> The ownership of at least the common stock should be
> substantially complete; or the balance not owned should
> consist either of shares left in the hands of managers
> or others for business purposes or of shares the owner-
> ship of which cannot be traced.[33]

Similarly in 1921 W. H. Bell argued that "consolidation of the accounts
is appropriate whenever the ownership in one company is all, or
substantially all, vested in another company". On the other hand,
Bell suggested that cases where ownership was in the range of 50%-95%
were "doubtful" and necessitated the exercise of judgment as to whether
"the true conditions are better expressed by individual or consolidated
statements.[34]

The view that consolidation was only appropriate for "substantially-owned" subsidiaries was to survive in the U.S. at least until

---

33.   Op.cit., p.182.

34.   Op.cit., p.144.

the 1930's.[35] When British companies started using consolidated
reporting in the early 1920's they followed early U.S. practices by
restricting the area of consolidation to substantially-owned companies.
For example, Nobel Industries, the first major U.K. company to publish
a consolidated report, seems to have only consolidated those of its
subsidiaries that were near to 100%-owned.[36] And in 1923 Sir Gilbert
Garnsey reported that "as a rule" the assets and liabilities were not
amalgamated unless the parent company owned 75% or more of the ordinary
capital.[37]

But in the 1920's, U.S. accounting writers shifted ground. Led
perhaps by Bennett,[38] Paton and Stevenson[39] or Kester,[40] most authors
of texts published in the 1920's claimed that consolidated statements
should encompass the holding company and all corporations it controlled
by virtue of ownership of a majority of the (voting) stock. Some texts
were quite explicit on this point;[41] others merely discussed consolidated

---

35. In 1929 Staub reported that "good practice requires that there must
    be a large stock ownership by the parent or sub-parent company to
    warrant inclusion of the subsidiary in a consolidated balance
    sheet and that ordinarily a bare majority ownership would not be
    regarded as [sufficient]". W. A. Staub, "Consolidated financial
    statements", in Proceedings of the international congress on
    accounting, 1929 and reproduced in The accountant, 7 Dec. 1929,
    p.732. In the late 1930's Daniels reported that some U.S.
    corporations only consolidated wholly-owned subsidiaries while
    others "established a definite percentage of stock ownership for
    consolidation, such as 50, 75 or 90 per cent, and consolidated
    only those companies so qualifying". M. B. Daniels, Financial
    statements (Chicago: American Accounting Association, 1939), pp.85-6.

36. "Balance sheets of holding companies", The incorporated accountants'
    journal, Oct. 1922.

37. Holding companies and their published accounts, op.cit., p.63.

38. Op.cit., p.456.

39. Op.cit., pp.592-3.

40. Op.cit., p.603.

41. e.g., The Commercial Research Bureau, Inc., Accountancy reports
    (Chicago: 1929), Vol.IV ("Depreciation, costs and consolidated
    balance sheets"), pp.381-2; Cox, op.cit., p.374; Guthman, op.cit.,
    p.399.

statements as though they dealt with all subsidiaries, without the
slightest allusion to the possibility of excluding any subsidiary
from the consolidation.[42] And so the literature quietly came to
promote the idea that consolidated statements should deal with
majority-owned subsidiaries.

However, while there were occasional (but rare) mentions of the
possibility of consolidating firms in which ownership was less than
50% but still sufficient to establish "control"[43] the existence of
"controlling" relationships was not generally regarded as being sufficient
to warrant consolidation.

This idea of extending the area of consolidation to 51%-owned
companies was soon echoed in the U.K. literature. Garnsey indicated
that a bare 51% holding could be sufficient to warrant consolidation;
"each case is a matter for individual judgment".[44] On the other hand,
Garnsey also stressed that even near-total ownership need not necessarily
warrant consolidation; he claimed that the "essential point is whether
or not there is real control by the holding company either direct, or
through the medium of another company in the group".[45]

---

42. e.g., Finney, op.cit., esp. Ch.II; Sunley and Pinkerton, op.cit.,
     p.447ff.

43. e.g., McKinsey and Noble prefaced their discussion of consolidated
     statements by defining the terms "holding company" and "subsidiary"
     in terms of "control". "Ownership of 51 per cent of the outstand-
     ing stock makes such control possible, although in some cases a
     smaller percentage gives the holding company sufficient voting
     power to elect directors of its own choice ...". It appears that
     these authors favoured consolidation of these "controlled" cor-
     porations. J. O. McKinsey and H. S. Noble, Accounting principles
     (Cincinnati: South-Western Publishing Co., 1935), p.628. Both
     Bennett and Kester indicated that the consolidation of minority-
     owned subsidiaries was carried out in practice; however Kester
     questioned whether this method gave a "true presentation of the
     facts of financial condition". Bennett, op.cit., p.457; Kester,
     op.cit., p.603.

44. Holding companies and their published accounts, loc.cit., p.56.

45. "Holding companies and their published accounts" (1926), loc.cit.,
     p.275.

Garnsey seems to have been thoroughly confused by the U.S. literature. On the one hand he accepted the British view that there was a need for a "legal" balance sheet and he described consolidated statements as one way of supplementing legal balance sheets and of providing "better" information than would be provided by one-line references to investments in subsidiaries. Yet on the other hand he reproduced arguments from the American literature to the effect that consolidated statements were concerned with depicting a "group" of companies.

Most discussions of the proportion of share ownership sufficient to warrant consolidation did not distinguish <u>direct</u> share-ownership and the <u>indirect</u> interests such as would arise with multi-tiered holding company structures.

It appears that U.S. Steel Corporation (which pioneered the use of consolidated statements) had several subsidiaries which were themselves holding companies. Evidently U.S. Steel's consolidated statements encompassed both subsidiaries and these "substantially owned" sub-subsidiaries.

When multi-tiered holding company structures became more common in the 1920's, many writers were then arguing that consolidated statements were intended to depict a "group" of companies and as such should encompass not only directly-owned subsidiaries but all "controlled" firms. But for those who argued that consolidated statements were amplifications of a holding company's statement, it was more difficult to delineate the percentage interests that might warrant consolidation. The following diagrams illustrate the difficulties facing those who saw consolidated statements as amplifications of holding company reports. In each of these illustrations, the symbol H indicates a "holding company", the terms S1, S2 and S3 represent "subsidiary" companies, while the arrows and percentages indicate the extent of shareholdings.

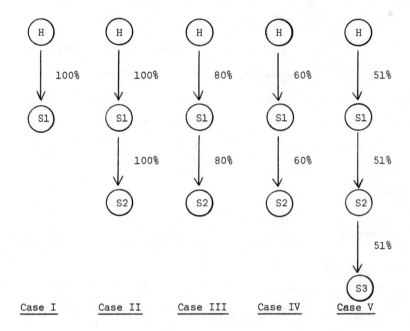

Case I   Case II   Case III   Case IV   Case V

Case I is the classic situation from which it was argued that consolidated statements would provide a convenient amplification of the holding company's reports. Case II introduces sub-subsidiaries; in this instance, the effective equity of H in S2 is 100%, and those who saw a need for consolidated statements would no doubt support the inclusion of S2 in the area of consolidation. Cases III, IV and V highlight some of the significant features of conflicting ideas about the aims of consolidated reports. In Case III, S1 is substantially owned by H, and S2 in turn is substantially owned by S1. On the "amplification" argument, H and S1 would be consolidated. But H's equity in S2 is only 64%, (80% of 80%), somewhat less than "substantial ownership". (It may be that cases such as this led American accountants who saw consolidated statements as amplifications to or substitutes for the holding company's report to abandon the "substantial ownership" idea and to substitute the "majority ownership" test). In Case IV, H's equity in S2 is (effectively) only 36%. Now consolidation of S2 would be hard to justify as an "amplification" of the holding company report, it would be easy to justify if one saw consolidated statements as depicting an "economic entity" of "controlled" companies. Case V further illustrates the consequences of "pyramiding"; H's effective equity is only around 13% yet the intercompany shareholdings could be sufficient to ensure that H company's management was able to control the election of S3's management and hence "control" S3. The greater number of tiers, the less the percentage ownership interest necessary to effect control. And this relationship could be magnified with the utilization of shares with differing voting rights.

The U.K. Companies Act of 1929 defined holding company relationships for the purpose of requiring disclosure of how subsidiaries' profits or losses had been "dealt with" in the accounts of holding companies. The definition established three tests. One spelt out that a company would be deemed a subsidiary if another firm directly or through nominees held more than 50% of its issued share capital. The other two tests were based on the ability of one corporation to control the management of another. The holding of shares entitling the exercise of more than 50% of the voting power or the power to appoint a majority of the directors of another company, would establish a holding-subsidiary relationship. However, these tests did not encompass so-called sub-subsidiaries.

The 1929 Act's definition of subsidiary was not designed to delineate the "area of consolidation" though in practice it was used for this purpose. The intention of the Greene Committee in framing this definition was to ensure that there was disclosure of the methods used by holding companies to account for investments in subsidiaries (in conventional financial statements). It was assumed that this form of disclosure would overcome the limitations of cost-based valuation and avoid misrepresentations. It soon became apparent that "disclosure" in this form was virtually useless. However the accounting profession chose to regard evidence of the inadequacy of this form of disclosure as suggesting

the need for an extension of the statutory definition of "subsidiary"
rather than as a reflection on cost-based valuation procedures.[46]

Again it must be emphasised that the concern with identifying
"controlled" companies in this context was in no way associated with
attempts to prescribe the ambit of consolidated statements. However
in later years some U.K. firms were to adopt the idea that consolidated
statements should encompass all "controlled" firms. Dunlop Rubber took
the lead in 1933 by consolidating "sub-subsidiaries", and this practice
was followed by a limited number of other firms. Meantime accounting
writers tended to approach questions of how to handle inter-coprorate
investments by discussing the meaning of the term "subsidiary"; the
fact that the Companies Act did not encompass "sub-subsidiaries" was
regarded as a deficiency of the legislation notwithstanding that the
inclusion of these companies in consolidated statements may not have
been appropriate.

In the U.S.A., the SEC's consolidation rules prohibited the
consolidation of all but majority-owned subsidiaries. On the face of
it this restricted consolidation to those firms in which direct
shareholdings aggregated more than 50%. But the rules also contained
a definition of "majority-owned".

> The term 'majority-owned subsidiary' means a subsidiary more
> than 50 per cent of whose outstanding voting shares is
> owned by its parent and/or the parent's other majority
> owned subsidiaries.

The effect of this definition was to describe a class of companies which
were not majority owned by a holding company. Further, "majority
ownership" was reinterpreted to mean the possession or control of a

---

46. See the report of the committee appointed by the Society of Incor-
     porated Accountants to investigate the implications of the Royal
     Mail case, in The incorporated accountants' journal, April 1932.

majority of votes, rather than ownership of a majority of equitable
interests. The rule was phrased in terms of majority ownership but was
then reinterpreted to be consistent with the aim of encompassing a set of
"controlled" companies.[47]

Thus by the end of the 1930's (i) the SEC rules clearly encouraged
the consolidation of "controlled" companies, (ii) the New York Stock
Exchange had (unsuccessfully) tried to persuade listed companies to do
likewise, and (iii) some U.K. firms were following the same approach.

Another matter at issue concerning the area of consolidation was
the propriety of consolidating companies engaged in different lines of
business. This does not seem to have attracted much attention in the
U.K. However several U.S. writers raised the matter during the 1920's.
The earliest cases which were discussed in the literature related to
subsidiaries which carried on the business of banking or were otherwise
engaged in regulated industries. For example, in 1927 Tinen claimed
that consolidated statements should cover the "entire organization", but
"an exception may be cited in the case of a bank owning a public utility"
in which case "separate cross-referenced balance sheets would give a
better picture" since "a combination of dissimilar items might be
misleading".[48] Later, Daniels suggested that "it may be undesirable"
to consolidate unrelated companies.[49] Paton indicated that in particular
situations, it would be "unwise" to use consolidated statements for firms

---

47. "This rigid rule follows the theory that if the registrant does not
    own, directly or indirectly, more than 50 per cent of the voting
    stock, definite control is really not in the hands of the registrant",
    T. F. Thompson, "Consolidation rules of the SEC", The New York
    certified public accountant, Jan. 1942, p.257.

48. J. V. Tinen, Advanced accounting (New York: Ronald Press Company,
    1927), para.41.

49. Op.cit., p.86. Conversely Daniels claimed that similarlity of
    business activities was sufficient to justify the inclusion of
    subsidiaries which were not substantially owned.

which were "unrelated ... from an operating standpoint".[50]

The SEC's rules allowed some flexibility in the determination of the area of consolidation but required that "the principle adopted in determining the inclusion or exclusion of subsidiaries" be disclosed in a note to the balance sheet. However the SEC expressly forbade the consolidation of subsidiaries engaged in certain classes of business - "life insurance, fire and casualty insurance, securities broker-dealer, finance, savings and loan or banking, including bank related finance activities".[51] These subsidiaries were to provide separate financial statements. Alternatively, if there were a number of such subsidiaries engaged in these activities, the SEC permitted the submission of "group" statements which aggregated the financial statements of unconsolidated firms.[52]

These formal SEC rules must be considered in conjunction with SEC administrative practices in order to get a sense of what was acutally required or permitted. The prohibition on consolidation of so-called finance companies was clear enough. An SEC-compiled summary of data compiled from the financial statements lodged by registrants during the period 1939-1942 indicates that it was not uncommon for consolidated statements to exclude certain subsidiaries - but the information provided in this document is not always sufficient to conclude the precise grounds for non-consolidation.[53]

---

50. Essentials of accounting, loc.cit., p.761.

51. Rule 4-09 of Regulation S-X. An exception was made in respect of totally-held insurance companies provided inter alia, they were primarily engaged in insuring risks arising in the ordinary course of business of parent companies and other subsidiaries. See Accounting Series Release No.18, Nov. 1940.

52. Note that Accounting Series Release No.141 (Feb. 1973) indicated that different types of insurance companies were not to be considered as "one group".

53. Securities and Exchange Commission, Data on profits and operations 1936-1942 (Washington, D.C.: 1944). See Vol.I, pp.129, 145, 243, Vol.II, pp.8, 233.

However there have been other reports that (in its early years of operations at least) the SEC took the view that subsidiaries engaged in entirely different lines of business need not be consolidated.[54]

Another matter which came into focus in the war years was the propriety of consolidating foreign subsidiaries. Evidently in the early 1900's, users of consolidated statements made no distinction between domestic and foreign subsidiaries:

> At that time there were no substantial restrictions on trade in any part of the world and between different nations, with the exception of tariffs, the effect of which was generally understood. Currency restrictions were practically unknown at that time, and currencies in general commercial use had a reasonably well-established value which did not fluctuate widely in their relation to each other ... In these circumstances the business activities, the availability of profits for distribution, and the realizability of assets in the liquidation of a business were not fundamentally different in the case of foreign subsidiaries from subsidiaries operating in the home country.[55]

In later years, the blocking of currencies, restrictions on foreign investment and finally the outbreak of hostilities led to a reconsideration of these practices. In the U.K., Dunlop Rubber excluded foreign subsidiaries from its 1934 consolidated statements on the ground that these firms were not under the parent's managerial control.[56] In the U.S., the American Institute of Accountants Committee on Accounting Procedure issued a pronouncement which suggested a variety of treatments: non-consolidation of foreign subsidiaries with accompanying summaries of foreign investments, consolidation with accompanying parent company statements which isolated investments in and income from foreign subsidiaries, or the presentation of two sets of consolidated reports, one including and the other excluding

54. See, e.g., Thompson, op.cit., p.259; W. H. Childs, Consolidated financial statements (Cornell University Press, 1949), p.72.

55. W. A. Staub, Auditing developments during the present century (Cambridge, Mass.: Harvard University Press, 1942), pp.95-6.

56. See The accountant, 4 May 1935, pp.656-9.

foreign subsidiaries.[57] These methods were proposed not only for war-
time conditions but also for general application. The bulletin
alluded to "exchange restrictions" and to risks associated with
foreign investments but did not indicate what criterion or criteria
were to be used to select one of these disclosure methods. The choice
was left to the judgment of practitioners.[58]

An early SEC Accounting Release asserted that consolidation "may
be misleading" if subsidiaries were operating under foreign currency
restrictions and war conditions". Once again the SEC allowed "flexibility" by permitting consolidation if this would not impair a "clear
and fair presentation" of the financial condition and results of
registrant and subsidiaries.[59] And once again the accounting literature
reflected conflicting views on the matter. Daniels argued that "important foreign subsidiaries should generally be consolidated,
regardless of complexities encountered".[60]

To recapitulate, the major questions which exercised the attention
of accounting writers and of those framing rules concerning the area
of consolidation were:

> (i) what percentage of stock ownership was necessary or
> sufficient to warrant consolidation; whether the
> exercise of control (or the ability to exercise
> control) was a necessary or sufficient condition for
> consolidation?
>
> (ii) whether consolidated statements should encompass all
> subsidiaries (as defined in (i)) or whether certain

---

57. Accounting research bulletin No.4 (Dec. 1939), "Foreign operations
   and foreign exchange".

58. Childs reports that "after the entrance of the United States into
   the war, the accounts of all foreign subsidiaries - even those
   located in allied countries with which there was some semblance
   of normal business relations - were usually omitted from the
   consolidated statements". Op.cit., p.242. For examples of the
   deconsolidation of foreign subsidiaries, see Data on profits and
   operations 1939-1942, loc.cit., Vol.1, pp.134, 163, Vol.II,
   p.205, Vol.III, p.93.

59. Accounting Series Release No.11, Jan. 1940.

60. Op.cit., p.88.

> subsidiaries should be excluded (a) because they
> were engaged in some business activity which was not
> consistent with that carried on by other related
> corporations, or (b) because they were domiciled
> in some foreign country?

Some attempt was made to resolve these questions by appeals to propositions about what consolidated statements purported to show. For example, the idea of an "economic entity" was used to support the consolidation of "controlled" corporations and the non-consolidation of firms engaged in unrelated business activities. However, quite different ideas about the aims of consolidated statements were held by different writers; correspondingly, various writers supported substantially different consolidation criteria.

The following table illustrates this point by outlining rules governing the specification of the area of consolidation which are consistent with the various aims of consolidated statements that were identified.

It will be recalled that this list of four aims was not intended to represent a comprehensive list of possibilities but only to provide a rough categorisation of the main arguments presented in the pre-1940 literature. Likewise it should be noted that the list of hypothetical rules that are related to these aims is not claimed to be comprehensive. Nor is it suggested that the rules listed are appropriate. The list merely indicates how different rules might flow from the adoption of one rather than another view of the function of consolidated reports.

Status and supposed function	Possible area of consolidation
1. Primary documents - to depict the financial position and performance of holding. companies	Holding company plus "substantially owned" subsidiaries.
2. Supplementary reports - to amplify the financial statements of holding companies.	Substantially-owned subsidiaries (only - excluding holding company) <u>or</u> (a series of group statements each covering) those subsidiaries engaged in a particular line of business <u>or</u> (a series of group statements each covering) domestic subsidiaries, foreign subsidiaries <u>or</u> holding company and all "material" subsidiaries.
3. Supplementary reports - to facilitate assessments of the ability of firms to meet their debts.	Holding company and all "controlled" subsidiaries <u>or</u> all companies which have guaranteed the indebtedness of other companies, plus the companies subject to those guarantees <u>or</u> some other combination - depending upon pattern of inter-company loans (e.g., all subsidiaries involved in inter-company loans but excluding the holding company, if it was not involved in loans. (N.B.: foreign subsidiaries might be excluded on ground that currency restrictions and/or jurisdictional limitations make resources unavailable to creditors).
4. Supplementary statements - to depict position and performance of "economic entities".	All corporations (or unincorporated associations) subject to (actually exercised) control. (N.B.: tests of control might be based on voting power or contractual rights). <u>or</u> all "controlled" corporations (or unincorporated associations) engaged in some specified business activity or activities.

However, it is a matter of record that few accounting writers recognised underlying conflicts in the specification of the aims of consolidated reporting; correspondingly, the specification of the "area of consolidation" was not often approached from the standpoint of ensuring consistency with one or other aim. In fact, the conflicting views were rarely aired.[61]

Without any analysis of the aims of consolidated reports, or any assessment of their utility, consolidated reporting was accepted as a good thing. Disagreements about underlying assumptions or over basic concepts were dismissed as merely indicating the need for the exercise of judgment in particular situations. So, by the end of the 1930's, accounting writers and regulatory agencies accepted a need to accommodate conflicting viewpoints. Thus the SEC proposed a general rule for consolidation but permitted registrants to adopt variations as they saw fit. Text books frequently alluded to the need for "judgment" and "the exercise of discretion" in relations to decisions about which companies were to be consolidated. And the main guidelines set down in statutes or regulations were compromises between the procedures that were consistent with one or other aim. Hence consolidated statements prepared in accord with these rules might come close to reporting on an "economic entity", or come close to providing a view of the solvency of related corporations - but they would not necessarily achieve either objective.

Minority interests

A second technical issue in relation to consolidation procedures concerned how to calculate and disclose the interests of "minority" shareholders. Text-book examples of consolidation procedures usually

---

61. Perhaps the only public discussion of such a conflict followed the New York Stock Exchange's attempt to persuade firms to consolidate all "controlled" corporations. (The firms in turn preferred to consolidate only "substantially owned" subsidiaries). See Childs, op.cit., pp.76-7.

illustrated the reporting of some form of "minority interest". The practice of separately identifying these items does not appear to have been questioned - though the segregation of minority and majority interests was not necessary or even consistent with some of the supposed objectives of consolidated reporting. One might suppose that reports on a multi-corporation "economic entity" would indicate the aggregate resources invested in an enterprise and the aggregate returns earned on those investments. In this context a disaggregation of shareholders' equity between minority and majority interests would be of no interest. Similarly, if consolidated statements were intended to assist creditors to assess the overall solvency of a group of corporations, then the relative interests of shareholders in particular companies would be irrelevant. On the other hand, the identification of minority interests might have some explanatory value, if consolidated statements were regarded as amplifications of the reports of holding companies. The dis-aggregation of shareholders' equity might help readers discern the association between "investments" and investment-income in the financial statements of parent companies, and balance sheet or income statement items in the consolidated reports. But even in this context it is by no means clear that the identification of minority interests in balance sheets and income statements would necessarily be the optimum way of showing the link between parent and consolidated reports.

One might also note that the term "minority-interest" could be a misnomer. In a multi-tiered holding company organization, a controlling interest in the holding company might only constitute a small proportion of the aggregate of the shareholders' equities in the various companies. Suppose that a holding company (H) held 51% of subsidiary (S1) which in turn held 51% of another company (S2). Also suppose that each company was successful in obtaining cash contributions from shareholders; H and S1 have invested their total funds in shares in S1 and S2 respectively; no costs were incurred in forming the companies and no interest has been earned subsequently. Balance sheets for the three firms and consolidated balance sheet could be as follows:

Balance sheet H

Shares in S1	$2,601	Shareholders' contribution	$2,601

Balance sheet S1

Shares in S2	$5,100	Shareholders' contribution	$5,100

Balance sheet S2

Cash	$10,000	Shareholders' contribution	$10,000

Consolidated balance sheet: H, S1 and S2

Cash	$10,000	Shareholders' contribution	$2,601
		Minority interest	$7,399
	$10,000		$10,000

Here, the "minority" interest holds the major equity in the "group".

When American accountants first began using consolidated statements, holding companies generally held close to 100% of subsidiaries' stock and in any event only the financial statements of subsidiaries which were wholly-owned (or nearly wholly-owned) were consolidated. The treatment of minority interests did not rate a mention in some early texts,[62] and as late as 1932 it was reported that "when very

---

62. Dickinson, op.cit.; Esquerre, op.cit. Montgomery indicated that that the presence of minority interest necessitated "some adjustment" of the consolidated profit and loss account, but did not illustrate any such adjustments or discuss balance sheet treatments. R. H. Montgomery, Auditing theory and practice (New York: Ronald Press Company, 1912), p.561. Paton and Stevenson provided an illustration of a consolidated statement encompassing a holding company and two other companies in which the former held "controlling interests"; however this consolidated statement contained no allusion to minority interests but simply listed "equities" starting with "capital stock", then showing liabilities, and concluding with "surplus". Op.cit., pp.595-6. Bennett indicated that it was desirable to disclose the extent of ownership of subsidiaries' common stock, either in the balance sheet or in a supporting schedule. He did not propose the identification of minority interests in the balance sheet but commented that "the minority interest in surplus profits is sometimes indicated ...". Op.cit., p.457.

small, the minority interest is commonly disregarded".[63]

However, with pyramiding operations, merger agreements and takeovers, American holding companies began to have larger "minority interests". And during the 1920's accountants began to consolidate majority-owned subsidiaries. With the adoption of this practice it became difficult to claim that a consolidated balance sheet depicted a holding company's financial position as it would have been if its subsidiaries were mere branches. With the consolidation of sub-subsidiaries in which the parent's equity might be far _less_ than 50%, the old rationale for consolidated statements became even more difficult to sustain. As Kester observed, the presence of minority interests meant that "manifestly, a consolidated balance sheet ... cannot be applicable alone to the holding company".[64]

However it is a matter of record that accountants did not reject the use of consolidated statements when there were minority interests. Instead, accountants placed more emphasis on the supposed aim of showing the position and performance of a "group" of corporations as a single entity. And yet, as noted above, if consolidated statements were concerned with the position and performance of a group of companies there was no point in distinguishing the interests of minority or majority shareholdings. The reason advanced for the disaggregation was that consolidated statements were intended for the shareholders of the parent company. So on the one hand consolidated statements were supposed to report on a "group", and on the other hand they concerned the parent company. To this extent, accounting writers sought to simultaneously support competing propositions about the aims of consolidated statements.

---

63. W. A. Paton (ed.) Accountants' handbook (New York: Ronald Press Company, 2nd ed., 1932), p.1041.

64. Kester, op.cit., pp.601-2.

With this background, the disagreements which emerged within
the literature concerning the methods to be adopted in preparing
consolidated statements were as follows:

(i) whether minority interests should be reported as a liability
or as part of the shareholders' equity,

(ii) whether the income reported in consolidated statements
... should be gross or net of the minority's share,

(iii) whether eliminations of inter-company profits arising from
transactions with minority-owned subsidiaries should be
concerned with the total profits or only the majority's
equity in those profits,

(iv) whether the minority's interest in "goodwill on consolidation" should be incorporated in reported balance sheet
figures.

The treatment of (iii) inter-company transactions and (iv) "goodwill"
will be touched on later in this chapter. At this point some
additional observations will be offered about items (i) and (ii).

While considerable space was devoted in the literature to the
question of whether or not minority interests were to be regarded as
"liabilities" the matter seems to have been of little practical significance since it was not customary for balance sheets to distinguish
categories of equities.

Daniels later reported that liabilities were "rarely totalled
in published balance sheets" so that it was "generally impossible to
tell whether the minority interest is considered as a liability or
not".[65] Moreover, the standard texts made no effort to discourage
this practice. Indeed, among those books which provide worked examples
of consolidated statements involving minority interests, one finds
that Montgomery[66] and Bennett[67] provided balance sheets with headings

65. M. B. Daniels, Corporation financial statements (Ann Arbor:
University of Michigan Bureau of Business Research 1934), p.111.

66. Op.cit., p.555.

67. Op.cit., p.458.

"assets" and "liabilities" but no sub-totals on the "liability" side.
Paton and Stevenson[68] and Paton[69] used the general headings "assets"
and "equities" without any grouping of the "equities", while McKinsey
and Noble[70] chose the heading "liabilities and proprietorship" - and
similarly did not bother to discriminate between liability and
proprietorship items.

However, the few discussions of this point indicate the difficulties
that authors had in explaining the presence of minority interests in
statements which supposedly showed the position of parent or group.
Sunley and Pinkerton, for example, ruminated that there was "a community
of interest, and yet in some instances ... a decided diversity of
interest" between minority interests and "the consolidated unit"; this,
they suggested, made the interest of the minority "somewhat similar to
the interest of a creditor", though it was clearly a stockholding interest
in the subsidiary if not in the consolidated unit.[71] Rorem indicated
that the interest of minority shareholders was a "special proprietorship item",[72] while the British writer Simons linked minority interests
with goodwill on consolidation as examples of fictitious items arising
only as "figures of adjustment".[73] Kohler plainly stated that "outside
stockholders and their shares of the surplus accounts ... should be
regarded as liabilities rather than as net worth",[74] while the
Accountants' handbook of 1932 went so far as to suggest that minority
interests should be shown as "deferred liabilities".[75]

---

68. Op.cit., p.596.
69. Op.cit., p.506.
70. Op.cit., p.632.
71. Op.cit., pp.461-3.
72. Op.cit., p.440.
73. Op.cit., p.89.
74. Op.cit., p.68.
75. Op.cit., p.1041.

Despite these fairly specific proposals it appears that not only did texts (and practitioners) commonly fail to distinguish liabilities from shareholders' equity but they also described or adopted methods of preparing consolidated statements which did not depict the aggregate minority interest. Three methods of treating the minority interest were commonly described. One showed particulars of "capital stock" (distinguishing that issued by the holding company and that issued by subsidiaries to minority interests) while the consolidated surplus was shown elsewhere on the balance sheet, undissected. The second method showed capital stock and surplus with suitable dissections between majority and minority interests, though capital and surplus were listed at different points in the balance sheet. Only the third method combined capital stock and surplus so as to show the aggregate of the minority interest.[76] The first two methods had the appearance of being transcriptions from the worksheets used to prepare consolidated statements, but they hardly presented data in a way that was readily amenable to analysis. Even the third method led to figures being ambiguously presented so that it was not clear whether the minority's interest was a liability or part of the shareholders' interest. As Childs later wrote, to those who saw consolidated statements as reports on the "majority interest", the minority interest was an accounting misfit to be pushed into some inconspicuous spot ...".[77]

---

76. For examples of the first two treatments, see W. M. Lybrand, "The accounting of industrial corporations", The journal of accountancy, Nov. 1908, p.40 (which was reproduced in Montgomery, op.cit., p.555); W. H. Bell, op.cit., pp.152-3; Bennett, op.cit., p.461; T. Conyngton, R. J. Bennett and H. R. Conyngton, Corporation procedure (New York: Ronald Press Company, rev.ed. 1927), p.963; Commercial Research Bureau, op.cit., Vol.IV ("Depreciation, costs and consolidated balance sheets"), pp.382-3. Writers who did aggregate the elements of the minority interests included Hatfield, op.cit., p.447 and McKinsey and Noble, op.cit., p.632.

77. Op.cit., p.54.

In the U.A., SEC rules resolved the matter to some extent by requiring the disclosure of minority interests, including particulars of the minority's interest in capital and in surplus. If nothing else, this led to the disclosure of the aggregate minority interest under one heading. But no ruling was made as to whether the minority interst should be treated as an outside liability or as part of shareholders' equity. This was to be a source of diversity in practice for many years to come.[78] There were similar variations in the practices adopted in Canada[79] and in the U.K.[80]

Turning to consolidated income statements, it will be recalled that many early texts gave little or no attention to the preparation of these reports. And, correspondingly, few texts discussed the form and content of consolidated income statements. However this changed as practitioners began consolidating majority-owned subsidiaries. The literature began to reflect differences of opinion concerning whether income statements should reflect "group" income or the income attributable to the "majority" interest. In respect of the latter objective, there was some disagreement about whether the income attributable to outside interests was to be regarded as (a) an expense or (b) an appropriation of income. The essential differences are

---

78 A review of American consolidated reporting practices in the 1950's showed that, out of 85 annual reports examined, 23 showed minority interest as a liability, 3 showed it as part of shareholders' equity, while the balance used other treatments. American Institute of Accountants, Survey of consolidated financial statement practices (New York: 1956), p.18.

79. A 1940 survey of Canadian practice "disclosed that a large majority of companies followed the practice of stating minority interests either as a separate group or grouped (though stated separately) with creditors". J. D. Campbell, as cited T. B. Robson, Consolidated and other group accounts (London: Gee & Company (Publishers) Limited, 3rd ec., 1956), p.77.

80. Robson listed 16 variations in the descriptions of minority interests, and indicated that there were similar variations in balance sheet location of these items. Ibid, p.77-9.

indicated in the accompanying illustration (which assumes dividend-based revenue recognition by the parent company).

Holding company

Trading income	$100,000
Dividend from subsidiary (60% owned)	60,000
	$160,000

Subsidiary company

Trading income	$200,000
Dividend paid	$100,000

Consolidated income statement

	"Group"	"Majority interest"	
		(a)	(b)
Net income	$300,000	$220,000	$300,000
Less			
Applicable to minority interest	-	-	80,000
	$300,000	$220,000	$220,000

American writers appear to have favoured the presentation of "group" income. Paton and Stevenson,[81] Paton,[82] McKinsey and Noble[83] and Porter and Fiske[84] all provided examples in which the consolidated income statemen did not show any deduction in respect of the share of profits attributable to minority interests. Kester also favoured this method, and attempted to justify it as follows:

> [The consolidated income statement] is not a profit and loss statement of the holding company for it includes

---

81. Op.cit., p.590.
82. Op.cit., p.472.
83. Op.cit., p.643.
84. Op.cit., pp.309-13.

> also items representing other interests. In some
> respects it is an unwieldy instrument, but it seems
> to be the best way in which to show the actual[85]
> condition of the holding company's operations.

Very few British writers discussed the preparation of consolidated income statements. One was Robson, who followed American precedent in describing a "group" statement.[86]

It appears that several American corporations prepared consolidated statements which ended up with a "majority interest profit"; accordingly, even though writers seemed reluctant to support it, this practice earned a place in text books.[87]

As Daniels later commented, the choice of methods did not matter much, provided a figure for combined aggregate profit was shown and the "distributions" to minority interests were divided as to dividends and equity in retained income.[88] But the disagreements were further symptoms of the uncertainty of accountants as to the aims of consolidated statements.

"Goodwill" or "negative goodwill" on consolidation

How should one treat the difference between the "cost" of acquiring shares in firms deemed subsidiaries, and the net asset backing or book value of those shares, when preparing consolidated statements? That was a frequently debated topic before 1940 - and it has remained a matter for debate ever since. It should be recognised also that there was (and is) no unanimity about what terminology was appropriate to

---

85. Op.cit., p.614.

86. T. B. Robson, "The construction of consolidated accounts ...",
     The accountant, 7 March 1936, p.372.

87. For an example of reports that deducted profit attributable to
     minority interests see Childs, op.cit., pp.141-2. For illustrations of the treatment of minorities' share of profit as an expense
     see ibid, p.141; Accountant's handbook, loc.cit., p.1070; M. B.
     Daniels, Financial statements, loc.cit., p.98. Note that Finney
     compromised by showing "group" profit in the income statement but
     also providing a schedule dissecting this profit between various
     interests. Op.cit., pp.118-9.

88. Op.cit., p.98.

describe these differences. "Goodwill on consolidation" is probably the most familiar term, and accordingly is used here.

Disagreements in the literature were concerned with:

(i) calculation of the "goodwill" item,

(ii) the balance sheet presentation of "goodwill".

(i) Calculation: Obviously the key elements in the calculation of "goodwill on consolidation" were the "cost" attributed to the acquisition of stock, and the corresponding book value or net asset backing of the stock acquired. In cases where subsidiaries' shares were acquired for cash, the cost was readily ascertainable. But where subsidiaries' shares were acquired through the issue of shares in the holding company (or other company in a "group) the matter was more complicated. At least five bases for calculating "cost" were proposed. The method most commonly illustrated or recommended by U.S. writers up until 1940 was that of regarding cost as equal to the par or stated value of the stock issued.[89] Other alternatives suggested at times were to regard cost as being either the book value of the shares issued or the book value of the shares acquired[90] - though the latter method would avoid the "goodwill" item altogether. Some U.S. and British writers paid more attention to the use of market prices of the issuing company's shares as an indicator of the effective cost - though an example provided by Garnsey suggested the need to look beyond estimates of cost obtained in this way to see whether it was justifiable to record the subsidiary's stock acquired in such a transaction at that figure.[91]

---

89. See, e.g., Esquerre, op.cit., p.449ff; S. F. Racine, Accounting principles (Seattle: The Western Institute of Accountancy, Commerce and Finance, 3rd ed. 1923), p.173.

90. See, e.g., Sunley and Pinkerton, op.cit., p.473ff; Kester, Advanced accounting, (New York: Ronald Press Company, 3rd ed., 1933), p.667.

91. Garnsey, Holding companies and their published accounts, loc.cit., pp.25-6. This method was also supported by Kester, Advanced accounting, loc.cit., p.667.

Another suggestion was that investments in subsidiaries should be recorded at the aggregate of the subsidiary's net tangible assets.[92]

Whatever basis was used to calculate cost, the "goodwill" (or "negative goodwill") item was taken as being the difference between that figure and the proportion of the subsidiary's equity attributable to the share holding. Of course, the net asset backing of subsidiaries' shares would be calculated from accounting data. Leaving aside the question of whether "goodwill" should be recorded as an asset, it can be readily recognised that the amount attributed to "goodwill on consolidation" might be a function of a choice of accounting methods rather than an indication of the significance placed on the benefits expected to flow from the acquisition of the subsidiary.

To illustrate, suppose H acquired a 100% interest in S for a cash consideration of $1,000,000. Suppose also that S Corporation held two assets; cash, and a machine which was used to process clients' goods in some way. Suppose further that S's balance sheet at the date it was acquired by H was as follows:

<u>S Corporation</u>

Cash	$500,000	Shareholders' equity	$800,000
Machine	300,000		
	$800,000		$800,000

Consolidation of S and H would lead to the identification of a balancing item of $200,000 - the difference between the consideration paid of $1,000,000 and the equity acquired of $800,000. It is easy enough to conceive of possible reasons why H paid $1,000,000. The machine might have been saleable for about $300,000 (the recorded figure) and H's

---

92. <u>Ibid</u>., pp.26-7; Simons, <u>op.cit</u>., p.64.

willingness to pay a premium could arise from that company's wish to acquire a profitable business, to gain entry to a market or to reduce competition. On the other hand, the machine might be virtually unsaleable and yet be very expensive to replace; given H's determination to enter this line of business, it might seem worthwhile to pay more than book values to obtain control of S. In all these cases, the book value of the assets would be irrelevant to H's decision. Correspondingly the figure (later) arrived at for "goodwill" would not at any stage have entered into H's deliberations. Further, the use of different accounting methods by S would have produced a totally different "goodwill" figure. In the example given, one might suppose that the machine's book value of $300,000 was obtained by using reducing balance depreciation at a rate of 50% per annum for two years on an initial depreciation base of $1,200,000. Assuming nil scrap value, and an estimated life of 12 years, straight line depreciation methods would have produced a book value of $1,000,000 for the machine. The "goodwill on consolidation figure produced under these conditions would not have been $200,000, but minus $500,000.

Understandably, writers' attitudes towards the handling of "goodwill" items were shaped somewhat by their attitude towards asset valuation. It will be recalled that in the U.K. in the early 1920's it was accepted that firms could revalue fixed assets up or down to reflect changes in their "value". Correspondingly, some early British advocates of consolidated statements indicated that they regarded the adjustment of asset magnitudes prior to the preparation of aggregative reports as an acceptable practice.[93] In the U.S.A., some writers on consolidation accounting were content to describe the mechanics of calculating goodwill on consolidation without any comment on the significance of

---

93. e.g., Garnsey, Holding companies and their published accounts, loc.cit., pp.62-3, 104; (anon.) "Consolidated adjustment", The accountant, July 1928, pp.59-63.

the numbers so calculated.[94] But the leading writers advocated that recorded values of subsidiaries' assets be examined critically, particularly to eliminate overvaluations.

For example, Lybrand suggested that discrepancies between the cost of the investment in subsidiaries and the book value of the stocks acquired could indicate overvaluation of subsidiaries' assets;[95] Kester suggested that subsidiaries' assets be adjusted by means of a depreciation reserve on the consolidated statement;[96] Kohler indicated that accountants should correct any "inaccurate bookkeeping"[97] while the Accountants' handbook (1932) strongly urged that upon acquisition of a subsidiary its assets should be revalued to current replacement prices.[98] The effect of these adjustments would be to recalculate the book value of subsidiaries' stock and hence affect the calculation of "goodwill".

Another source of disagreement related to "goodwill on consolidation" concerned whether the minority interest in this "asset" should be acknowledged in a statement supposedly depicting the affairs of a group of companies. Proponents of the inclusion of the minority's interest assumed that "goodwill on consolidation" was an asset of

---

94. e.g., Racine, op.cit., p.202; McKinsey and Noble, op.cit., pp.629-33.

95. Op.cit., p.508.

96. Op.cit., p.604-5. A similar adjustment was proposed by the Commercial Research Bureau's 1929 text: "if ... the purchase price is less than the market value of the stock, as shown by the balance sheet, it may be assumed that the balance sheet figures are inflated and such a discount would ordinarily be credited to the Goodwill Account on the consolidated balance sheet". Op.cit., Vol.IV, p.378.

97. Op.cit., pp.66-7. Kohler also suggested that if any "excess" could not be attributed to under- or over-valued assets or to assessments of a subsidiary's earning power, then "the inclusion of the subsidiary with the consolidated group might lead to substantial inaccuracy in interpretation". (p.67).

98. Op.cit., p.1043.

significance and not merely a balancing item.

As an illustration of this proposal, suppose that a firm paid $1
million for a 75% interest in a subsidiary with a reported shareholders'
equity of around $933,333 - so that the 75% interest was represented
by an equity of $700,000. The calculation that would typically be made
when consolidating reports of the holding and subsidiary companies would
lead to a "goodwill" item of ($1,000,000 - $700,000) or $300,000. But
some authors claimed that since $300,000 represented the goodwill for
a 75% interest, the total goodwill should be recorded at $400,000 -
with the interest of minorities being correspondingly increased by
$100,000 over and above what was recorded in the subsidiary's books.
This argument was advanced most strongly by Hatfield[99] and was touched
on by Porter and Fiske[100] - though both agreed that the recording of a
"full" goodwill figure was not commonly adopted by practitioners.

(ii) Balance sheet presentation: Most text book treatments of "goodwill on consolidation" illustrated the placement of this item in the
assets section of a consolidated balance sheet.[101] Several writers
took pains to emphasise that "goodwill on consolidation" should be
aggregated with other goodwill items rather than appear separately.[102]
Conversely, if the purchase price was less than the corresponding net
equity of subsidiaries, it was frequently suggested that the "negative
goodwill" be deducted from the totals of "goodwill" in the aggregative

---

99. Op.cit., pp.447-8.

100. Op.cit., p.304.

101. e.g., Dickinson, op.cit., p.177; Kester, op.cit., p.604.

102. e.g., Dickinson, op.cit., p.177; Racine, op.cit., p.202; Finney,
op.cit., p.33; Garnsey, Holding companies and their published
accounts, loc.cit., pp.64-6; de Paula, op.cit., p.59; Simons,
op.cit., pp.91-3. One text indicated that subsidiaries' "goodwill"
was "frequently merged with other items under the head of property",
Commercial Research Bureau, op.cit., Vol.IV, p.378.

statement.[103] In the event that "negative goodwill" on consolidation
exceeded the aggregate of subsidiaries' goodwill, it was variously
recommended that the difference be deducted from recorded asset values
("since it merely serves as an offset to inflated asset values")[104] or be
shown as part of shareholders' funds.[105]

However there were several variations on these recommendations
to be found in texts. The major source of these differences was the
conflict between accountants who regarded "goodwill" as an asset which
should properly be included in balance sheets, and those who regarded
such "intangibles" with distrust, or who regarded "goodwill on consolidation" in particular as a mere balancing item. For example, both the
Accountants' handbook (1932) and Porter and Fiske argued that the term
"goodwill" should only be used in cases where appraisals of subsidiaries'
assets indicated that the acquisition price was indeed in excess of the
"real" value of the acquired company's assets.[106] Otherwise terms such
as "excess of investment in subsidiaries over book value purchases"
were to be preferred. Another alternative (suggested by the Accountants'
handbook) was to "disregard current values" of subsidiaries' assets and
to regard any difference between the cost of these intercorporate
investments and the net asset backing of those shares not as "goodwill"
but as a mere balancing item (which was to be labelled accordingly).
Similarly Kohler stressed that the item should be labelled "excess
from consolidation with subsidiaries" or "consolidation excess" and
not merged with the goodwill of individual companies. Moreover, he

103. e.g. Finney, op.cit., p.34; Commercial Research Bureau; op.cit.,
     Vol.IV, p.378; Garnsey, Holding companies and their published
     accounts, loc.cit., p.66.
104. Commercial Research Bureau, op.cit., Vol.IV, p.378; Bell and
     Graham, op.cit., p.435.
105. Finney, op.cit., p.74; Porter and Fiske, op.cit., p.304.
106. Accountants' handbook; loc.cit., pp.1043-5; Porter and Fiske,
     op.cit., pp.303-5. See also Sunley and Pinkerton, op.cit.,
     pp.479-80.

urged the disaggregation of "consolidated excess" and "consolidated surplus" since the former "may become a loss ..."[107] Some accountants regarded the "goodwill" item as a "loss" rather than an "asset". For example, Porter and Fiske claimed that it was a common practice to show any "excess of investment in subsidiaries over book value" as a deduction from shareholders' equity.[108] Some years later Moonitz also observed that few firms alluded to goodwill but rather handled discrepancies between cost and the book value of subsidiaries' stock as a write-off against consolidated surplus.[109] Of course, by the 1940's the SEC's hostility to the writing-up of fixed assets would have been fairly evident. And it seems that many firms were reluctant to report "goodwill" as an asset. (The SEC rules at that time quite clearly stated that any goodwill retained on the books was to be identified and separately disclosed - so goodwill could not be "buried" by aggregating it with other assets). Moonitz noted that firms were reluctant to show "any goodwill at all" though it is not clear from his remarks whether firms commonly wrote-off goodwill against shareholders' funds or whether they simply avoided the term "goodwill" in favour of alternatives. The latter seems more likely. In 1949 Childs reported that a survey of some 200 reports filed with the SEC revealed that in no case was the term goodwill used to describe the excess of cost over equity on the face of the consolidated balance sheet.[110]

Finally, it should be noted that the amount calculated for "goodwill" upon qcquisition of subsidiaries' stock would, ceteribus paribus,

---

107. Op.cit., p.67.

108. Op.cit., p.305.

109. M. Moonitz, The entity theory of consolidated statements (American Accounting Association: 1944), p.60.

110. Op.cit., p.89. See also W. A. Paton (ed.), Accountants' handbook (New York: Ronald Press Company, 3rd ec., 1947), p.1081 for comments about the "burying" of the goodwill on consolidation under other headings.

be retained in subsequent balance sheets. Kester noted that acquisitions of additional stock in a subsidiary would require further calculations and hence adjustment of the aggregate goodwill item appearing in this consolidated statement.[111] Otherwise there was little further discussion in the standard texts of the subsequent treatment of goodwill. In particular, the question of whether or not goodwill should be "written off" was not raised.

*   *   *   *

Disagreements about the calculation and presentation of "goodwill on consolidation" were obviously linked with disagreements about the appropriate bases for the recognition and valuation of assets. However these disagreements can also be seen as reflecting uncertainty about the aims of consolidated statements.

For example, Hatfield's proposals that goodwill be recorded at the "full amount" (i.e. including the minority interests' share) were consistent with claims that consolidated statements were intended to depict the affairs of a group of companies. (Indeed, this unpopular notion was later revived by M. Moonitz in his Entity theory of consolidated statements). Other proposals to the effect that goodwill on consolidation should be clearly labelled so as to identify it as a balancing item were consistent with the view of consolidated statements as an amplification of a holding company's reports. Claims that goodwill should be deducted from shareholders' equity were consistent with support for consolidated statements as a representation of liquidity or solvency. Opposition to the subtraction of goodwill from the shareholders' equity were consistent with claims that consolidated reports should be clearly linked with holding company statements so that they could amplify the latter documents.

---

111. Op.cit., pp.554-8.

The extent of these disagreements suggest that practitioners faced formidable difficulties when endeavouring to prepare consolidated statements. The number and variety of these difficulties indicate the underlying uncertainty about the aims of consolidated reporting, and also illustrate how little had been achieved by efforts to resolve these difficulties. Consolidated statements became part and parcel of accounting practice despite the fact that the rationale of these reports had not been fully explicated.

Pre-acquisition profits

In 1904 at the International Congress on Accounting, A. L. Dickinson had first warned against the deception that could be practiced should the pre-acquisition profits of subsidiary companies be treated as distributable income of a holding company. Legally, any dividends paid out of a subsidiary's pre-acquisition profits were distributable by the holding company as dividends, but Dickinson urged that these items be treated as reductions of the cost of inter-corporate investments rather than credits to surplus.[112] Other writers made similar observations and it became accepted that dividends "out of pre-acquisition profits were not to be regarded as income. Indeed, in 1932 the American Institute's Committee on Co-operation with Stock Exchanges listed the treatment of pre-acquisition profits as an example of one of the few "principles" of accounting. The Committee asserted that a dividend declared out of pre-acquisition surpluses could not "properly be credited to the income account of the parent company". That was straightforward enough. But the Committee's discussion of pre-acquisition profits was to have broader implications for the preparation of consolidated statements. The Committee went on to claim that it was an accounting "principle" that "earned surplus of a subsidiary created prior to acquisition does not form part of the consolidated earned surplus

---

112. Dickinson, op.cit., pp.190-1.

of the parent company and subsidiaries".[113] This contention was quite
different from the matters discussed by Dickinson and others, even though
superficially it concerned pre-acquisition profits. The rules proposed
by Dickinson seemed to have been designed to prevent the manipulation
of income calculations in the parent's books in the context of cost-based
valuation of inter-corporate investments. If the 1932 Committee was
concerned with the manipulation of profit data then it might have
spelled out this concern and approached the matter in one of several
ways. In particular, the manipulation of profits through the use of
dividend-based revenue recognition might have been avoided by the use of
equity accounting procedures (which by 1932 had been fully described in
the Accountants' handbook and in many leading texts, including those by
Racine, Finney and Kester).

However it seems that the Committee was not concerned with the
manipulation of profit data but with the use of a method of compiling
consolidated statements in which the investment in subsidiaries on the
holding company's books was offset against the par value of the
subsidiaries' shares (rather than book value). The practical effect
of this was to vary the amount of "goodwill on consolidation". This
is illustrated below. In the following examples, suppose that H Co.
acquired stocks in a subsidiary (S1, S2, S3 or S4) on January 1, and
initially valued these investments at cost. In Cases 1 and 2, a 100%
stockholding was acquired. Two consolidated statements are prepared
in these examples. Consolidated balance sheet "A" is prepared using
the customary procedure of eliminating the entire shareholders'
equity in the subsidiary's books. Consolidated balance sheet "B"
follows from the elimination of only the par value of the subsidiary's
stock.

---

113. As cited by G. O. May, Twenty-five years of accounting responsibility (New York: Price, Waterhouse & Co., 1936 ed. by B. C.
Hunt; later reprinted by Scholars Book Co., 1971), p.121. Emphasis
added.

Case 1
100% ownership

"Goodwill" on consolidation

	H Co. Balance sheet	S1 Co. Balance sheet	Consolidated balance sheet A	Consolidated balance sheet B
	$	$	$	$
Assets				
Cash	900,000	80,000	980,000	980,000
Shares in S1 Co.	100,000	-	-	-
"Goodwill on consolidation"	-	-	20,000	25,000
	1,000,000	80,000	1,000,000	1,005,000
Liabilities	-	-		
Shareholders' equity				
Contributed capital	500,000	75,000	500,000	500,000
Surplus	500,000	5,000	500,000	505,000
	1,000,000	80,000	1,000,000	1,005,000

Case 2
100% ownership

"Reserve" on consolidation

	H Co. Balance sheet	S1 Co. Balance sheet	Consolidated balance sheet A	Consolidated balance sheet B
	$	$	$	$
Assets				
Cash	900,000	140,000	1,040,000	1,040,000
Shares in S2 Co.	100,000	-	-	-
	1,000,000	140,000	1,040,000	1,040,000
Liabilities	-	-	-	-
Shareholders' equity				
Contributed capital	500,000	120,000	500,000	500,000
Surplus	500,000	20,000	500,000	520,000
			1,000,000	1,020,000
"Reserve on consolidation" (or "Excess of book value of shares in subsidiary at date of acquisition over eensideration paid")			40,000	20,000
	1,000,000	140,000	1,040,000	1,040,000

In Case 1, the only difference between the consolidated statements A and B is that the latter shows a higher "goodwill on consolidation" figure, and a higher "surplus" (undistributed profits) figure. In Case 2, the surplus figure is again higher, with the difference again being reflected in the "balancing item" which here is termed "reserve on consolidation" (though other terms have been used for that purpose).

Method B may have been fostered by Dickinson's original description of consolidation procedures. Dickinson had referred to the goodwill item as "the amount by which the aggregate book value to the holding company of the stocks of subsidiary companies exceeds the par value of that stock".[114] Later Dickinson amended this description by alluding to the difference between values on the holding company's books and "the par value of that stock and the surplus at the date of acquisition".[115] But it seems that the original version was accepted and adopted by some U.S. corporations. And, even though the American Institute's committees claimed that there was an accepted "broad principle" favouring Method A, it appears that until the late 1930's some firms continued to include the pre-acquisition profits of subsidiaries in the shareholders' equity section of consolidated statements. In September 1937 the SEC issued Accounting Series Release No. 3 "to prevent write-ups arising in the consolidation of accounts by a parent company with those of its subsidiaries through the elimination of only a portion of the investment account". The American Institute's 1932 statement was concerned with the "over-statement" of surplus. But the SEC opposed the inclusion of pre-acquisition surpluses because of its opposition to asset write-ups.

The exclusion of subsidiaries' pre-acquisition surpluses from the shareholders' equity section of consolidated statements would not be

114. "Some special points in corporation accounting", The accountant, Oct. 7, 1905, p.409. Emphasis added.
115. Accounting practice and procedure, loc.cit., p.177. Emphasis added.

consistent with particular aims of consolidated reporting. If one viewed
consolidated statements as amplifications of the reports of holding
companies, then the major reason for excluding the pre-acquisition
surpluses of wholly-owned subsidiaries might be to ensure that the
shareholders' equity sections were identical - thus linking the two
statements.[116] But if consolidated statements were regarded as depicting
the affairs of a "group" of companies then it could be argued that the
total surplus of the component companies should be aggregated. Alternatively, if one argued that consolidated statements should reflect the
performance of an economic entity then one could suppose that the
consolidated statements should distinguish between that portion of shareholders' equity which was earned before and after the formation of the
group. This could require disaggregation of both the surpluses of both
subsidiaries and the holding company according to whether they were earned
before or after the purchase of subsidiary stock.

The rule most commonly accepted seems to have been aimed at
identifying that portion of accumulated profits which was attributable
to the interests of the holding company. This was not the same as the
amount of profit legally distributable by the holding company - for
the customary treatment of dividends from subsidiaries in the parent
company's books was certainly not consistent with that objective. However
the presence of minority interests in subsidiaries produced complications.

Cases 3 and 4 show consolidated statements under these conditions.

---

116. Judging from comments by Webster, this was in fact the justification
    offered for the practice. Op.cit., p.263.

Case 3
75% ownership
"Goodwill" on consolidation

	H Co. Balance sheet	S3 Co. Balance sheet		Consolidated balance sheet
	$	$	$	$
Assets				
Cash	900,000	80,000		980,000
Shares in S3 Co.	100,000	–		–
"Goodwill on consolidation"	–	–		40,000
	1,000,000	80,000		1,020,000
Liabilities	–	–		–
Shareholders' equity				
Contributed capital	500,000	75,000		–
Surplus	500,000	5,000		–
Majority interest				
Contrib. capital			500,000	
Surplus			500,000	1,000,000
Minority interest				
Contrib. capital			18,750	
Surplus			1,250	20,000
	1,000,000	80,000		1,020,000

Case 4
75% ownership
"Reserve" on consolidation

	H Co. Balance sheet	S4 Co. Balance sheet		Consolidated balance sheet
	$	$	$	$
Assets				
Cash	900,000	140,000		1,040,000
Shares in S4 Co.	100,000	–		–
	1,000,000	140,000		1,040,000
Liabilities	–	–		–
Shareholders' equity				
Contributed capital	500,000	120,000		–
Surplus	500,000	20,000		–
Majority interest				
Contrib. capital			500,000	
Surplus			500,000	1,000,000
Minority interest				
Contrib. capital			30,000	
Surplus			5,000	35,000
Excess book value of shares in subsidiary at date of acquisition over consideration paid				5,000
	1,000,000	140,000		1,040,000

In these examples only one form of a consolidated balance sheet is
illustrated: a statement which distinguishes majority and minority
interests and which shows contributed capital and undistributed surplus
for each category. Note that the minority interest includes pre-
acquisition surpluses. The shareholders' equity in S3 totalled $80,000,
of which 25% or $20,000 is attributable to outside interests. In S4,
the equity of minority shareholders was 25% of $140,000, or $35,000.
The acquisition of a 75% shareholding would in no way affect the extent
of the equity of the remaining shareholders.

Strictly, the American Institute's statement and the SEC's Release
required the total exclusion of pre-acquisition surpluses from the
consolidation. To be consistent with these rulings $1,250 of the equity
of minority shareholders in S3 would be eliminated, with a corresponding
reduction in "Goodwill on consolidation". Similarly, the minority
interest in S4 would be reduced by $5,000. However these adjustments
would hardly be consistent with the aim of depicting either the affairs
of a "group" or of representing the relative status of majority and
minority shareholders in the associated enterprises.

One way of observing the American Institute's "principle" and of
meeting the SEC's requirements without producing any distortion of the
minority's interests would be to remove this item from the shareholders'
equity section altogether. It is difficult to say whether this "solution"
was consciously considered - but the fact is that accountants eventually
adopted the practice of reporting minority interests as a "quasi-liability"
and of calculating these interests inclusive of pre-acquisition profits.
Clearly this treatment was not consistent with reporting the position
and performance of a "group" of companies - for to satisfy this supposed
objective of consolidated statements there would be no point in
distinguishing categories of shareholders' interests, let alone grouping
any part of these interests with liabilities. Nor was the "liability"

classification consistent with the aim of providing information to
creditors - for this practice would distort representations of
liquidity and solvency. And it is hard to see how this treatment would
further the supposed aim of depicting the affairs of holding companies.

Inter-company transactions

Several of the early discussions of consolidated reports in the U.S.
focussed on balance sheets and made only passing reference to consolidated income statements - possibly because there was little to be said
of a technical nature about the preparation of these documents. Even so,
it was usual for mention to be made of the (supposed) need to eliminate
the inter-company profit component of inventory valuations.[117] However,
as the literature expanded there were more discussions of consolidated
income statements and it is apparent that writers often disagreed about
how to treat transactions between subsidiaries or between subsidiaries and
parent companies. There was near unanimity about the desirability of
preventing consolidated income statements from being puffed by profits
on inter-company transactions. But when the literature became concerned
with both balance sheets and income statements, it was clear that there
were disputes about how to "eliminate" inter-company profits. Dickinson
suggested that consolidated earnings statements should totally exclude the
amount of sales and expenses that were attributable to inter-company
transactions. Correspondingly, Dickinson outlined a procedure for
reducing inventories by the extent of profit on intra-group sales[118]
(though he indicated that the total elimination of all inter-company
transactions had "probably ... never yet been attempted").[119] On the
other hand Lybrand suggested that consolidated income statements should

---

117. e.g. Bennett, op.cit., p.468; Webster, op.cit., p.265; Conyngton,
Bennett and Conyngton, op.cit., p.956.

118. "Some special points ...", loc.cit., p.410; Accounting theory and
practice, loc.cit., pp.181-2.

119. "Some special points ...", loc.cit., p.410.

show <u>gross</u> income and expenses (without elimination of intra-group

transactions). However this was put forward as a matter of convenience:

> While on the surface it would seem that there is a
> duplication of gross earnings under this method it is
> probably the only practical way ... where there is a
> large number of companies with very many manufacturing
> processes.[120]

Another variation (noted by Kester) was that of recording inventories at

the aggregate of balance sheet figures, but setting against this a

"Reserve for inter-company profits" created by a charge against consoli-

dated surplus.[121] This procedure differed only in respect of balance

sheet presentation and did not exclude inter-company profits from

consolidated income statements.

Most writers agreed that it was desirable to totally eliminate

both the revenues and the expenses arising from inter-company transac-

tions. Hence revenues and expenses appearing in consolidated income

statements would only relate to the sale of goods or services to customers

outside the holding company-subsidiary company network. Correspondingly,

further adjustments were necessary in cases where items sold from one

company to a related company were regarded by the purchaser as a fixed

asset. Dickinson (influenced no doubt by his experience with the U.S.

Steel Corporation) pointedly warned about the need to check whether

inter-company transactions involved items used "in construction". Later

other writers discussed the need to adjust depreciation charges in

relation to the amount of inter-company profit included in the depreciation

base.

The common rationale for these practices rested on two assumptions.

---

120. Lybrand, <u>loc.cit.</u>, Jan 1909, p.229. This passage was approvingly
     reproduced by Montgomery, <u>op.cit.</u>, pp.559-60 and by S. Walton in
     "Consolidated statements", <u>The journal of accountancy</u>, March 1918,
     pp.228-9.

121. R. B. Kester, <u>Accounting theory and practice</u>, Vol.II, <u>loc.cit.</u>,
     p.610. This procedure was similar to that described earlier
     by Conyngton, Bennett and Conyngton, <u>op.cit.</u>

The first concerned asset valuation, and the idea that "profits" should only be recognised in accounting when "realised". The second concerned the function of consolidated statements. The idea of eliminating profits on inter-company transactions was supposedly to avoid the inclusion of profits which had not been "realised" in transactions with outsiders, given the assumption that consolidated statements reflected the performance of a "group" of companies. Correspondingly, it was claimed that assets should be valued at "cost to the group". It should be noted that insistence upon such eliminations would not necessarily be consistent with other ideas about the aims of consolidated reports - such as amplifying a holding company's reports, or reflecting group solvency for the benefit of creditors.

There were some dissident voices. In the early 1930's, Sunley and Pinkerton commented that "the real purpose" of these eliminations should not be lost sight of. That was:

> to prevent a manipulation of profits through the
> mechanism of affiliated companies.

These authors suggested that if there was "good evidence" of the absence of intention to manipulate, then "the principle of eliminating inter-company profits should not be carried to absurd lengths". Likewise in connection with profits on "construction", they pointed to the complexities which could arise in attempting to adjust recorded values, and suggested that "it is not unusual to obtain competitive bids on the work in order to show that the affiliated company would have had to pay just as much or more if it had purchased the asset elsewhere".[122]

However, the process of eliminating these profits became an accepted procedure. It will be recalled that the only U.K. and Australian disclosure rules relating to consolidated statements were those issued by stock exchanges and in either case the rules did not deal with technical

---

122. Sunley and Pinkerton, op.cit., pp.459-60.

matters. In the U.S., the SEC refrained from formally making eliminations mandatory, but did require disclosure of "the amount, and the
effect upon any balance sheet item, of profits and losses resulting
from transactions with affiliated companies which had not been eliminated.
(If it was not possible to give an accurate figure without under effort
or expense, an estimate and explanation were required). Likewise,
explanations were required in respect of the non-elimination of inter-
company profits from consolidated income statements. There was at least
one early SEC decision indicating that non-elimination rendered financial
statements misleading,[123] and it seems reasonable to suppose that
eliminations were required by the SEC in the course of the review of
documents lodged for filing.

But there were disagreements about the appropriate way to handle
inter-company eliminations in cases where there were substantial outside
interests in subsidiaries.

It was claimed by some writers that transactions involving
partly-owned subsidiaries should be regarded as being "realised" from
the viewpoint of the minority shareholders - at least when it came to
asset valuations. For example, while some American writers argued that
inventory values should be reduced by the full amount of inter-company
profits,[124] writers such as Finney in the U.S. and Garnsey supported
the elimination of only that percentage of inter-company profits which
could be attributed to the majority: the balance was "realised".[125]

Clearly this disagreement can be associated with different views
about the aims of consolidated statements. Stempf claimed that the

---

123. Associated Gas and Electric Co. (1942), 11 S.E.C. 975.

124. Stempf, op.cit., p.369; Kohler, "Some tentative propositions
     ... ", loc.cit., p.66.

125. Finney, op.cit., p.103; Garnsey, Holding companies and their pub-
     lished accounts, loc.cit., p.71.

the total elimination of unrealised inter-company profit was consistent with "the single-company theory of consolidated statements" - the view that consolidated statements endeavoured to reflect the performance of a "single economic entity". Similarly Kohler talked of reflecting "the unitary position of the combined enterprises". Conversely it was claimed that reporting minority interests at their "full" amount (and hence not reducing asset valuaions by supposedly unrealised profits) was consistent with providing ancillary information to the holding company's share-holders.

In either case the parties to the disagreement accepted that "cost" was the appropriate basis for asset valuation and hence for calculating the extent of equity interests. Another basis of asset valuation (par-ticularly one based on the use of market prices) would have eliminated the need for these calculations and adjustments.

The difficulties which flowed from trying to calculate "cost" in these circumstances can readily be appreciated from an examination of the elimination processes that might be used in relation to sales between a series of majority-owned subsidiaries.

Suppose that a holding company (H) has stockholdings in three subsidiaries (A, B and C) of 60%, 75% and 90% respectively.

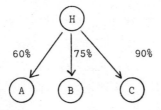

Suppose also that A Co. deals in goods which cost $1,000 per unit to fabricate and which are sold for $2,000 per unit. (For the sake of simplicity, disregard the basis of calculating production costs and also the costs associated with selling and administration - though obviously the treatment of these expenditures would affect calculations

of "inter-company" profits).

During 19x1, A fabricated 5 units and sold 4 - one each to H, B,

C and an outside customer. A's records would thus show: Sales $8,000,

Cost of sales $4,000, Inventory $1,000. But when the income statements

of H, A, B and C are consolidated, data would appear as follows:

Sales	$2,000
Cost of sales	1,000
Gross margin:	$1,000

This is straightforward: only the "outside" sales would be recorded.

However the calculation of inventory is less straightforward. Inventory

data would appear in the companies' records as follows:

Inventories

A	(cost)	$1,000
H	(cost)	2,000
B	(cost)	2,000
C	(cost)	2,000
		$7,000

Given that "unrealised" inter-company profits were to be eliminated,

one rule that was described in the literature was that of eliminating all

inter-company profits, regardless of proportionate interests.[126] Adoption

of this rule would mean that inventories in the consolidated balance

sheet would be shown at the sum of $4,000: 4 units at $1,000, each.

An alternative (and more commonly described rule) was that of

deducting from the aggregate recorded "cost" data the majority interest's

share of vendor's profits on transactions with affiliates.[127] This would

---

126. See, e.g., Dickinson, Accounting practice and procedure, loc.cit.,
     p.182; Porter and Fiske, op.cit., p.300; this method was noted (but
     criticised) by Finney, op.cit., p.104 and the Accountants' handbook
     (1932), loc.cit., p.1041

127. See, e.g., Garnsey, Holding companies and their published accounts,
     loc.cit., p.136; Bell and Graham, op.cit., p.441; Finney, op.cit.
     p.103; G. H. Newlove, Consolidated balance sheets (New York: Ronald
     Press Company, 1926), pp.289-90; Sunley and Pinkerton, op.cit.,
     pp.465-6.

lead to the consolidated balance sheet including inventories at a figure calculated as follows:

Inventories

A (cost)		$1,000
H, B and C		
Cost	$6,000	
less		
60% A's profit on sales	1,800	4,200
		$5,200

Identical goods would thus be recorded in the consolidated statement at different prices - notwithstanding that their "cost" (of manufacture) was identical - supposedly because A's recorded profit of $1,000 per unit was "unrealised".

A more complex method of eliminating inter-company profits involved the calculation of the <u>majority interest's share of profits "earned" on sales to its own "interests"</u>.[128] This method is easier to illustrate than describe. In the above example, the value of inventories for the consolidated balance sheet would be calculated as follows:

Inventories

A (cost) $1,000

H (cost $2,000 <u>less</u> intra-group profit
i.e. $\frac{60}{100}$ x $1,000) 1,400

B (cost $2,000 <u>less</u> intra-group profit
i.e. $\frac{60}{100}$ x $\frac{75}{100}$ x $1,000) 1,550

C (cost $2,000 <u>less</u> intra-group profit
i.e. $\frac{60}{100}$ x $\frac{90}{100}$ x $1,000) 1,460
$5,410

Once again, identical goods would be recorded at different prices - in this case, ranging from $1,000 to $1,550 per unit. And it will be realised that these eliminations were adjustments to data relating to

---

128. See, e.g., Sunley and Pinkerton, <u>op.cit.</u>, p.466.

transactions with <u>subsidiaries</u>. Supposing transactions involving the
sale of identical goods had been with 40% or even 50%-owned companies -
no such eliminations would take place.[129] Also note that the third method
described could have the effect of eliminating less than 50% of profits
on inter-company transactions - a factor which is not in itself of any
great significance but which points to the arbitrariness of the procedure in
the light of comparisons that could be made with other situations. For
example, suppose a similar transaction giving rise to a $1,000 profit took
place between companies D and E which had a common holding company, H1.

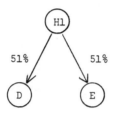

Profit eliminated would be $(\frac{51}{100} \times \frac{51}{100} \times \$1,000)$ or approximately $255
- 25.5%. But suppose a similar transaction took place between companies
H2 and F, or between companies I and J:

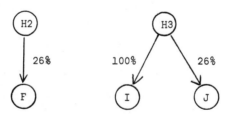

In these situations no profit eliminations would have been carried out -
even though the parent companies' equity in those unrealised profits
would be of a similar proportion to that of H1 in the previous example.

---

129. However rules outlined by professional associations of accountants
     in the 1970's in connection with the use of "equity accounting" pro-
     cedures have prescribed the elimination of profits arising from
     transactions between "associated" companies. See the following
     chapter.

Whatever procedure was used to adjust the values attributed to inventories or other assets, there would necessarily be an equal adjustment to shareholders' equities. If the adjustments were made in respect of unrealised profits on inventories, then it seems reasonable to suppose that these modifications to book values would disappear when the goods in question were actually sold. (Though they might well be replaced by adjustments in respect of subsequently acquired inventories). However if the adjustments were made in connection with the sale of "fixed" assets then the elimination of inter-company profits would have a long-term effect on reported data, given the use of conventional valuation procedures. Depreciation would have to be recalculated for consolidation purposes to reflect adjustments to the depreciation base. This would lead to differences between consolidated profits and the aggregate of parent and subsidiary companies' profits.[130] But while textbooks routinely advised the elimination of inter-company profits from inventory or fixed asset values, they did not commonly discuss the effect of these eliminations on the accounting reports of later periods. Few texts discussed the complications which could arise when goods were transferred from one partly-owned subsidiary to another. And virtually no attention was given to other transactions (such as the payment of "management fees") between related but not wholly-owned companies.

No doubt the complexities which could arise in such situations led Sunley and Pinkerton to caution accountants against losing sight of the "real objective" of forestalling the manipulation of profits through inter-company transactions at phony prices. But even these writers did not pause to consider that the style of adjustment carried out in the process of preparing consolidated statements had little to do with the proposition that profits were "realised" when they were converted into cash or debts. Whereas the general view of realisaton was that profits either

---

130. In terms of rules promulgated by professional associations in the 1970's this would also necessitate adjustments to income tax expense.

were or were not realised in particular situations, the consolidation rules could treat profits as being _partly_ realised. Indeed, a sale from a 75%-owned subsidiary to an 80%-owned subsidiary could lead to a profit being treated as totally unrealised, or 25% realised or 40% realised, depending upon the method being used to eliminate inter-company profits.

U.S. experience with public utilities and other corporate groups during the 1920's and early 1930's seems to have encouraged adherence to cost-based valuation and the elimination of inter-company profits on consolidation. As was noted in an earlier chapter, the Federal Trade Commission's investigations of the Insull group and other public utilities led some to propose a ban on the writing-up of fixed assets as a means of countering manipulation of financial reporting.[131] It seems highly likely that, in this climate, the taking of profits on transactions between subsidiaries was regarded as being equivalent to a write-up and hence was to be offset by appropriate profit eliminations.[132] In 1936 T. H. Sanders (who had been recruited from Harvard to assist the SEC formulate policies on accounting matters) described the SEC's rules on the treatment of inter-company items as being extremely flexible. "The one thing insisted upon is that the practices adopted shall be disclosed".[133] But later rules required disclosure of the effect of non-eliminated profits and losses arising from transactions with affiliated companies; if

---

131. See, e.g, testimony of R. E. Healy (later an SEC commissioner), Hearings before the committee on banking and currency, United States Senate, 73rd Congress, April 1934.

132. Actually elimination procedures would probably have been ineffective in the Insull case because inter-company transactions were negotiated through dummy intermediaries, so that what were in effect inter-company transactions appeared to be at arm's length.

133. T. H. Sanders, "Influence of the Securities and Exchange Commission upon accounting principles", The accounting review, March 1936, p.69.

eliminations were carried out, no notation was required.[134] It seems
likely that when the SEC began its campaign to actively discourage
write-ups, the Commission's staff may have encouraged the total
elimination of inter-company profits. In any event, a survey of
documents filed with the SEC prior to 1949 revealed that in all cases
inter-company profits had been eliminated entirely from every balance
sheet examined.[135]

In the U.K., on the other hand, there seemed to be more support for
proportional, rather than total, eliminations of inter-company profits.
Among early writers, Cash[136] and Robson [137] did not canvass the question
of what eliminations were appropriate for transactions involving majority-
owned subsidiaries - but they described the need for eliminations and
(perhaps unintentionally) implied that eliminations would be of the
aggregate profit involved. But both Garnsey[138] and Simons[139] regarded
proportional illustrations as appropriate and provided extended
illustrations of this practice. And whereas the evidence available
from SEC filings suggests that U.S. accountants soon abandoned proportional eliminations, it appears that British writers continued to
to regard the choice of methods as a debateàble matter. U.K. disclosure

---

134. See L. H. Rappaport, SEC accounting practice and procedure (New
     York: Ronald Press Company, 2nd ed., 1959), pp.252, 259. Note
     that these rulings applied to both consolidated data and data
     contained in the reports of unconsolidated subsidiaries.

135. Childs, op.cit., p.116.

136. W. A. Cash, "Consolidated balance sheets" (an address at the
     1929 International Conference on Accounting), The accountant, 7
     Dec. 1929, p.737.

137. T. B. Robson, "The construction of consolidated acounts - some
     points ...", The accountant, March 1936.

138. "Holding companies and their published accounts", The accountant,
     13 Jan. 1923, p.58.

139. Op.cit., pp.106-21.

rules or professional recommendations avoided recommending one or other

technique, and text books in the post-war period have continued to

describe (if not necessarily support) both total eliminations and some

form of proportional eliminations.[140] Similarly, Australian writers

have continued to describe proportional-elimination methods[141] (even

though some early professional recommendations indicated preference for

total eliminations).

However, in both the U.S. and the U.K. the corresponding treatment

of the minority interest seems to have remained an unsettled issue.

Some writers have argued that a proportion of inter-company

profits should be deducted from the minority interest (treating this as

a balancing item rather than an indication of the extent of this class

of shareholders' equity) while others have claimed that the minority

interest should be left at book figures with any necessary adjustment

taken up elsewhere in the shareholders' equity section. There seems

little need to explore these technicalities further since it is apparent

that there were extensive disagreements about what consolidation

procedures were appropriate.

And, once again, it seems reasonable to attribute these disagree-

ments to conflicting ideas about the aims of consolidated statements.

---

140. A. MacBeath and A. J. Platt, Group accounts and holding companies (Lon-
     don: Gee & Company (Publishers) Ltd., 1951), p.41; T. B. Robson, Con-
     solidated and other group accounts (London: Gee & Company (Publishers)
     Limited, 3rd ed., 1956),p.43; D. J. Bogie, Group accounts (London:
     Jordan & Sons Limited, 2nd ed., 1959), p.118; E. Stamp, The elements
     of consolidation accounting (Wellington, N.Z.: Sweet & Maxwell (N.Z.)
     Ltd., 1965), pp.43-4; G. A. Lee, Modern financial accounting (London:
     Thomas Nelson and Sons Ltd., 1973), p.404.

141. See, e.g., G. E. Fitzgerald and A. E. Speck, Holding companies in
     Australia and New Zealand (Sydney: Butterworth & Co. (Australia)
     Ltd., 2nd ed. 1950), p.29; ibid., 3rd ed. 1957), p.47; R. L. Bowra
     and F. L. Clarke, Holding companies and group accounts in Australia
     and New Zealand (Sydney: Butterworths Pty. Ltd., 1973), pp.50-2;
     L. N. Lee and L. A. McPherson, Consolidated statements and group
     accounts (Sydney: The Law Book Company, Ltd., 1963), pp.122-52.

The idea of total eliminations was commonly associated with arguments to the effect that consolidated reports depicted an "economic entity", for by totally eliminating all the inter-company profits the reports were concerned with cost to the group. Conversely, while arguments for proportional eliminations seem to have been tied in with particular views about "realisation", they were also commonly linked with the idea that consolidated statements amplified the reports of a holding company.

It must of course be acknowledged that the complexities which developed in this area of practice were a product of cost-based valuation rules. If assets were valued by reference to market prices of one kind or other, then there would be no need to carry out these elimination procedures.

Review and resume

An attempt has been made to identify the main, disputed issues about consolidated statements in the accounting literature up to the end of the 1930's. By this time consolidated statements were both widely accepted and widely used in the U.K. and the U.S.A.

It is useful to distinguish _fundamental_ and _technical_ issues. The fundamental issue in dispute about consolidated statements concerned the _function_ of these documents. Other matters - the scope of consolidated statements, the treatment of minority interests or pre-acquisition profits, the elimination of profits on inter-company transactions - can be seen as technical questions arising from the adoption of one or other idea about the function of this form of report.

A review of the British and American literature in this period led to the identification of the following propositions about the aims of consolidated statements:

1. to depict the financial position and performance of holding companies;

2. to amplify the financial statements of holding companies;

3. to facilitate assessments of the ability of firms to meet their debts;

4. to depict the position and performance of "economic entities".

It is not claimed that any of these four propositions is an assertion of the _appropriate_ function of consolidated reports. The list simply provides a convenient basis for examining the arguments considered by the accounting profession and by those concerned with framing disclosure rules.

The evidence suggests that some accounting writers and regulatory agencies tended to emphasise one or other of these "aims" of consolidated statements, and to correspondingly support proposals for technical rules (e.g., concerning the area of consolidation) that were consistent with that assumption. Other accounting writers reproduced passages from leading texts in an entirely uncritical fashion. This led some writers to simultaneously support inconsistent ideas about the objectives of consolidated reporting. Similarly, disclosure rules occasionally prescribed or permitted practices which were consistent with one or other function, so that the end result was a set of rulings which would not fully satisfy any particular objective.

The evidence also indicates that very few commentators apprehended that text books on the disclosure rules contained any disagreement about the objectives of consolidated reports. This situation seems to have arisen because the jargon used to describe consolidation practices was extremely ambiguous. One of the most popular explanations of consolidation accounting was that these statements depicted a holding company and its subsidiaries "as if" they were a single organization. Another description was that consolidated statements depicted the affairs of several corporations as a "group". Both of these descriptions could be taken as supporting conflicting ideas about the objectives of consolidation accounting. Indeed, the popularity of these descriptions may have exacerbated the conflict. As has been described earlier, consolidated statements were originally designed for situations in which holding companies either owned 100% or near to 100% of subsidiaries' stock. But some writers became preoccupied with the idea of depicting the affairs of a "group" and so attempted to widen the ambit of consolidated statements to encompass "controlled" corporations. Other writers focussed on the meaning of the term "subsidiary" rather than on the outcome of adopting particular criteria for determining the scope of consolidation. Subsequently accountants began to prepare consolidated statements which not only encompassed wholly-owned or substantially-owned firms but also firms which were majority-owned or merely "controlled". This shift in accounting practice was accompanied by support for the idea that consolidated statements were reports on corporate "groups". The end result was that around 1940 consolidated statements had become firmly accepted as a vehicle for corporate reporting even though questions about the aims, status, and procedures appropriate for consolidated reporting had not been resolved.

On one point there was a consensus. Accounting writers differed about what consolidated statements should encompass and what they should show and whether they were necessary. But they did agree that consolidated were not sufficient. Reporting practices in the U.S.A. (as opposed to SEC filing requirements) appeared to sanction the presentation of consolidated statements alone. But with this exception, it was generally held that either consolidated statements were to supplement parent company reports, or vice versa.

One of the major shifts in accounting practice since 1940 has been the abandonment of this position. Consolidated statements have come to be regarded as primary statements which can stand alone.

SECTION V

Ch. 16 Confused ideas and practices: Consolidated reporting since 1940

By 1940, U.K. and U.S. accountants had firmly adopted consolidated
reporting - even though the profession had yet to resolve such questions
as what these statements were intended to show, when they should be
used and how they should be prepared.

Subsequent experience with consolidated reporting has continued to
reflect confusion about the objectives and adequacy of consolidated
reports. Post-1940 disclosure rules and the recommendations of professional bodies have reduced the range of variations in consolidation
techniques that was evident in the 1930's. But a comparison of rules
adopted in different countries or jurisdictions reveals marked differences.
And the particular rules adopted within a given country can still be seen
to lack internal consistency, relative to one or other of the supposed
"aims" of consolidated reporting.

This chapter reviews developments in consolidated reporting since
1940. The review is fairly brief since the issues that appear from a
review of recent literature and from an analysis of disclosure rules and
professional recommendations are substantially the same issues that were
evident before 1940.

Legislation and regulations

In the U.S.A., the SEC did not make far-reaching changes to its
regulations dealing with the use of consolidated reports. It maintained
its requirements for the submission of consolidated statements in conjunction
with parent company reports. These consolidated statements were only to
encompass majority-owned subsidiaries, but not banks or (with some exceptions) insurance companies. The SEC continued to permit firms to exercise
some discretion in selecting the ambit of consolidated statements and to
require ancillary disclosures for non-consolidated subsidiaries.

The SEC made one change to the technical rules governing consolidation procedures when it prohibited the consolidation of subsidiaries in a "promotional, exploratory or development stage".[1] The SEC also required auditors to comment on the "principles" followed by firms in determining the inclusion or exclusion of subsidiaries.[2] Other SEC rules concerning financial disclosure by firms engaged in diversified activities may be interpreted as affecting decisions about the area of consolidation; these will be examined later in this chapter.

While the SEC maintained a general requirement for the filing of both consolidated and parent company statements, the Commission introduced certain "concessions". These concessions indicate that the SEC had refined its views about the status of these reports. The changes in the disclosure rules were consistent with the attitude that consolidated statements are primary documents, and that the holding company statements supplement consolidated reports, not vice versa. In 1947 the SEC resolved that when the parent's assets or revenues represented 85 per cent or more of the consolidated assets and revenues, respectively, then either consolidated statements or the parent's individual statements could be filed - it was unnecessary to file both.[3] Later, the instructions accompanying Form 10-K (the principal annual report form to be filed by all listed and some unlisted companies) noted that parent statements could be omitted when one or other of the following conditions prevailed:

> (a) The registrant was primarily an operating company, and all subsidiaries included in the consolidated financial statements were totally held subsidiaries.

> (b) The registrant's total assets, exclusive of investments in and advances to the consolidated subsidiaries,

---

1. Accounting Series Release No. 65 (June 21, 1948).

2. Accounting Series Release No. 32 (March 10, 1942).

3. Release No. 3908 under the Securities Exchange Act of 1934, as cited W. H. Childs, Consolidated financial statements (Cornell University Press, 1949), p.257.

> constitute 85 per cent or more of the total assets
> shown by the consolidated balance sheet filed, and
> the registrant's total gross revenue (or sales) for
> the period for which its income statement would be
> filed, exclusive of interest and dividends received
> from consolidated subsidiaries, constitute 85 per
> cent or more of the total gross revenue (or sales)
> shown by the consolidated income statement filed.[4]

The Commission also maintained wide discretionary powers to dispense with
the submission of statements or data as it saw fit, and these powers
were occasionally used to permit registrants to omit the filing of
parent-company statements.[5]

In the U.K. and commonwealth countries, post-1940 legislative changes
have been of greater significance in introducing and extending the use
of consolidated statements. Despite widespread criticism of the shortcomings of the 1929 U.K. Companies Act (particularly with respect to
its rules dealing with holding company reporting), this statute remained
in force until the late 1940's. Moreover, it served as a model for
companies legislation in New Zealand (1933) and in several Australian
states: Queensland (1931), South Australia (1934) and New South Wales
(1936) - and these statutes were to survive until the late 1950's and
early 1960's.

In 1945 a Company Law Amendment Committee (the "Cohen Committee")
was appointed to review the U.K. legislation. Not unexpectedly the
Committee devoted some attention to the reporting practices of holding
companies. For more than fifteen years there had been agreement within
the financial community on the need for reform in this area. Likewise,

---

4. As cited, L. H. Rappaport, SEC accounting practice and procedures
   New York: Ronald Press Company, 2nd ed., 1959), p.208.

5. Rappaport described a case in which the SEC permitted the non-
   inclusion of parent statements. A parent and a "significantly-
   owned" subsidiary were engaged in complementary activities and the
   profits of the subsidiary were largely a function of arbitrarily-
   determined transfer prices; the statements were to be used in
   connection with an issue which would lead to the redemption of all
   the subsidiary's outside debt. Ibid., p.107.

British accountants had accumulated almost twenty years experience
with consolidated reporting and the valuation of inter-corporate investments. However, the Cohen Committee did not examine local accounting
practices in any detail, but instead looked to American and Canadian
views for guidance. Whereas British accountants had regarded consolidated reporting as a means of supplementing parent company statements to
overcome the limitations of cost-based accounting, American practitioners
viewed consolidated reports as primary documents aimed at reporting on
group "entities". The Cohen Committee did not stop to examine these
differences in outlook. It placed great significance on America's and
Canada's long experience with holding companies, and reproduced traditional
American assertions about the aims of consolidated reports. Consolidated
statements were said to be "the best means of showing the financial
position and results of the group as a whole".[6]

Consistent with this view of consolidated statements, the Committee
argued that in defining "subsidiary" the "question of control should
as a general rule be decisive." Further, the Committee endeavoured to
encourage the general use of consolidated statements by requiring
directors' explanations and auditor's comments on departures from this
form of disclosure.

However, the legislation which finally appeared did not seem to aim
at showing the affairs of a "group" as much as requiring a form of report
which supplemented or amplified a holding company's report. Moreover, the
legislation made the use of alternative forms of disclosure more readily
available. The alternatives specified in the 1948 Companies Act were:

>   (a) more than one set of consolidated accounts dealing
>   respectively with the company and one group of
>   subsidiaries and with other groups of subsidiaries

6. <u>Report of the Committee on Company Law Amendment</u> (London: H.M.S.O.,
   1945), p.70. Similar observations about the aims of consolidated
   statements had been made in submissions by the Institute of Chartered
   Accountants in England and Wales.

(b) separate accounts dealing with each of the
subsidiaries

(c) statements expanding the information about the
subsidiaries in the company's own accounts[7]

(d) any combination of the above forms.

Directors were to form an "opinion" that consolidated statements were

inappropriate if they should choose to adopt an alternative form of

presentation.

> If the company's directors are of the opinion that it
> is better for the purpose
>
> (a) of presenting the same or equivalent information
> about the state of affairs and profit and loss of
> the company and those subsidiaries; and
>
> (b) of so presenting it that it may readily be appreciated
> by the company's members;
>
> the group accounts may be prepared in a form other than
> that required by the foregoing subsection.[8]

The Act provided no indication as to what criteria might be used by

directors in forming such a "judgment".

It was later reported that most holding companies found that

consolidated statements incorporating the results of parent and all

subsidiaries "served their purpose best".[9] Thus the 1948 Companies Act

seems to have fostered the use of consolidated reports in the U.K.,

The 1948 Act's provisions were copied in New Zealand in 1955, but

it was not until 1961 that Australian states introduced similar

provisions. And then, contrary to British and American practices, the

---

7. One text suggested that this method could be applied "in circumstances where the investment in subsidiaries is of a peculiar
nature" - as, for example, when "the investment in the subsidiary
company was originally purchased for £100,000, representing the
cost of acquiring a patent ... [for which] no revenue had yet
been received ..." and where the investment in the subsidiary had
been written down to a nominal value. A. MacBeath and A. J. Platt,
Group accounts and holding companies (London: Gee and Company (Publishers) Ltd., 1951) p.16.

8. U.K. Companies Act, 1948, s.151(2). S.150 also extended total relief
from the obligation to submit group accounts under certain circumstances.

9. T. M. Robson and S. N. Duncan, Consolidated and other group accounts
(London: Gee & Company (Publishers) Ltd., 4th ed., 1969), p.102.

Australian legislation did not permit the omission of individual
companies from the consolidation. The Australian requirement was based
on legislation introduced as early as 1938 in the state of Victoria,
and required the submission of either consolidated statements or the
separate statements of subsidiaries. The Australian tests for determining
the area of consolidation were also distinctive. The 1961 uniform state
legislation included a definition of "subsidiary" which employed criteria
similar to those used in the U.K. act (i.e. the definition specified
alternative tests of (a) majority stock ownership, or (b) control of
the composition of another corporation's board of directors) but with
the addition of a test concerned with control of a majority of the
voting power of another corporation. But the Australian legislation then
specified that only majority-owned subsidiaries (or sub-subsidiaries)
could be consolidated - a restriction similar to SEC requirements.[10]

The overall effect of these Australian rules was substantially
different from U.K. or U.S. precedents. Consolidated statements were
treated as supplementary disclosures which amplified a holding company's
reports; they dealt with all subsidiaries (not merely those engaged in
specified activities and regardless of their liquidity or operating performance). Those who framed these rules had evidently ignored arguments
about the need to look to relationships involving "control" in order to
identify an "economic entity" or "group".[11]

Subsequent proposals for amendments to British and Australian

---

10. See, e.g., N.S.W. Companies Act, 1961,s.6(i) and Ninth Schedule,
    clause 4(7).

11. The uniform legislation was at odds with the only authoritative
    document issued by the Australian profession on the subject.
    "Notes on the preparation of consolidated statements", the first
    of a series of Statements on accounting practice issued by the
    Australian Society of Accountants in 1956, indicated that exclusion
    of subsidiaries from consolidation could be warranted on a number
    of grounds, including dissimilarity of business operations or the
    absence of effective control over foreign subsidiaries (pp.5-6).
    This statement is discussed further below.

legislation have maintained points of difference about consolidation rules. A U.K. company law amendment committee appointed in 1960 (the "Jenkins Committee") recommended changes to the statutory definition of "subsidiary" in order to better-implement the Cohen Committee's recommendations that "the question of control be decisive".

> We recognise that one result of this change will be that a company may have 90 per cent or more of the equity share capital of another without that other being its subsidiary. In such a case there will be no obligation to consolidate the accounts of the two companies - and indeed the presentation of consolidated accounts would not meet the requirement of the Act ...[12]

The Jenkins Committee did not approach its discussion of the definition of subsidiary by (a) considering the aims of consolidated reports and then (b) defining the term "subsidiary" in a way that was consistent with those aims. The scope of consolidated statements was apparently "determined" by the Committee's opinions on a range of matters. As the Committee stated, the statutory definition of subsidiary was linked with several provisions of the Act.

> The definition of a subsidiary or holding company is important in company law in relation to accounts; to the ownership and acquisition of shares (section 27); to the restriction on a company's giving financial assistance for the acquisition of its shares (section 54); to the disqualifications for appointment as auditor (section 161(3)); to the power of inspectors appointed by the Board of Trade (section 166); to the prohibition of loans to directors (section 190); to the duty to disclose Directors' shareholdings and emoluments (sections 195-6).[13]

Nevertheless the Committee's conclusions that "control" was the appropriate test of a holding-subsidiary relationship can be interpreted as acceptance of the proposition that consolidated reports were intended to deal with "groups" of companies.

---

12. Report of the Company Law Committee (London: H.M.S.O., 1962), p.54.

13. Idem.

The Jenkins Committee was attempting to reinforce the Cohen Committee's earlier recommendations. Byt the Committee's proposals were ignored. The 1967 U.K. Companies Act left the 1948 Act's definitions of the relationship between holding and subsidiary companies unchanged.

While British disclosure rules retained the status quo, the Australian companies legislation was finally "liberalised" to permit firms greater flexibility in the selection of reporting methods. Australian states adopted the 22-year old British provisions relating to "group accounts" which gave firms a wide choice of methods of presenting supplementary information about subsidiaries. Moreover the Australian legislation extended the application of these provisions to all subsidiaries, not merely "majority owned" firms, as had formerly been prescribed. (Consequently the Australian definition of holding/ subsidiary relationships was wider than that in the U.K. legislation as it embodied an additional test of control - "voting power").

Recommendations of professional bodies

After the 1940's and 1950's professional associations of accountants took a more active role in encouraging and regulating the use of consolidated statements.

The American Institute's Committee on Co-operation with Stock Exchanges had accepted the need for consolidated data in 1932 (when the Committee made submissions to the New York Stock Exchange concerning "broad principles of accounting"). Later a joint committee representing the American Institute and the American Society of Public Accountants advised the newly-formed Securities and Exchange Commission that there was a need for either separate statements for subsidiaries or consolidated statements, "whichever will more clearly set forth essential facts". But little more was said about consolidated reporting at this stage. Some technical matters were discussed in The journal of accountancy by the Institute's director of research, Carman G. Blough. While the

American Institute initiated a series of Accounting Research Bulletins
as early as 1939, it was not until 1959 that one of these Bulletins
dealt directly with consolidation accounting.

Around 1940 the Institute of Chartered Accountants in England
and Wales established formal machinery for communicating "official"
views on accounting matters to members. Reliance had earlier been placed
on the publication of model answers to examination questions, and of
submissions made to company law reform committees. However in 1941 the
Institute established a Taxation and Financial Relations Committee which
initiated the preparation of recommendations on accounting matters.[14]
Initially these official Institute recommendations were described as
materials which might assist members who might be called upon to advise
as to "what is regarded as the best practice". While these statements
were not couched as directives, they appear to have been of some
influence on accounting practices.

Recommendation No. 7 (1944) was titled "Disclosure of the financial
position and results of subsidiary companies in the accounts of holding
companies".[15] It commenced with the assertion that when a company held
"controlling interests" in other firms:

> a true appreciation of the financial position and
> the trend of results of the group as a whole can be
> made only if the accounts of the holding company
> as a separate legal entity take into account or are
> supplemented by information as to the financial position
> and results of the subsidiary undertakings.

But having acknowledged that holding companies' records could take into
account particulars of subsidiaries' performance, the Recommendation
proceeded to ignore this possibility and only discuss ways of "disclosing
supplemental information". The Recommendation claimed that the use of

---

14. See S. A. Zeff, Forging accounting principles in five countries
     (Champaign, Ill.: Stipes Publishing Co., 1972), p.7ff. for an
     account of the formation and activities of this committee.

15. The recommendation was initially published in The accountant,
     12 Feb. 1944, pp.74-5.

consolidated statements was "most suitable for general application"
and so affirmed the Institute's support for this form of reporting.
In the process the Recommendations included a fairly radical
suggestion: that consolidated profit and loss statements might
encompass a different set of subsidiaries to those included in
consolidated balance sheets. This proposal, while contrary to the
supposed aim of reporting on a "group", was entirely consistent with
(say) efforts to overcome the limitations of cost-based valuation so
as to more-accurately show the performance of a holding company, while
at the same time trying to depict the aggregate liquidity of a number
of related companies.

Whatever the merits of this proposal, the Recommendation was
soon superseded. After the 1948 Companies Act came into force the
Institute's Taxation and Financial Relations Committee drafted a further
statement on the use of consolidated accounts, though in this instance
the Council of the Institute was not prepared to issue an official
recommendation, ostensibly because of the "absence of any long
established practice on many of the points involved".[16]

This 1949 statement was concerned with procedural matters rather
than with the case for (or the occasion for using) consolidated statements. It was written as a guide for practitioners as to how best
prepare consolidated reports in order to comply with the 1948 Companies
Act. Yet in so doing the statement clarified the British profession's
perspective on the aims of these reports. It was said that a consolidated balance sheet "has practical meaning and value only as showing
the position of the group as a whole so far as concerns the members of
the holding company".[17]

---

16. Preamble, "Group accounts in the form of consolidated accounts",
    The accountant, 28 May 1949, p.431.

17. Idem. Emphasis added.

This statement of the aims of consolidated reports seems to have followed the terminology used by draftsmen of the 1948 Act. S.152(1) stated that "group accounts laid before a company shall give a true and fair view of the state of affairs and profit and loss of the company and the subsidiaries dealt with thereby as a whole", "so far as concerns members of the company". This section, it will be realised, dealt with all forms of "group accounts" prescribed by the act, and so the reference to "members of a holding company" did not necessarily deal with consolidated statements. Moreover this phrase had not been used in the Cohen Committee's discussions of holding company accounting.[18]

In one sense, the claim that consolidated statements should depict group affairs from the viewpoint of holding company shareholders was simply descriptive of the well-established practices of identifying minority interests and isolating the holding company's share of "group profit". At the same time, this claim could be interpreted as de-emphasising the long-established view that consolidated balance sheets were intended to represent group liquidity for the benefit of creditors. Indeed, the Institute Committee stressed that consolidated statements

---

18. Origin of the proposition that consolidated statements were concerned with showing the affairs of a group of companies "so far as concerns the members of the holding company" may perhaps be T. B. Robson's description of U.S. and Canadian practice. Robson (of Price, Waterhouse & Co.) wrote the successor to the pioneering English text by Sir Gilbert Garnsey (also a Price, Waterhouse partner). He described consolidated reports as the U.S. and Canadian solution to the problem of "how best to present the position and earnings of a holding company group ... to those who are interested in it as shareholders in the holding company". Robson avoided the point that U.S. and Canadian practitioners regarded consolidated reports as primary documents rather than as a means of amplifying a holding company's statements, though he expressly described the function of consolidated statements in the U.K. as being that of "amplification". T. B. Robson, Consolidated accounts (London: Gee & Company (Publishers) Limited, 1946), pp.7-8.

might be of little significance to creditors.

> To the creditors and the outside shareholders
> of any of the subsidiaries in the group a consoli-
> dated balance sheet may disclose little or no informa-
> tion regarding their particular interests, relating
> as these do to individual entities within the group.

And yet in the U.S. the use of consolidated statements has been supported
by both present and potential creditors of holding companies and
subsidiaries! The 1949 Institute Committee statement can thus be seen
as a further reflection of disagreement about the objectives of
consolidated reporting. Moreover one can further note that British writers were later to claim that consolidated statements did in fact enable
readers of financial statements to assess the liquidity and financial
standing of a group.[19] Despite these disagreements and contradictions,
the 1949 statement's description of the aims of consolidated statements
was often reproduced in later publications.[20]

The earliest pronouncement from an Australian professional accounting body on consolidation matters owed as much to American as to British
ideas about consolidated reports. In 1956 the Australian Society of
Accountants issued the first in a short-lived series of Statements on
accounting practice. Titled "Notes on the preparation of consolidated
statements"[21] the document was not issued as an official recommendation
or ruling but only as a statement of the views of a "Research Committee".
While it included positive recommendations on particular points (e.g.

---

19. e.g. T. B. Robson, Consolidated and other groups accounts (London:
    Gee and Company (Publishers) Ltd., 3rd ed., 1956), p.15.

20. e.g. Institute of Chartered Accountants in Australia, "Auditors'
    reports on group accounts", May 1968 (though this statement
    did not specifically deny that consolidated statements are of
    relevance to creditors); see also W. J. Kenley, A statement of
    Australian accounting principles (Melbourne: Accounting Research
    Foundation, 1970), p.87.

21. Published as a supplement to The Australian accountant, April 1956.

the terminology to describe "goodwill on consolidation", the elimination of inter-company profits, the propriety of setting-off debit and
credit bank balances), it seems to have been primarily intended to
explain consolidated reporting to practitioners who were not familiar
with this form of report.

The Society's statement described the aims of consolidated statements as being to show the affairs of a "group" of companies - but
it did not specify precisely what these reports were intended to represent
or the particular users of financial statements that they were intended
to serve. The U.K. contention that consolidated statements showed the
affairs of a group "so far as concerns members of the holding company"
was watered down to brief comment that consolidated reports portrayed
group results "from the standpoint" of the holding company's interests
- a proposition which did not preclude the implication that consolidated
statements were of relevance to other parties. And perhaps the most
notable feature of the statement was that it avoided discussing when
consolidated statements were useful, desirable or necessary.

By the time that the American Institute issued Accounting Research
Bulletin No. 51 in 1959, the use of consolidated reports was so well-
established that it may have seemed unnecessary to spell out why
consolidated statements were useful and what they were intended to
represent.   Certainly ARB 51 did not canvass these questions. The
Bulletin's preamble asserted that "there is a presumption that consolidated statements are more meaningful than separate statements". This
"presumption" was not analysed or questioned.

ARB 51 seemed to have been aimed at setting down what was "accepted"
rather than evaluating or endeavouring to support particular positions.
One finds in ARB 51 the first clear statement from the American profession
that consolidated statements were to be regarded as primary documents.
This was a reversal of the position taken in submissions to the SEC in

the 1930's. True, stock exchanges and financial analysts had placed
greater significance on consolidated rather than parent company data.
And corporate reporting practices had reflected this emphasis. A 1956
American Institute survey of the use of consolidated statements in
annual reports to shareholders discussed the appearance of parent company statements under the heading, "Supplementary financial statements".

> In only five cases out of the 329 [respondents to a
> questionnaire] were financial statements of the parent
> company submitted in the annual reports, in addition to
> the consolidated statements. One of these discontinued
> the practice in the following year ...[22]

But the Bulletin made no attempt to indicate why consolidated
statements should be regarded as primary documents. It simply commented
that parent company statements might be useful "in some cases".

> In some cases parent company statements may be needed,
> in addition to consolidated statements, to indicate
> adequately the position of bondholders and other
> creditors of preferred stockholders of the parent ...

In summary, the statements of accounting bodies in the U.K., the
U.S. and Australia have provided some authoritative support for the use
of consolidated reports. The profession's statements have taken the
form of "recommendations" or pronouncements on what was deemed to be
"best practice". They have not included reasoned arguments indicating
why the use of consolidated reports was to be preferred to other forms
of reporting.

While the statements of the various professional associations of
accountants have agreed on the need for consolidated reporting, these
recommendations have followed from conflicting assumptions about the
aims and objectives and status of these reports. As such, the recommendations or pronouncements have perpetuated the conflict in ideas
that was evident in the accounting literature before 1940.

---

22. American Institute of Accountants, Survey of consolidated financial
statement practices (New York: 1956), p.10.

The 1970's saw the first results of efforts to standardise accounting practices on an international basis. In 1966 an agreement between the leading professional associations in the U.K., Canada and the U.S.A. led to the establishment of the Accountants' International Study Group (AISG); in 1973 this body published a report on the use of consolidated statements.[23] As has already been described, there were substantial differences between British and U.S. (or Canadian) attitudes towards the function of consolidated statements, and these differences were reflected in conflicting sets of disclosure rules. The AISG was confronted with this evidence.

The matters considered by the AISG are indicated by the section headings of the report:

        Need for consolidated statements
        Limitations of consolidated financial statements
        Support for present practices
        Concepts of consolidated financial statements
        Consolidation criteria
        Miscellaneous consolidation topics
        Minority interests
        Parent company statements
        Component company statements
        Intercompany eliminations
        Income taxes
        Conclusions

The AISG's report set down details of the statutes, regulations and professional recommendations operative in the three countries. It even noted that there were "two general concepts of consolidated financial statements" and thus acknowledged that there were fundamental differences in the rationale for consolidated reporting. But instead of exploring these matters further the AISG chose to regard the differences in rules as merely temporary imperfections. The differences in arguments were brushed aside. The AISG seemed intent on reaching agreement at all costs. It managed to do so by means of a series of propositions,

---

23. Accountants' International Study Group, Consolidated financial statements (1973).

which expressed members' beliefs or opinions. The report asserted that "financial statements of companies with subsidiaries should be prepared on a consolidated basis because they are likely to be the most informative presentation". Why this was "likely" was not explained. It was said that "equity" methods of valuing inter-corporate investments were not "valid substitutes" for consolidation. Again, the "invalidity" of equity methods or the specific advantages of consolidated reporting were not explained. And, after noting that quite different criteria were used in the three countries to determine the scope of consolidated statements, the AISG avoided discussing whether these rules were based on conflicting premises and instead sought to find elements which were common to the rules.

The AISG was in a position to identify unresolved issues about the preparation of consolidated reports - but seems to have devoted its efforts to the preparation of a communique outlining points on which accountants from different countries could agree.

In June 1973 further steps were taken to secure the standardisation of accounting practices with the establishment of the International Accounting Standards Committee (IASC) with a membership which initially included representatives of accounting bodies in Australia, Canada, France, Germany, Ireland, Japan, Mexico, Netherlands, the U.K. and the U.S.A. In December 1974 the IASC issued a draft statement titled "Consolidated financial statements and the equity method of accounting".[24] In place of the AISG's tentative statements the IASC put forward firm directives. Whereas the AISG had suggested that consolidated statements were likely to be more informative, the IASC asserted that "a parent company should issue consolidated statements". The AISG had been non-commital about whether subsidiaries could be excluded from consolidation on the grounds (say) that their activities were unrelated to those of other firms; the IASC declared that the only grounds for exclusion were those where "control is likely to be temporary" or where a subsidiary is subject to long-term restrictions on the transfer of funds.

---

24. Published as a supplement to The management accountant, Jan. 1975.

It appears that the emphatic tone of the IASC document was not an expression of a newly-formed consensus about the aims of consolidated reports or of how to achieve those aims. No new analysis was presented and no new evidence about the utility of one or other form of data was offered.

As it happened, the IASC soon changed its views. In March 1976 the Committee approved the publication of International Accounting Standard No.3, "Consolidated financial statements". This document contradicted the exposure draft's claims that consolidated statements should encompass all of a holding company's subsidiaries. It stated that "better information for the parent company shareholders and other users may be provided by presenting separate financial statements in respect of subsidiaries engaged in dissimilar operations" (para. 37). The basis of this assertion was not explained; it appears that the IASC was simply attempting to accommodate the conflicting viewpoints of its members.

To some extent, IAS 3 and the statements issued by other professional associations have reduced the range of alternative procedures that an accounting practitioner might face when preparing consolidated reports. But since these accounting standards have not been based on a thorough analysis of the aims of consolidated reports, they have not resolved issues, but only removed them.

The "entity theory" of consolidated reports

A feature of the post-1940's literature has been the almost universal acceptance of the proposition that consolidation statements are concerned with depicting the affairs of a "group". As has been described in Section III much of the American literature of the 1930's glossed over the aims and objectives of consolidated reporting. Several early texts described consolidated statements as depicting the situation that would exist "if" a holding company and its subsidiaries were a single firm. Soon the "if" was dropped; some writers argued that consolidated reports were concerned with depicting the affairs of a "group" of companies.

The proposition that "consolidated statements depict the affairs of a group" does not constitute a statement of function. It may describe the process of preparing these reports, but it does not indicate the aims of this mode of communicating financial data, the parties to whom the information might be communicated or the specific matters that the reports supposedly communicate. Even so, the idea of depicting the affairs of a "group" of companies has been used to justify specific accounting practices.

The major contributor to this acceptance of the "group" idea appears to have been M. Moonitz. In July 1942 The accounting review published a brief article in which Moonitz explored the procedural consequences of approaching consolidated statement preparation from the standpoint of preparing exhibits "as though the companies were legally as well as economically mere administrative subdivisions of one concern".[25] He offered no evidence or argument in support of this assumption. And while he noted that "the premise stated is not the only one on which a consistent theory may be built" (instancing assumptions that "the affiliated corporations constitute a co-partnership" or that consolidated statements "are mere statistical compilations whose purpose is to clarify and amplify the statements of a parent company") he made no attempt to evaluate these alternatives. Moonitz was only concerned with exploring one way of clearing up what he described as a confusing array of alternative and sometimes contradictory and inconsistent procedures".

Moonitz's analysis may perhaps have been influenced by the approach adopted by his University of California colleague, H. R. Hatfield. Certainly Moonitz's proposals for the calculation of "goodwill on consolidation" in situations where there were minority interests were similar

---

25. "The entity approach to consolidated statements", loc.cit., p.237.

to those advanced in Hatfield's writings.[26] But Moonitz extended Hatfield's analysis to argue that "control" was the appropriate test of consolidation, to support the total elimination of all inter-company
profits, and to oppose the treatment of minority interests as
liabilities.

Moonitz later extended his examination of procedures consistent
with the "entity" hypothesis in The entity theory of consolidated statements, published by the American Accounting Association in 1944.[27] Here,
Moonitz attempted to support his assumption about the aims of consolidated
reports, though again he did not attempt to consider the strengths of the
case in support of other hypotheses about the aims of consolidated reports.

What support was offered?

Moonitz claimed that the historical background to the adoption of
consolidated statements justified his assumption that they were concerned
with depicting the affairs of an "entity" of closely affiliated
corporations. He claimed that consolidated statements had developed as "a
supplement, a complement, an addition to but not a substitute for the
statements of individual corporate units" (p.10); they depicted the
affairs of an "economic entity".

The material presented in Sections II and III of this study clearly
conflicts with Moonitz's conclusions. In particular, the U.S. history
of consolidated reporting shows that consolidated statements were used
as substitutes for parent-company reports. It has been suggested that
this may have been consistent with the aim of indicating the consequences
of mergers, and perhaps to further the interests of promoters. Consolidated statements were not regarded as dealing with economic entities but with
the affairs of parent corporations. It will be recalled that early

---

26. See H. R. Hatfield, Accounting - its principles and its problems
     (New York: D. Appleton and Co.,1927; reprinted 1971 by Scholars
     Book Company), pp.447-8.
27. Reprinted in 1951 by The Foundation Press, Inc., Brooklyn.

usage of consolidated statements was confined to cases involving wholly-
or substantially-owned subsidiaries. And (in the light of accounting
dogma about the need to value inter-corporate investments at cost)
consolidated statements were regarded as a far more satisfactory
vehicle for communicating financial information than parent-company
statements. There were signs in the 1920's and 1930's that U.S.
accountants had come to regard consolidated reports as amplifications
of holding company reports. There is precious little evidence of any
support among practitioners, regulatory agencies or accounting writers
for the proposition that details about the affairs of an "economic
entity" composed of "controlled" corporations would be a useful adjunct
to a holding company's financial statements. Indeed, it was only when
academic writers endeavoured to develop a "theory" of consolidated
statements that this idea was advanced in any detail.

The U.K. background to the use of consolidated statements was
even more plainly unrelated to the "economic entity" idea. U.K.
accountants were concerned with amplifying the reports of holding companies and to overcome the limitations of conventional, cost-based
methods of accounting for inter-corporate investments.

Whatever the flimsiness of the "case" in support of the "entity
theory of consolidated statements", it appears that Moonitz's writings
have had a profound effect on the accounting literature and hence on
accounting practices.

Acceptance of the "group entity" argument

Those who have framed disclosure rules and the recommendations of professional bodies appear to have accepted the "entity theory" as a suitable description of the aims of consolidated reporting. One illustration
of the consequences of adopting the "entity" idea is available from a
consideration of the rules formulated to handle the ubiquitous "goodwill
on consolidation". While there has been some support from professional

bodies to label this item with such terms as

> excess of cost of investment in subsidiary over the
> net equity acquired[28]

it was consistent with the "entity theory" to regard the holding company's

payments over and above the book value of subsidiaries' assets as being

the purchase by a group entity of "goodwill". The latter view was

later adopted by the American profession. In 1966 the Accounting

Principles Board ruled that goodwill on consolidation should be written

off against income over a maximum period of 40 years - a ruling that

treated the goodwill item as an asset of a group rather than as a balancing

item arising from the mechanics of consolidation.

Another disputed issue - the extent to which profits on intra-

group transactions should be eliminated where subsidiaries were not

wholly-owned - was likewise resolved by an appeal to the group entity

notion. The suggestion that only the majority interests' equity in

such transactions should be eliminated was not advanced with any great

frequency after 1940.[29] And disclosure rules or professional recom-

mendations commonly spelled out that all inter-company profits or

losses were to be eliminated in consolidations.[30] A further complica-

tion arising from intra-group transactions concerns situations in which

---

28. See, e.g., Australian Society of Accountants, "Notes on the prepara-
    tion of consolidated statements", loc.cit.

29. Texts which discussed or endorsed this argument included Robson and
    Duncan, op.cit., p.81; L. N. Lee and L. A. McPherson, Consolidated
    statements and group accounts (Sydney: The Law Book Company Ltd.,
    1963), pp.125-9.

30. e.g., Australian Society of Accountants (1956), pp.10-11; (1968),
    pp.14-15; American Institute of Accountants, ARB 51, para.14. See
    also American Accounting Association, Committee on Concepts and
    Standards, "Consolidated financial statements", The accounting review,
    April 1955, p.197. In Australia, companies legislation required total
    eliminations; see, e.g., N.S.W. Companies Act, 1961, Ninth Schedule,
    clause 4. British disclosure rules did not require eliminations but
    simply indicated the need for "such adjustments (if any) as the
    directors of the holding company think necessary". 1948 Companies
    Act, Eighth Schedule, clause 17; 1967 Companies Act, Second
    Schedule, clause 17.

parent or subsidiaries are taxed on profits which (for consolidation purposes) are eliminated. From the standpoint of the "entity theory" (and given acceptance of the so-called realisation convention), intra-group transactions were not "realised" and as such should be eliminated. Any taxes paid on these "unrealised" profits could be seen (from a group view) to be prepaid - an asset. The deferral of these taxes was in fact recommended by ARB 51.[31]

Purchase v. pooling debate

In some respects the controversy over the use of purchase or pooling methods of accounting for business combinations might be seen as a further reflection of support for the group entity notion.

Under purchase accounting, the assets and liabilities of an acquired form are recorded (through revaluations in the company's books or through working-paper adjustments) at so-called "fair market value"; under pooling accounting, these items are maintained at book values. Correspondingly, the choice of one or other method is linked with different treatments of the pre-acquisition profits of the acquired company (which could seriously affect the reported income of the acquiring firm for the current and prior years); moreover the choice of methods could seriously affect subsequent income calculations (through variations in depreciation charges and the amortization of goodwill).

As outlined in Sections II, III and IV, disputes over the appropriate basis of asset valuation, the recording of stock issues, the treatment of pre-acquisition profits and the calculation of goodwill have had a long history. The purchase v. pooling debate simply placed these issues into packages. American accountants adopted, as a key test for determining which package of rules was to be used in a given situation, the question of whether a business combination resulted in a new economic enterprise.

---

31. However ARB 51 did offer the alternative of reducing the amount of inter-company profit to be eliminated (para.17).

This test was incorporated in the American Institute's Accounting
Research Bulletin No.40 (1950) and formed the basis of subsequent,
more detailed rulings (ARB 43, 1953; ARB 48, 1957; APB 6, 1965; APB
10, 1966 and APB 16, 1970). Similarly, the test was implicitly adopted
in an exposure draft issued by the English Institute in 1971 (ED 3)
dealing with the choice of treating business combinations as acquisitions
or mergers.

In placing such store on the rather vague notion of an economic
enterprise, the profession was clearly borrowing from the set of terms
introduced earlier to describe the process of consolidation accounting.
The preparation of consolidated statements had been described as a process
of preparing documents "as if" a number of firms constituted a single
enterprise; later a preoccupation with technical processes led accountants
to see the aim of consolidated statements as actually being to depict
the affairs of a group entity. The purchase and pooling debate can be
viewed as a further expression of accountants' preoccupation with concepts
and techniques - as opposed to a concern for the utility of published information. The choice of purchase or pooling accounting was said to turn
on whether or not there were grounds for supposing that a merged enterprise
constituted a new enterprise in some general, economic sense.

However the key issues underlying the purchase or pooling debate
concerns asset valuation or the calculation of legally distributable
surplus - issues which are more general than the special problems associated with reporting on the affairs of holding companies. Further, the
purchase v. pooling debate was not peculiar to holding/subsidiary company
relationships; the rules developed in this area were said to be applicable
to mergers consummated through the purchase of assets, the transfer of
assets to a new corporation, and to mergers between unincorporated
associations. And the controversy about the choice of methods for handling
business combinations had little bearing on the rationale for aggregating

the financial statements of incorporated, legally-separate entities -
except in the sense that the propriety of consolidation accounting was
taken for granted. Hence the controversy is not examined in any depth
in this study.

It is simply noted that the purchase v. pooling debate is in one
sense an outcome of acceptance of the "group" idea.

Inconsistent arguments

This is not to suggest that all recommendations and rules developed
in the post-war years have been consistent with the "group entity"
proposition. In fact, accountants have developed several rules which
are inconsistent with the aim, of depicting the affairs of a "group"
but which might make more sense if one viewed consolidated reports as
amplifications of parent-company statements. For example, under the tax
laws of various jurisdictions the payment of dividends from subsidiary
to holding company (or from subsidiary to subsidiary, etc.) would
attract taxes. From a "group" point of view, the profits of subsidiaries
could validly be aggregated to represent the performance of an economic
entity, ignoring (for that purpose) any taxes which might be levied on
cash transfers (i.e. dividends) within the group. But from the
viewpoint of the holding company it could be supposed that gains from
inter-corporate investments in a given period could be related to the
net amount which could be distributed from subsidiary to holding company.
Without attempting to explore the validity of this argument, it may
be noted that British and Australian professional bodies have adopted
this "parent company" viewpoint in developing rules to handle taxes.[32]

32. See, e.g., Institute of Chartered Accountants in England and Wales,
    Recommendations N19 (1959), paras.50-3; Institute of Chartered
    Accountants in Australia, Statement on Accounting Practice DS 4
    (Oct. 1974), para.29. The latter recommendation indicated that
    taxes could be ignored if "there is strong evidence that the
    holding company intends to leave the profits of the subsidiary
    indefinitely in the latter's hands".

Other rulings which seem inconsistent with the "group entity"
proposal were those prohibiting the setting-off of asset and liability
items in consolidated balance sheets. To illustrate this issue,
suppose that one subsidiary had a bank overdraft and another had cash
holdings. The question would then arise as to how these items should be
treated in a consolidated balance sheet.

From the point of view of a "group", it would be perfectly proper
to simply show the net balance of the two items. But from the point of
view of attempting to represent the liquid position of a series of
related companies (a subtly different objective), this practice could
conceal significant data. Some professional recommendations have placed
greater weight on the aim of depicting liquidity in this context. In
1949 the Institute of Chartered Accountants in England and Wales
asserted that "overdrafts and credit balances should not normally be
set-off against each other on consolidation".[33] Later Australian
company laws similarly prohibited these set-offs,[34] while professional
recommendations precluded the setting-off of "future income tax benefits"
against "deferred income tax".[35]

A further issue which reflected the profession's equivocal attitude
towards the group-entity argument concerns the area of consolidation.
In many respects the profession's rulings or recommendations on this
matter might be seen as consistent with the entity idea. Yet in other
respects they could be seen as consistent with attempts to represent
liquidity - or to amplify a holding company's statement. The following

---

33. Op.cit., para.5. However, the Australian Society (1956) indicated
     that "where all companies within the group have the same bankers
     there would normally be no objection to combining all bank balances
     and setting-off overdraft against credit accounts". The English
     Institute sanctioned set-offs only if that would be done by the bank
     by reason of some arrangement with the companies concerned.

34. e.g. N.S.W. Companies Act, 1961, as amended, Ninth Schedule, clause 5.

35. Institute of Chartered Accountants in Australia, Statement on
     Accounting Practice DS 4 (Oct. 1974), para.28.

table illustrates this point by enumerating some of the criteria which

were cited in the recommendations of accounting bodies as justifying

the exclusion of particular subsidiaries from the consolidation. (The

table excludes certain recent proposals for the non-consolidation of

"controlled" but not majority-owned subsidiaries: these proposals will

be considered later in this chapter in connection with equity accounting).

Grounds for excluding subsidiaries from consolidation

Results would be "misleading".
   Australian Society 1956.

Publication of consolidated data harmful to company or subsidiaries.
   Australian Society 1956.

Business so different could not be treated as part of group.
   Australian Society 1956.
   AICPA 1959 ("but weigh against unnecessary detail")
         (Note: CICA 1972, IASC 1974 "not a valid reason for exclusion").

Control likely to be temporary.
   AICPA 1959
   CICA 1972
   IASC 1974

Accounting practices different from those of parent, other subsidiaries.
   Institute T and FR 1949 (e.g., overseas companies).
   CICA 1972   (e.g., regulated industries).

Restrictions on international remittances.
   Institute T & FR 1949
   AAA 1955
   CICA 1972
   IASC 1974 ("long term restrictions").

Violent fluctuations in exchange rates.
   Institute T & FR 1949.

Minority interests large in relation to majority interest.
   AAA 1955
   AICPA 1959

Inability to exercise control.
   Australian Society 1956 (e.g., foreign companies).
   AICPA 1959; CICA 1972 (e.g., reorganization or bankruptcy).
   AAA 1955 (e.g., "some reason, or law, custom or economic condition").

The list highlights disagreements between some professional bodies.

For example, the AICPA and the Australian Society both claimed that

dissimilarity of business activities was sufficient grounds to exclude

a subsidiary from consolidation, whereas the Canadian Institute and the

IASC reached a contrary conclusion. This conflict is consistent with
disagreements about whether the objective of consolidated statements
is to report on an "economic entity" or to amplify the reports of a
holding company. (Alternatively, the conflict might be viewed as
reflecting disagreements about whether consolidated statements were
intended to depict the affairs of a group of corporations under <u>unified</u>
<u>control</u> or an economic entity, engaged in a <u>unified business</u>). Similar
comments might be made about the proposal to exclude "temporarily held"
subsidiaries: from the point of view of reporting on the extent to
which particular interests were in command of economic resources, every
"controlled" corporation should be included; whereas it could be claimed
that an "economic entity" included only those subsidiaries which were
part of a cohesive unit. And one can note that even when there was
agreement about particular rules the professional bodies concerned could
have reached those conclusions on the basis of differing assumptions.
For example, the IASC implied that the exclusion of temporarily-
controlled subsidiaries was warranted for the purpose of determining the
scope of a "controlled" organization; the CICA stated that the non-
consolidation of those firms was justified because increases in the
shareholders' equity would not normally accrue to the holding company.

Inconsistencies can also be observed within individual recommendations. For example, the AAA's 1955 statement and the AICPA's ARB 51
(1959) both suggested that a large minority interest could render
consolidated statements misleading - a proposition at odds with the
avowed aim of depicting the state of a "group" or "economic entity".
However exclusion of such subsidiaries (or the abandonment of consolidation procedures) might be seen as consistent with the aim of amplifying
the affairs of a holding company. Likewise the English Institute's claim
that exchange fluctuations or restrictions on overseas remittances could
justify the non-consolidation of a foreign subsidiary was totally

inconsistent with the idea of depicting the affairs of companies operating under the domination of a central interest.

It is difficult to avoid the conclusion that professional bodies have been confused about the precise aims of consolidated statements. But the task of analysing the function of these reports has been avoided. Accountants have assumed that consolidated statements are useful, and then endeavoured to formulate rules or recommendations that would accommodate conflicting ideas or opinions.

Consolidation of loss-making subsidiaries

The propriety of consolidating loss-making subsidiaries was called into question in Australia in the 1960's. The disclosure rules then in force in various Australian states were so framed as to require the inclusion of all subsidiaries in any consolidated statements that might be prepared.

Following some well-publicised company crashes during the 1960's, state governments initiated investigations of the circumstances surrounding the failure of several prominent firms. Some of these failures had followed soon after the publication of financial reports which depicted the firms in question as being profitable and financially sound. The investigators' reports publicly questioned the utility of generally accepted accounting principles and the effectiveness of customary audit procedures.

Some extracts from these reports follow:

> ... the Reid Murray reports and accounts were in law free to conceal and in fact not infrequently did conceal losses of huge proportions suffered by individual subsidiaries by setting them off against large 'profits' which were said to have been made by other subsidiaries.
> In order to have any real understanding of the affairs of the Reid Murray group it was clearly necessary to understand the affairs of at least the principal functioning subsidiaries (e.g. Robert Reid and Hicks Atkinson) and groups of subsidiaries (e.g. the Paynes

Properties group) within the group.[36]

> ... from 1958 onwards Factors relied for its profits
> on Rockmans, Holeproof (N.Z.) and Holeproof (Australia).
> It is also clear that from its business of hire pur-
> chase, factoring, land development, building erection,
> uranium mining, deposits at call, money lending and
> investment, it earned insignificant profit - but suffered
> substantial losses ...
> None of this can be seen from a perusal of the published
> Consolidated Accounts of Factors.
> Neither in the 9th Schedule nor in any other section of
> the Companies Act 1961 is there any requirement that a
> "holding" company shall publish with its consolidated
> accounts figures showing the profit or loss earned by
> each subsidiary or even each group of subsidiaries whose
> accounts are consolidated with those of the holding company.
> If a holding company has subsidiaries with diversified
> activities, as Factors did, it would be beneficial to
> those reading the accounts if information was given at
> the same time showing the profit or loss earned by the
> individual subsidiaries or groups of subsidiaries.[37]

> No doubt the problems arising from a general consolida-
> tion of the accounts of all companies within a group seem
> as difficult of solution as they are easy of recognition.
> Nevertheless, it seems that some attempt will, sooner or
> later, have to be made to require the provision of
> accounting information in sufficient detail so as to avoid
> the presentation of a distorted or unreliable picture
> where disparate results are achieved in widely different
> activities carried on within the one group.[38]

The major theme of these comments was not criticism of the inclusion

of loss-making subsidiaries in consolidated statements. The inspectors

claimed that the data included in the consolidated reports were inadequ-

ate or insufficient to enable an assessment of the performance and pros-

pects of the firms in question. The objections raised about the

consolidated statements could well have been satisfied by the use of

---

36. Final report of an investigation ... into the affairs of Reid
    Murray Holdings Ltd. ..." (Melbourne: Victorian Government Printer,
    1966), p.36.

37. Interim report of an investigation ... into the affairs of Factors
    Ltd. ..." (Melbourne: Victorian Government Printer, 1966), p.176.

38. Report of an investigation ... into the affairs of Neon Signs
    (Australasia) Ltd. ..." (Melbourne: Victorian Government Printer,
    1966), p.224.

"equity" methods to value inter-corporate investments. Alternatively,

supplemental disclosures could have drawn attention to the losses of

subsidiaries, especially where those losses threatened the survival

of related firms. However, the Australian Society of Accountants con-

cluded that the way to overcome the inadequacy of the consolidated

figures was to relax the statutory requirement for "total" consolidations.

> General Council ... suggests that provisions similar
> to those of the United Kingdom Companies Act be
> introduced into the Australian legislation to permit partial
> consolidation where, in the opinion of the directors
> and the auditor, this procedure is preferable in order to
> present the members of the parent company with a true
> and fair view of the result of operations and the financial
> position of the consolidation.[39]

Similar observations were expressed two years later when the Australian

Society issued its revised version of "Notes on the preparation of

consolidated statements". Again, the Society suggested that "information

relating to the position and operations of a group of companies might

be more effectively communicated by means of more than one set of

consolidated statements" or by the "separate statements of one or more

subsidiaries which, for good reason, have been excluded from the con-

solidation".[40] And the hope was expressed that Australian disclosure

laws would shortly be modified to permit these practices.

However, these suggestions for law reform were not immediately

implemented. Hence firms were obliged to continue the practice of

including all subsidiaries in their consolidated statements. Some firms

responded to this requirement by engaging in the devious practice of

"deconsolidation" - of selling parcels of shares sufficient to reduce

39. Australian Society of Accountants, Accounting principles and practices discussed in reports on company failures (Melbourne:
Australian Society of Accountants, 1966), pp.20-1. Note that
this survey of the criticisms of government-appointed inspectors
was produced before publication of the three reports cited above.
However the Society had considered interim reports relating to
two of the three cases cited.

40. Loc.cit., p.3.

their holding to less than the 50% specified in the legislation. This
enabled firms to avoid including unprofitable subsidiaries in the
consolidated statements. Conversely, in good times the shareholding
could be restored to a "majority" interest.

The manipulation of consolidated data that took place in these
circumstances would not have been possible had "equity" rather than
cost-based valuation methods been used to record inter-corporate
investments. However, at the time, equity methods were apparently
regarded as unacceptable. The Australian Society of Accountants responded by drafting recommendations which condemned the practices of
deconsolidation or non-consolidation. This was, in effect, a complete
reversal of the position taken in the Society's 1966 and 1968 statements
which had claimed that partial consolidation could be the most informative way of supplementing the reports of holding companies. Contrary
to the 1966 and 1968 proposals, the 1969 draft recommendations asserted
that consolidated statements should encompass all "subsidiaries or
other segments of a group which are subject to the one ultimate decision-
making power". This line of argument was in the tradition of claims
in the American literature that consolidated statements were concerned
with depicting a "group". However, elsewhere in the same draft statement,
the purposes of consolidated statements were linked with the avoidance
of distortions or manipulations likely to arise from dividend-based
revenue recognition - a view of consolidated statements which was
consistent with the aim of amplifying holding company reports. Evidently
the Society was thoroughly confused about the aims of consolidated
statements.

Symptoms of this confusion were also evident in successive drafts
of the one statement. The first version[41] condemned de-consolidation

41. Australian Society of Accountants, "Consolidated financial state-
    ments and the practices of de-consolidation and non-consolidation",
    1969, 7pp.

as likely to distort the financial statements of a holding company;
a later draft[42] alluded to distortion of the financial statements of a
group. Neither of these draft statements was finally issued as a firm
recommendation. But the drafts do appear to have influenced amendments
to the statutory disclosure rules. The Society's view was that "control"
was a necessary and sufficient condition for consolidation - in contrast
to the then-existing statutory rules which permitted consolidation of
majority-owned subsidiaries only. 1971 amendments to the companies
legislation of various states accommodated this proposal (though not to
the extent of permitting consolidation of controlled, unincorporated
ventures). However, while the Society flatly stated that the presentation of partially consolidated statements, or sets of consolidated data
or the separate financial statements of subsidiaries "cannot be considered
as adequate financial reporting", the company law amendments which
were introduced in 1971 expressly sanctioned all of those methods of
reporting.

This seems to indicate that issues debated in the 1930's and
1940's were still very much alive in the 1970's.

Consolidated statements and disclosure by diversified companies

While Australian accountants were considering how to ensure that
corporate reports disclosed significant trends in the performance of
one or more subsidiaries of a holding company, American accountants
were devoting their attention to the issue of how best to report on the
activities of diversified companies. The debate was prompted initially
by complaints from economists about the limited usefulness of corporate
reports as a guide to the profitability of individual industries, since
more and more corporations were engaged in a wide range of activities.

---

42. Australian Society of Accountants, "Omission of subsidiaries from
consolidated statements" (exposure draft), The Australian accountant, Nov. 1969, pp.487-90.

The debate was joined by security analysts who professed difficulty in assessing the likely profitability of conglomerate enterprises. Continuation of the debate was assured when the SEC threatened to use its powers to introduce disclosure rules of its own devising unless industry and the accounting profession could promptly formulate appropriate, acceptable solutions.[43]

This debate took place in a context in which consolidated statements were the major vehicle for corporate reporting. The question of how to best present detailed information about the major activities of a group was approached from the standpoint of how best to supplement consolidated statements. But the debate was accompanied by a significant shift in attitudes towards consolidated reporting.

American accountants had long accepted that a lack of homogeneity of operations was a valid ground for excluding subsidiaries from consolidation. This proposition had been supported to some extent by SEC rules. Regulation S-X had prohibited the consolidation of insurance companies (except under very limited circumstances) and similarly provided that the reports of banks and bank holding companies could only be consolidated with the reports of other banks or bank holding companies. Later the SEC amended its consolidation rules with respect to commercial, industrial and mining companies in the promotional, exploratory or development stages; these companies were to provide data not on a consolidated basis, but were "to show the information for the registrant and each of its subsidiaries in parallel columns".[44] Now these rules may not have been primarily aimed at isolating the performance of major segments of a business. In fact, the provisions dealing with banks and insurance companies appear to have been designed to prevent a misleading

43. See K. F. Skousen, "Chronicle of events surrounding the segment reporting issue", Journal of accounting research, 1970, pp.293-9.

44. These amendments were foreshadowed in Accounting Series Release No. 65, dated 21 June 1948.

impression being given of a firm's liquidity and asset structure. The
rules concerning unseasoned companies applied even if all related
companies were engaged in identical activities. But these rules
established the principle that consolidated statements need not cover
all subsidiaries. Moreover, a clause in the original Regulation S-X
encouraged flexibility in determining the scope of consolidated reports.
The principles of inclusion or exclusion to be followed were to "clearly
exhibit the financial condition and results of operations of the
group or groups" (emphasis added). Of course this appearance of flexibility may have been somewhat illusory in the light of SEC review
procedures whereby the Commission's staff assessed the acceptability of
financial statements lodged for filing. In 1959 L. H. Rappaport indicated
that the SEC "probably" would not insist on the consolidation of a
subsidiary which was in a business "totally different from that of the
parent and the parent's other subsidiaries". Nor was the SEC likely to
insist on "consolidating a finance subsidiary with a manufacturing
company".[45] But whatever the probabilities of rulings of one sort or
another in particular situations, the fact remains that the SEC did on
occasions sanction the non-consolidation of subsidiaries on the ground
that their activities differed from those of other firms in the group.

The American Institute also supported this practice. ARB 51 (1959)
described decisions about the area of consolidation as matters of
"policy" which should be concerned with the presentation of data which
were the "most meaningful in the circumstances".

> The reader should be given information which is
> suitable to his needs, but he should not be burdened
> with unnecessary detail. Thus, even though a group
> of companies is heterogeneous in character, it may
> be better to make a full consolidation than to present
> a large number of separate statements. On the other
> hand, separate statements or combined statements would

---

45. Rappaport, op.cit., p.268.

> be preferable for a subsidiary or a group of
> subsidiaries if the presentation of financial
> information concerning the particular activities
> of such subsidiaries would be more informative ...
> than would the inclusion of such subsidiaries in
> the consolidation.

As late as 1973, the AICPA's Accounting Principles Board Opinion

No.18 ("The equity method of accounting for investments in common

stock") reaffirmed this support for the use of sets of statements for

diversified companies. Also in 1971, the Accountants' International

Study Group (which included American representatives) described this

practice without any critical or adverse comment.

Turning to Canada, statements prepared by the Research Committee

of the Canadian Institute of Chartered Accountants suggested that

aggregative statements could be prepared in respect of several, uncon-

solidated subsidiaries.[46]

Australian accountants had been slow to adopt the idea that

dissimilarity of business operations was a ground for non-consolidation

- mainly, it seems, because the statutory rules in force since 1938

in the state of Victoria and since 1961 in other states had expressly

provided that consolidated statements were to cover all subsidiaries,

without exception. The Australian Society of Accountants had criticised

these provisions in 1966.[47] But in 1968 the Society published (un-

official) recommendations on consolidated reporting, which included

the following observation:

> Most accountants would agree that, in many cases,
> information relating to the position and operations
> of a group of companies might be more effectively
> communicated by means of more than one set of
> consolidated statements; or, perhaps, by presenting,

---

46. Canadian Institute of Chartered Accountants, "Consolidated financial
    statements and the equity method of accounting", as revised 1972,
    para.1600.04.

47. Accounting principles and practices discussed in reports on company
    failures, loc.cit., pp.20-1.

along with the consolidated statements, the separate
statements of one or more subsidiaries which, for
good reason, have been excluded from the consolidation.[48]

These comments were made at the same time as a committee appointed by

state Attorneys General (the "Eggleston committee") was evaluating

proposals for company law reform. It appears that both the Institute

of Chartered Accountants and the Australian Society of Accountants

supported the introduction of U.K.-style provisions for holding company

reporting. And, in 1971, Australian states introduced amending legisla-

tion along these lines. The amendments enabled holding companies to

adopt alternative forms of disclosure if they did not wish to prepare

consolidated statements encompassing a holding company and all sub-

sidiaries.[49] (Similar provisions had been adopted in New Zealand in

1955).

U.K. and Australian commentators supported the arrangement of

group data in terms of the major business activities carried on by a

set of related companies. They suggested that the presentation of

several consolidated accounts "would probably be most suitable where a

group of companies consisted of, for example, three distinct sections

of companies ...".[50]

Ironically, the Australian legislation which permitted the

---

48. Notes on the preparation of consolidated statements, loc.cit., p.3.

49. The statutes formally required all-inclusive consolidated statements but then sanctioned the presentation of other combinations
of consolidated and separate statements as would present "the same
or equivalent information" in a form that would be "readily
appreciated by the company's members". See, e.g., N.S.W.
Companies Act, 1961-72, s.151.

50. MacBeath and Platt, op.cit., p.15. For other comments about the
suitability of presenting more than one set of consolidated statements for diversified companies, see Lee and McPherson, op.cit.,
p.367; Bowra and Clarke, op.cit., p.29. Earlier in the U.K. the
Jenkins Committee had claimed that these "group account" provisions enabled the presentation of information concerning the
derivation of profits and the asset-holdings of firms which were
operating in different industries or in different geographical
areas. Report of the Company Law Committee, loc.cit., p.149.

non-consolidation of subsidiaries came into force just as there were

moves (in Australia and elsewhere) to support the "total consolidation"

approach that had been required in the legislation just abandoned.

In July 1971 the Australian Society issued an "exposure draft" titled

"Accounting for material investments in other companies by consolidation

and by the equity method".[51] This draft was first reproduced, and then

endorsed,[52] by the Institute of Chartered Accountants. It included the

following assertion:

> Several separate consolidations of segments of an overall
> group must be considered in themselves an unsatisfactory
> method of reporting group results - unless the segmental
> consolidations are accompanied by an additional total
> consolidation covering the whole group as an investment
> entity.

The Australian Society had demanded segmental consolidations in

1966 but damned them in 1971. And other accounting bodies had similarly

changed their minds about the desirability of excluding particular sub-

sidiaries, apparently in the light of the 1960's American proposals

for separate supplementary reports about the activities of diversified

businesses.

The Canadian Institute, which in 1972 had indicated support for

segmented consolidated data, asserted in 1973 that differences in

business activities did not constitute "a valid reason for exclusion

of a subsidiary from consolidation".[53] When the International Account-

ing Standards Committee issued its exposure draft on "consolidated

financial statements and the equity method of accounting" in December 1974,

---

51. The Australian accountant, July 1971, pp.257-63.

52. "Exposure draft", The chartered accountant in Australia, Aug. 1971,
    pp.18-24. The Oct. 1971 issue of The chartered accountant reported
    that the Institute's Accounting Principles Committee "agrees with
    the accounting principles embodied in the exposure draft and therefore
    a separate draft statement will not be published by the Institute"
    (p.31).

53. Canadian Institute of Chartered Accountants, "Long term inter-
    corporate investments", 1973 amendment, para. 3050-10.

it carefully excluded "dissimilarity of business" from its list of
grounds justifying the exclusion of particular subsidiaries. In 1974 the
SEC also changed its rules governing the scope of consolidated statements by removing prohibitions on the consolidation of subsidiaries
engaged in "financial activities" - life insurance, fire and casualty
insurance, securities broker-dealer, finance, savings and loan or
banking and related activities.[54]

This change in official views about the propriety of one of the long-
standing rules for consolidation did not come about as a result of
extended analysis of the aims of consolidated reporting. On the contrary,
many recently-published texts had continued to note that the scope of
consolidated reports could (or should) be determined by reference to the
degree of heterogeneity in the assets and operations of the related
companies.[55] Some criticism had been levelled at the non-inclusion of
finance companies on the ground that this practice distorted representations of liquidity and gearing and concealed the interest burden
effectively faced by a "group" enterprise.[56] But it appears that the key

---

54. Separate financial statements were still to be presented for each
subsidiary (or group of subsidiaries) engaged in those businesses.
See Accounting Series Release No.154, April 19, 1974. In Dec.
1974 the SEC clarified the condition that separate statements would
generally be required for firms engaged in leasing, factoring and
mortgage banking, and foreshadowed further amendments liberalising
the test whereby these supplementary disclosures could be dispensed
with for "immaterial" subsidiaries. (Securities Act Release 5548).

55. See, e.g., R. Wixon, W. G. Kell and N. M. Bedford (eds.),
Accountants' handbook (New York: Ronald Press Company, 5th ed.,
1970), pp.234-6; C. H. Griffin, T. H. Williams and K. D. Larson,
Advanced accounting (Homewood, Ill.: Richard D. Irwin, Inc., 2nd
ed., 1971), pp.211-2. See also W. B. Meigs, A. N. Mosich and E. J.
Larsen, Modern advanced accounting (New York: McGraw-Hill Book Com-
pany, 1975), p.165; P. Grady, Inventory of generally accepted
accounting principles for business enterprises (New York: American
Institute of Certified Public Accountants, Accounting Research
Study No. 7, 1965), p.318.

56. See V. L. Andrews, "Should parent and captive finance companies be
consolidated?" The journal of accountancy, Aug. 1966,
pp.48-56.

factor in prompting the change was the sudden growth in the number of "conglomerate" enterprises during the stock market and merger boom of the early 1970's. The conglomerates' financial statements included the reports of firms which were engaged in a wide variety of businesses. It seemed inconsistent to accept (or expect) consolidated statements from conglomerates, while prohibiting the consolidation of finance-related subsidiaries.[57]

The change in consolidation rules indicates that there had been a shift in ideas about the role of consolidated reports. More significance was attached to the idea of reporting on a "group" of "controlled" corporations than to the idea of reporting on an "economic entity" (in the sense of a set of firms carrying on related activities).

Along with this shift in ideas, there were shifts in the <u>accounting context</u> in which consolidated reports are presented. Since 1940 there have been changes in the status of consolidated statements, and changes in the profession's attitudes towards the use of equity methods for valuing inter-corporate investments.

Valuation of inter-corporate investments

Consolidated statements were introduced, and then popularised, in the light of a set of ideas about asset valuation, revenue realisation and the calculation of distributable income. At the time that consolidated statements were first used on either side of the Atlantic, accountants generally supported the idea that assets (particularly fixed assets) should not be written up. And if write-ups did take place, it was generally held that the resultant surpluses were not to be regarded as income.

In this setting, consolidated statements had a distinct role, relative to parent company reports. Both in the U.K. and Australia, consolidated

---

57. Meigs, Mosich and Larsen, op.cit., p.165.

statements were plainly viewed as a means of overcoming the limitations
of conventional methods of accounting for inter-corporate investments.
Cost-based valuation, dividend-based revenue recognition (and, for fixed
assets, the non-recognition of fluctuations in value until they appeared
"permanent") meant that the financial statements of holding companies
could be uninformative or misleading. In the U.S.A. the profession's
attitude to consolidated reporting was somewhat more complex in view
of the diversity of accounting practice and the inactivity of state or
federal governments in regulating corporate reporting. Cost-based
valuation was not so highly regarded in the U.S. as it was in the U.K.
Moreover, holding companies were not obliged to publish a "legal"
balance sheet. Nevertheless, several leading accounting writers - notably
Montgomery, Lybrand and Dickinson - based their support for consolidated
statements on the argument that these reports avoided the objections which
could be levelled at holding company reports which showed investments
"at cost".

By the 1940's, consolidated statements were accepted vehicles for
corporate reporting both in the U.K. and the U.S.A., though the accounting
profession had not yet resolved questions about the aims and status of
these reports. However, in both countries, consolidated statements were
being used in the context of fairly similar ideas about the treatment of
inter-corporate investments in the accounts of holding companies.

Since 1940 there have been far-reaching shifts in the profession's
approach to inter-corporate investments.

After experimenting with asset valuation procedures in the 1920's,
British accountants came to accept the framework of applying different
sets of valuation procedures to "fixed" and "current" assets. This
framework was applied to inter-corporate investments. Regardless of
whether these shareholdings were marketable, or whether they constituted
1%, 10%, 50% or even 100% of the issued capital of the investee-companies,

the first step in valuing these assets was to classify them as fixed
or current. Those regarded as fixed assets were valued at cost, or
cost-derivatives; those regarded as current were valued with reference
to current market prices (or contemporary assessments of "value").[58]

Some British writers were critical of cost-based valuation and
favoured the use of a form of "equity" accounting for handling investments in subsidiaries. The most commonly-described "equity" method
involved the systematic adjustment in the holding company's books of
the recorded values of investments by adding to or subtracting from
initial cost an appropriate proportion of subsidiaries' losses or undistributed profits. (Few writers bothered to consider whether cognisance
should also be taken of non-operating gains or losses, such as would
arise from the revaluation of fixed assets). Opponents of this cost-based
equity method claimed that it led to the recognition of "unrealised" income.

However, with the popularisation of consolidated statements, few
U.K. firms bothered to use "equity" methods and few writers gave the
matter much attention. Consolidated statements were regarded as an
alternative way of conveying information about a holding company's investments - and, in the light of other supposed advantages, consolidated
reporting was clearly the preferred alternative.

While some American valuation practices were significantly different
from those adopted in the U.K. (particularly in relation to the assign-
ment of values to newly-acquired assets) it seems that American practitioners were equally concerned to avoid the recognition of "unrealised"
profits. Hence American writers followed British arguments to the effect

---

58. This approach to the valuation of inter-corporate investments was
     eventually spelt out in The Institute of Chartered Accountants in
     England and Wales' Recommendation N20, "Treatment of investments
     in the balance sheets of trading companies", Nov. 1958. As des-
     cribed in Ch.3 this approach was regarded as "best practice"
     well before the 1930's.

that assets should be valued on differing bases depending upon whether they were classed as fixed or current. In the 1930's the policies of the newly-established SEC contributed to a firmer adherence to cost-based valuation for fixed assets. Notwithstanding the consensus among accounting writers that the writing-up of fixed assets was justified in certain circumstances, the SEC imposed an informal ban on all upward revaluations, and progressively tightened its administrative processes to the stage where upward asset revaluations were regarded as taboo, despite the fact that there had been no formal SEC pronouncement or American Institute recommendation dealing with the topic directly.

U.S. approaches to the valuation of inter-corporate investments have been influenced by this antipathy towards upward asset revaluations. The use of "equity" methods by public utility corporations was expressly banned by the SEC - though not for other registrants. The SEC introduced a general requirement that financial statements disclose the basis of determining the valuation of investments in affiliates. It seems reasonable to suppose that SEC attitudes towards upward asset revaluations would have deterred many registrants from adjusting asset values by the amount of undistributed profits of subsidiaries - though it does not appear that the SEC actually prevented firms from using this method.[59] However at this stage in the development of U.S. accounting practices, the statements of parent companies were not regarded as being of great significance, and consolidated statements were treated as the primary reports. As noted in earlier chapters, text-book discussions of the valuation of investments in subsidiaries often described both cost and equity methods, but regarded the choice as insignificant since parent company reports might not be published. Equity accounting was

---

59. In a number of instances the SEC held that parent statements were deficient insofar as they failed to recognise losses incurred by subsidiaries. See Rappaport, op.cit., p.281.

regarded more favourably as a means of handling unconsolidated subsidiaries.

Texts produced after 1940 maintained this attitude. Lewis's Consolidated statements described both cost valuation procedures and what
he termed the "adjusted value" method for recording in the books of the
parent company.[60]   In 1948 Newlove produced a new text, Consolidated
statements, which repeated his 1926 description of the "actual value
method" for handling intercorporate investments.[61]   Noble, Karrenbrock
and Simons similarly provided examples of consolidation procedures using
both the cost and equity methods.[62]   Mason claimed that "as an economic
unit" a parent company could update its investment account to record
profits and losses of a subsidiary - and besides, that method aided
"the calculations called for by the consolidated statements".[63]   Most
contributors to the literature did not get very excited about the
desirability of using one rather than another method. Half-hearted
opposition to equity accounting was expressed by C. G. Blough (the SEC's
first Chief Accountant) who claimed that many accountants "felt" that
the practice of accruing earnings or losses of subsidiaries on the books
of a parent company should be discouraged.[64]   One of the few writers

60. E. J. B. Lewis, Consolidated statements (New York: Ronald Press
     Company, 1942), pp.67-8, 74.

61. G. H. Newlove, Consolidated statements (Boston: D. C. Heath and
     Company, 1948), p.31. Newlove also claimed that any gains arising
     from undistributed earnings of subsidiaries should be recorded "as
     a separate division of earned surplus" in the parent's record since
     these gains were "not available for the declaration of parent company
     dividends". Idem.

62. H. S. Noble, W. E. Karrenbrock and H. Simons, Advanced accounting
     (Cincinnati: South-Western Publishing Company, 1941), pp.638ff.

63. P. Mason, Fundamentals of accounting (Chicago: The Foundation
     Press. Inc., 1942), p.366. However he acknowledged that these
     adjustments would "not ordinarily" be formally recorded in the
     parent's books (p.367).

64. C. G. Blough, Practical applications of accounting standards (New
     York: American Institute of Certified Public Accountants, 1957),
     p.417.

to actively support equity methods was M. Moonitz who included an
"extended digression" on the subject in his Entity theory of consolidated statements. W. A. Paton, who was editor of the AAA monograph series,
strongly disagreed with Moonitz's argument and inserted an extended
footnote to Moonitz's text in which he claimed that equity methods and
consolidation accounting were alternatives:

> ... the main reason for the preparation of such statements
> is to show the stockholders of the parent or dominant
> company what the amount of the controlling equity is,
> assuming corporate lines to be erased, and if this is done
> in terms of the regular accounts of the holding company
> there is not much point to going further.[65]

There were often reports of equity methods being used in the U.S. during
the 1930's and 1940's for both subsidiary[66] and non-subsidiary investments.[67] But it seems that the attitude of most American accountants
towards equity accounting methods was that expressed by Kohler in 1938:

> No practical benefits are derived from accruing profit and
> loss from subsidiaries on the books of the controlling
> company.[68]

However the frequency with which firms presented consolidated
statements which omitted one or more subsidiaries seems to have caused
concern about the utility of those reports, and led to authoritative

---

65. Op.cit., p.46. Elsewhere Paton emphasised that cost-based valua-
    tion procedures should be retained by parent companies in order
    to reflect the position of a separate legal entity, and to avoid
    showing an investment account composed of elements valued on
    different bases. See W. A. Paton and W. A. Paton, Jr., Asset
    accounting (New York: The Macmillan Company, 1952), pp.137-8.

66. See, e.g., E. A. Kracke, "Consolidated financial statements",
    The journal of accountancy, Dec. 1938, p.385.

67. "Accrued profit on an investment" ("The commentator" column,
    edited by W. D. Cranstoun), The journal of accountancy, 1938,
    p.324.

68. E. L. Kohler, "Some tentative propositions underlying consolidated
    reports", The accounting review, March 1938, p.68. (Kohler's
    paper was said to represent "in the main" the opinions of the
    executive committee of the American Accounting Association.) See
    also "Profits and losses of subsidiary company", ("Accounting
    questions" column), The journal of accountancy, 1933, pp.75-6.

support for equity methods. The American Institute's Accounting
Research Bulletin No.51 expressed a preference for the use of adjusted
data to value unconsolidated subsidiaries in consolidated statements.

> The preferable method [of dealing with unconsolidated
> subsidiaries in consolidated statements] is to adjust
> the investment ... to take up the share of the controlling
> company or companies in the subsidiaries' net income or
> net loss, except where the subsidiary was excluded because
> of exchange restrictions or other reasons which raise the
> question of whether the increase in equity has accrued to the
> credit of the group.

Some members of the American Institute's Committee on Accounting Procedure
felt that the proposal was not sufficiently strong and that equity
accounting should be regarded as the only acceptable way of valuing
investments in subsidiaries. But note that these recommendations applied
to consolidated statements, and not necessarily to parent company reports.
It might be supposed that this restriction reflected the view that write-
ups should not be regarded as giving rise to income: equity accounting
was acceptable for consolidated statements but was not necessarily
acceptable for income calculations in a corporation's own "legal" reports.
However it seems more likely that consolidated reporting was so entrenched
in U.S. accounting practice that the Institute Committee did not bother
to discuss the methods used in parent companies' books. Parent company
reports were not published; hence the parent's bookkeeping procedures
were irrelevant.

The American Institute's Accounting Principles Board later hardened
this preference for equity accounting to a firm recommendation. The
APB resolved that equity accounting methods should be used in consolidated statements for all unconsolidated domestic subsidiaries:

> If, in consolidated financial statements, a domestic
> subsidiary is not consolidated, the Board's opinion
> is that ... the investment in the subsidiary should be
> adjusted for the consolidated group's share of accumulated
> undistributed earnings and losses since acquisition.[69]

_____

69. APB Opinion 10 ("Omnibus opinion"), Dec. 1966, para.3.

Both ARB 51 and APB 10 seem to show little concern for matters of "principle". Indeed, a note to APB 10 seemed to acknowledge that the Board's rulings were merely ad hoc responses to perceived abuses; it referred to accounting research studies "on the broader subjects of accounting for inter-corporate investments and foreign operations" as being in progress. APB 10 was only to be as a temporary policy decision, pending the completion of a more thorough investigation. (By the time the APB was disbanded the promised research study had still not appeared). But it soon became apparent that the ARB 51 and APB 10 rulings were not sufficient to avoid abuses or anomalies, and the APB was obliged to extend its rulings to cover joint ventures, investments in associated companies, and foreign subsidiaries. In March 1971 the Board published Opinion 18, "The equity method of accounting for investments in common stock". Once again the APB avoided discussing general questions about asset valuation - and again the APB excused this omission by referring to on-going research into inter-corporate investments and foreign operations. Even so, the implicit theme of Opinion No. 18 was that cost-based valuation of inter-corporate investments was inadequate. The adjustment of cost data was seen as an improvement. However the adoption of cost-based equity accounting was advocated without any detailed evaluation of alternatives (particularly the use of net asset backing rather than adjusted-cost data - or even the use of market selling prices in cases where inter-corporate investments took the form of publicly-traded securities).

APB 18 also extended the ambit of equity accounting to parent company statements - but only when such statements were "prepared for issuance to stockholders as the financial statements of the primary reporting entity".

The fact that APB 18 was prepared to recommend equity accounting for parent companies seems to indicate that little importance was

placed on the one-time bogey of recognising gains arising from
inter-corporate investments before those gains were "realised". The
restriction on the application of equity accounting to parent company
reports seems to have been a concession to those who objected to the
practice. Otherwise the APB seemed intent on removing from consolidated
statements some of the distortions introduced by adherence to cost-based
valuation.

The American support for equity accounting which was finally expressed
in APB 18 was a remarkable departure from the position taken in earlier
years. And there was a similar switch in British attitudes. Many British
writers had opposed the use of equity accounting on the ground that the
adjustment of asset valuations constituted the recognition of "unrealised"
revenues. But in January 1971 this approach was abandoned. The Institute
of Chartered Accountants in England and Wales issued Statement of Standard
Accounting Practice No.1 (SSAP 1)[70] which required the use of equity
methods to record the performance of both subsidiaries and associated
companies.[71] Like the earlier U.S. pronouncements (ARB 51 and APB 10)
the U.K. ruling was concerned with consolidated statements only, not
parent company statements. This emphasis in the American pronouncements
may have arisen because consolidated reports were typically the only
statements published. However the U.K. restriction arose from an
attempt to preserve the "realisation" idea: it was claimed that the
inclusion of undistributed profits in company statements would "be
in breach of the principle that credit should not be taken for investment
income until it is received or receivable". While the U.K. statement

70. "Accounting for the results of associated companies", issued in
    association with the Scottish and Irish Institutes, and published
    in Accountancy, Feb. 1971, pp.61-5.

71. Associated companies were defined as being those firms in which
    the investing company participated in "commercial and financial
    policy decisions", and either had an interest which was "effectively
    that of a partner in a joint venture or consortium", or held a
    long-term interest in excess of 20% of the "equity voting rights".

sanctioned equity accounting "where the investing company has no subsidiaries, or otherwise does not prepare consolidated accounts", it was said to be necessary in these situations for the investing company to "adapt its profit and loss account, suitably titled, to incorporate the additional information". In other words, equity accounting was not to be used to calculate the income of an investor-company "as a legal entity".

Since 1971, recommendations approved (or being considered) in Canada, Australia and New Zealand have also sanctioned equity accounting in some form or other.

The 1974 New Zealand statement closely followed the U.K. text. It emphasised that "the basic purpose of equity accounting" was "to show more truly and fairly the return on total shareholders' funds ...". But it recommended that equity accounting be used in consolidated statements only; the use of equity accounting by parent companies was claimed to be contrary to "accepted practice".[72]

In Canada, a 1972 "research recommendation" supported a cost-adjusted equity method for unconsolidated subsidiaries, and for other long-term investments in the records of investor-companies.[73]

The Australian Society of Accountants produced an exposure draft in 1971 which recommended the use of equity methods in consolidated statements (or, where no consolidated statements were prepared, in separate "equity statements").[74] The proposals were for the valuation of investments in associated companies at their underlying "net asset

---

72. Statement of Standard Accounting Practice No.2, "Accounting for associated companies (equity accounting)", Accountants' journal, Dec. 1974, pp.176-82.

73. Canadian Institute of Chartered Accountants, "Long term inter-corporate investments", Oct. 1972 (section 3050).

74. "Accounting for material investments in other companies by consolidation and by the equity method", The Australian accountant, July 1971. This draft was later endorsed by the Institute of Chartered Accountants in Australia. See note 52, above.

backing" rather than at an adjusted-cost figure. However, following

changes to the statutory definitions of "subsidiary" and to requirements

for the publication of "group accounts", the Society and the Institute

combined to produce a new proposal in September 1973.[75] Unlike the

1971 draft, the 1973 proposals were intended to be applied to subsidiaries

as well as to associated companies - and to be used not only in con-

solidated statements but also in the books of account and published

statements of "the investor company as a legal entity". The 1973

draft abandoned the support for a "net asset backing" equity method in

favour of a cost-based calculation. And, without argument or explanation

the 1973 draft urged the use of equity accounting rather than consolidation

procedures for "controlled" but not majority-owned subsidiaries.

The resurgence of interest in equity accounting methods since the

1950's seems to underline the fact that accountants of the 1920's and

1940's did not remove the problems associated with inter-corporate

investments by their adoption of consolidated reporting. Elements of

the rules or proposals for equity accounting also point to continuing

confusion among accountants as to the aims of various methods of

reporting on inter-corporate investments. The Australian profession's

support for the idea that consolidated statements were intended to

depict the affairs of a "group" of companies was hardly consistent

with its support for the non-consolidation of minority-owned but

"controlled" subsidiaries. There was obvious conflict between British

and Australian views on the propriety of using equity accounting pro-

cedures in investor-company statements. But the major manifestation

of confusion about the underlying rationale of equity accounting was

the support for the proposition that managerial "influence" over the

75. Proposed statement of accounting standards, "The use of the equity
     method in accounting for investments in subsidiaries and associated
     companies", supplement to The Australian accountant, Oct. 1973.

affairs of an investee company was of relevance to the application of equity methods. The Canadian statement indicated that equity methods should be used for the valuation of investments in firms which were not subsidiaries but which were "effectively controlled" by the investor. The British, Australian and New Zealand statements claimed that equity methods should be used to account for investments in "associated companies", and the statements defined associated companies as firms over which an investor exercised "significant influence". These proposals were not the outcome of an analysis of the problems of attempting to value inter-corporate investments. In fact, equity accounting was not approached as a valuation procedure but as a means of extending the ambit of consoli-dated reports or of removing the anomalies in consolidation accounting. This approach also led to the application to equity accounting of the consolidation techniques of inter-company eliminations. These techniques had been justified as a means of ensuring that "group" financial state-ments only showed the profits arising from transactions between a group and outside parties. The use of these techniques in equity accounting may have seemed consistent with the view that reports prepared using equity procedures were intended to depict the affairs of an "economic entity" where that was defined as a set of firms under a common "influence" On the other hand the elimination of profits arising from transactions between (say) subsidiaries and non-subsidiaries was certainly not justified by the proposition that consolidated reports were intended to depict a "group entity". Alternatively, one might suppose that the across-the-board eliminations were consistent with the aim of amplifying the financial reports of a holding company since the procedures would avoid the over-statement of asset and income figures.

In short, there were serious inconsistencies between proposals for the use of equity accounting - and many of these can be seen as echoing long-standing inconsistencies in the literature on consolidated statements.

Status of consolidated reports

As noted earlier in connection with the statements or recommendations of accounting bodies, accountants in different countries have held
different views about the status of consolidated statements (relative to
the reports of holding companies). American (and Canadian) accountants
have long regarded consolidated statements as primary reports, while
British, Australian and New Zealand accountants have viewed consolidated
reporting from a different perspective due to disclosure rules which have
required the publication of holding company reports and treated consolidated statements as only one way of providing supplementary information.

In the U.K. and commonwealth countries, some of the users of financial
data have come to place greater emphasis on consolidated data than that
indicated by the statutory rules or the profession's recommendations.

The 1948 U.K. Companies Act permitted the total or partial incorporation of group accounts into a holding company's own balance sheet and
profit and loss account. Initially, only a few firms took advantage of
this provision but in 1956 Robson reported that a large number of firms
presented their profit and loss accounts (if not their balance sheets)
in a hybrid form.[76] And in 1973 Lee reported that the consolidated
profit and loss account normally displaced the holding company's
account: firms reported a group profit and then indicated how much
was attributable to the holding company.[77]

Australian rules have not permitted the publication of "hybrid" financial statements, but it is clear that stock exchanges and the financial
press have come to place far greater emphasis on consolidated financial
data than on the figures obtainable from holding company statements.

---

76. T. B. Robson, Consolidated and other group accounts (London:
    Gee & Company (Publishers) Limited, 3rd ed., 1956), p.97.

77. G. A. Lee, Modern financial accounting (London: Thomas Nelson and
    sons Ltd., 1973), pp.396-7.

Moreover, this emphasis on consolidated data has been acknowledged in professional statements dealing with other matters. Several accounting standards or recommendations dealing with the publication of funds statements or earnings-per-share statistics have specifically stated that these disclosures are to be based on consolidated rather than holding company data.[78]

---

78. e.g., The Institute of Chartered Accountants in England and Wales, Statement of Standard Accounting Practice 3, "Earnings per share" (May 1972), para.8; Statement of Standard Accounting Practice 10, "Statements of source and application of funds" (July 1975), para.5. The Institute of Chartered Accountants in Australia, Technical Bulletin F.1 "Statement of source and application of funds" (Jan. 1971), para.5; Technical Bulletin F.5, "Earnings per share (Dec. 1973), para.6.

Resume

By 1940 consolidated reports had become an accepted vehicle for corporate reporting on either side of the Atlantic (and in some commonwealth countries). But practices had developed before accountants had sorted out the aims of this form of statement. A review of the pre-1940 accounting literature indicated that accountants and those who framed disclosure rules were uncertain about what consolidated statements were intended to show. And this uncertainty was reflected in an array of inconsistent and confused practices and rules.

Since 1940 this confusion has continued, though accounting writers developed a superficially-sensible explanation of consolidated reporting. It was commonly said that consolidated statements depicted a "group" of companies as a single entity. This proposition was sufficiently vague to accommodate conflicting ideas about the aims of these reports. However, what was originally intended as an analogy (showing related companies "as if" they were a single organization) has become a rigid framework for consolidation practice. Rules have been framed with the object of securing the preparation of reports dealing with a "group" of companies - despite the fact that individuals buy shares in or lend money to individual corporations, not to "groups".

Despite the apparent consensus concerning the aims of consolidated statements, the underlying disagreements about the scope and content of these reports have not been resolved. These disagreements have led to inconsistencies in disclosure rules and in the profession's rules for the preparation of consolidated statements.

The promulgation of rules prescribing the form and content of con-solidated statements may have stifled debate on these questions. In 1948 one writer commented that the major contributions to the literature on consolidated reports had been made by a handful of writers.[79]

---

79. G. H. Newlove, op.cit., p.viii.

The same could be said of the literature since then - in the U.S.A. or elsewhere. There has been very little analysis of conflicting ideas about consolidated reports. There has been very little recognition that such a conflict exists. And virtually no attention has been paid to the significant shifts in attitudes towards consolidated reports that have taken place in the last 30 years.

There have been three types of changes since 1940.

First, there have been far reaching changes in the status of consolidated statements. In the early 1940's American writers were virtually unanimous that consolidated statements were not, by themselves, sufficient disclosures. Indeed, most writers regarded consolidated statements as supplements to parent company reports. True, some saw it the other way round, and regarded parent company reports as supplements to group data. But there was certainly agreement that consolidated reports should not be presented on their own. Some writers speculated that this state of affairs would not last. Moonitz suggested that legal changes might make "groups" of companies the primary unit of organization and accountability. Only then, he said, could consolidated statements legitimately be regarded as primary documents. But the law has not recognised "groups" of companies as the primary unit of organisation and accountability. However, the stock exchanges, the financial press and the accounting profession have placed greater emphasis on consolidated statements than on parent company reports, so that consolidated statements have nevertheless become the primary vehicle for corporate financial reporting.

Second, there have been substantial changes in the scope of consolidated statements. Accountants have come to accept the case for the total consolidation of holding company and subsidiaries and now permit only a few exceptions to this rule. The exclusion of subsidiaries from consolidation on the ground that they are engaged in dissimilar industrial activities has fallen into disfavour.

Third, the acceptance of equity accounting methods has produced a major change in the context in which consolidated statements are prepared. While the English Institute has maintained its opposition to the reporting of "unrealised" gains on investments as part of the income of holding companies, other professional bodies have either explicitly or implicitly accepted the practice. Hence the proposition that consolidated statements are intended to overcome the limitations of conventional valuation methods has lost much of its significance. If holding companies are able to use equity methods, then the case for the use of consolidated reporting must rest on different grounds.

SELECTED BIBLIOGRAPHY

Accountants' International Study Group, Consolidated financial statements (1973).

American Institute of Accountants, Survey of consolidated financial statement practices (New York: 1956).

Andrews, V. L., "Should parent and captive finance companies be consolidated?" The journal of accountancy, Aug. 1966.

Angell, J. W., "The Illinois blue sky law", Journal of political economy, 1920.

Anon, "Balance sheets of holding companies", The incorporated accountants' journal, Oct. 1922.

Anon, "A history of the American Institute of Accountants", Fiftieth anniversary celebration (New York: American Institute of Accountants, 1937).

Anon, "Consolidation adjustment", The accountant, July 1928, pp.59-63.

Ashworth, R., "Some aspects of group finance", The incorporated accountants' journal, March 1933.

Ashby, F. B., The economic effect of blue sky laws (Philadelphia: University of Pennyslyvania, 1926).

Atwood, A. W., The stock and produce exchanges (New York: Alexander Hamilton Institute, Modern Business series, 1921).

Australian Society of Accountants, Accounting principles and practices discussed in reports on company failures (Melbourne: 1966).

Ayres, A. U., "Governmental regulation of securities issues", Political science quarterly, 1913.

Barton, A. E. Australasian advanced accountancy (Sydney: The Law Book Company of Australia Ltd., 7th ed., 1922).

Baxter, W. and Davidson, S., (eds.) Studies in accounting theory (Homewood, Ill.: Richard D. Irwin, Inc., 1962).

Bedford, N. M., Perry, K. W. and Wyatt, A. R., Advanced accounting (New York: John Wiley & Sons. Inc., 3rd ed., 1973).

Bell, W. H., Accountants' reports (New York: Ronald Press Company, 1921).

Bell, W. H., Auditing (New York: Prentice-Hall, Inc., 1926).

Bell, S. and Graham, W. J., Theory and practice of accounting (Chicago: American Technical Society, 1937).

Benington, H., "Limitations", The accountant, Sept. 1916.

Bennett, R. J., Corporation accounting (New York: Ronald Press Company, 1919).

Bentley, H. C., The science of accounts (New York: Ronald Press Company, 1911).

Berle, A. A. Jr., "Accounting and the law", The accounting review, March 1938.

Bierman, H. Jr., Financial and managerial accounting (New York: The Macmillan Company, 1963).

Binder, B. H., "Uses and abuses of subsidiary and associated companies", The accountant, 26 March 1932.

Binder, B. H., "Holding companies' profit and loss accounts", The accountant, 13 May 1933.

Blough, C. G., Practical applications of accounting standards (New York: American Institute of Certified Public Accountants, 1957).

Bliss, J. H., Financial and operating ratios in management (New York: Ronald Press Company, 1923).

Boddington, A. L., "Company amalgamations, absorptions and reconstructions", The accountant, 26 April 1924.

Bogie, D. J., Groups accounts (London: Jordan & Sons, Ltd., 2nd ed., 1959).

Bonbright, J. C. and Means, G. C., The holding company (New York: McGraw-Hill Book Company Inc., 1922).

Bowra, R. L. and Clarke, F. L., Holding companies and group accounts in Australia and New Zealand (Sydney: Butterworths Pty. Ltd., 1973).

Brundage, P. F., "Some shortcomings in consolidated statements", The journal of accountancy, Oct. 1930.

Brundage, P. F., "Consolidated statements" in T. W. Leland (ed.), Contemporary accounting (New York: American Institute of Accountants, 1945).

Carey, J. L., The rise of the accounting profession (New York: American Institute of Certified Public Accountants, Vol. I, 1969).

Carter, E. M., "What is an annual balance sheet?" The incorporated accountants' journal, 22 Oct. 1910.

Carter, G. R., The tendency towards industrial combination (London: Constable & Company Ltd., 1913).

Carter, R. N., Advanced accounts (London: Sir Isaac Pitman and Sons Ltd., 1922).

Cash, W. A., "Consolidated balance sheets", The accountant, Dec. 1929.

Castle, W. H., "Points on company accounts", The accountant, 28 June 1924.

Chambers, R. J., "Consolidated statements are not really necessary", The Australian accountant, Feb. 1968.

Chatfield, M., A history of accounting thought (Hinsdale, Illinois: The Dryden Press, 1974).

Chaykin, I. J. and Zimering, M., Advanced accounting problems (New York: John Wiley & Sons. Inc., 1958).

Childs, W. H., Consolidated financial statements (Cornell University Press, 1949).

Cilliers, H. S., Rossouw, S. and Touche, A. G., Consolidation of financial statements (London: Butterworths, 1969).

Clephane, W. C., The organization and management of business corporations (St. Paul, Minnesota: West Publishing Company, 1905).

Cole, W. M. (with A. E. Geddes), The fundamentals of accounting (Boston: Houghton Mifflin Company, 1921).

Colesworthy, H. E., "Amalgamations", The incorporated accountants' journal, Oct. 1921.

Commercial Research Bureau, Inc., Accountancy reports (Chicago: 1929).

Conyngton, T., Bennett, R. J. and Conyngton, H. R., Corporation procedure (New York: Ronald Press Company, rev. ed., 1927).

Corbin, D. A., Accounting and economic decisions (New York: Dodd, Mead & Company, 1964).

Cox, H. C., Advanced and analytical accounting (New York: Ronald Press Company, 1920).

Cropper, L. C., Bookkeeping and accounts (London: Macdonald and Evans, 1911).

Cutforth, A. E., Audits (London: Gee & Company, 1908).

Cutforth, A. E., "Amalgamations", The accountant, 1 April 1933.

Daniels, M. B., Corporation financial statements (Ann Arbor: University of Michigan Bureau of Business Research, 1934).

Daniels, M. B., Financial statements (Chicago: American Accounting Association, 1939).

de Bedts, R. F., The new deal's SEC (New York: Columbia University Press, 1964).

de Mond, C. W., Price Waterhouse & Company in America (Privately printed, New York, 1951).

Densham, F. W., "Depreciation of assets and goodwill of limited companies", The accountant, 28 May 1898.

Dewing, A. S., The financial policy of corporations (New York: Ronald Press Company, rev. ed., 1926).

Dickinson, A. L., "The profits of a corporation", Official record of the proceedings of the Congress of accountants (New York: George Wilkinson, 1904). (Reprinted in The incorporated accountants' journal, Nov. 1904).

Dickinson, A. L., Accounting practice and procedure (New York: Ronald Press Company, 1914).

Dickinson, A. L., "Some special points in corporation accounting", The accountant, 7 Oct. 1905.

Dickinson, A. L., "Notes on some problems relating to the accounts of holding companies, The journal of accountancy, 1906.

Dickinson, A. L., "The American Association of Public Accountants", The accountant, 28 Nov. 1925.

Dicksee, L. R., Auditing - a practical manual for auditors (London: Gee & Company, 1892).

Dicksee, L. R., "Published balance sheets and accounts", The accountant Nov. 1920.

Dicksee, L. R., "Published balance sheets and window dressing", The accountant, 17 April 1926.

Edwards, J. D., History of public accounting in the United States (East Lansing: Bureau of Business and Economic Research, Michigan State University, 1960).

Eiteman, W. J., Dice, C. A. and Eiteman, D. K., The stock market (New York: McGraw-Hill Book Company, 4th ed., 1966).

Esquerre, P. J., The applied theory of accounts (New York: Ronald Press Company, 1914).

Esquerre, P. J., Accounting (New York: Ronald Press Company, 1927).

Eggleston, D. W. C., Modern accounting theory and practice (New York: John Wiley and Sons, Inc., 1930).

Fabricant, S., Revaluations of fixed assets, 1925-1934 (New York: National Bureau of Economic Research, Bulletin No. 62, 1936).

Fairbairn, W. J., The consolidation of accounts (Cape Town: Juta & Company, Ltd., 3rd ed., 1968).

Finney, H. A., Consolidated statements for holding company and sub-sidiaries (New York: Prentice-Hall Inc., 1922).

Finney, H. A., Introduction to principles of accounting (New York: Prentice-Hall Inc., 1932).

Fitzgerald, G. E. and Speck, A. E., Holding companies in Australia and New Zealand (Sydney: Butterworth & Company (Australia) Ltd., 2nd ed., 1950).

Fitzgerald, A. A. and Fitzgerald, G. E., Form and content of published financial statements (Sydney: Butterworths, 2nd ed., 1960).

Foulke, R. A., The sinews of American commerce (Dun & Bradstreet, Inc., 1941).

Foulke, R. A., Practical financial statement analysis (New York: McGraw-Hill Book Company Inc., 1945).

Freeman, H. C., "The statement of accounts of holding companies", The journal of accountancy, Sept. 1914.

Freeman, M. V., "A private practitioner's view of the development of the Securities and Exchange Commission", The George Washington law review, Oct. 1959.

Garnsey, Sir Gilbert, "Holding companies and their published accounts", The accountant, 6 Jan. 1923.

Garnsey, Sir Gilbert, Holding companies and their published accounts (London: Gee & Co. (Publishers) Ltd., 1923).

Garnsey, Sir Gilbert, "Insurance companies' accounts", The accountant, 3 Jan. 1925.

Garnsey, Sir Gilbert, "Holding companies and their published accounts", The accountant, 20 Feb. 1926.

Garnsey, Sir Gilbert, Holding companies and their published accounts, (London: Gee & Co. (Publishers) Ltd., 3rd edn. by T. B. Robson, 1936).

Gentry, J. A. and Johnson, G. L., Finney and Miller's principles of accounting - advanced (Englewood Cliffs, N.J.: Prentice-Hall, Inc., 1971).

Gerstenberg, G. W., "Special phases of corporation law", The journal of accountancy, Oct. 1909.

Gibson, R. W., Disclosure by Australian companies (Melbourne: Melbourne University Press, 1971).

Gilman, S., Accounting concepts of profit (New York: Ronald Press Company, 1939).

Goggin, W. J. and Toner, J. V., Accounting - principles and procedure (Cambridge, Mass.: Houghton Mifflin, 1930).

Grady, P., (ed.) Memoirs and accounting thought of George O. May (New York: Ronald Press Company, 1962).

Grady, P., Inventory of generally accepted accounting principles for business enterprises (New York: American Institute of Certified Public Accountants, Accounting Research Study No. 7, 1965).

Graham, B. and Meredith, S. P., The interpretation of financial statements (New York: Harper and Brothers, Publishers, 1937).

Greendlinger, L., Accounting theory and practice (New York: Alexander Hamilton Institute, 1910).

Greendlinger, L., Financial and business statements (New York: Alexander Hamilton Institute, 1922).

Greene, W. A. "The report of the company law amendment committee",
The accountant, 13 Nov. 1926.

Griffin, C. H., Williams, T. H. and Welsch, G. A., Advanced accounting,
(Homewood, Ill.: Richard D. Irwin, Inc., 1966).

Guthmann, H. G., The analysis of financial statements (New York:
Prentice-Hall, Inc., 1925).

Haslam, A., "Balance sheets of public companies", The accountant,
1 June 1927.

Hatfield, H. R., Modern accounting (New York: D. Appleton and Co.,
1916).

Hatfield, H. R., Accounting - its principles and problems (New York:
D. Appleton and Co., 1927).

Hawkins, D. F., Corporate financial reporting (Homewood, Ill.:
Richard D. Irwin, Inc., 1971).

Hawnt, F. M., "The plea for greater detail in balance sheets of limited
companies", The incorporated accountants' journal, Dec. 1914.

Healy, R. E., "Address before the Controllers Institute of America,
Jan. 31, 1934", The controller, Feb. 1935.

Healy, R. E., "The next step in accounting", The accounting review,
March 1938.

Hendriksen, E. S., Accounting theory (Homewood, Ill.: Richard D.
Irwin, Inc., 1965).

Hickey, D., "Company law defects - suggested amendments", The accountant,
1 Nov. 1924.

Herr, J. P., "The appreciation of assets - when is it legitimate?"
The journal of accountancy, Nov. 1906.

Himmelblau, D., Principles of accounting (New York: Ronald Press
Company, rev. ed., 1934).

Hoagland, H. E., Corporation finance (New York: McGraw-Hill Book Co.
Ltd., 3rd ed., 1947).

Hodge , A. C. and McKinsey, J. O., Principles of accounting (Chicago:
University of Chicago Press, 1920).

Howitt, H. G., "Present day demands on auditors and the effect of the
Companies Bill thereon", The accountant, 28 Jan. 1928.

Huebner, S. S., "Scope and functions of the stock market", The annals
of the American academy of political and social science, May 1910.

Jenkinson, W. M., "Some debatable matter in accounting and auditing",
The accountant, 20 March 1909.

Jenkinson, W. M., Bookkeeping and accounting (London: Edward Arnold
2nd ed., 1912).

Jenkinson, W. M., "Some notes on the audit of different businesses", The accountant, 19 April 1913.

Jones, E., The trust problem in the United States (New York: The Macmillan Company, 1922).

Jones, E. W., "Company amalgamations", The accountant, 21 Nov. 1925.

Keen, F. N. "The balance sheet of a limited company", The accountant 16 April 1898.

Keen, F. N., "Balance sheet values", The accountant, 11 Jan. 1908.

Keister, D. A., Corporation accounting and auditing (Cleveland: The Burrows Bros. Company, 12th ed., 1907).

Kenley, W. J., A statement of Australian accounting principles (Melbourne: Accountancy Research Foundation, 1970).

Kennedy, R. D., Financial statements (Chicago: Richard D. Irwin, Inc., 1946).

Kerr, D. S., "Consolidated balance sheets", The accountant, Nov. 20 1915.

Kerr, H. M. B., "A talk on pooling agreements", The incorporated accountants' journal, March 1926.

Kester, R. B., Accounting theory and practice (New York: Ronald Press Company, 1922).

Kester, R. B., Accounting theory and practice, Vol. II (New York: Ronald Press Company, 2nd ed., 1925).

Kester, R. B., Advanced accounting (New York: Ronald Press Company, 3rd ed., 1933).

Kester, R. B., Principles of accounting (New York: Ronald Press Company, 4th ed., 1939).

Kieso, D. E., Mautz, R. K. and Moyer, C. A., Intermediate principles of accounting (New York: John Wiley and Sons, Inc., 1969).

Kirshman, J. E., Principles of investment (Chicago: A. W. Shaw Company, 1924).

Kitchen, J., "The accounts of British holding company groups: development and attitudes to disclosure in the early years", Accounting and business research, Spring 1972.

Kohler, E. L. and Morrison, P. L., Principles of accounting (Chicago: A. W. Shaw Company, 1928).

Kohler, E. L., "Some tentative propositions underlying consolidated reports", The accounting review, March 1938.

Kracke, E. A., "Consolidated financial statements", The journal of accountancy, Dec. 1938.

Ladd, D. R., Contemporary corporate accounting and the public (Homewood, Ill.: Richard D. Irwin, Inc., 1963).

Lagerquist, W. E., Investment analysis (New York: The Macmillan Company, 1921).

La Salle Extension University, Principles of accounting (Chicago: 1920).

Leake, P. D., "Depreciation and wasting assets", The accountant, 3 July 1915.

Lee, G. A., Modern financial accounting (London: Thomas Nelson and Sons Ltd., 1973).

Lee, L. N. and McPherson, L. A., Consolidated statements and group accounts (Sydney: The Law Book Company Ltd., 1963).

Lewis, E. J. B., Consolidated statements (New York: Ronald Press Company, 1942).

Lindsay, M. M., Holding companies and consolidation statements (Boston, Mass.: The Bentley School of Accounting and Finance, 1946).

Lisle, G., Accounting in theory and practice (Edinburgh: William Green and Sons, 1899).

Lloyd-Dodd, F. T., "Industrial and business amalgamations", The incorporated accountants' journal, Nov. 1926.

Loomis, P. A., "The Securities Exchange Act of 1934 ...", The George Washington law review, Oct. 1959.

Lough, W. H., Business finance (New York: Ronald Press Company, 1917).

Lybrand, W. M. "The accounting of industrial enterprises", The journal of accountancy, Nov.-Dec. 1908, Jan. 1909.

MacBeath, A., and Platt, A. J., Group accounts and holding companies (London: Gee and Company (Publishers) Ltd., 1951).

MacFarland and Ayers, R. D., Accounting fundamentals (New York: McGraw-Hill Book Co., Inc., 1936).

McKinsey, J. O. and Noble, H. S., Accounting principles (Cincinnati: South-Western Publishing Company, 1935).

MacNeal, K., Truth in accounting (Philadelphia: University of Pennsylvania Press, 1939).

Macrosty, H. W., The trust movement in British industry (London: Longmans, Green & Co. 1907).

Magee, B., Accounting (London: Gee and Company (Publishers) Ltd., 8th ed., 1971).

Mason, P., Fundamentals of accounting (Chicago: The Foundation Press, Inc., 1942).

Masters, J. E., "Financial statements as a basis of credit", The journal of accountancy, May 1915.

Mathews, G. C., "Address before the Illinois Society of Certified Public Accountants, Jan. 18, 1935", (Washington D.C.: Securities and Exchange Commission, mimeo.).

Mauriello, J. A., Accounting for the financial analyst (Homewood, Ill.: Richard D. Irwin Inc., 1967).

May, G. O., "Improvement in financial accounts", Dickinson lectures in accounting (Cambridge, Mass.: Harvard University Press, 1943).

May, G. O., Financial accounting - a distillation of experience (New York: The Macmillan Company, 1961).

May, G. O., Twenty-five years of accounting responsibility (New York: Price, Waterhouse and Company, 1936, ed. by B. C. Hunt, later reprinted by Scholars Book Co., 1971).

Mead, E. S., "The genesis of the United States Steel Corporation", Quarterly journal of economics, 1901.

Mead, E. S., "Capitalization of the United States Steel Corporation", Quarterly journal of economics, 1902.

Mead, E. S., Corporation finance (New York: D. Appleton and Company, 5th edn., 1924).

Meeker, J. E., The work of the stock exchange (New York: Ronald Press Company, 1922).

Meigs, W. B. and Johnson, C. E., Accounting: the basis for business decisions (New York: McGraw-Hill Book Company, Inc., 1967).

Meigs, W. B., Mosich, A. N. and Larsen, E. J., Modern advanced accounting (New York: McGraw-Hill Book Company, Inc., 1975).

Mofsky, J. S., Blue sky restrictions on new business promotions, (New York: Matthew Bender, 1971).

Montgomery, R. H. and Staub, W. A., Auditing principles (New York: Ronald Press Company, 1923).

Montgomery, R. H., Dicksee's auditing (New YOrk: Ronald Press Company, rev. American ed., 1909).

Montgomery, R. H., Auditing theory and practice (New York: Ronald Press Company, 1912).

Montgomery, R. H., "Federal control of corporations", The journal of accountancy, Oct. 1912.

Moonitz, M., "The entity approach to consolidated statements", The accounting review, July 1942.

Moonitz, M., The entity theory of consolidated statements (American Accounting Association, 1944).

Moonitz, M. and Jordan, L. H., Accounting: an analysis of its problems (New York: Holt, Rinehart and Winston, 2nd ed., Vol. II, 1964).

Moulton, H. G., The financial organization of society (Chicago: University of Chicago Press, 2nd ed., 1925).

Murphy, M., "Arthur Lowes Dickinson: pioneer in American professional accountancy", Bulletin of the business historical society, Inc. (later known as Business history review), April 1947.

Murphy, M., Selected readings in accounting and auditing (New York: Prentice-Hall, Inc., 1952).

Navin, T. R. and Sears, M. V., "The rise of a market for industrial securities 1887-1902", Business history review, 1955.

Newlove, G. H., Consolidated balance sheets (New York: Ronald Press Company, 1926).

Newlove, G. H., Consolidated statements (Boston: D. C. Heath and Company, 1948).

Noble, H. S., Karrenbrock, W. E. and Simons, H., Advanced accounting (Cincinnati: South-Western Publishing Company, 1941).

Page, E. D., "Balance sheet valuations", The journal of accountancy, April 1916.

Parkinson, H., "Disclosure in published accounts", The accountant, 19 June 1937.

Paton, W. A. and Stevenson, R. A., Principles of accounting (New York: The Macmillan Company, 1920).

Paton, W. A., Accounting (New York: The Macmillan Company, 1924).

Paton, W. A. (ed.), Accountants' handbook (New York: Ronald Press Company, 2nd ed., 1932).

Paton, W. A., Essentials of accounting (New York: The Macmillan Company, 1938).

Paton, W. A. (ed.), Accountants' handbook (New York: Ronald Press Company, 3rd ed., 1947).

Paton, W. A. and Paton W. A. Jnr., Asset accounting (New York: The Macmillan Company, 1952).

de Paula, F. R. M., "The form of presentation of the accounts of holding companies", The accountant, 15 Dec. 1934.

de Paula, F. R. M., "Some further notes on auditing", The accountant, 22 March 1913.

Pegler, E. C., "The principles of auditing", The accountant, 14 Feb. 1914.

Porter, C. H. and Fiske, W. P., Accounting (New York: Henry Holt and Company, 1936).

Prickett, A. L. and Mikesell, R. M., Principles of accounting (New York: The Macmillan Company, 1937).

Pyle, W. W. and White, J. A., Fundamental accounting principles (Homewood, Ill.: Richard D. Irwin, Inc., 5th ed., 1969).

Racine, S., Accounting principles (Seattle: The Western Institute of Accountancy, Commerce and Finance, 3rd ed., 1923).

Rappaport, L. H., SEC accounting practice and procedure (New York: Ronald Press Company, 2nd ed., 1959.

Reed, R. R., "Blue sky laws", in Encyclopaedia of the social sciences (New York: The Macmillan Company, 1930).

Reeve, F. E. and Russell, F. C., Accounting principles (New York: Alexander Hamilton Institute, 1922).

Reynolds, F. J. (ed.), The American business manual (New York: P. F. Collins and Sons, 1914).

Ripley, W. Z., Main street and Wall street (Boston: Little, Brown, and Company, 1929).

Robinson, M. H., "The distribution of securities in the formation of the United States Steel Corporation", Political science quarterly, 1915.

Robson, T. B., "The construction of consolidated accounts ...", The accountant, 7 March 1936.

Robson, T. B., Consolidated accounts (London: Gee & Company (Publishers) Ltd., 1946).

Robson, T. B., Consolidated and other group accounts (London: Gee & Company (Publishers) Ltd., 3rd ed., 1956).

Robson, T. B., and Duncan, S. N., Consolidated and other group accounts (London: Gee & Company (Publishers) Ltd., 4th ed., 1969).

Rorem, C. R., Accounting method (Chicago: University of Chicago Press, 2nd ed., 1930).

Saliers, E. A., (ed.), Accountants' handbook (New York: Ronald Press Company, 1923).

Saliers, E. A., Accounts in theory and practice (New York: McGraw-Hill Book Company Inc., 1920).

Sanders, T. H., "The influence of the Securities and Exchange Commission upon accounting principles", The accounting review, March 1936.

Sanders, T. H., "Accounting aspects of the Securities Act", Law and contemporary problems, 1937.

Sanders, T. H., Hatfield, H. R. and Moore, U., A statement of accounting principles (New York: American Institute of Accountants, 1938).

Schultz, B. E., The securities market (New York: Harper and Brothers, Publishers, 2nd ed., 1946).

Schwartz, B. (ed.), The economic regulation of business and industry - a legislative history of U.S. regulatory agencies (New York: Chelsea House Publishers, 1973).

Seatree, W. E., "Consolidated balance sheets" (correspondence), The accountant, 4 Jan. 1930.

Securities and Exchange Commission, Data on profits and operations 1936-1942 (Washington, D.C.: 1944).

Shaw, J. C. (ed.), Bogie on group accounts (Bristol: Jordan and Sons Ltd., 3rd ed., 1973).

Simons, A. J., Holding companies (London: Sir Isaac Pitman and Sons Ltd., 1927).

Smith, C. A., "Accounting practice under the Securities and Exchange Commission", The accounting review, Dec. 1935.

Smith, D. D. R., "Principles and problems in consolidation", Proceedings - Tenth International Congress of Accountants (Sydney: 1972).

Sobel, R., The big board (New York: The Free Press, 1965).

Spicer and E. C. Pegler, Practical auditing (London: Foulks Lynch and Company 1911).

Stamp, E., The elements of consolidation accounting (Wellington: Sweet and Maxwell (N.Z.) Ltd., 1965).

Staub, W. A., "Consolidated financial statements", Proceedings of the international congress on accounting, 1929 (reproduced in The accountant, 7 Dec. 1929).

Staub, W. A., "Some difficulties arising in consolidated financial statements", The journal of accountancy, Jan. 1932.

Staub, W. W., Auditing developments during the present century (Cambridge: Mass:: Harvard University Press, 1942).

Stempf, V. H., "Consolidated financial statements", The journal of accountancy, Nov. 1936.

Sterrett, J. E., "Legislation for the control of corporations", The journal of accountancy, Feb. 1910.

Stewart, A., "Accountancy and regulatory bodies in the United States", Fiftieth anniversary celebrations (New York: The American Institute of Accountants, 1937).

Stockwell, H. G., How to read a financial statement (New York: Ronald Press Company, 1922).

Storey, R. K., "Revenue realization, going concern, and measurement of income", The accounting review, April 1959.

Strachan, W., "Some remarks on balance sheets and profit and loss accounts", The incorporated accountant's journal, May 1903.

Strachan, W., "The audit of financial and land companies' accounts", The incorporated accountants' journal, Dec. 1906.

Sunley, W. T. and Pinkerton, P. W., Corporation accounting (New York: Ronald Press Company, for the American Academy of Accountancy, 1931).

Taylor, A. W., Investments (New York: Alexander Hamilton Institute, 1924).

Thompson, T. F., "Consolidation rules of the Securities and Exchange Commission", The New York certified public accountant, Jan. 1942.

Tinen, J. R., Advanced accounting (New York: Ronald Press Company, 1927).

Vallance, A., Very private enterprise (London: Thames and Hudson, 1955).

Vance, L. L. and Taussig, R. A., Accounting principles and control (New York: Holt, Rinehart and Winston, 3rd ed., 1972).

Wade, H. H., Fundamentals of accounting (New York: John Wiley and Sons, Inc., 1934).

Walker, R. G., "Group accounts", The chartered accountant in Australia, Sept. 1970.

Walker, R. G., "Asset classification and asset valuation", Accounting and business research, Autumn 1974.

Wall, A. and Duning, R. W., Analysing financial statements (New York: American Institute of Banking, 1930).

Wallis, R. W., Accounting: a modern approach (London: McGraw-Hill Publishing Co. Ltd., 1970).

Walton, S., "Consolidated statements", The journal of accountancy, Mch. Apl. May 1918

Walton, V., "Some thoughts on accounts and financial statements", The accountant, 26 June 1926.

Webster, G. R., "Consolidated accounts", The journal of accountancy, Oct. 1919.

Werntz, W. W., "Some problems as to parent companies", The journal of accountancy, June 1939.

Wildman, J. R., Principles of accounting (Brooklyn, N.Y.: The William G. Hewitt Press, 1913).

Wilkinson, N., "Valuation of assets", The accountant, 22 August 1925.

Wilkinson, R. H. E., "Balance sheets", The accountant, 1 August 1914.

Witty, R. A., "Some defects of company law with special reference to the work of accountants", The accountant, 18 June 1932.

Wixon, R. (ed.), Accountants' handbook (New York: Ronald Press Company, 4th ed., 1961).

Wixon, R., Kell, W. G. and Bedford, N. M. (eds.), Accountants' handbook (New York: Ronald Press Company, 5th ed., 1970).

Woodbridge, F. W., Elements of accounting (New York: Ronald Press Company, 1924).

Wright, A. W., "Consolidation of balance sheets in holding company accounting", The journal of accountancy, Jan. 1914.

Wynon, Sir Albert W., "Holding and subsidiary companies" Proceedings of the International Congress on Accounting (London: 1933).

Yamey, B. S., "The case law relating to company dividends" in W. T. Baxter and S. Davidson (eds.), Studies in accounting theory (London: Sweet and Maxwell Ltd., 2nd ed., 1962).

Zeff, S., Forging accounting principles in five countries (Champaign, Ill.: Stipes Publishing Company, 1972).

INDEX

THE DEVELOPMENT OF
CONTEMPORARY ACCOUNTING THOUGHT

An Arno Press Collection

Baldwin, H[arry] G[len]. **Accounting for Value As Well as Original Cost** *and* Castenholz, William B. **A Solution to the Appreciation Problem.** 2 Vols. in 1. 1927/1931

Baxter, William. **Collected Papers on Accounting.** 1978

Brief, Richard P., Ed. **Selections from Encyclopaedia of Accounting, 1903.** 1978

Broaker, Frank and Richard M. Chapman. **The American Accountants' Manual.** 1897

Canning, John B. **The Economics of Accountancy.** 1929

Chatfield, Michael, Ed. **The English View of Accountant's Duties and Responsibilities.** 1978

Cole, William Morse. **The Fundamentals of Accounting.** 1921

Congress of Accountants. **Official Record of the Proceedings of the Congress of Accountants.** 1904

Cronhelm, F[rederick] W[illiam]. **Double Entry by Single.** 1818

Davidson, Sidney. **The Plant Accounting Regulations of the Federal Power Commission.** 1952

De Paula, F[rederic] R[udolf] M[ackley]. **Developments in Accounting.** 1948

Epstein, Marc Jay. **The Effect of Scientific Management on the Development of the Standard Cost System** (Doctoral Dissertation, University of Oregon, 1973). 1978

Esquerré, Paul-Joseph. **The Applied Theory of Accounts.** 1914

Fitzgerald, A[dolf] A[lexander]. **Current Accounting Trends.** 1952

Garner, S. Paul and Marilynn Hughes, Eds. **Readings on Accounting Development.** 1978

Haskins, Charles Waldo. **Business Education and Accountancy.** 1904

Hein, Leonard William. **The British Companies Acts and the Practice of Accountancy 1844-1962** (Doctoral Dissertation, University of California, Los Angeles, 1962). 1978

Hendriksen, Eldon S. **Capital Expenditures in the Steel Industry, 1900 to 1953** (Doctoral Dissertation, University of California, Berkeley, 1956). 1978

Holmes, William, Linda H. Kistler and Louis S. Corsini. **Three Centuries of Accounting in Massachusetts.** 1978

Horngren, Charles T. **Implications for Accountants of the Uses of Financial Statements by Security Analysts** (Doctoral Dissertation, University of Chicago, 1955). 1978

Horrigan, James O., Ed. **Financial Ratio Analysis—An Historical Perspective.** 1978

Jones, [Edward Thomas]. **Jones's English System of Book-keeping.** 1796

Lamden, Charles William. **The Securities and Exchange Commission** (Doctoral Dissertation, University of California, Berkeley, 1949). 1978

Langer, Russell Davis. **Accounting As A Variable in Mergers** (Doctoral Dissertation, University of California, Berkeley, 1976). 1978

Lewis, J. Slater. **The Commercial Organisation of Factories.** 1896

Littleton, A[nanias] C[harles] and B[asil] S. Yamey, Eds. **Studies in the History of Accounting.** 1956

Mair, John. **Book-keeping Moderniz'd.** 1793

Mann, Helen Scott. **Charles Ezra Sprague.** 1931

Marsh, C[hristopher] C[olumbus]. **The Theory and Practice of Bank Book-keeping.** 1856

Mitchell, William. **A New and Complete System of Book-keeping by an Improved Method of Double Entry.** 1796

Montgomery, Robert H. **Fifty Years of Accountancy.** 1939

Moonitz, Maurice. **The Entity Theory of Consolidated Statements.** 1951

Moonitz, Maurice, Ed. **Three Contributions to the Development of Accounting Thought.** 1978

Murray, David. **Chapters in the History of Bookkeeping, Accountancy & Commercial Arithmetic.** 1930

Nicholson, J[erome] Lee. **Cost Accounting.** 1913

Paton, William Andrew and Russell Alger Stevenson. **Principles of Accounting.** 1918

Pixley, Francis W[illiam]. **The Profession of a Chartered Accountant and Other Lectures.** 1897

Preinreich, Gabriel A. D. **The Nature of Dividends.** 1935

Previts, Gary John, Ed. **Early 20th Century Developments in American Accounting Thought.** 1978

Ronen, Joshua and George H. Sorter. **Relevant Financial Statements.** 1978

Shenkir, William G., Ed. **Carman G. Blough: His Professional Career and Accounting Thought.** 1978

Simpson, Kemper. **Economics for the Accountant.** 1921

Sneed, Florence R. **Parallelism in Two Disciplines.** (M.A. Thesis, University of Texas, Arlington, 1974). 1978

Sorter, George H. **The Boundaries of the Accounting Universe** (Doctoral Dissertation, University of Chicago, 1963). 1978

Storey, Reed K[arl]. **Matching Revenues with Costs** (Doctoral Dissertation, University of California, Berkeley, 1958). 1978

Sweeney, Henry W[hitcomb]. **Stabilized Accounting.** 1936

Van de Linde, Gérard. **Reminiscences.** 1917

Vatter, William J[oseph]. **The Fund Theory of Accounting and Its Implications for Financial Reports.** 1947

Walker, R. G. **Consolidated Statements.** 1978

Webster, Norman E., Comp. **The American Association of Public Accountants.** 1954

Wells, M. C., Ed. **American Engineers' Contributions to Cost Accounting.** 1978

Worthington, Beresford. **Professional Accountants.** 1895

Yamey, Basil S. **Essays on the History of Accounting.** 1978

Yamey, Basil S., Ed. **The Historical Development of Accounting.** 1978

Yang, J[u] M[ei]. **Goodwill and Other Intangibles.** 1927

Zeff, Stephen Addam. **A Critical Examination of the Orientation Postulate in Accounting, with Particular Attention to its Historical Development** (Doctoral Dissertation, University of Michigan, 1961). 1978

Zeff, Stephen A., Ed. **Selected Dickinson Lectures in Accounting.** 1978